I0823146

*Praise for*

# Finding the Third Way

"With a refreshingly candid insider's reflection on a time when a sense of higher purpose and shared respect shaped the hard work of politics and governing, Lanny Davis offers hope that we can restore integrity and civility to our nation's public life."

**John R. Kasich,** former two-term governor, Ohio, and United States congressman (R-OH)

"It's hard to argue with Lanny Davis's thoughtful call for decency, pragmatism, and—most importantly—listening to people instead of reflexively and defensively demeaning each other. Making a point against your perceived enemies may feel good, but making a difference is the better way."

**Gavin Newsom,** governor, California

"From his days at Yale, Lanny Davis developed relationships—and lifelong friendships—with future American political titans. Lanny's good cheer, solution-oriented pragmatism, and ability to gain the trust of so many put him in the room with many influential people who determined the future course of this great nation. American political discourse would be infinitely better if more of us conducted ourselves like Lanny."

**Charlie Dent,** former United States congressman (R–PA)

"When it comes to the past fifty years of national politics in America, Lanny Davis has seen—and been right in the middle of—it all. Rooted in history, fueled by conviction, and deeply personal, *Finding the Third Way* is more than a political memoir. It's the blueprint we need to heal our fractured democracy."

**Eric Swalwell,** United States congressman (D–CA)

"Lanny Davis's book on the 'Third Way' approach—to focus on results, not rules—is what we need in this country—now more than ever."

**Hon. Rahm Emanuel,** former United States congressman (D–IL), mayor of Chicago, and White House chief of staff

"When I think of Lanny Davis, the word 'Democrat' is about fifth or sixth on the list, after more important descriptors like patriot, pragmatist, problem-solver . . . and friend. He's the guy I'd want in a foxhole and a person I've called when I was in a jam. In *Finding the Third Way*, Lanny has an answer to the crisis of the current polarized politics of our country—to encourage Trump supporters and non-Trump supporters, Democrats and Republicans, liberals and conservatives, to look for and find common ground or at least to be able to disagree agreeably."

**Michael Smerconish**, SiriusXM and CNN host

"Lanny Davis invites us to take a walk with him as he shares his appreciation for the value of connection, the importance of solutions, and the requirement that we be 'uniters, not dividers.' *Finding the Third Way* offers unique insight into a lifelong journey to create civility and an appreciation for common ground. And no one has been a better example of that than Lanny Davis!"

**Michael Steele,** former lieutenant governor, Maryland

"Lanny Davis is the consummate political professional who understands D.C. politics inside and out. His insights are always invaluable."

**Jim Acosta,** national news correspondent

# FINDING *the* THIRD WAY

## LESSONS IN THE POLITICS OF CIVILITY FROM MY JOURNEY THROUGH HISTORY

LANNY J. DAVIS
WITH CARL M. CANNON

www.amplifypublishinggroup.com

*Finding the Third Way: Lessons in the Politics of Civility from My Journey Through History*



The author has tried to recreate events, locales, and conversations from their memories of them. In order to maintain their anonymity in some instances, the author has changed the names of individuals and places, and may have changed some identifying characteristics and details.

The views and opinions expressed in this book are solely those of the author. These views and opinions do not necessarily represent those of the publisher or staff. The publisher and the author assume no responsibility for errors, inaccuracies, omissions, or any other inconsistencies herein. All such instances are unintentional and the author's own.

**For more information, please contact:**
RealClear Publishing, an imprint of Amplify Publishing Group
620 Herndon Parkway, Suite 220
Herndon, VA 20170
info@amplifypublishing.com

Library of Congress Control Number: 2024925883

CPSIA Code: PRFRE1025A

ISBN-13: 979-8-89138-335-7

Printed in Canada

*To, most importantly—Carolyn Atwell Davis, a brilliant,
beautiful, indefatigable wife, mom, friend, attorney,
and tough but fair counselor of more than forty years,
who made it all possible for me and still does.*

*To our amazing children, their spouses, and our grandchildren.*

*To, especially, President William Jefferson Clinton
and First Lady, Secretary of State, and U.S. Senator
Hillary Rodham Clinton, whose friendship over five decades
changed my life (and the nation's) for the better
and immeasurably enhanced and made possible
my incredible journey through history.*

*And to Carl Cannon, who co-wrote this book with brilliance—
he gave me the key overall themes emerging
out of my life, which he saw better than I, and remained
a trusted friend and constructive critic throughout.*

"First of all," he said, "if you can learn a simple trick,
Scout, you'll get along a lot better with all kinds of folks.

You never really understand a person until you
consider things from his point of view . . ."

"Sir?"

"Until you climb into his skin and walk around in it."

—**ATTICUS FINCH TO HIS DAUGHTER, SCOUT,**
*To Kill a Mockingbird,* by Harper Lee, 1960

You want progressive change?
Then stop talking only to people who agree with you.
Find a way to persuade, not attack, people who don't.

—**ALLARD K. LOWENSTEIN,**
speech at Yale Law School, October 1967

The builder lifted his old gray head.
"Good friend, in the path
I have come," he said,
"there followed after me to-day
a youth whose feet must pass this way.
This chasm that has been as naught to me.
To that fair-haired youth may a pitfall be.
He, too, must cross in the twilight dim.

"Good friend, I am building this bridge for him."

—**WILL ALLEN DROMGOOLE,**
"The Bridge Builder," 1898

# CONTENTS

# FOREWORD

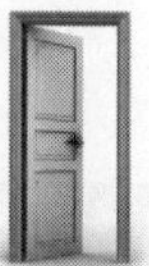

## BILL CLINTON
### 42ND PRESIDENT OF THE UNITED STATES

## AL FROM
### FOUNDER OF THE DEMOCRATIC LEADERSHIP COUNCIL

We come from very different backgrounds. One of us comes from a small town in rural Arkansas, the other from a medium-sized, old industrial city in northern Indiana. We were both inspired by the spirit and civic ethic of President John F. Kennedy. Neither of us came from money, but we are both beneficiaries of the American Dream. Our belief that all Americans should be able to chase that dream eventually brought us together to work to change our country for the better.

After the Democratic Party's three landslide losses in presidential elections in the 1980s, we joined forces in the Democratic Leadership Council to revitalize America and redefine our party—with an agenda designed to meet our current challenges and able to win the support of a majority of the American people. That effort animated the New Democrat movement and was critical to President Clinton's winning the White House in 1992.

At its core were the principles that shaped our own political philosophies and guided our careers—opportunity for all, responsibility from all, and a community of all our people. Those principles were at the heart of what President Clinton called the New Covenant. We believed that government's responsibility was to provide the opportunity for every American to rise as far as his or her talents would allow—and that the people's responsibility was to take advantage of those opportunities and give something back to their country and communities.

With the help of a lot of dedicated people who often knew more about important issues than we did, we developed an agenda of bold and innovative ideas to further those principles. Then we travelled to about two dozen states—red, blue, and swing states—before the 1992 campaign began to talk to a cross section of Americans about how we could refine those ideas to best serve their needs.

As president, Bill Clinton put those ideas into action—and the American people were all the better for it. The result was eight years of peace and prosperity.

This approach to governing and problem-solving came to be called the Third Way. We rejected governing from extremes. But we didn't just try to split the difference between the Left and the Right. As former British Prime Minister Tony Blair—whose New Labour movement embraced the Third Way—often said: The Third Way is not a compromise between liberalism and conservatism; it is the modernization of liberalism.

Because our ideas transcended the old labels, they earned the support of voters from all sides of the political spectrum.

Despite the anger, vindictiveness, and polarization that have often been successful in contemporary politics, we still believe that ideas matter, that what you stand for matters, and that honorable compromise can emerge from serious differences. We believe constructive cooperation can be achieved through debates that are civil and honest, where people have our country's best interests at heart.

Lanny Davis is our compatriot in Third Way politics. He has been a friend to both of us for more than half a century—long before we even knew each other. Lanny has lived a lifetime of service to his country—and now he's written about how his incredible life experiences led him to believe in the Third Way and the importance of civility in politics.

Lanny spent much of his political life as a deep-blue Democrat. But throughout his remarkable career, he has befriended, worked with, and learned from leaders on both sides of the political aisle.

He wrote this book after the 2024 election, and in the epilogue, he exhorts political leaders on both sides—even in these most difficult and highly polarized times—to learn from, listen to, and respect each other.

Many might see the title of Lanny's book and react—this is not the right time to write about finding common ground. We're facing a radical assault on our democracy, our Constitution, our public servants, and our humanitarian, economic, and security alliances around the world.

Today's polarizing abuses of power and lack of compassion in our politics should remind Americans that we need civility and the effort to find common ground now more than ever. That's what Lanny Davis is trying to say in this book.

PREFACE

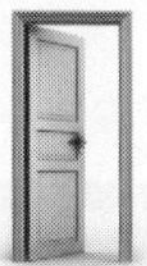

# AN IMAGINARY WALK THROUGH THE YALE CAMPUS: 1963–1971

I am imagining taking a series of strolls across the Yale campus sometime between 1963 and 1971. I am imagining whom I would have seen and what we might have said during my seven years at Yale for college and law school had such a tour not been imaginary.

We're traveling through time, so the walk isn't strictly sequential. In my mind the first stop is a stone and redbrick edifice at 202 York Street in New Haven. This is the Hadden Building, home of the *Yale Daily News* and named after the dashing and brilliant Briton Hadden, who died in 1929 at age thirty-one, just as he and Henry Luce—both former editors of the *News*—were building *TIME* magazine into a media powerhouse.

I have just come from the Payne Whitney Gymnasium, located several blocks away. The gym is named after another Yalie, like me, a Delta Kappa Epsilon (DKE) man. Whitney survived being rammed at sea in 1911 by the sister ship of the *Titanic* but collapsed after a tennis match on his estate at age fifty-one and died an hour later from what *The New York Times* termed "acute indigestion."

I'm too young at the time to realize I'm surrounded by so many ghosts. I'd only gone to the gym to confirm that my name was on the list to play on the Yale freshman basketball team. I had completed a week of tryouts and had no doubt, as a former cocaptain of the Newark Academy basketball team, that I would make the frosh squad. I look up at the list posted on the door, my eyes passing over the *A*'s to the *C*'s and looking under the *D*'s for my name.

It is not there. What? Impossible! It must be a mistake!

It isn't. Crushed, but only temporarily, I arrive ten minutes later at the Hadden Building. I'm in the offices of the oldest collegiate daily newspaper in the country. The place seems to be empty, except for a janitor cleaning up. I ask him where the office of the "chairman" is. He motions up the stairs, down the hall to the end. I walk up the stairs, down the hall, and knock on the closed door. I hear a voice say, "Come in." I poke my head in and see, sitting at his desk in the large, luxurious, wood-paneled office, someone I knew as the famous *Yale Daily News* chairman. I'm impressed.

"Are you Joe Lieberman?" I ask, nonsensically, as I knew it was him and recognized him from the photo I had seen in the newspaper many times.

He nods and asks, "How can I help you?"

"How do I get to become chairman of the *News*?"

He smiles and then gives me the answer—the punch line of an old vaudeville line about a tourist in New York City who stops a passerby and asks, "How do I get to Carnegie Hall?" The puckish New Yorker answers, "Practice, my boy—practice." Lieberman pauses after my question and says, "Write, my boy—write."

I ask Lieberman, who would become one of my best friends and godfather to my oldest son, what he wants to be when he grows up.

"I don't know," Joe might have replied if he, too, were a time traveler. "Maybe I'll get elected to six terms as a United States senator from Connecticut. Then in my fourth-term race for the Senate, I will lose the Democratic primary and still win as an independent. And I'll win with support from a leading conservative Republican senator and Vietnam War hero from Arizona."

"Oh, come on, Joe," I say. "You are letting your imagination go too far."

"Actually, maybe I'll do even more than that," he adds with a smile. "Maybe someday I will come within about three hundred votes in the state of Florida of becoming the first Jewish vice president of the United States, dashing my hopes of waiting out two terms of an incumbent Democratic president to then become the first Jewish president."

"Now," I think, "you are really off in fantasyland, Joe."

■ ■ ■

As my imaginary walk continues, I run into George Pataki, a classmate and friend. George had been elected chairman and later served as speaker (in our senior year, 1966–1967) of the Conservative Party of the Yale Political Union.

George waves at me, and we stop to chat. "Hi, George. So where are you headed after graduation?"

"Well," he answers, "I am thinking of someday getting elected mayor of Peekskill, New York. And then someday running for governor—and winning!"

"Peekskill? Isn't that a little Republican town upstate? That's not exactly a great base from which to get elected governor of a Democratic state," I reply.

But George, ever the optimist, is undeterred.

Even more shocking, he continues: "Also, the man I think I will defeat is someone who is a bleeding-heart liberal like you. His name is Mario Cuomo."

*That's ridiculous*, I thought. *A conservative Republican from Peekskill is going to win governor of New York over a popular incumbent liberal Democrat?* But I wouldn't have talked that way to young George

Pataki. He was too easy to like, and I would have wished him well, despite me being—as George noted—a committed lifelong Democrat.

"You'll see, Lanny," he says. "Just wait."

■ ■ ■

Walking alongside Pataki is another classmate and friend—J. ("Jay") Harvie Wilkinson, who surprised many when he was elected president of the largely liberal Yale Political Union in our junior year. But not me. He and I had strongly disagreed on the 1964 presidential campaign choices. He supported Arizona senator and GOP nominee Barry Goldwater. I supported Lyndon Johnson. But despite our different presidential preferences, when we debated, Jay always seemed able to hear and weigh what I was saying—and vice versa. I could see why liberals in the political union had supported him.

I ask him whether he is going to run for political office someday. He says he might but that he also "kind of liked the idea of being a judge someday—calling balls and strikes, with the U.S. Constitution as my only touchstone."

Little could I have imagined that nearly sixty years later, in the second decade of the twenty-first century, the now Honorable J. Harvie Wilkinson—chief judge of the U.S. Court of Appeals for the Fourth Circuit, appointed to the bench by conservative President Ronald Reagan—would make national headlines calling out unconstitutional conduct by a Republican president, Donald J. Trump. In an April 2025 opinion described by *The New York Times* as "scathing," Judge Wilkinson, writing for a unanimous three-judge circuit court panel, challenged Trump's claim that he had the power to deport undocumented persons by executive order without due process of law.

"This should be shocking not only to judges but to the intuitive sense of liberty that Americans far removed from courthouses still hold dear," he wrote.

■ ■ ■

Onward I walk. I see a tall, long-haired, and preppy-looking guy wearing a sport coat with patches on the sleeves. It is John Kerry, Wilkinson's predecessor as president of the Yale Political Union. Kerry was known to tell people, often early into their first meeting, that his middle initial was "F"—giving him the familiar initials of the young president John F. Kennedy, who had been assassinated a few months into our freshman year in November 1963. (Kennedy was a Harvard man, yes, but also a U.S. Navy PT boat commander in World War II. This latter-day JFK knows his Kennedy history well and has plans of his own.)

"Hi, John," I say. "I hear you are going into the navy and want to get assigned to a PT boat in Vietnam. Why would you volunteer to go to Vietnam and, worse, ask for such a dangerous assignment? You could get killed." I wait to see if he'll acknowledge wanting to follow the path of the other famous JFK.

"I have a long way to go, Lanny," John Kerry's avatar answers, quoting my favorite Robert Frost poem. "And miles before I sleep."

"What are your plans after Vietnam?" I ask gingerly.

"Well, I might move to Boston like you-know-who and run for Congress as an anti-war candidate, then seek a Senate seat and serve with Ted Kennedy before I run for president," he says. With the benefit of hindsight, the incarnation of 1960s Kerry could have added, "But I will lose the popular vote in a close election and the Electoral College even more narrowly to your fraternity brother, George W. Bush."

The younger me finds this unlikely. "Too bad, John," I'd probably say. "If that happens, sorry about that."

"Not to worry. After that I will become secretary of state, like Thomas Jefferson."

"Really?" I respond to this unlikely-sounding scenario. "How will you get that appointment?"

"Well, I won't support your future law school friend Hillary Rodham Clinton when she runs for president—even though she and her husband, a former president, will campaign for me when I lose in 2004 to your buddy Dubya."

"Really? Didn't Bill Clinton ignore his physicians and come to Philadelphia five days after quadruple bypass heart surgery on the last weekend before the 2004 election to campaign for you at a late-night rally? How could you not endorse Hillary?"

"The Clintons certainly will feel that way, but I'll support an extremely talented junior U.S. senator from Illinois," he says. "That man will then get elected and become the first African American president. He'll name me secretary of state."

I undoubtedly would have cheered the prospect of an election result that would have focused the country on the moral stain of slavery, but I am skeptical . . . and curious. "Any guess as to what his name will be, John?"

"Yes," he says. "Barack Hussein Obama."

"Barack Hussein Obama?" I repeat. Seriously? I wonder what kind of dream I'm in.

■ ■ ■

Kerry then points his finger knowingly at someone familiar to me. The next person on my imaginary walk has a big smile on his face as he walks toward us. I immediately recognize the man Kerry had pointed out. George W. Bush always had a way of walking that was, well, a kind of swagger but not off-putting. Just confident. And always friendly. George was my fraternity brother at DKE. He was also a good friend and comember of the closely knit Davenport College residential college community, one of twelve back then (now fourteen) within the larger Yale University. George waves and gives me a quick embrace. That's George Bush, all right—always a big smile and a hug.

"How's your dad doing?" I ask him.

His father, George H. W. Bush, had been a member of the U.S. House of Representatives from Houston, Texas, when I first met George in 1964, when I was a sophomore and he was a freshman. That year, his dad was defeated in a race for a U.S. Senate seat by Democrat Lloyd Bentsen.

George pitched on the freshman baseball team but never came close to his father's exploits. His dad was captain of the team after serving as a World War II combat pilot in the Pacific—a star first baseman who led Yale to the finals of the first-ever collegiate World Series in 1947, losing to the University of California. Then he led the team to a second straight World Series final in 1948, this time losing to the University of Southern California. That year, the elder Bush (then known as "Poppy") greeted Babe Ruth on Yale Field in a pregame ceremony, one of the last public appearances by the Bambino. In 2021 the school would name the baseball diamond after Bush Sr.

I think Dubya knew early on that he couldn't live up to his dad's athletic achievements, but he went on to compete in inter-residential sports competitions, playing for various Davenport College teams, including football and rugby.

As we passed each other this day, I asked, "What're you thinking of doing after graduation, George?"

Of course, no one I knew thought of George as having any serious political aspirations. He was well liked by almost everyone—a rare thing on a campus filled with big egos and competitive overachievers. But we didn't connect the dots very well, did we? What we couldn't see then, although the signs were surely there, was that his authenticity, likability, and ability to read people and be sensitive to their aspirations would take him far in politics—all the way to the top.

"I just saw Kerry and Pataki," I tell young Bush. "They're political comers, but I'm sure you don't have any political ambitions."

He gives me that special George W. grin. I knew that expression, and it was genuine. But I would learn that there was more behind it than affability. Something about that grin should have told us all that he realizes something that nobody else, including me, knows or appreciates.

"Oh, you know me, Lanny. I'm the master of underachievement and underexpectations," he says. "I may surprise all of you and especially my family someday and get elected president of the United States!"

"Sure, George," I say, not wanting to offend him. I really liked this guy. A lot. But president of the United States? George Bush?

No way.

■ ■ ■

Now my imaginary walk jumps ahead to the spring of 1971. Though I had already graduated from law school, I was still in New Haven and volunteering in the Senate campaign of the Reverend Joseph Duffey, an anti–Vietnam War Democrat. I expected to leave after the November elections to join the budding 1972 presidential campaign of Maine Senator Edmund S. Muskie.

I still had friends at Yale Law who were one or two years behind me. The most impressive was a young woman I'd first met on registration day in September 1969, when I was in my third (and final) year and she was just entering as a first-year. She had already gained national attention for a brilliant senior class speech at Wellesley College's graduation ceremony.

Her name then was Hillary Rodham.

We spot each other on my walk that beautiful spring day as she is emerging from the front entrance of Yale Law School on Wall Street. We hug and say a big hello as she asks about the "babies." (She was always amazed that I married and had two children so young, at the age of twenty-four.)

I ask her, "How's your social life going?"

"I met a special guy," she says.

"Hillary, this sounds serious."

"It's serious, all right. I think this is for real."

"What's the lucky guy's name?"

"Bill Clinton."

"Hmmm." I had heard that name in the campus buzz, even though I was no longer a student. "Is that the guy from Arkansas, the one everybody says is already a real political comer? The one who just arrived on campus from a Rhodes Scholarship?"

"Yup, that's the one."

"So what's he like?" I ask her, always feeling a bit protective about Hillary even then. We had become good friends.

"He's brilliant, charming, pretty handsome—not that looks really matter—but he has something special."

"What is it?"

"Lanny, when he talks to you, even among a large group of people, you feel like you are the only person in the room he is talking to. And he seems interested in you—truly interested, not like most guys who spend most of their time talking about themselves. I can't wait for you to meet him. I know you two will get along."

"So you think he's going places?" I ask.

"Absolutely," she says. "Someday he will be the first president of the United States from our baby boomer generation."

"Wait a minute. No way. *You* are going to be the first president of the United States from our generation, the first female president in U.S. history." That's what I thought almost immediately after meeting her for the first time the year before.

"Wait until you meet Bill," Hillary parries. "You'll see what I mean."

■ ■ ■

As if on cue, we hear a foggy male voice with a Southern accent coming out of the law school. The last guest on my imaginary walk.

"Hi, Hill!" Bill Clinton says.

There he was—bearded and with longer hair than I imagined a future president of the United States would have. *Nah,* I thought. *Not this guy.*

Then he shakes my hand warmly, and we start talking—exactly what Hillary had predicted would happen.

This guy was like a vacuum cleaner. I found myself telling him all about myself, my background, my family, whether I liked dogs and cats—and all the time, for that moment, I felt like I was the only one on the face of the earth he was talking to or cared about.

*Wow,* I thought. *Maybe this guy is going to go far in politics someday.*

I was drawn to him like iron filings to a magnet the first time I met him. And ever since. And I understood what Hillary saw in him.

But could I possibly imagine, in the furthest fantasies of my imagination, that someday this guy would become president of the United States and would be succeeded by my fraternity brother Dubya? And that Dubya's dad, who also went on to become president, would someday become close to Clinton after losing to him? And that, despite major political differences, Dubya would become close with Bill (as both would often remind me, thanks to my friendship with both) and Bush might someday be asked whom he would vote for in the 2016 presidential election—a contest between his brother, Jeb, seeking the Republican Party nomination, and Hillary Clinton, the likely Democratic nominee? And that Dubya would respond, "That would be like choosing between my brother and sister-in-law!"?

*Oh, come on,* I would have thought. No chance of that ever happening.

■ ■ ■

In the course of my imaginary walk, I meet at least three future governors, three future senators, two future secretaries of state, and two future presidents of the United States, one succeeding the other.

I could have walked on and on while my imagination soared about the many others I met in law school and college who would go on to become federal judges, Supreme Court justices, leaders of major corporations, and famous faces in the arts and Hollywood.

But it's better to stop here. After all, this is just a hypothetical walk over eight years in one day. Who would have thought then that I knew all these future American leaders during those several years at Yale, many of whom would become lifelong friends?

I can't explain why so many future American political leaders attended Yale during this period rather than other colleges in the turbulent and historic decade of the 1960s. Why not Harvard, Stanford, UCLA, or the University of Iowa? I have some theories, but most of them merely reflect a bias in favor of my school.

It's a well-known phenomenon, however, that clusters of influential people pop up in history from time to time in various places. My view is that once this is apparent, the bunching of such individuals tends to be reinforcing: Heightened competition raises the level of discourse and achievement, for one thing. In our case at Yale during the momentous sixties, in addition to pushing each other to do better, I also think we helped each other.

At times I've felt like Woody Allen's fictional Leonard Zelig. Through the intrigues of magical realism, Zelig impresses F. Scott Fitzgerald at a Long Island garden party, displays his baseball talent at the New York Yankees' spring training camp, serves a stint in Al Capone's Mob in Chicago, and sits ably for a set with an African American jazz combo. Zelig is a chameleon, however, and I am often seen as (and accused of) being much too opinionated and argumentative to be likened to him. Perhaps Forrest Gump is a better analogy. Tom Hanks's memorable character in the movie runs into Elvis Presley, John Lennon, and Presidents Kennedy, Johnson, and Nixon. That's getting closer to my story. But Gump is an amiable sweetheart of limited intellectual ability who doesn't really comprehend what's happening around him. So that doesn't seem like a fit either.

Both roles were literary devices by filmmakers trying to make broader points. I've wondered whether there was a larger lesson in my experience. It's hard to see the work of Providence in the college admission process, but was interacting with all these people at Yale merely a coincidence? Or just good luck?

Mostly, I think of it as a series of doors that opened. I believe I walked through them with good intentions—that I tried to meet the obligations these opportunities afforded me. I can draw one conclusion, however: If not for these accidental friendships forged during my years at Yale with future U.S. leaders, I would not have ended up in so many "rooms where it happened."

I witnessed—and sometimes, at least marginally, may have influenced—the course of U.S. history. Along the way, I gained rare insights into what happened behind the curtains and why, while accumulating some lessons I'd like to impart as America and the world head into an uncertain and increasingly contentious future.

I also realize that by learning to like and admire those whose politics turned out to be much different than mine during my journey through time, it is possible to stick to your principles and still be able to find common ground. To disagree agreeably. To argue strenuously on camera and be friendly off.

Especially, I learned, decades before "red" and "blue" were used to define Republican- and Democratic-oriented states on the media's political map, that it was possible to have a combination of the two colors—"purple"—to govern a nation that celebrates our differences, not exploits them for selfish purposes.

That is why I originally decided to write this book. In the aftermath of the 2024 election, with our nation even more divided and polarized, the greater need for civility and compromise in American politics made the message even more important.

If I am asked what I want Democrats to take away from this book, here is my answer: We must find a better way to win over voters who have abandoned us than shaming people who don't agree with us.

We can and should oppose politicians like Donald Trump when they challenge democracy and our Constitution. But we can do so and still respect the vast majority of those who voted for him (with the exception of outright bigots and extremists). We need an alternative to the orthodoxy of our liberal Democratic base (of which I consider myself a card-carrying member) and compromising our core principles to win over Trump voters.

The answer to me is clear: We need to focus on solutions, not labels or playing identity politics. We need—as Bill Clinton first said to me many years ago and then practiced as a successful two-term president—neither left nor right but a "third way." That's where solutions are found.

## CHAPTER 1

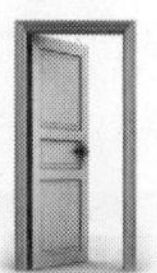

# "YOU CAN'T ROOT FOR THE YANKEES—THEY'RE REPUBLICANS!"

My father, Mortimer Davis, taught me two great lessons in life. Both were about tolerance. I learned how to treat other people—people with differences from me—and how *not* to. I'm grateful to him for both examples.

I was born on December 12, 1945, in Jersey City, the most populous city in Hudson County, the most populous county in New Jersey. My hometown is located between the Hudson River on the east and the Hackensack River on the west, across from Manhattan and Brooklyn, bounded on the north by Bergen County (North Bergen) and on the south by Bayonne. At the time, it had about 330,000 people. Seven decades later, the population had dropped to some 250,000.

I arrived exactly thirty years—to the day—after Sinatra was born in neighboring Hoboken. My mother, Frances (everyone called her "Fran"), often reminded me of our shared birthday. She had a warm spot for Sinatra because when he was young, he'd sing for a few dollars at the Jersey City Jewish Community Center. That made him more than a famous performer. In her telling it made him a mensch. So whenever I was about to blow out my birthday candles, Mom would say, "To Frank too."

Not to be outdone, Dad would remind me that December 12 was a date with more direct significance to our family: It was the date my father was discharged from his World War II service in the U.S. Army. He didn't see combat and wasn't shipped abroad. But he was proud of his time in uniform. He was an army dentist, filling cavities and doing root canals before the young soldiers were shipped out to war. "Soldiers can't afford to get a bad toothache in battle," he would explain as he described the role he played in the war.

On that same day, my mom and dad were scheduled to move into our new home at 115 Bentley Avenue, Jersey City, New Jersey. Of course, my mom couldn't be there for the move. She was in the Margaret Hague Hospital, bringing me into the world.

Here is what my dad wrote about the day I was born in a short memoir he wrote about his dad and his family:

> *On December 12, 1945, Lanny was born. I left for Fort Dix, New Jersey, to get discharged, and the moving men moved us in the house [on 115 Bentley]. It was not just an ordinary busy day for us. I planted Papa in the house for the moving men, and after seeing Fran and my new son in the hospital, took off for Dix. The house cost us $8,000, and, of course, Papa gave me the dough, a down payment of $2,000. He also arranged a mortgage for me.*

The hospital where I was born was named after the mother of the famously corrupt Democratic Party boss of Jersey City, Mayor Frank Hague, who ran the city as his own private fiefdom from 1917 through 1947. (Mayor Hague once declared after someone insisted on quoting the law to him, "I am the law!")

I must have been only five or six years old when this incident happened, but I remember it—vividly. A cranky old man lived two houses away from our Bentley Avenue home, down the slope toward Westside Avenue. I was playing with a friend, and our "game" was to run through this man's backyard, knowing that he would bark at us to keep off his property. The game was to irritate him. It worked, as my paternal grandfather was soon to find out.

My dad often proudly told me that my grandfather Frank Davis was a loyal political supporter of Mayor Hague and was paid for a "no show" job. I later learned he actually had a good job—a well-established photography studio on Avenue A in Bayonne—and made enough money to send my dad and his siblings to college and my dad to dental school at Rutgers University.

But it was also true that Grandpa Frank had political connections and was "close" to Mayor "I Am the Law" Hague. He would take his wallet out, open it up, and show us a genuine Jersey City Police Department badge. It was gold and shiny, and I was so impressed. He loved my reaction. "Don't do anything wrong, Lanny," he would say in a mock-menacing tone, "or I could have you arrested." I believed him.

But it was not me who had to face Frank's wrath on the day my friend Billy Levy and I irritated the older man next door so much that he came running out of his house, screaming with a horrible, scary face as he chased us.

We ran and ran, hearts beating, crying as we ran toward my house, up the front steps, and straight into the arms of Grandpa Frank, who was standing at the door.

"What's the matter, boys?" he asked. "Who scared you?"

When we told him, he took me by the hand and asked me to show him the house where the man lived. "No, Grandpa, please—I am afraid," I said.

"Oh yeah?" my grandpa said. He stood up, took out his wallet, opened it up, and there it was—that big gold police badge.

"Take me to his house and show me the door," he said.

He took Billy and me by the hand, and we walked together past our driveway next to the house, two houses down, and up the steps. As we resisted and tried to pull away, my grandpa knocked loudly on the door.

The old man answered, scowled at the two of us, and looked at my grandpa.

"Well, what do you want?" he said. "These two young scoundrels are deliberately disturbing me by running across my back lawn."

My grandpa stared coldly at him. "This is my grandson," he replied. "And this is his friend. I'm Frank Davis." His wallet was open. The old man looked at my grandpa and then noticed the gold badge.

"Well, I didn't break the law," he said, stammering.

"You threatened my grandson and his friend, and I might just arrest you," my grandpa said without a blink. "Unless you apologize right now to them."

Then he got down on his knees and looked up at the man. "Now I am their size. Why don't you try to scare me?" he said.

The man seemed to hesitate, as if trying to decide whether Grandpa was for real. I think he decided he was. "Well, okay, I didn't mean to scare them. They're just little kids. I'm sorry, boys. Just don't scream and run across my back lawn," he said.

My grandpa wasn't there to make concessions. "I don't care what they do—you can't chase young boys and try to scare them," he said. "I will let it go this time, but you'd better not do it again."

And we left. My heart was no longer beating fast. Instead, it was filled with awe—and love—for my grandpa.

"You really told him off, Grandpa," I said. "You scared him."

Grandpa Frank laughed. "Yes, he won't be bothering you anymore. You can count on that."

I must admit, though, we decided not to run across the older man's backyard again.

More than fifty years after my birthday, the day we moved into that house, I returned to visit 115 Bentley Avenue. My wife of thirty years was with me. It was a Sunday morning, and we parked the car in front of Temple Beth-El, the synagogue where I had completed my bar mitzvah ceremony some four decades before. I paused in front of the synagogue as memories flooded me of the many hours spent there during the Jewish High Holy Days. I recalled milling about in front of the synagogue, socializing with girls and friends who had ducked out of religious services to mingle and flirt. A sin? Not really. Raging teenage hormones are not a mystery to God. The space in front of the synagogue wasn't as big as I remembered it. The synagogue building itself looked so small.

Then we headed down Bentley Avenue to 115. The walk took much less time than I remembered. We almost passed it. Had Bentley Avenue shrunk?

And there it was. I saw the same front lawn, the same front porch, and the same alleyway to the right of the house to the garage. Now there was no screened porch. No sign reading, "Dr. Mortimer Davis, DDS" on the front lawn.

I looked for the sharp-edged bricks that circled the weeping willow tree on the front lawn. They were gone, but their memory remained. One night, after coming home from dinner with my sister and parents, I ran from the driveway up the steps across the lawn, stumbled, and fell face-first onto those bricks. The next thing I remember was my father holding me in the living room and hearing, "Are you okay?" repeated over and over again. I was dizzy and stunned and crying, but I was all right.

The memory of that pain in my forehead was as clear at that moment as if it had just happened. The memory of my dad holding me in his arms was even clearer.

Then I looked at the sidewalk halfway to the front porch. The memory was so vivid I broke out laughing. It seems there was this dog named Cookie who lived somewhere up Bentley Avenue. When I was young, probably in second or third grade, my dad and I left one morning so he could drive me to school.

As we walked down the stairs from the front porch, turning left onto the sidewalk to the curb, my dad shocked me with a very loud shout: "*Nooooooo!*" He was yelling, I realized, because Cookie was apparently at the end of a big—can't find a better word—poop. Her rear end was crouched down, and the poop was about to drop to the ground. Ugh. But when my dad yelled, "*Nooooooo!*" Cookie reacted with obvious fright. In a nanosecond, she seized the poop in her mouth and tore up the street, followed by my screaming dad. We burst out laughing, amazed at what Cookie had just done. The shock of the situation overcame what would have been a moment of revulsion.

My dad and I were so amazed by Cookie's act that we could not stop laughing—and hugging, somehow knowing this was a shared moment we would never forget.

When I got to the backyard, which I remember was big enough to play baseball with a rubber ball and a broomstick for a bat, I was in disbelief. The grass I remembered was mostly dirt, and it was so cramped. How had we played stickball here? I looked at the places where we had placed stones to represent first base, second base, and third base, just to check my memory. How could it have shrunk over time?

Finally, we knocked on the front door. A young man answered, his wife and young children behind him. I explained who I was and that this had been my boyhood home and apologized for disturbing him on a Sunday morning. He immediately invited us in. He and his wife graciously asked whether I wanted to take a look through the house. We accepted gratefully. We walked up the front staircase to the second floor. On the left was the little den, followed by the small bedroom that had been my parents' "master" bedroom. Across the hall were the small bathroom and the bedroom where my sister had slept. Then down the hall, we reached the back staircase that led to what had been my room.

Then we went down the backstairs to the little kitchen, where memories flooded back of my mom cooking breakfasts and lunches. From there, we went down the steps to the basement, which my dad and mom had "finished" with wooden panels and linoleum (and a fireplace!) in time for my bar mitzvah.

As we left and thanked the young couple who now resided at 115 Bentley, I was filled with sadness, nostalgia, wonder—and grief. I missed my parents, both of whom had passed by then.

As we drove away, I thought again about how small everything had become: the size of Bentley Avenue, the house at 115, the backyard, the basement, my room—everything. How was that possible? It couldn't be that the laws of physics allowed houses, streets, and rooms to shrink over time. The answer, of course, is that all seemed bigger when I was little and smaller now that I was grown. I was filled with memories and sadness at growing up.

My dad really disliked his first name—and his childhood friends knew it. So even though he went by "Mort," they relentlessly sang out, "Mortimer . . . Mortimer . . ." Dad told me his reaction was to "punch them in the nose," whether they were big or small. I doubted that since my dad, a slender five feet, ten inches tall, was not exactly the "punch them in the nose" type. Anyway, he also claimed his middle name was "Caryl," but he wouldn't answer when I asked him if he made up that name and spelling. He was born on June 22, 1918, in Bayonne, New Jersey.

I've learned this, and more, from my dad's attempt at a brief family history (which I mentioned earlier), which was completed in April 1992, four years before he passed away in October 1996 at the age of seventy-eight. He wrote it on an old-fashioned typewriter. He tried using the early version of a word processor but hit the wrong button and erased almost the entire manuscript and had to start all over again. The book, titled *Izzy*, was really about his father. Here is how the book begins:

> *Ten years before the Johnstown Flood, eight years after the Great Chicago Fire, just fourteen years after the Civil War*

> *ended, my father, Frank M. Davis, was born on January Fourth, 1879, in Newark, New Jersey. He was not named Izzy, of course. That change came much later. His given name was Israel Michael, and he was called Izzy by his family and friends until he married and settled down in Bayonne, New Jersey, at the age of twenty-three.*

Much of the family tree at my grandfather's level can be found in this little seventy-eight-page book. (My oldest son, Seth, took it upon himself to publish it as a softcover book with a photograph of my grandfather's early twentieth-century photo shop on Broadway in Bayonne, "Davis Photos.") During my early years, however, some of my cousins thought my grandfather's name was "Mike," and some thought, as Tama and I did, that his name was "Frank." No matter.

The little book is a trove of family history going back at least to my grandfather's parents (my dad's great-grandparents): Lewis Davis and Hanna Marx, who were married on December 13, 1864. One way we know this is because we have a fiftieth wedding anniversary photograph of Lewis and Hanna holding cards taken by my grandfather at his photo studio in 1914. The caption under the two kindly looking seniors reads, "Playing the game of love."

Dad had two elder brothers and one older sister. His oldest brother, Sonny, joined my grandfather in the photography business. Sonny had two sons, Ira and Ted, my first cousins. I never got to know Ira well, but Teddy was the older brother I never had—and remains so to this day.

Dad's second-oldest brother was Harry, a brilliant pianist who got as far as one concert in Carnegie Hall and then opened a music school in Westchester, New York. He gave me my earliest piano lessons there. My father was also a musician—a violinist who later learned how to play the saxophone, clarinet, and piano.

His older sister, my aunt Beattie, was a beautiful and successful fashion designer who became famous in the women's clothing business. Beattie and her husband, Lew Bodenstein, who partnered with my grandfather in the photography business, had one daughter, Lois. Lois was drop-dead gorgeous well into her eighties. She married a conservative Republican named Gene Bierer, a military man and graduate of West Point who achieved the rank of colonel before retirement. I loved and respected Gene, although he and my father argued about politics constantly.

Besides bristling at the name "Mortimer," Dad was also supersensitive when anyone called him "Mister."

"I am to be called 'Dr. Davis,'" he would insist, even to close friends. "I am a doctor dentist, but so what?" he'd say. "I am just as entitled to be called 'doctor' as a 'doctor doctor.'"

Mom and Dad were secretly married, I believe, sometime in 1936, when my dad was nineteen and my mom a year younger. For at least a year, they kept their marriage a secret. They lived apart in their respective parents' homes—my mom's in Jersey City and my dad's in Bayonne.

Then after they let out the secret, they got "officially" married on August 9, 1937, with a big party, a wedding cake, and photographs for posterity. It is no exaggeration to say that my young, thin-waisted, and buxom mother was dazzlingly beautiful in a white, lacy wedding dress. At the "official" wedding, my parents announced their secret, to screams of excitement and—so my dad told me—knowing nods from most of the men (and all the women) in the room.

The only explanation they ever gave my sister, Tama, and me about why they decided to get married but keep it a secret and live apart was, "We wanted to wait till we could afford it." This was an evasion. In those days "nice girls" didn't have premarital sex. My parents didn't want to wait, and it had nothing to do with money.

On the date of my birth, when my parents moved into our house at 115 Bentley, my dad immediately put a sign on the lawn, "Dr. Mortimer C. Davis, DDS," with his plan to start earning a living in his own home to save office rent. It was not for another twenty years that he moved the dental office out of the house and into an office about ten blocks away.

My mother was my dad's dental office manager from the first day he opened his practice. She ran all aspects of the dental office, keeping the appointments, calling patients to remind them of their visits, and collecting the bills—usually cash in those days.

After summer vacation, when I was in middle school and had summer reading that I was supposed to complete but had not, my dad would drive down to Montgomery Street, with a view of the Hudson River, to the main Jersey City library. There, we could get what came to be known as "CliffsNotes"—short summaries of big classic books that most kids are supposed to read over the summer for their next grade in elementary or high school but almost never actually read. I discovered I could get away with not reading most of the summer reading books by finding the "Classic Comic" version and passing the quick quiz to see if I had done my reading.

Every time we went to the main library, my dad would see the Jersey City waterfront tenements, empty warehouses, and docks filled with rats, insects, dirt, and garbage. He would always repeat the same line: "Lanny, I could buy all this waterfront land up from Hoboken to Bayonne for ten cents an acre or less, and someday, by the time you grow up, we will be millionaires." (In those days the biggest number anyone could think of to describe being filthy rich was "millionaire." I don't think I ever heard the word "billionaire" until decades later.)

Today, in the 2000s, that land is prime territory for multimillion-dollar condos for zillionaire Yuppies and Wall Street financiers. My dad would quip more times than I could count, "Lanny, you can decide the best investment strategy by following what I do: When I buy, you sell. When I sell, you buy."

■ ■ ■

Grown men weep at the iconic scene in *Field of Dreams*, when Kevin Costner's character asks his reincarnated father, "Hey, Dad, want to have a catch?" Although I get a lump in my throat when I see that movie, too, I didn't have to visit Iowa or depend on magical realism to bond with my father over baseball.

A typical afternoon coming home from elementary school in the 1950s entailed young Lanny Davis entering the front door of his Jersey City house, waving to the patients in the living room/waiting room, and sticking his head into the door. I would see my dad working, the patient's mouth often uncomfortably held wide open with a hard metal brace.

"Hey, Dad," young Lanny would mouth silently. "Wanna have a catch?"

Dr. Davis would respond by giving me a nod and a wave, gesturing with his hand as if to say, "Give me a minute." Then I would hear him say to the patient, "Excuse me, I need to use the restroom," leaving the patient stuck with the metal brace and a mouth stretched open. Then the dentist would morph effortlessly into the best father a boy could have.

By then I had already grabbed my baseball glove and raced outside to the narrow driveway next to our house. Minutes later my dad would appear with his old, shabby glove on his right hand—he was a lefty—and we'd start throwing the ball back and forth. The ritual was to make believe we were in the middle of a real baseball game. Our team was the New York Giants. Our usual opponent was the Giants' archrivals: the Brooklyn Dodgers. Dad would take on the tone of a baseball announcer—one in particular: the legendary Russ Hodges, the Giants' radio announcer, who famously screamed, repeatedly, after Bobby Thomson hit his walk-off, game-winning home run against Ralph Branca and the Brooklyn Dodgers in 1951: "The Giants win the pennant! The Giants win the pennant! The Giants win the pennant!"

He would throw me a ground ball, imitating Hodges in announcing that a sharp ground ball was hit to Giants shortstop Alvin Dark (me). I would scoop it up and throw it sidearm, and my dad would yell, "He's out!" Then a fly ball. I would go back and, at the last second, drop my hands to my stomach and perform a basket catch just like my idol, Giants' center fielder Willie Mays. My dad would shout, "Say hey, Willie!"—the famous 1950s moniker used to invoke "the Say Hey Kid."

At some point, when we'd get carried away and the bases were loaded, with the dangerous Dodgers center fielder, Duke Snider, up to bat, my father would realize that about ten minutes had passed. He would think about his poor patient, stuck with the iron-locked jaw, waiting for him to return. Then he would say, "Oh my god. I've got to go. Don't miss this catch, or the Dodgers will win!"

And he would throw a high fly ball to me as he ran up the steps and crossed the lawn to go back into the dental office. I backed up, back, back, down the driveway, onto Bentley Avenue. Forget about any cars coming that might run me over and kill me—I was not going to miss that fly ball and let the Dodgers win the game! Of course, I also had to go back fast enough and far enough to make the Willie Mays basket catch. My hands cupped at my waist, and like Willie, at the last second, I would open them up and catch the ball in my "basket."

After catching it, I'd feel certain I heard the cheers of tens of thousands of fans at the Polo Grounds, the Giants' home field in Harlem on the East River, across from the Bronx and the despised Yankee Stadium.

The last time I saw my hero at the Polo Grounds—the last time anyone played baseball there—was Sunday, September 29, 1957.* My dad took me to see Willie Mays play his last game in New York for the New York Giants. The next season, the Giants were moving to San Francisco. We expected all 54,555 seats in the old Polo Grounds on Coogan's Bluff in the Bronx, just across the ravine from Yankee Stadium, to be filled. Instead, the stands seemed virtually empty. It seemed that Giants fans were angry about the move to San Francisco, and, to make matters worse, the Giants were mired in sixth place. Only about eleven thousand fans showed up.

* Originally written and published in *The Hill* newspaper on December 15, 2008.

But there was an advantage to the sparse turnout. My dad was able to take me to the empty seats right behind the Giants' dugout, near the rail to the field. None of the ushers seemed to mind. So close to Willie!

In the first inning, when No. 24 came up to bat, my dad urged me to yell, "Say, 'Hey, Willie!'" and I did. He turned, looked, and smiled at me! I swear he did. Then he proceeded to get a single. But the game didn't go well for the Giants. They were down 9–1 going into the bottom of the ninth when Willie came up with one out. *Thank goodness,* I thought, *he won't be the last out in the last inning.*

"Oh please, please," I prayed to the gods of baseball, "let Willie hit a home run in his last at bat at the Polo Grounds." It was not to be. Willie hit a one-hopper to the pitcher, and he was quickly thrown out. Yet he hustled all the way to first base and beyond. *Oh my, oh my*, I thought.

My hero hustled to the very end. Two outs. And then came the last batter, grounding out to shortstop, and it was over. As fast as that. Suddenly, I saw No. 24 literally leap up the steps of the Giants' dugout, right in front of me, so close I could almost touch him, and there he was, tearing full speed toward center field to the safety of the clubhouse and the team locker room. As soon as I saw Willie burst out of the dugout, I had only one thought: I have to shake Willie's hand and thank him and say goodbye. I have to!

Without the slightest hesitation, I jumped over the rail and ran after him. I ran as hard as I could. A few other people had the same idea—like virtually all of us lining the railings for the last out. A few people (it seemed like a few thousand) stopped, as I did, to get souvenirs from the field. I grabbed a handful of Polo Grounds infield dirt—the same dirt, I thought, that Willie might have stepped on. I put it in my pocket. I kept that dirt in a paper cup in my desk drawer for years.

Other fans grabbed the infield bases. Others were tearing down the outfield walls. It was a mob, and it was a mess. I ended up sitting on the first step of the steep staircase to the clubhouse, with nearly all eleven thousand fans behind me, all of us shouting, "We want Willie! We want Willie!"

Then suddenly it hit me: Where is my dad?

I looked around to see if I could find him. I couldn't.

First, I thought there was no reason to be afraid—after all, I was twelve years old, so why should I be afraid of temporarily being separated from my father? Then I changed my mind as I looked at the screaming mob of strangers behind me. I was petrified. But at that very moment, I felt a hand on my shoulder. When I turned, it was my dad.

"How did you know where I was?" I asked him.

"I knew where you would be," he said quietly, with a wisdom I didn't appreciate at the time.

And then—it happened. Willie Mays came for a curtain call, waved to all the delirious thousands of shouting fans, and then . . . and then . . . he looked down the stairs, looked at me, and pointed his finger at me, as if to say, "Hi, kid. Bye, kid."

As I recalled this memory over the years, I wanted to believe he looked at me, just me—my hero Willie. Looking back, I realize I had experienced an important lesson in life. I was both happier and sadder in that moment than I had ever been in my life, and those feelings were not necessarily a contradiction.

In 2010 the only official biography of Mays, titled *Willie Mays: The Life, the Legend*[†] was published. Shortly afterward I received a phone call from Robert Siegel, the host of a popular National Public Radio show. Coincidentally, I was at the airport in San Francisco, the city where the Giants had made their home after abandoning New York.

"Have you seen the Willie Mays bio yet?" Siegel asked, knowing I was still a devoted Willie Mays fan nearly four decades after he retired.

"No, why?" I replied.

"Go to the bookstore at the airport," he said. "I am sure it will be out front by the register. Buy it and turn to page 266."

I did so, and I opened the book to that page. And there it was: an account of Willie's last game in the Polo Grounds, with a sentence that

---

† James S. Hirsch, *Willie Mays: The Life, the Legend* (New York: Scribner, 2010).

began, "Watching the game was twelve-year-old Lanny Davis, who had come with his father to say farewell to Willie." Then on page 267 were quotations from my column in *The Hill* and other descriptions of the scene of fans ripping up the stadium for souvenirs and the shouts of "We want Willie!" at the bottom of the clubhouse stairs in deep center field.

Five decades later I finally had my chance to shake Willie Mays's hand. I was told a few days beforehand that he would be a special guest at a San Francisco fundraiser for a presidential campaign I had helped organize for Hillary Clinton. She could not make it, but her husband was there to speak on her behalf. Bill Clinton and Mays had met when Clinton was president, raised money for each other's foundations, and became golfing buddies.

I was ushered into a room in the private home where the fundraiser was being held, and there he was. Willie was standing with President Clinton. I started to cry. I could barely get out a sentence about how much I loved him and had been his fan since I was little. Clinton was laughing at how moved I was.

I handed Willie a paper that my young son Josh had written as a school assignment about his dad's boyhood hero, Willie Mays. The biography had a photo that Josh had taken from the internet of Willie as a young Giants ballplayer. I asked Willie if he would autograph Josh's essay. He scrawled on the first page above his photo, "To Josh—Willie Mays, #24." President Clinton, with delight, leaned over and scrawled with his pen: "I'm a Willie Mays fan, too." To say the least, I saved my son's essay with those two autographs behind a sealed frame, and it still hangs in my office.

I mentioned earlier in this chapter that grown men cried while watching *Field of Dreams* when Ray Kinsella, played by Kevin Costner, asked his magically-come-back-to-life father to play catch. I wasn't being hyperbolic. I saw that movie in 1989 and sobbed at the scene.

When the theater lights went on, I saw I wasn't alone. Like men all over America, I went to a phone booth (no cell phones then) and called my dad at his Miami Beach retirement home. Hearing his voice, I started crying again.

"Lanny? What's the matter?" he said. "Dad," I blubbered through sobs and tears. "Dad, I love you."

This alarmed him even more.

"What is the matter?" he said. "Are you hurt? The kids?"

Now I heard my mom in the background also sounding worried, so I quickly told him that we were fine and that I had seen a movie that made me think of him—a film he had to see.

I tried to explain that I didn't want to be like Ray Kinsella, who wished he'd told his father while he was still alive how much he loved him. Through my tears, I just repeated, "Just wanted you to know I love you."

My parents saw the movie the next day, and Dad phoned to say, "Now your mom and I know why you called. I love you too. Remember the catches in the alleyway we used to have?" he asked.

"Yes," I said. "I do remember. I love you, Dad."

I learned over the many years since that joy and sadness are not only part of life—one almost always follows after the other and then back again. So now I know, with the wisdom of hindsight, that when such a moment of pure joy occurs, never forget it—always treasure it, because in real life it won't last forever. Surely, some sadness will inevitably follow.

So remember those moments of joy as best as you can, and, if possible, write them down so you won't forget them. Now I finally have.

■ ■ ■

Music was a central part of my dad's life. After politics, it was his second most important preoccupation. He played violin in the local symphony orchestra at the Jersey City Jewish Community Center. He also played in a "string quartet" with another violinist, a viola player (a slightly larger, richer form of the violin), and a cellist in our living room. He loved compositions by Mozart the best.

One night, when I was about four or five, he was tuning up for his three other members, using the A string—the traditional string that orchestras use to synchronize the tone of their instruments. As he played the A string for his colleagues to tune from, I said, "Uh-uh," moving my head back and forth in a *no* motion.

My father was puzzled. "What did you say, Lanny?"

"Uh-uh," I said again, shaking my head when I heard the sound of his bow across his string. He then tightened the string, meaning he raised the tone slightly (or "sharpened" the tone). No again, I indicated. Then he loosened the string slightly. Now I nodded, indicating yes—just right. The other three members of the quartet were now sitting and staring at me, stunned.

"I think he has absolute pitch," one said in shock.

"Perfect," also known as "absolute," pitch appears rarely in humans. Apparently about one in ten thousand people has it. It possibly comes from genetic traits, the key element being the ability to hear a note and know what it is automatically, without even understanding how or why you know.

People with perfect pitch are also able to memorize what they hear quickly and then play music by ear.

Because I memorized my classical pieces so quickly, I was lazy about practicing sight-reading—to look up and read the notes on the page of new music. I memorized it too quickly and didn't have to make the effort. To this day I still cannot read music.

What I could do was hear a popular song on the radio—especially singable songs from Broadway musicals by such composers as Rodgers and Hammerstein (*The Sound of Music*, *Oklahoma!*, and *Carousel*) or Lerner and Loewe (*My Fair Lady* and *Camelot*)—and play them by ear on the piano without sheet music.

My dad was so proud of me as he showed me off to his music-playing friends and bandmates. I heard him whisper, "My genes, not Fran's" (meaning he took the credit, and my mother did not deserve any). And though I also heard the praise, the truth is, when I was playing by ear, I didn't feel talented at all. It was so easy, and the chords and notes came to me so naturally. I almost felt I was cheating. I still think that today when people express amazement when I am playing any song with chords by ear without sheet music.

Being Morty Davis's kids also meant that my sister, Tama, and I got to see all the 1950s Broadway classics, usually on opening night. The one that became my favorite was *Damn Yankees*, a 1955 musical by Richard Adler (with lyrics by Jerry Ross) about an older man named Joe Boyd who lived in Washington, D.C., and rooted for the Washington Senators, who always lost to the New York Yankees.

Baseball and music, music and baseball—what could be better for my dad and me together in a Broadway theater? And the plot! Perfect! Joe Boyd makes a deal with the devil and transforms into a young superstar named Joe Hardy. He gets to play for the Senators and make the last play to ensure that the Senators finally beat the Yankees for the American League pennant!

Then Satan sends him back to be an old man again because he wasn't supposed to make that play. And even after the devil made him old again, he had another chance at that last play, and he did catch the last out and won the pennant for the Senators anyway.

Every song in that show is memorable to me today as I write, some sixty years later: "You Gotta Have Heart," "Whatever Lola Wants," and "A Man Doesn't Know" (my father's favorite song and one of his favorite lyrics).

And then there was the late-nineteenth-century composer Giacomo Puccini and his two operas, which Dad would have me sit and listen to while reading the librettos, *La Bohème* and *Tosca*. Why? Because Puccini wrote beautiful melodies, just like Richard Rodgers, Dad would say. Once

I heard the beautiful arias—powerful solos with beautiful, memorable melodies—I could play them on the piano by ear. And voilà! Dad was proud of me again.

Besides having a catch, my dad would also always be there for me when I was playing the piano. I took classical piano from the age of three or four from my dad's brother, Harry Davis. In the 1930s and 1940s, Uncle Harry was a highly regarded classical pianist who once played in Carnegie Hall. One bad review discouraged him, however, so he quit playing concerts and turned to private teaching. One of my uncle's most famous teachers, who gave me many lessons when I was older, was Brooklyn-born prodigy Bernard Nierow, who became internationally famous under his Anglicized name, Peter Nero.

Dad would expect me to go downstairs to the basement after our catches in the alleyway to practice my classical pieces before my next lesson. I usually did, at least before I became a teenager and switched to playing jazz and popular music in a band. I switched because I noticed most of the pretty girls liked to hang out around the piano player at school dances. (Yes, it worked: I met my wife, Carolyn—brilliant, beautiful, and talented, with natural vibrato in her singing voice—while playing the piano for an amateur singing group. She was impressed that I could play by ear and change keys for her to sing her audition song in her preferred key! In answer to not-so-humorous questions from friends of mine who couldn't understand how such a drop-dead gorgeous woman could fall for me, given my scrawny body and not-overwhelming good looks, to say the least, I would always say, "My piano playing did it." Sometimes when Carolyn heard the same questions, she would say, "He has perfect pitch and could change the key in his head so I could sing the song! That was it!")

So there I was, in the basement, a floor below where my father was standing at the dental chair, operating a loud drill that could break an eardrum. He also had classical music blaring in the background, and usually my mother was nearby talking loudly on the telephone to a patient to remind him/her of an appointment or gossiping with a girlfriend. Also nearby was the lab technician, John Fabula, a Hungarian immigrant, pounding away at making a crown or a gold inlay. Yet somehow, amid all that noise, all that din, if I hit a wrong note while I was practicing, say, F rather than F sharp on the keyboard, I would almost immediately hear a shout from my dad. His voice bounced off the walls of his office and carried down the stairs to the basement: "F sharp!"

Go figure. A miracle. A noodge to the extreme. My dad.

■ ■ ■

But that obsessiveness, that sense of wanting things to be perfect, had a flip side to it. My dad was possessed by politics, and although politics is an art, it is not a science and rarely even great art. It ain't Mozart, in other words. It's not even baseball. It's the art of the possible. It's messy and entails compromises. My dad wasn't a compromiser.

He was a New Deal Democrat who loved Franklin Roosevelt and loathed those who didn't. He used the word "hate" frequently in front of nearly anyone he identified as a Republican—with only a few exceptions. He revered Senator Jacob Javits, a liberal Republican from New York. (It didn't hurt that Javits was Jewish.) Dad also always voted for Republican Senator Clifford Case of New Jersey, explaining, "He's a liberal, and we need a few of them in the Republican Party."

Dad couldn't get enough of politics, which he followed by faithfully reading the columnists in the *New York Post*, which leaned left in those long-ago days. Every night over dinner, he would hand me columns by Jimmy Wechsler, Murray Kempton, Marquis Childs, and so many others. They were all liberal Democrats and anti–Dwight Eisenhower. I noticed that Dad could find politics in everything, even things that weren't political at all. For example, I was not allowed to root for the New York Yankees. They didn't really compete with the New York Giants because they were in the American League. And rarely did the Giants make the World

Series and even have a chance to play the Yankees, who seemed to almost always win the Series.

Yet in our house, God forbid you should be a Yankees fan or say anything good about the Yankees in front of my dad. Why? Simple. Here is his direct quote: "The Yankees have all the money, they win all the time, they're Republicans!" End of story. I suppose that in this way, he was a man ahead of his time. In twenty-first-century America, we have Republican and Democratic fast-food restaurants, Republican and Democratic radio stations, and Republican and Democratic churches.

My dad also had a habit of personalizing political differences. I noticed, especially when I grew older, how many friends he lost when they offered a political opinion with which he disagreed. And God forbid they should be conservatives. I watched my father in horror, over dinner or at social events, quarreling with an old friend he discovered happened to be a Republican. Afterward I noticed that he and my dad were not together anymore. He was persona non grata as far as my dad was concerned.

I remember thinking, *There's something wrong with that.* At one point I made a conscious vow: I will never turn politics into something personal. I will never hate someone because we have political differences. This was the vow I made in my younger years, wanting to be the opposite of my dad in this one important respect.

I haven't always kept that promise, but I've always remembered it, even to this day. And when I failed to keep it, I always vowed to try not to repeat that mistake.

■ ■ ■

My father would be the last one to think of himself as intolerant of others. On the contrary, he believed (as I do) that Democrats—at least outside the old South—epitomized tolerance. The modern Democratic Party showed the way on racial progress, was accepting of Jews, expanded immigration to the Third World, prioritized human rights in foreign policy, embraced women's rights, supported organized labor, challenged McCarthyism, and led the way on environmental protection. It was hidebound conservatives who resisted these enlightened positions—and who were therefore problematic in my father's eyes. I get that. But as Bill Clinton, another Democrat who would be an important influence in my life, liked to say, we should love our political adversaries, for they "show us our faults."[‡]

What I'm saying is that my father's intolerance came from a place of wanting a better world for the less fortunate. In this sense he was not unlike the "woke" young progressives today, who are so vitriolic when talking about anyone with whom they disagree.

I would also say, in defense of my father, that the injustices in this country when he was growing up were tangible and manifest. His generation didn't have to conjure up "microaggressions" or embrace a zany dialectic that paints everyone of European descent as a closet "white supremacist." Segregation was real in this country. Sixty Black people were lynched in this country the year my father was born (compared with four whites).

The seminal movie in our house when I was growing up was *To Kill a Mockingbird*, based on Harper Lee's Pulitzer Prize–winning novel published in 1960. The movie, which is about standing up against racial prejudice, came out in 1962, starring Gregory Peck as lawyer and father Atticus Finch. After the movie, my dad took out a copy of the book and turned to a page in chapter 3, and he read it aloud to my sister and me.

Atticus's young daughter, Scout, had told him about an unpleasant experience she had with an elderly neighbor who took offense at something Scout had done.

‡ Clinton was paraphrasing Benjamin Franklin. Riffing off the New Testament, Franklin's puckish advice in *Poor Richard's Almanack* is to "Love your Enemies, for they tell your Faults."

"First of all," Atticus said, "if you can learn a simple trick, Scout, you'll get along a lot better with all kinds of folks. You never really understand a person until you consider things from his point of view . . ."

"Sir?"

"Until you climb into his skin and walk around in it."

Through the years I read that passage to my children and grandchildren. I thought of it often. It was easy to memorize but not easy to do. So you see, my father was imparting the right lesson. He just didn't take the final step—and apply his wisdom to Republicans.

Another lesson my dad taught us was from a different movie, this one much older, made in 1947. Directed by Elia Kazan, it was also filmed in black and white, based on a best-selling novel, and coincidentally also starred Gregory Peck. It was called *Gentleman's Agreement* and won many Academy Awards, including Best Picture and Best Director.

It's a story about a widowed magazine writer named Philip Schuyler Green (played by Peck) who wanted to write a story about anti-Semitism. So he decided he needed to experience it firsthand. He had just moved to New York City and was unknown to most people, so he rendered his last name as "Greenberg." He used it when introducing himself in various social situations: shops, restaurants, cocktail parties, and hotels. The stares, the hostility, and his experiences when people heard his last name as Greenberg provided graphic, visceral evidence of anti-Semitism and its impact on Jews experiencing it.

One of the film's pivotal scenes is when Peck/Green is checking into an upscale resort hotel, the Flume Inn, and the reservation is made under his real last name, Green. But when he is signing in at the hotel registration desk, he corrects the clerk and signs in as "Greenberg." Suddenly, the clerk pauses, says he needs to check on room availability, and goes into a room behind the registration desk. He returns to tell Green, "Sorry, I was mistaken. We have no rooms."

Green is furious, but he is escorted out of the hotel.

Later, Green's fiancée (played by actress Dorothy McGuire, whose character name is the very WASPish Kathy Lacy) is present when Green's son Tommy comes home from school crying. When Green asks his son why he is crying, his son tells him some kids at school were mocking him for being Jewish. Green's fiancée, McGuire/Lacy, assures Tommy that he shouldn't worry about being called "a dirty Jew" because he's not Jewish and that this is merely his father's writing method. Sensing what today we'd call a "teachable moment," Green tells his son to ignore her. The point of the story is how wrong such ethnic slurs are—not that they were misapplied.

Other stresses arise for the couple: Kathy takes Phil to meet her parents, but when he won't reveal the charade, several of the guests cancel. Kathy also meets Phil's best friend, fellow U.S. Army combat veteran Dave Goldman, who is Jewish. Despite having returned from the war, Goldman is redlined out of finding housing, and Kathy won't rent her parents' cottage to him for fear of offending bigoted neighbors. Phil, not liking what he is seeing in this woman, breaks off the engagement. She then meets with Dave and tearfully asks him, "Do you think I'm anti-Semitic?"

"No, Kathy, I don't," Dave replies.

To bolster her credentials of not being a bigot, Kathy then tells Goldman about "a vicious story" a man told her at dinner that made her "ill with shame."

"What kind of story, Kathy?" Dave says. He has to coax it out of her, and it's not pretty. A man she identifies as "Lockhart" tells a crude racist joke that includes the words "kike" and "coon." Kathy is horrified but says nothing. Neither do the other guests.

As Dave Goldman teases this story out of Kathy, the eponymous meaning of the movie's title becomes clear. That's the "gentleman's agreement," but it's something no true gentleman—or decent American—would ever agree to. It's a pact to remain silent in the face of injustice, to not make waves in supposedly polite society. To remain silent. The "nice people" didn't laugh, Kathy tells Dave, but as she repeats the story, she realizes how hollow it is. Phil tried to tell her, but she didn't see it until she lost him.

"They are more than nasty little snobs, Kathy," Phil told her earlier in the film. "You call them that, and you can dismiss them. It's too easy. They're persistent little traitors to everything this country stands for and stands on, and you have to fight 'em! Not just for the 'poor, poor Jews,' as Dave says, but for everything this country stands for."

But *Gentleman's Agreement* is a romantic escape and a parable about prejudice, so Kathy sees the light, Phil takes her back, and Dave Goldman and his family stay in Connecticut and presumably live happily ever after. In our family the point of this movie was not the love story; it was how to resist the "gentleman's agreement." My father told my sister and me that silence is not acceptable. Not once but many times throughout our lives. Working this out aloud as she talks to an American combat veteran, a Jew, Kathy Lacy says, quite rightly, "Behind that joke, there's Flume Inn, and Darien and Tommy and those kids. If you don't stop with that joke, where do you stop?"

Left unsaid—and it didn't need to be said because this movie was released only two years after the liberation of Auschwitz—is that the horrific lesson behind that joke was the Holocaust.

Some twenty-first-century conservatives are fond of ridiculing the excesses of "woke" culture among progressives, especially young people. A particular target is the phrase "Silence is violence." Overstated, yes, and sometimes employed on the wrong side, such as when many on the left unleashed vitriol on Israel instead of Hamas after the gruesome attacks of October 7, 2023. But history shows us that silence in the face of bigotry *can* lead to violence, and what my father taught us is that silence is not an option when you hear someone use hateful words against people based on their race, religion, or ethnic origin.

"You have to speak up, no matter what," my dad taught me early and often. "Just ask the speaker to respect you and not repeat those words in front of you. Then you stake your ground for yourself—and let the other person know how you feel. Make it clear where you stand on bigotry."

That is a lesson I have remembered throughout my life, and many times I have asked people using racist and religiously bigoted words to stop, to not repeat those words in my presence. Rather than making a personal attack against the speaker, I found that approach had a greater effect and registered better with them. And when those occasions happen, I always think of my father and silently say, "Thank you, Dad."

## CHAPTER 2

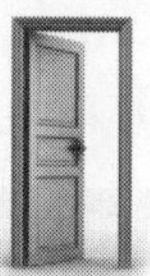

# MOM

There is a subgenre of humor about Jewish mothers, and one consistent trope is that they are overbearing, which can be another way of saying they love their kids intensely. It can also mean they are not women to be trifled with. I can relate to both stereotypes.

First and foremost, you didn't mess with my mom. She was funny, kind, lovable, and a great friend to all. But most of all, she was tough. She knew who she was and what her boundaries were—as anyone who crossed her quickly discovered.

She was brilliant, a great writer, and savvy with people of all stripes. Had she lived in the twenty-first century, not in the mid- to late twentieth century, she would have had a successful career in medicine, law, politics—you name it. Instead she was born in 1919, one year before women could even vote in this country.

As it was, she ended up as a top-rate secretary (with typing and shorthand skills), a medical officer administrator, and ultimately, a full-time office manager and administrator for my dad's dental practice. At the same time, she was a full-time—virtually 24/7—mom, friend, and grandmother, available to help and be a mother to all who were in need—both humans and four-legged stray animals.

Sometimes, when she walked by my dad while he was drilling someone's tooth or performing some other procedure, she offered unsolicited advice right in front of the patient, such as "Morty, you're not drilling in the right place."

My father's reaction, let us say, was not always positive. That didn't bother my mom, who also didn't worry about the patient's reaction.

"You'll be fine," she would say to the patient, tapping him or her on the shoulder while ignoring my dad.

We had live-in help, what today would be called a "nanny." Some stayed for years and lived in the fourth-floor little attic bedroom. One, whom I shall never forget, was named Heidi. She stayed for only a few days. More about her later.

■ ■ ■

My mother, Fran Goldberg, daughter of Jennie and Joe Goldberg, was born in Jersey City. I believe that her mother, Jennie, whom we called "Bubby," came from Latvia. Her father, Joseph Goldberg, whom we called "Pop," was born in the borderlands between western Russia and Poland.

I know little about my mother's childhood or teenage years. I think she went to Lincoln High School, on the eastern side of Jersey City. Her dad, Pop Goldberg, ran a hand-laundry and sewing shop in a lower-income neighborhood and scratched out a living. I remember their place in Jersey City was a narrow three-story townhouse in a compact lower-working-class neighborhood, much of which was Irish Catholic. I recall my mom referring to some of her best friends as Irish girls who sometimes took her to Christmas Eve Mass.

What is definite is that she was a gorgeous young woman. Photos of her in a bathing suit after she married my dad make it pretty clear why my dad insisted on marrying secretly before they could afford a house.

She had an older brother, Louis, and a younger brother, Joseph. Lou was handsome and had a deep, resonant singing voice. He married a vivacious gentile named Loise and moved to a Cleveland suburb when I was young. They had three sons—my first cousins Bob, Richard, and Larry, who was my age. Lou died in his late forties, I think—so young, even back then—from a heart infection that I think would have been handled without much difficulty with today's medical resources. My mother cried and cried when we heard about Uncle Lou's death. She was his "hero," she told me.

I remember her other brother as dark and handsome with a mustache that seemed to dazzle and attract women. But Uncle Joe was always strapped for money. He had an amazing aptitude for electronics, and had he had the money to go to college, he could have gone to a place such as MIT. But he only went to high school, joined the army during World War II, and fought in Europe. I used to watch in awe as he repaired a television set or a radio and even took apart an automobile engine and put it back together—all self-taught.

But when he got home after the war, Joe struggled to earn a living. He opened a TV-radio repair shop, which failed after a while. He ultimately ended up as a floor salesman at a department store in Yonkers, New York. My mom, I suspected, slipped him cash whenever she could (without, I guessed, telling my dad). Uncle Lou and Uncle Joe at some point changed their last names to "Gilbert" from "Goldberg." I assume this was because "Gilbert" was less obviously Jewish than "Goldberg." I never thought about it at the time, but when I was growing up, anti-Semitism was pretty strong, which is why my dad insisted we watch *Gentleman's Agreement*.

■ ■ ■

The simple fact was that my mother viewed every human being and four-legged stray cat or dog as her responsibility to worry about and take care of—and they all somehow knew it. This meant our house became a mecca for many of them once word spread among humans and strays. Starting with the stray cats and dogs, we always had one or two dogs inside our house (but no cats). My father might have been allergic to cats—or maybe he just didn't want to work as hard as one does to earn a cat's love. But this didn't keep my mother from her mission. Every night, as the sun went down, Mom would go to our back porch to put down scraps of food and water for Jersey City's stray cats and dogs. Sometimes there were dozens.

When it came to human beings who were lonely and homeless, Mom stopped short of bringing them all into the house to live with us. But countless times I saw her pass a homeless person on the street asking for money, and she never failed to reach into her pocketbook to give them a coin or a dollar. My father also had a soft spot for homeless people, but sometimes he would complain to my mother about "encouraging" them not to get a job. My mom would look at him with scorn.

"You think it's so easy to be out there begging for money to eat and a place to sleep?" she would ask my dad. "Why don't you try it for a night or two, and you'll change your mind?"

(Throughout my life I would always do the same and found myself repeating Mom's line to anyone I was walking with who made the same complaint about encouraging them.)

Then there was Johnny.

Johnny was probably in his mid-forties when I first met him, working around the house doing odd jobs. I never figured out where Mom even met him. He was small, about five feet tall, and smelled bad, presumably because he had no home and nowhere to bathe or shower. But he would show up at the house nearly every day, and my mother would give him odd jobs to do. When I came home from school, after I had a catch with my dad, Johnny would wink at me and take out an old baseball from his pocket and a well-worn baseball mitt. We would head for the driveway to toss the ball back and forth. The baseball would sting if I caught it in the center of my baseball glove. He threw hard and true.

I never wondered, as I did later, where Johnny had learned to play baseball so well or how he became homeless and down and out.

All I knew was that my mother was kind to him, and he helped around the house by fixing things and cleaning up the backyard. When the weather got cold, my mother set up a blanket and pillow in the shed leading downstairs to our basement. While there wasn't much heat, it was warm enough to allow him to sleep. My dad would complain about the "Johnny smell" in the shed. But Johnny was taken care of, thanks to my mother.

One night, and we knew it was bound to happen, she went too far. Mom would sometimes let him sit at our kitchen table, which we used for dinner when my dad's dental office was still in the house. He would eat quickly before my dad finished his last appointment and leave. The lingering odor caused us to worry that my dad would realize that Johnny had been at the table, but he never said anything. Then one evening my dad ended his last appointment early and came into the kitchen to find Johnny sitting *in his chair*! It was a bad scene. Frightened by my dad shouting his disapproval, Johnny jumped up and ran out of the house.

My mother ignored my dad's ongoing fury and just continued to make dinner. When he was finished shouting, he asked her, "What do you have to say about this?"

"About what?" she answered.

That was Mom.

■ ■ ■

My list of professions she would have mastered should include investigative reporter. Or private detective. Dad intuited this early on, thankfully, and therefore learned to tell the tale. I should have listened to him. I also noticed that Dad feared her ability to know everything—and to see through every lie.

I was at a New York Giants baseball game one weekend with my dad when I was thirteen or fourteen, just old enough to know I had hormones and the birds and the bees, when a gorgeous-looking young woman in a tight sweater walked by. Nearly every man in our section of the stands stared, leaned, and followed her every step. My dad did the same.

All of a sudden, he turned to me and noticed that I was noticing.

"Did you see me looking at that woman, Lanny?" he asked me.

"Yes, Dad."

He seemed a little nervous.

"And you know I love your mother, right?" he asked.

"Yes, Dad."

"And you know I would never do anything with that woman because I love your mother, right?" he persisted.

"Yes, Dad—if you say so."

When I added "if you say so," with obvious sarcasm, he paused for a moment.

I will never forget his exact words in reply. I have repeated them again and again to friends who heard this story, including my children.

"Listen, son, this is advice I want you to remember for the rest of your life. You may be married someday and love your wife, but you may see a woman like that, and you may want that woman, and you may imagine doing something with that woman, but you shouldn't. You shouldn't! Do you know why, my son?"

I sat silently, waiting.

"Because if you do, you're *gonna get caught*!"

He went on to remind me that my mother was the world's greatest sleuth. "Better than Sherlock Holmes!" he insisted.

"Never try to fool your mom," he reminded me often. "She will figure it out. I promise you."

■ ■ ■

Like every other teenager with only one thing on his mind, I decided to ignore that advice. It was three or four years later when I had a girlfriend from summer camp who lived in Montreal, Québec. Her name was Babs. She was the first girl to whom I said, "I love you," and the first I ever made love to, a fact that young people of my generation did not share with our parents.

I left camp in late August 1962 and immediately began planning a clandestine trip to Montreal to see her again. So I planned the perfect crime, going to Montreal to visit Babs for the weekend (a fourteen-hour drive from Jersey City, I calculated) and prove my dad wrong—show that I could get away with lying to my mom, and she would not catch me.

So I planned the caper carefully, weeks ahead of time, trying to foresee every contingency. I enlisted several friends in the plot. The cover story for my parents was a trip to the Jersey Shore for the weekend.

Anticipating that she would try to call me to be sure I was really at the beach, I instructed my comrades that when the call came in, they should tell her I was at the store getting milk. Then they would call me—I gave them the telephone number of Babs's home in Montreal—and I would then call my mom right back. There were no cell phones back then, let alone GPS tracking devices tagged into your phone, so it was a perfect plan, at least to a seventeen-year-old boy. She would never know.

The morning I left, a Friday, I got up early, made my bed, made breakfast, put the dishes away, and kissed Mom goodbye as I walked out the door. I got into the car and drove nonstop to Montreal. I left at 8:00 a.m. and arrived at 10:00 p.m. That's right, a fourteen-hour drive, almost all without stopping, to the house of Babs's parents. The sex drive will motivate a teenager that way. So when I arrived, all I was thinking about was what I expected to happen the rest of the night and throughout the weekend with Babs.

What I didn't expect was what actually happened when I opened the door. Instead of Babs, ready for an intense kiss to greet me, her mother answered the door, looking at me sternly. My heart skipped a beat. She didn't say hello. She said, "Your mom called."

"What?" I asked. "She called here? When?"

"Late this morning. She said you would be arriving tonight, and you should call her as soon as you got here."

Babs was standing behind her mom, looking more fearful than disappointed.

I went to the phone and called home. In my near panic, I actually thought about telling her that I was out getting milk, as I had planned, until I remembered I was calling her from Montreal, Québec, from Babs's house. The jig was up!

With dread, I waited for someone to answer the phone. I heard a very calm voice. My mom.

"Go to bed and leave tomorrow morning. You are coming home."

And she hung up.

I was mortified. Exhausted. But I never had a thought to call her back to appeal her verdict. I knew I was sunk. I did try to have some time alone with Babs that night anyway so the pain and the misery would at least be worth it. But Babs's mother wasn't cooperating. She sent Babs upstairs to her bedroom and me downstairs to the basement.

Yes, I admit, Babs sneaked down during the night, and we at least had a chance to, well, a gentleman never tells. (I was proud as a teenager when I heard girls tell me, "You have a reputation for not talking." I smiled. It was a reputation that paid excellent dividends.)

Still, as instructed by Mom, I was on the road early, leaving at dawn and arriving home before dark. I still can't believe I made it without falling asleep at the wheel. Well into my adulthood, with teenagers of my own—who I knew were occasionally pulling fast ones on me—I wondered, *How did my mom figure it out? How did she defeat what I thought was the perfect crime?*

Finally, when she was in her seventies, I put it to her directly.

"How did you figure out I had gone to Montreal?" I asked her. "And how did you figure it out so quickly?"

"You made three mistakes," she said without hesitating, as if it had happened the day before.

"Three? Which ones?"

"First, you made your bed," she said, indicating that such fastidiousness was itself suspicious.

"Second, you made your own breakfast and put the dishes away," she said. "Now I knew you must be up to something."

Then she said there was a final clue—the one that led her to the inevitable conclusion.

"As you left the house, you kissed me goodbye, and as you walked to the car, I saw you skip, so happy. Then I knew."

So that was it. Not one, not two, but three clues—and she knew, given my age and hormones, that I had acted uncharacteristically civilized, sweet, and loving. Therefore, I was headed for Babs and Montreal.

I couldn't resist asking her, "How could you make me drive back? That was dangerous. I could have died, falling asleep at the wheel to drive back the very next day. You never would have forgiven yourself."

She looked sad. I was immediately sorry for my outburst.

"You are right," she said. "I never should have. I have regretted that all my life."

I loved her for her honesty, as well as her willingness to admit her error, after all these years.

Then she added, "Your dad knew too. He just didn't tell me. And he knew that I would figure it out. That's how I kept him in line through the years."

I looked at my dad. He held his hands in the air as if to say, "You see?"

I recalled that moment in the Polo Grounds at the Giants game from thirty years before. And that amazing woman in the tight sweater.

He knew what I was remembering—I was certain of it. And from his eyes, I could tell he was afraid I might tell my mom about that and his advice. Of course, I didn't. That was a special father-son secret. Although, as I think about it, she might have known that too.

■ ■ ■

To say that my mother was demanding when she was in a restaurant and ordering her predinner favorite alcoholic beverage, as well as with regard to the quality of the service and the rest of the meal, would be a classic understatement.

Although she was never rude to the waitstaff, she could be a tremendous pain in the ass, which is exactly how my dad would put it: "Fran, would you stop being a pain in the ass?"

If anything, rather than being rude, she would irritate Dad (and embarrass us as kids once in a while) by being too friendly. By the end of the meal, Mom had typically learned the waitress's age, marital status, children, health issues, and even her sex life (followed by whispered advice, woman to woman).

The most memorable moment of my mother's restaurant escapades is known in our family as the "Perfect Rob Roy" incident. Sometime in the late 1980s, my wife, Carolyn, and I were visiting my parents at their retirement home in Miami Beach. The ritual was for all of us to go to dinner for the "early bird special" when it was still daylight and prices were discounted for seniors.

At a restaurant overlooking Biscayne Bay, we were seated at a table near the bar. A waitress, unaware of what was about to happen to her, cheerfully approached the table to ask for predinner drink orders.

My dad usually ordered a whiskey sour, and my mom a Scotch on the rocks. But then she suddenly turned to the waitress and said, "Could you ask the bartender if he knows how to make a Perfect Rob Roy?"

"Oh, I'm sure he does," the waitress said.

My mother was skeptical. "Just be sure you emphasize the word 'perfect' to him."

To this day I do not know where my mother heard of that drink or why she ordered it. A Rob Roy is essentially a Manhattan but with Scotch instead of rye whiskey or bourbon, mixed with vermouth and bitters. It's chilled and served with a garnish. (For the uninitiated, a "Perfect" Rob Roy is not a definition of excellence; it's the name of a variation of that cocktail: A Rob Roy has sweet vermouth. A dry Rob Roy naturally substitutes dry vermouth. The "perfect" version has equal parts sweet and dry vermouth.)

You probably see where this is going. When the waitress returned, the drink was in a tall glass, with a big fishbowl at the top filled with a caramel-colored liquid and a cherry stem hanging outside. My mother took a sip as the waitress watched, smiling.

"Nope," Mom said. "This is a Rob Roy, but it's not perfect. Please tell the bartender I said 'Perfect' Rob Roy."

The waitress seemed disappointed but eager to please my mom, although as she turned toward the bar, I could see the bartender, an older man, looking at her quizzically. The waitress quietly explained the situation to him. He looked up at my mom, shrugged, and tried again.

Back came the waitress, this time looking at my mom and waiting with expectation.

"Try this one," she said. I turned slightly to eye the bartender. He was ignoring other customers at the bar, waiting to see my mother's reaction.

She sipped, paused, and said, "Nope. This is not a Perfect Rob Roy."

The waitress quickly picked up the glass and went back to the bar. This time the bartender reacted with obvious irritation. Who could blame him?

Two minutes later the waitress came back.

Incredibly, my mother sent back imperfect Rob Roys three or four more times, with my dad getting more and more irritated each time—the bartender even more so—while the waitress tried to remain polite.

Finally, after what I think was the fifth try, I was more worried about my father doing violence to my mom than about the mental state of the waitress or the bartender as we waited for my mom to take a sip of the newly delivered Perfect Rob Roy.

The waitress, too, looked like she wasn't breathing. Carolyn and I were nervous, too, as we waited for a sound from my mom after she took her sip.

"Perfect!" she exclaimed.

We all exhaled—me, my wife, my dad, and especially the waitress. I turned to the bartender. He put his fist in the air like he had just won the Masters golf tournament. My mom motioned toward him with an "okay" sign with her hand. And so it goes. Life with Fran Davis in a restaurant.

As we left, my mom told my dad to be sure to leave a big tip for the waitress and an extra tip to the bartender, and my dad muttered to me quietly, "So because your mom is a pain in the ass, I have to pay extra?"

On our way out, I saw my mom whisper in the waitress's ear. The waitress smiled broadly, and I swear she seemed to blush.

I asked my mom, "What did you say to the waitress?"

"None of your business," she said to me firmly. "It was about how she should take care of her husband tonight to make him happy."

Then she walked off with confidence and joy that she had gotten her Perfect Rob Roy and had helped another waitress perfect her sex life.

■ ■ ■

Our mother could be controlling, which was tough on her children in their teenage years. She was especially overprotective of my sister. More on that in the next chapter. But when it came to grandchildren, as they say in Brooklyn, "Fuhgeddaboudit!"

My two oldest children, Marlo and Seth, and my sister's daughter, Jennifer, all called her "Mom-Mom."* After a weekend with her, they would be so spoiled it would take weeks to get them over the bad habits that came from having a grown-up say yes to every request.

No matter how much I scolded my mother about the bad effects our children's visits showed after spending time with her, it didn't matter. She was Mom-Mom, and they loved her so intensely, so unconditionally, and

---

* Our two younger sons, Joshua Benjamin and Jeremy Joseph, were born in 1998 and 2005 (respectively), after my mom passed away. They have heard most of my stories about her many times.

since that was all that mattered to her, that was the end of that story. She would wave her hand and say, "Oh, you're just jealous they love me so much."

She might have been partially right, although in a way neither Mom nor I would deign to say aloud. If Tama and I were "jealous," it wasn't because our kids loved their grandmother so much. It was that perhaps we wished that the unconditional love she lavished on her grandchildren had been more present in our own home while we were growing up.

My mother was a great fan of Bill and Hillary Clinton, as was my dad—not only because they were loyal Democrats but also because they knew of my friendship with both Clintons. Sadly, my dad passed in October 1996, two months before I went to work in the White House. But my mom lived another fourteen months, passing away in late November 1998.

She was going downhill quickly after my dad died from a severe stroke. She had progressive heart failure, and we could have kept her alive for more years, perhaps, with a heart transplant or partial surgery. But nope, she was not interested. Without saying so directly, she made it clear to us that with Dad gone, she was ready for whatever came next. I am not sure she believed in the eternal soul and a concept called "heaven" or the "afterlife" (as I think I do), but I believe she did.

As she weakened and lost weight, and we could see the end coming in the summer and fall of 1997, I knew her greatest wish would be to come to the White House and meet her all-time political hero, Hillary Clinton. Mom was an instinctive feminist without ever using the word. But I knew she loved watching and listening to Hillary and always commented to me that she would definitely be the first female president, and she would love to meet her. She knew about my longtime friendship from Yale Law School days.

So in early October 1997, Hillary said to me one day, knowing that my mom was heading downhill, "Why don't you invite her to the White House if she can make the trip, and I will be able to meet her, and we can exchange Lanny stories?"

Hillary had a twinkle in her eyes when she said, "Lanny stories," so I did not necessarily want them exchanging "Lanny stories" without me in the room.

So I asked my mom if she would be up for a trip, and she said, "Of course." Taken to the plane at Miami Airport in a wheelchair and fussed over by all the flight attendants (I imagined that by the end of that flight, they had all gotten marital or sex life advice), she was met at Reagan National Airport by a White House intern who had volunteered to meet her and brought into my office in the Old Executive Office Building, across from the West Wing.

I rang the First Lady's office to get the message through to Hillary that my mom had arrived.

"I will call Mrs. Clinton," Hillary's assistant told me. "Take your mom, and she will meet you in the Map Room in ten minutes."

The Map Room, as I explained to my mother as we made our way along the columned walk next to the Rose Garden, is where Franklin D. Roosevelt gave his fireside chats during the Great Depression and also where he tracked the movements of Allied forces during World War II. FDR might well have been in that room the day Mom's brother Joe landed on the beaches of Normandy.

As we made our way over, I gave my mother the pre-Hillary set of rules and regulations I had devised in advance.

"Now, Mom, when you see Hillary, please just say, 'Hello, Mrs. Clinton,' and let her talk about her life in the White House and as First Lady—and you can ask her about what it's like and so on. But please do not talk about me, how talented I am playing the piano, what a good job I did at my bar mitzvah, and the time I tried to get away with the perfect crime and you caught me. Just say, 'Hello Mrs. Clinton,' chitchat awhile, and then 'Thank you, Mrs. Clinton,' after fifteen minutes or so, okay?"

Mom eyed me warily. "I won't embarrass you, I promise," she said.

I repeated my speech. She nodded and said, "I promise."

She was so excited about just being at the White House, "in the real residence," as she kept repeating, that I relaxed and was so happy to give her this thrill at what I knew were the closing days of her life.

Then Hillary arrived, her usual effervescent, smiling, warm, and laughing self, greeting my mom with a big hug, relaxing both her and me, and saying something like, "How nice it is to finally meet the mother of Lanny Davis—and try to figure out how you put up with Lanny all these years!"

My proud Jewish mother beamed like, well, a proud Jewish mother.

Mom laughed and said, "I have so much to tell you about Lanny." Then realizing she had started down the path of breaking her promise, she looked at me warily, seeing my look of disapproval, and said, "Tell me what it's like to be First Lady," and I relaxed a bit.

Hillary sat her down on the couch in the Map Room, and within minutes they were talking like old friends, laughing together at some of Hillary's stories about life in the White House. She referenced the early days when she first met me in law school and how we became friends, and I could see my mother enjoyed hearing about those days.

Instead of fifteen minutes with the First Lady, the meeting lasted almost an hour. Classic Hillary. She was in the middle of multiple meetings and visits from senior diplomats and officials and in the Oval Office with President Clinton, yet she blew all these commitments off to spend time with my mom.

As we got up to leave, and I was ready to breathe a sigh of relief and was so happy things had gone so well, my mother seemed to pause as we said goodbye. My mother, according to the script, was supposed to say "Goodbye. Thank you so much, Hillary, for spending time with me." Over and out.

Instead, she seemed to have something on her mind, something she wanted to say. My heart skipped a beat. I could tell she was thinking about something, and I was pretty certain it was off script.

Hillary was wearing a bright-yellow pantsuit, and suddenly I could tell that my mother was taking note of it, peering at her yellow jacket and pants and back again to her jacket.

Then with no warning, Mom said, "Hillary, didn't I see you wear the exact same outfit on *Larry King* last week?"

Hillary seemed as surprised by the question perhaps as I was, and Mom instantly realized she had erred. She glanced at me nervously, biting her lip with obvious anxiety. But Hillary Clinton burst into a spontaneous belly laugh. It was the same laugh we all loved to hear in law school when we were hanging out, and we all laughed ourselves and realized we were laughing at Hillary's laugh, which made us laugh even more.

"Oh, Fran," Hillary said, reaching out to take both of my mother's hands. "You are right. And so observant. I *did* wear this same suit last week on Larry King's show. Yes, I did. I am *so* glad you noticed and remembered."

As gracious as Hillary was, my mother still looked anxiously at me, worried about my reaction. Of course, Hillary picked that up right away too.

"Oh, don't mind Lanny, Fran. I am so happy you noticed my pantsuit—it's one of my favorites. I will take care of Lanny—don't worry about him!"

She hugged my mother, and my mother hugged her back, still eyeing me nervously.

There is a God in heaven: At the very moment my mother made her comment to Hillary, the official White House photographer walked into the room to take a parting set of photos of the three of us. He caught the candid shot of my mother precisely as she and Hillary held their hands out together, just as Hillary heard my mother's question about her outfit, and my mother was looking off nervously to her left at me, biting her lip.

A moment to remember, a moment that captured my mother off script, and of course, a moment that captured why Hillary Clinton is so adored by so many of her friends—because she is such a great friend.

My mom and I walked out of the White House through the upper floor north portal entrance, the famous columned entrance facing Pennsylvania Avenue that everyone knows. As we went down the driveway arm in arm, she couldn't stop talking about how exciting it was for her to see the White House, especially the way "Hillary hugged me. I can't wait to tell all the girls!" (referring to her coterie of seventy- to eighty-plus-year-old girlfriends she hung out with in her Miami Beach home now that my dad was gone).

■ ■ ■

Weeks later, in early November, as Thanksgiving approached, my sister flew to Florida to spend the holiday with my mom. The plan was for me to fly down the following week. My mom had been hospitalized to get some extra oxygen and blood to rejuvenate her failing heart, as she did every few months.

As I was about to leave the White House compound for the day, I called the hospital to see when she would be checking out to go home. When the nurse picked up the phone, I knew something was wrong.

"Who is this?" I heard a stressed-out voice ask me.

"This is Lanny, Fran Davis's son. May I talk to my mom?"

There was a long pause.

"I'm so sorry, Lanny," she said. "Your mom went into a Code Blue emergency—cardiac arrest. We tried to revive her. She passed a few minutes ago. But she passed without pain and peacefully. And a smile on her face."

I started to cry. I felt faint and had to sit down. But then I contemplated those comforting words: "with a smile on her face."

I raced to my car from the White House. While driving home I called Carolyn on my bulky White House cell phone and told her the news. I asked her to book a plane for both of us to fly to Miami early the next morning.

As soon as I hung up, my phone rang. No caller ID. It was a familiar voice, someone I considered one of my best friends, always there for me in moments of pain or difficulty or just plain needing a friend to be there.

"I just heard," Hillary said. "I will never forget the look on your mom's face when she knew she had messed up. Love . . . and fear. But she was so proud of you. She sure loved you. Don't forget that."

When I thought of the description of Mom's smile at the last moments of her life, I knew this was the way she wanted to go—filled with memories of her family first in her mind, our love for her, and her love for us.

And I was pretty sure what Mom was thinking that made her smile in the end: "Soon I will join Morty's sweet soul . . . and be able to nag him for eternity."

# CHAPTER 3

# MY "YOUNGER" SISTER, TAMA

In recent years a biological miracle occurred. My older sister, Tama (born fifteen months before me—August 29, 1943, versus December 12, 1945), became my *younger* sister, Tama. Don't ask me how. Maybe a genetic mutation? Maybe a mistake birth-certificate error?

The truth is less dramatic, of course, and more charming. Some years ago, when I was introducing my older sister, Tama, she smiled sweetly and said, "You mean younger sister." And that was that. The main point to understand about my sister and our childhood is that for several reasons it was very difficult to be the sister of Lanny Davis in our household. Acquiescing to our private little joke was the least I could do.

Let me start with this mea culpa: When I was a preteen, I was a brat, a snitch, and embarrassing to her in front of her friends and especially her boyfriends. I was also often self-centered. And, not coincidentally, I was spoiled by my parents, who, in the casual sexism of the time, favored me over my sister in all kinds of subtle ways.

It was not only inevitably damaging to her self-esteem and a sign of less-than-great parenting, but it was also objectively unfair. Tama was superior in many self-evident ways. For starters, I thought she was smarter than I was. By the time she was a teenager, she was drop-dead gorgeous. She was also funny, athletic, and musically talented. She was a voracious reader, knowledgeable about almost everything, and a great and loyal friend to her girlfriends. Tama was also a magnet for contemporary young men and some considerably older ones, such as college-age boyfriends while she was in high school.

Yet my parents' attitude toward their two children made it difficult for Tama to be my older sister. Take piano playing, for example. She was good. We both took lessons from the same teacher, and the rule my father imposed was that we would learn to play different classical pieces so it would be a competition. My dad's instinct was sound, but when I turned out to be a better piano player than Tama, we were always compared in front of family and company anyway. I was always praised more than Tama, and neither my parents nor I gave much thought to how this made her feel.

In my defense I turned out to be a talented classical pianist, above my years in skill. Some people thought I could become a professional. I practiced hard, too, but I was also lucky. As mentioned previously, I was born with the genetic rarity of "perfect pitch" (meaning I could hear a note with my eyes closed and know what it was, allowing me to memorize quickly, and when I learned to play popular songs, I could hear the chords to play). This gave me an advantage Tama did not have.

I don't remember the details, but I do remember the hurt I caused my sister. When we were both preteens, I was privy to something she regarded as a "great big personal secret"—one she did not want my parents to know about. I can't recall what it was. I just remember the awful thing I did. It causes me to shudder when I think about how I became a blackmailer so easily. Almost every time Tama and I had an argument, I would threaten to tell Mom about "it" (whatever that was). At one point I started to go to tattle on her, and Tama shrieked in pain, even terror, begging me, "Please, no, don't!"

Why didn't I hear her terror? Why didn't I care that I was going to hurt my sister? In any event I ratted out Tama, who ran to her room wailing and crying.

To this day I feel shame thinking about that. As I write these words, I still feel it. The memory is painful. It wasn't easy for Tama to be my older sister.

Yet I also remember being so grateful to her for helping me with my antisocial, insecure inability to make friends with kids I didn't know, or even with kids I did know. Tama seemed to have no such fear. Kids in our neighborhood would be in front of our house on Bentley Avenue, playing stickball in the street. Tama would go right out, and sure enough, she would be playing.

I would watch her from the window of the waiting room to my dad's dental office, envying her ability to just go out and start playing with kids she didn't know or barely knew. Sooner or later she would call out to me, knowing I was watching through the window. "Come on, Lan, play with us."

Slowly, but easier each time, I would come outside, watch for a while, and then start playing. And while I rarely, if ever, expressed it to her, I was grateful.

Another source of gratitude is that she was not only bigger and taller than me when we were preteens; she was also tougher and had more courage. For example, there was one boy my age, an Irish kid, who liked to bully me because he knew I never stood up to him. One time, when I missed a ball hit to me, he mocked me and called me "little Yid" or "little Jew," or some such anti-Semitic trope. I ignored it. *Nothing I could do about it,* I thought. Tama did not. She had remembered and better understood the lesson my father had taught us when he made us watch *Gentleman's Agreement*—silence is not a legitimate option when it comes to bigotry.

"Don't you dare call my brother that name," Tama said, slightly bigger than the kid who would pick on me, "or I will punch you in the nose."

Simply put, despite the many reasons for her to resent me for the favoritism shown to me by my parents or my own selfish behavior, Tama has always been there for me when I needed her most. It's true to this day, and it was true when I was about fifteen and she lied to protect me from my parents' wrath.

It happened when I first tried to get drunk at a party and drank out of a bottle of warm Scotch, guzzling swallow after swallow. And yes, at first it felt great. Unlike my usual self at that age, I was suddenly outgoing and flirtatious with girls and having a great time.

Then I didn't feel so good. Someone managed to take me home—I think it was an older brother from the party, who might have been the one who supplied the alcoholic beverages. It was after midnight. My parents were away for the weekend. My sister was home with her boyfriend. When I came into the house, she recognized my condition right away and rushed me to the bathroom as I showed signs of a major upheaval of everything in my stomach, mostly empty except for the Scotch.

She stood there, held my forehead, and then put me into bed. Most importantly, she didn't say a word to my parents.

Why didn't she threaten me to tell, as I did years before about her secret?

Because she just never would. It would have broken her honor code to protect her younger brother—or a friend or even a stranger who was in trouble who needed help. Later, when I worked for President Clinton in the White House, Tama told me how proud she was of me. When I had setbacks and was being publicly attacked, she was always one of the first to call me and cheer me up, with the inspiring words "Fuck them!"

That was my sister, Tama—always there when I needed her. I can't say the same in reverse. I wasn't entirely all bad and selfish. Sometimes I was so proud of Tama I would cry. I remember one moment when she competed, as an eighth grader, in the Hudson County elementary school spelling bee. It was a big deal—public school kids and private school ones, too, mostly Catholic parochial schools and one private school called "Jersey Prep."

The private school kids almost always won that spelling bee, but my sister won the contest to represent her public school, Joseph H. Brensinger Elementary, at the countywide contest. So there we were, in a large high school auditorium, filled from front row to back with the parents of the two hundred or so countywide competitors, and Tama was on the stage, way in the back row, hardly visible.

Round after round, each time she was asked to spell a word, increasingly more difficult, I would hold my breath, and she did it, again and again! The group on stage grew smaller and smaller as erroneous responders left the stage. My heart was beating faster and faster. My parents were smiling, clearly proud. Finally, it came down to Tama and one other kid in the final round. One mistake and the other one wins.

Three or four words passed. Each one spelled them right. Some of the words I had never heard before. Then came a word I was sure I had never heard: "degeneracy."

Definition: a word or expression that describes perverted or immoral activity. My sister was called on first. She hesitated. My heart thumped faster and harder. I had a feeling this was the one she didn't know.

She took a big breath.

"D-E-G-E-N-E-R . . ."

She hesitated.

"O-S-Y."

There was a pause by the judges that seemed like an eternity.

"Sorry," she was told. Tama was calm. Amazing. She was calm. She looked at her competitor, waiting to see whether she got it right and what error she had made. The other girl confidently spelled the word correctly: "D-E-G-E-N-E-R-A-C-Y." An *A*, not an *O*.

"Correct," the judge said.

The audience cheered. The winning girl graciously hugged my sister. My sister smiled. No tears from Tama. Meanwhile, I was crying. When

I remember that day, I realize now how much I loved my sister even if I didn't often show it. It's a good lesson for younger brothers about older sisters you don't get along with (or dads and moms you don't spend enough time with when they are alive): Express it at the time. Don't wait until it's too late.

I recall one bad crisis between my mom and Tama when my mom learned that Tama, while attending Lincoln High School in Jersey City, was hanging out with a boy named Johnny Murphy. You would think my sister had committed the most cardinal sin known to humankind. Murphy? An Irish boy? A Catholic boy? To be precise, a *non-Jewish boy*?

"You are not going out with that boy!" I heard my mom scream. Her daughter screamed back. I never stopped to ask "What's wrong with her going out with a non-Jewish boy?" My mom often told us that when she was growing up, her neighbors and best friends were Irish Catholics. She often told us that she had gone to Christmas Mass with them when she was growing up. What was the big deal? I wondered.

But it was a big deal. I later learned that it stemmed from a fear among some Jewish people that by intermarrying, the Jewish community would disappear. Forget about the irrationality of that notion. Sometimes Jews convert to Christianity in marriage, sometimes the Christian converts to Judaism, and sometimes it's live and let live. But this was a decade after the Holocaust. Such fears were not irrational. They were logical and visceral. Even the word getting out that a son or daughter was "dating" a non-Jewish person was a big deal for Jews of my parents' generation.

It caused a lot of tension for Tama as she was growing up and says something about the smothering control my mother (more than my father) exercised over her, especially as she entered her teen years, when I'd overhear comments about how boys her age and older were really attracted to her.

She eventually ended up with a boyfriend during her junior and senior years in high school, a "nice Jewish boy" (as my mother would say) named Samuel Reiken, who went to Princeton. So when she went to visit him at

Princeton, my mother could let herself feel pleased—no longer worrying about where Tama was sleeping or whether she had a chaperone as a high school girl at an all-men's college. Even when she was selected and photographed in a two-piece bathing suit as the "playmate" of a Princeton magazine, my mother didn't seem to mind. She even seemed proud.

After high school, Tama briefly went to college but married young (although not to Sam Reiken) and started a career after moving to New York City in financial services and planning as a sales and marketing director.

Tama had a beautiful daughter, my niece Jennifer. Ultimately, after her second marriage didn't work out, she met the true love of her life, Robert Teitelbaum—a teddy bear of a man who was a brilliant investment manager at one of the major Wall Street firms. They lived together for years in what amounted to a common-law marriage but with love and devotion to each other that were rare.

They traveled all over the world on vacations and enjoyed New York dinners and parties. Tama was happier than I had ever known her to be. Then in 1998, suddenly, in his late sixties, Bob Teitelbaum was playing tennis at a club in lower Manhattan. As he stood at the net in a doubles match, he suddenly fell to the tennis court rubber matting—a massive heart attack. The friend who was with him told Tama, "He was gone before he hit the mat."

If you've got to go, Bob did it without pain and quickly. That was twenty-six years ago as of this writing (2024), and she has never stopped mourning him or loving him. Now as we grow older, she lives in Southern California near my niece and three grandchildren. I don't call her enough, but she is and remains my big sister (though, I can't forget, my *younger* sister); I couldn't want a better one.

I know one thing for sure in the last years of our lives: We have rediscovered each other. About time. She actually tells me she loves me. I say the same back to her. For me, especially, I wish I'd had the wisdom a long time ago to say these words more often.

## CHAPTER 4

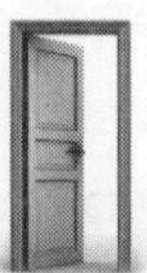

# NEWARK ACADEMY

When I decided to go to a small, private prep school in Newark, I had to say goodbye to my best friends from Public School #17, who would be attending Lincoln High, the Jersey City public high school where Tama was already a freshman. It was Tama who convinced me that Newark Academy would be better for my future.

Although Tama did great at Lincoln High, she told me that the classes were huge, the academic reputation would be problematic if I wanted to go to an Ivy League college, and I would have little chance of ever starting on the varsity basketball team. So I opted for Newark Academy, surprising my parents and adding another to the hundreds of reasons I owe so much to my "younger" sister.

I learned that to be admitted to Newark Academy, I had to learn first-year Latin and pass the year-end exam given to eighth-graders. That meant a three-month crash course by a private tutor to teach me Latin. I also learned that there was a dress code. I had to wear a dress shirt, tie, and blazer every day and learn to say "sir" when I talked to every teacher or administration official.

Then there was the commute. To arrive by 8:30 a.m. sharp, I had to be at the corner of Bentley Avenue and the Boulevard by 7:00 a.m. to catch the 108 bus to Newark Pennsylvania Station, then get off the bus and walk to the nearby Newark City Subway, an aboveground rail line. Then I had to wait for the subway and take a ten-minute above-ground train ride to First Street in the relatively downtrodden Roseville section of Newark, where the school was located.

The academy was founded before the American Revolution, in 1774, and then was subsequently burned to the ground by the British. It is the seventh-oldest private high school in the country. The building where I graduated on First Street was opened in 1929. In 1964, the year after I graduated, Newark Academy moved to a college-sized, sixty-eight-acre campus in Livingston, New Jersey.

Another aspect of attending Newark that made me especially uncomfortable was being told that I had to attend a fifteen-minute "chapel" religious service every day. I had to arrive in the auditorium no later than exactly 8:30 a.m., or doors would be shut, and after-school detention penalties would follow. The place was founded as a Protestant "Congregationalist" institution, meaning the chapel was filled with Christian prayers and hymns, and the service always ended with a move to small panels that opened for kneeling and praying to Jesus Christ. Since I was Jewish, I was told that I need not kneel on the panels if I did not wish to pray to Jesus.*

I complained about this chapel requirement and the Christian component to my parents. They inquired and learned that it was optional for me. I could instead go to my "homeroom" classroom to pray silently or sit

* My parents always taught me that while we Jews did not believe in the divinity of Jesus, we did consider him to be an inspirational rabbi who changed the world and was one of the holiest human beings ever to be born—in the pantheon with Abraham and Moses, who gave us the Ten Commandments and the Torah when he came down from Mount Sinai.

quietly in meditation for the fifteen minutes the chapel service was occurring. Then a surprising thing happened. I decided to attend chapel on my first day at Newark—and liked it. Even the immediate move to my knees on the little platform in front of me at the end of the service to pray, which I was told I did not need to do, I did anyway. I never missed another chapel service.

Sixty years later, I still remember the peaceful sensation I felt by attending chapel. I even enjoyed singing Christian hymns. My favorite was "Onward, Christian Soldiers" and "The Navy Hymn" ("Eternal Father, Strong to Save"). I found that I looked forward to the chapel every morning.

The one part of Newark Academy I was convinced I could never reconcile was the all-male student body. No girls. My reaction was to use the expression I often heard from people from Brooklyn when my dad took me to the Polo Grounds in Upper Manhattan to see the New York Giants play the Brooklyn Dodgers: "Fuhgeddaboudit."

Yet, incredibly, I even came to like, or at least tolerate, the absence of girls at the school. There was the advantage, at least, of not worrying about boy talk or locker-room talk in front of girls or even worrying about my hair or how I looked. Within several weeks of my first freshman year, I came to a shocking realization: I loved attending Newark Academy. I loved the teachers. I loved knowing I could make the basketball team.

So I learned to like, then love, my new school. Truly love it. There were days when I got off the City Subway on First Street, walked the half block to Newark Academy, and literally felt my heart lift as a sense of joy overcame me. Surely one reason is that the school was so small (our class had thirty-four boys, and the entire upper school had fewer than two hundred), which meant I had a chance to play not only high school basketball but also baseball and tennis.

Our varsity basketball team played against private schools of similar size in northern New Jersey, and I averaged about ten points per game, playing what is now called the point guard position. I wasn't big, but I played hard on both ends of the floor, which endeared me to our coach,

Bob Hendrickson, who complimented me on my "intense hustle." My biggest problem, he would also point out, was that I fouled too frequently on defense and often fouled out before the game was over. I also sometimes hollered at my teammates in frustration when I felt they weren't hustling as much as I was. Coach Hendrickson would yell, "Davis, knock it off!" even during regular games in front of my mother, who would scold me on the way home to be quiet, play my own game, and stop harping on my teammates. I tried and tried to restrain myself from this obnoxious habit.

Then came junior year, and Fran Pinchot.

Frannie, as we called him, transferred in as a senior. Coach Hendrickson found him playing in an inner-city Newark neighborhood, mostly with Black kids. He was white, but he said he didn't know who his father was, and he thought he was probably a Black man. No matter. When we first met on the basketball court on the first day of practice in my junior year, he stood about six feet one inch and dunked the ball with ease. We had never seen anyone on our team or any opposing team dunk at all—and jump so high his elbow was above the rim.

Fran and I became close friends, and I shone as point guard after he joined our team, allowing me to break the record for assists in a single game—or so I was told by Coach Hendrickson after Frannie scored sixty points in one game. My job was mainly passing the ball to Fran. Nothing to brag about, though boast I did.

Fran Pinchot also had the highest arc jump shot I have ever seen. He lofted the ball so high that when it came down, it was almost vertical through the hoop, meaning the swish through the hoop he produced was as soundless as any I have ever seen or heard. In 1961, with Pinchot leading the way, little Newark Academy went to the New Jersey small-school private school state championship in Lawrenceville and won—marking the first time ever. Again, Pinchot set a scoring record, and again, I racked the assists by passing the ball to him.

Later in life, Fran Pinchot coached Trenton High School to a state championship and still to this day is remembered as one of the greatest

New Jersey high school coaches. Some years after that, Fran suffered a family tragedy, retired, and went into seclusion. He wanted his privacy and, I was told, wouldn't take phone calls or go out very much.

A dinner was organized to honor Coach Hendrickson's tenure as both Newark Academy football and basketball coach for over four decades. Basketball and football players through all those years came back for the occasion. When I got the word that Fran Pinchot was not coming, it didn't feel right to celebrate without him. It took me a while, but I found his phone number. He first said no when I pleaded with him to come to the dinner, but he finally relented when I reminded him that if it weren't for me, he never would have broken all those scoring records at Newark Academy.

His response was, "Yeah, you learned to just throw me the ball."

We both laughed, and he agreed to come.

I had finished my high-profile work as President Clinton's defender in the media on campaign finance controversies and impeachment. So when it came time for the toast, I rose to thank Fran Pinchot for coming, thanked Coach Hendrickson for his inspiring coaching and leadership, and then gave my punch line: "If President Clinton were here, I think he would want to thank Coach Hendrickson, too, for teaching me to play tough defense."

That got a good laugh, especially from Pinchot. I could see he was glad he had come. He raised his glass and tipped it toward me, and I tipped mine back to him. It was a good moment and a good memory to see that Fran was back—a smile on his face, perhaps for the first time in a while.

■ ■ ■

I don't know anyone who doesn't recall at least one teacher, whether from elementary school, high school, or college, who didn't make a lasting impact on their lives. At Newark Academy I had two such teachers. To this day I appreciate how they affected my life for the better. The first was Blackwood Parlin. Known as "Blackie" Parlin to his peers (and "Mr. Parlin" to his students), he taught U.S. history and had such a major impact on us that we voted unanimously to dedicate our senior yearbook to him.

The dedication began with "Gentlemen, take out a piece of paper." Those were the ominous words Mr. Parlin would utter to indicate that a spot quiz was coming on the overnight reading. The thing is, we were usually prepared. Mr. Parlin was the kind of teacher you didn't want to disappoint. More importantly, he made the material fascinating—and challenging. He wouldn't just explain U.S. history; he would force us to think through the implications of what we were learning.

I will never forget that he assigned us to read the actual *The Federalist Papers* and the actual proslavery, pre–Civil War writings of South Carolina Senator John C. Calhoun, a racist slaveowner. But Mr. Parlin reminded us that even during the Civil War, most Northerners were also racist and that even Abraham Lincoln's Emancipation Proclamation freed the slaves only in the Confederacy and not those slaves living in the border states that did not secede.

As we discussed how America, which took pride in its Declaration of Independence assertion that "all men are created equal," could have ever allowed slavery to occur, Mr. Parlin reminded us that racism has been part of the American ethos before the founding and to the then-present day (this was the early sixties).

His lessons about institutional racism and his challenge to each of us to examine our souls and decide how racist we really were (without allowing us to get away with denying all racist instincts), in retrospect, show how much ahead of his time he was—long before "antiracism," Black Lives Matter, or the heyday of Civil Rights Movement for that matter.

It was Mr. Parlin who most indelibly stoked my interest in politics. He taught us that positive change in American history was usually achieved through political action, even while conceding that politics has often been dirty, corrupt, and depressing.

I will never forget the day he forced us all to read Theodore Roosevelt's famous 1910 speech, "The Man in the Arena"—delivered less than two years before TR's decision to run again against his handpicked successor, William Howard Taft, on an independent Progressive Party ticket. (Splitting the Republican vote, Roosevelt came in second, allowing Democratic candidate Woodrow Wilson to be elected president with a plurality of the vote. It was, in a way, a precursor of the three-way 1992 election that brought the Clintons into the White House.)

"The Man in the Arena" struck me then—and still does today—as the perfect counterpoint to the cynicism so many Americans express toward politicians of both parties. As we read each line in class, I kept thinking: *He is right.* If only the risk-averse people—those afraid to be criticized or dare to do or say anything bold—decide to become politicians, then how will the United States meet the challenges of the moment? Who will run the country when we grow up and are old enough to become political leaders—only the worst among us?

> *It is not the critic who counts; not the man who points out how the strong man stumbles, or where the doer of deeds could have done them better. The credit belongs to the man who is actually in the arena, whose face is marred by dust and sweat and blood; who strives valiantly; who errs, who comes short again and again, because there is no effort without error and shortcoming; but who does actually strive to do the deeds; who knows great enthusiasms, the great devotions; who spends himself in a worthy cause; who at the best knows in the end the triumph of high achievement, and who at the worst, if he fails, at least fails while daring greatly, so that his place shall never be with those cold and timid souls who neither know victory nor defeat.*

So during my sophomore year, in the middle of the 1960 presidential campaign between Republican Vice President Richard Nixon and

Democratic Massachusetts Senator John F. Kennedy, I decided to get "into the arena." I came up with the idea that Newark Academy's upper school (meaning the high school, grades nine through twelve) should have a mock election vote for president.

My first impression of Jack Kennedy came four years before when I watched him on TV in August 1956. I was ten years old, watching the Democratic presidential nominating convention with my father. He told me that the relatively young Senator Kennedy was seeking the vice presidential nomination on the ticket with former Illinois Governor Adlai Stevenson. Dad was already a big Kennedy supporter. But Kennedy lost his bid to Tennessee's populist and better-known U.S. senator, Estes Kefauver, much to my dad's great disappointment.

I was smitten when the young-looking Senator Kennedy, with that iconic shock of thick brown hair swept across his forehead, took the podium and graciously announced his support for Senator Kefauver and the Democratic ticket. I didn't know the word "charismatic" in those days, but he had it.

When JFK became the nominee in 1960, running against Nixon, I couldn't imagine how anyone would not vote for the dynamic young Kennedy over someone my dad called "Tricky Dick." I did not know exactly why, but I figured if my dad called him that, he must not be very good. That was enough for me.

So I went to the headmaster of Newark Academy, Robert Butler, and asked if we could have an election for president among the high school–aged students. He agreed. Knowing I was a Democrat (everyone knew, I guess), he found someone who was for Nixon, and the two of us spoke to the entire student body on behalf of the two candidates. I don't remember what I said and what issues I emphasized about why everyone should vote for Kennedy, but I do remember the last line I wrote, intentionally, to be a big punch line that would arouse loud applause and maybe a standing ovation. Of course, I knew that Kennedy would win the mock election. After all, we were all young people, he was young, and he was running against Tricky Dick.

So in full confidence of the outcome, I ended my five-minute speech with this call to action: "The name of John F. Kennedy is rising in importance throughout this nation and will carry him to the presidency and the White House. *Let us rise with him!*"

Thunderclap! A huge standing ovation! At least that was what I expected from my classmates. Instead, I received tepid applause.

What? I wondered. Maybe they weren't paying attention.

When the proponent of Nixon finished his speech, he didn't exactly get a rousing response, either, which made me feel better. But the clapping seemed louder than the applause that followed my speech. Still, I had no doubt about the outcome. JFK would win by a landslide among young people in our student body, much less among intelligent young people attending a school such as Newark Academy.

Then the shocking announcement was made over the school loudspeaker by Mr. Butler: "The results of the election vote for president are—Richard Nixon: 120 votes; John Kennedy: 60 votes."

What? Inconceivable! How could that be?

I marched down to Mr. Butler's office to ask him if there was some mistake. No, he assured me, Nixon had won by a decisive two-to-one margin.

When I got home that night, crushed and disappointed, I asked my father how that result could be possible. He didn't seem surprised. Most of the parents of Newark Academy students, he reasoned, were wealthier than the average person, as they could afford to send their sons to private school. And wealthier people, as he reminded me when he had described his antipathy for the New York Yankees, were Republicans. Ergo, John Kennedy was bound to lose among students who voted like their parents.

"Voted like their parents?" I asked. "Why would they not think for themselves and be persuaded by my speech?"

My dad shrugged and simply said, "John Kennedy will be elected our next president. Just watch."

What he didn't bother to point out was that I, too, was voting like my parents. I learned for the first time, and would learn many more times in the future when I became more deeply involved in politics, that voters make decisions on whom to support based more on culture, family, and emotional influences than candidates' stands on the issues or the two political parties' policy positions.

My dad understood this elemental truth about American politics, but he didn't want to teach it to me that bluntly. He must have figured I would learn it someday for myself.

■ ■ ■

Mr. Parlin taught me another lesson I never forgot, but this one wasn't about politics. It was about character and being too quick to assume my own talents were superior to others. The subject, of all things, was basketball foul-shooting.

Mr. Parlin, I came to learn the hard way, had one talent that seemed to be belied by his nonathletic physical appearance. After all, he was only about five feet eight, was paunchy around the middle even for a young man, and wore black-rimmed glasses. He was, in other words, an unlikely-looking basketball player. As it turned out, he loved basketball and was a close friend of Coach Hendrickson. That should have been a clue.

One day during my senior year, at the end of basketball practice, Mr. Parlin entered the gym, sat, and watched. Coach Hendrickson turned to me, whom he regarded as one of the better (and certainly cockier) foul shooters on the team, and challenged me to a foul-shooting contest with Mr. Parlin—best out of ten—in front of the team. I tried not to laugh, as I loved Mr. Parlin as a teacher. But I thought Coach was joking. Patronizingly, I said to Mr. Parlin, "I will give you 'plus five out of ten,' and we will have the contest."

Mr. Parlin was not offended. Nor did he take me up on the offer of giving him a huge advantage.

"No, that's okay, Mr. Davis," he said. "Just head-to-head, no pluses or minuses. Nothing at stake—just pride. You go first."

I looked at Coach Hendrickson, doubtful because I did not want to embarrass this teacher I loved so much.

"Go ahead, Davis," the coach said, "take him on straight up."

So I stood at the foul line as the team gathered to watch me, along with other students who seemed to have heard about the challenge and drifted into the gym.

I proceeded to shoot seven out of ten, about what my average was. Satisfied, I turned to Mr. Parlin and again asked if he wanted a handicap.

He just smiled, walked to the foul line, bent his knees slightly, and positioned his right hand slightly behind the ball with his left hand at about eleven o'clock, providing offsetting pressure. Swish went the first shot. Swish went the second. Then swish, swish—four in a row, all net.

*Wow, lucky,* I thought.

I looked at Coach Hendrickson. He wasn't looking at me. He was staring at Mr. Parlin. Two more. Swish. All net.

*What is happening?* I thought.

Next one, another swish. Now he was seven for seven. We were tied! I was dumbfounded.

His eighth shot missed, just off the back rim. His ninth shot missed again, this one off the front rim. I breathed a little easier, thinking he had a run of incredible luck, and at least we would be tied, assuming he missed the next one, as I expected. Shot number ten: swish.

I had lost. I was humiliated. I tried to shake his hand and smile like a good sport. I did shake his hand, but I didn't smile.

I stared at Coach Hendrickson. He stared back.

As I left for the locker room, listening to the crowd cheering for Mr. Parlin, I walked past the coach. "Next time don't be so cocky," he said. "And get 80 percent, not 70 percent."

About a half century later, I returned to Newark Academy and had the honor of being the commencement speaker for the class of 2013 on the anniversary of our graduation. A few days before, the phone rang at my office, and I picked it up.

A voice said, “Hi, Lanny, it’s Blackie.”

“Who?” I asked.

“Blackie. Blackie Parlin.”

“Oh my goodness,” I said. “Mr. Parlin. How great to hear from you.”

“Please don’t call me Mr. Parlin,” he said. “You are old enough now to call me by my nickname that everyone else uses: Blackie.”

I tried calling him “Blackie” several times in the conversation. Each time I stammered and ended up using “Mr. Parlin.” I just couldn’t call him by any other name.

“I hear you are coming to school next month to be our commencement speaker,” he said. “I hereby challenge you to another foul-shooting contest.”

“You’re on,” I said.

We met in the late morning, before the graduation ceremony, in the gym. A small crowd of my classmates who came to attend our fiftieth reunion dinner and to hear my commencement speech gathered in the gym to witness the “rematch” between Mr. Parlin and me. It was anticlimactic. Mr. Parlin, fifty years older, had a bad back. I was also fifty years older, but I had two young sons who kept me at least in shape to shoot foul shots.

We hugged after the contest, and he said, “Finally you can get your pride back after all these years.”

That night, at our reunion dinner, I asked him to sign a copy of my 1963 senior year yearbook, next to the first page where his dedication was published. He wrote, “I hereby, in sound mind and body, swear . . . that Lanny soundly defeated me in a return basketball match. Lanny learned from my 1963 coaching advice. I am proud to know you, Lanny.”

I laughed. I cried.

■ ■ ■

The second teacher who had the most impact on me to this day was my English teacher for my sophomore and senior years, T. Charles Abbey, known to his faculty friends as "Charlie" but to all of us only as "Mr. Abbey." I grew to like him, admire him, and then love him.

The day after my defeat on the foul line by Mr. Parlin, I entered Mr. Abbey's classroom, and by his understanding and sympathetic smile to me, I realized he had heard the news about my humiliation. (I soon realized in our small school, everyone knew about it.) So I came into his class that day looking downtrodden, and he noticed. He smiled and said, "Not to worry—you've learned a good lesson."

Mr. Abbey was more than a great teacher when it came to understanding poetry, literature, and especially Shakespeare. He taught me how to write. My first lesson in great writing that he imparted—as readers of this memoir can already attest—is a hard one to follow: Shorter is better; use the fewest words possible to express yourself. It's an old adage, dating from the eighteenth century: "If I had more time, I would have written less."†

This was the exercise used by Mr. Abbey: He would give us a topic as we entered the class every other week or sometimes more, and he would say, "Okay, exactly one hundred words. Not a hundred and one. Not ninety-nine. If you don't write the essay in exactly one hundred words, you get a failing grade."

Of course it was always too long, sometimes twice as long. *Cut a hundred words from my perfect essay? That is impossible,* I thought. Sometimes I expressed my frustration to Mr. Abbey.

He would merely smile. "I'm sure you will find the unnecessary words—or cut whole sentences," he would reply.

I did. And I had to admit, it usually read better that way. The day after my embarrassing free throw shooting contest with Mr. Parlin, Mr. Abbey taught me another lesson. It came in the form of a challenge. We had been reading in class Shakespeare's *Julius Caesar.* In consoling me

† The sentiment is often attributed to Mark Twain, but Twain never said it. Its provenance dates to French mathematician and philosopher Blaise Pascal.

about losing my pride on the basketball court (to a teacher!), Mr. Abbey told me to turn to act 3, scene 2, lines 73–108.

I opened to that section and saw it was Mark Antony's famous funeral oration in "honor" of Brutus, the "honorable man." Mark Antony began by explaining that he had "come to bury Caesar, not to praise him."

"What do you want me to write?" I asked him.

"An essay about what Mark Antony is trying to say about Brutus and his fellow patriots who killed Caesar in the name of freedom," Mr. Abbey replied, with no irony in his voice.

"And what does that have to do with my loss to Mr. Parlin?" I asked.

"You can figure that out after you write your essay," Mr. Abbey said. "I'll give you five hundred words, max. Due tomorrow morning."

That night I reread Marc Antony's famous oration. I had believed, as the other boys in the class did, that we understood Shakespeare's point: Caesar had become a military dictator, and the group of small *d* democrats in the Rome Senate, led by Brutus, decided they needed to kill him to save democracy from a military tyrant.

I couldn't figure out the connection to the shooting contest. Mark Antony was praising Brutus and his colleagues, whom I didn't consider "conspirators." They were doing their patriotic duty to save Rome's democracy from an autocrat. I kept going over the passage until I detected the strain of a more interesting nuance. Instead of praising Brutus, as Shakespeare's words indicated if you took them literally, perhaps the Bard's Mark Antony was making a more subtle point: that Brutus and his group were blinded by their own arrogance.

Something clicked, and I started writing. I focused on the first reference to Brutus being an "honorable man"—and focused on all the other times he had used that expression.

*The noble Brutus*
*Hath told you Caesar was ambitious:*
*If it were so, it was a grievous fault,*

*And grievously hath Caesar answer'd it.*
*Here, under leave of Brutus and the rest—*
*For Brutus is an honourable man;*
*So are they all, all honourable men . . .*

I kept reading. There it was again and again.

*Brutus is an honourable man . . .*
*Did this in Caesar seem ambitious?*
*When that the poor have cried, Caesar hath wept:*
*Ambition should be made of sterner stuff:*
*Yet Brutus says he was ambitious;*
*And Brutus is an honourable man.*

I explored the hidden meaning of "For Brutus is an 'honourable' man" in my paper, rendering it that way—with single quotes around the word "honourable." Mr. Abbey told me the following spring that those internal quotations, implying that Shakespeare intended them ironically, helped convince a faculty committee at Newark Academy to give me the best English essay award at our graduation ceremony. I had no clue I would win the award. I hadn't even submitted the essay for the competition. Later in life, though, as I became more involved in politics, I saw again and again the pitfalls of succumbing to hubris. Moreover, I became exceedingly wary of those who insisted on judging those with whom they disagreed as "evil" rather than "wrong."

If those had been my only two interactions with the faculty—my free throw debacle with Mr. Parlin and Mr. Abbey using Shakespeare to get me to confront my own arrogance—Newark Academy would have been worth every penny my parents paid in tuition. But they weren't, of course. I had hundreds of such interactions, as did every boy there, and the entire faculty had thousands of such "teachable moments" in their careers.

That is why I have always believed teachers are the most important underpaid individuals in our society. If I had my way and were a benevolent dictator for five minutes, I would issue an executive order forever tripling all teachers' salaries immediately.

After my graduation ceremony, Mr. Parlin and Mr. Abbey both congratulated me. Mr. Parlin leaned in and said, "You see, losing to me in foul-shooting isn't the end of the world. It made you better. Now you understand that Brutus was not such an honorable man."

But I was determined to be one and left Newark Academy for Yale, determined to make a difference in the world and to do so as "an honorable man."

■ ■ ■

My experience at Newark Academy has a nice postscript—two, actually. Fifty years after graduating in 1963, while speaking at commencement, I reprised my story about challenging Mr. Parlin, who was still teaching part-time at the school and still very popular.

I also regaled the class of 2013 with life lessons imparted for decades to Newark Academy athletes by the revered basketball and football coach Bob Hendrickson. I had called him at his retirement home in Arizona and convinced him to get on a plane, on my tab, to attend the graduation ceremony. I picked him up at the airport, and we shared old times. I reminded students that Coach Hendrickson had led our basketball team in 1962 to the first New Jersey State Prep School championship in our division in the school's history. After the game, I told them, Coach Hendrickson praised my defense, which he said turned the momentum and helped us win the game—but he was also quick to humble me when I was too full of myself.

I also mentioned that while working in the White House and after I left during Bill Clinton's impeachment ordeal, I spent a lot of time on television defending the president. The night of the day he was acquitted by the U.S. Senate, there was a celebration at the White House residence, and my wife, Carolyn, and I were invited. I relayed how President Clinton came over to me and referenced my anecdote about Coach Hendrickson's comments about my defense in the 1962 championship game.

"Tell your basketball coach, Coach Hendrickson [yes, I told the audience, President Clinton actually remembered the name!], thanks for teaching Lanny Davis great defense!"

I segued from that vignette to the themes of my talk, which were the importance of finding common ground, listening to other people, and not being too quick to judge. We are all in this together. That's what a Jewish boy who went to Christian services in the morning, set an assist record for passing the ball, and learned how to play defense in a good cause learned in school. But my education wasn't through.

CHAPTER 5

# SUMMER CAMP: LEARNING TO BURY THE HATCHET

*I didn't go back to camp so I could write a book.*
*I wrote a book so I could go back to camp.*

**SETH DAVIS,** *Equinunk, Tell Your Story: My Return to Summer Camp*

I have lived a rich and interesting life. I was married twice, both times to strong, beautiful women; raised two sets of kids; and advised two presidents of the United States. I have appeared on television too many times to count and written hundreds of newspaper columns and several books. I have helped people and institutions in the middle of severe media crises, from Martha Stewart to Penn State University, practiced law at the highest levels, and been blessed by a lifetime of cherished friendships.

But the most important, impactful experiences in my early life were my summer camp years—as a camper, counselor, and parent.

The two summer camps I attended were located forty-five miles from each other in the northeast corner of Pennsylvania. There, in the valleys of the Poconos, hundreds of clear-water lakes make an ideal geographic location for summer camps. The first one I attended was Camp Echo Lark from 1957 to 1961, beginning when I was eleven in a tiny village called Poyntelle. The second, Camp Equinunk, I attended as a counselor in 1964 and 1966. My two oldest children, Marlo and Seth, were campers in the 1980s, and my two youngest sons, Josh and Jeremy, were campers there two decades later. Our oldest son, Seth, stayed on as a counselor for several years.

Seth took the first stab at explaining the mystique of the Pocono camps when he returned a dozen years later. A staff writer for *Sports Illustrated* at the time, Seth spent seven weeks as a senior bunk counselor for kids fourteen and fifteen years old. His ensuing book, *Equinunk, Tell Your Story*, documented what happened inside the bunkhouse and on the ball fields, as well as the highs and lows, the beginning, middle, and end of a camp season. It's a well-written story, and I recommend the book to everyone, but I can sum up in a single word what made my camp experience so momentous for me: *friendship.*

It wasn't until my second summer, in the Cadet Group, that my bunkmates at Camp Echo Lark started to think about girls. We were twelve and thirteen. This was the summer we started to realize there was an advantage to having a girlfriend.

The couplings began during the first weekly socials held at a big cabin called the "canteen," which featured a soda fountain and jukebox blaring rock and roll. Few of us danced to the upbeat songs. We waited for the ballads so we could slow-dance with the girls. Our moves were limited off the dance floor, too, although a few of us attempted to sneak out the back door for a few minutes of learning how to kiss. That was about as far as we knew how to go.

Then came, usually in the third or fourth week, the midsummer "switch," when one partner in the couple would abruptly opt to try someone else. It could be crushing when you were the recipient of the decision. It usually happened when you showed up at the social and simply saw your girlfriend sitting at a table with another boy. That was it. Over and out. (Of course, boys would do the same abrupt switch, too, without any explanation or prenotice.) It was sometimes painful or, at least, embarrassing.

By the time we were senior campers (fourteen and fifteen), our hormones began raging. Although still mostly focused on winning on the ball fields, the socials took on greater importance—with a serious focus on making progress around the base paths in the parlance of the day. When we got back to the bunks, those of us with real girlfriends were called upon to report our progress after sneaking out the back door of the canteen. First base was serious kissing, and second and third were advanced touching, so to speak. And making it all the way to home plate? Well, we could dream, but no one dared to even make the claim. The best chance of making real progress was sneaking out in the middle of the night to go to the girls' camp, fetch our girlfriends from their bunks, and spend some time on a blanket under the stars. To get from the boys' camp to the girls' camp at Echo Lark, you had to cross a big open field. Obviously, when the moon was out, there was a serious risk of getting caught by counselors assigned to look for "raiders."

The real risk of getting caught was the next morning. That was when we told a few people about our postmidnight "raid," and within minutes, the word would spread throughout the camp. Then the dreaded loud voice from headquarters on the public address system would come, an angry head counselor announcing, "Lanny Davis, Lanny Davis, come to the HQ. *Now!*"

Fortunately, the worst penalty for that infraction was not being sent home; it was being "docked" from one or two future socials. And so I learned the advantage of being silent and not telling my friends anything when they asked me, "What did you get?"

Discretion had other benefits too. My sister, Tama, taught this important life lesson with these words: "If you don't talk to other guys about what you do with girls, I promise you the word will spread among the girls, and you will reap the benefits."

She was right. There were times in high school when I was trying to make my way around the bases with a girl, and she would say to me, "I hear you don't talk to other guys."

"Of course not," I said.

■ ■ ■

During my year in the Cadet Group, one level below the seniors, in the summer of 1959, at age thirteen, we had a great group of athletes, especially in softball. There was my best friend, Richie Singer, my "roomie" (in the bunk next to mine). He was already over six feet tall, with dark red hair and a sweet and powerful left-handed swing, recording many home runs (on the softball field, I mean). Richie was so different from me. I was a fast-talking, overenergized Jersey City boy. He was a slow-talking, slow-moving, low-energy Long Island boy. But we became inseparable as friends and cronies. Richie and I hung out together all the time, always there for each other when the other was having problems—with girls, with counselors, with growing up. He was my first true best friend. He and I both learned a lesson from a boy named Jimmy Cantor, who was not only advanced as a softball player / power hitter. He was also further down the road of maturity than the rest of us.

We first noticed this because after "Taps" was broadcast on the PA system, meaning "Lights out," Jimmy would be concentrating with a flashlight under the covers. At first we thought he was reading. Then we noticed that he had a stack of *Playboy* magazines close at hand and that reading wasn't exactly the activity he was pursuing. But back to softball. I was pretty cocky as a shortstop. I used to challenge the counselors to hit me ground balls as hard as they could to try to get the ball past me, and I prided myself on rarely making an error if it were at all within reach. We challenged the "mighty seniors" to play us, but they laughed us off and declined. Then the younger "Inters" challenged us, and we laughed them off the way the seniors had done to us. But in the dining room, the girls' camp Inters began shouting a cheer, mocking the Cadets for being afraid to play them. Word spread around camp that maybe the cocky Cadets were all talk. So we finally agreed to play a softball game after dinner against the younger campers. Our attitude was this: Let's embarrass them so they'll call off the seven-inning game early.

But things didn't turn out that way. We weren't hitting, and we were winning only 4–1 as the Inters came up for the last at bat in the bottom of the seventh. A couple of base hits and errors later, the score was tied 5–5 with two outs and runners on first and third. The next batter hit a soft ground ball to shortstop. It was an easy one. Noticing the runner from first was close to second, I decided to throw to first base for the final out, but I guess I was thinking too much in those seconds and stopped concentrating on the ball, which went under my glove and through my legs. Game over. Unfortunately, the entire camp, girls and boys of all ages, were attending this big face-off between the cocky Cadets and the ambitious Inters. Much of the camp rushed to the field to congratulate the exultant Inters.

As for us, the cocky, powerful Cadets campers, we slunk off the field and made it back to the bunk. As for me, I headed for my bed and pillow. The sobs began, and I couldn't stop. Tragedy! Maybe the end of my life—forever! The other kids and our two counselors came into the bunk, saw me, heard my sobs, and each patted me on the back while mumbling encouraging words. My counselor, who was the coach of our softball team, sat for a while and said, "It can happen to anyone. It was a bad hop."

That helped me a little but not enough to ease my pain of humiliation. Finally, Richie Singer, my best friend forever, came into the bunk, got undressed into his pajamas, and got into bed, silent. I noticed the silence. Then "Taps" played on the camp loudspeaker, and the lights went out. The only sound in the bunk was from me, still crying but more softly. Singer still said nothing. I was still in my baseball clothes and hadn't moved.

I waited and waited for Singer to talk to me. Nothing.

Finally, after what seemed like hours, with most of the kids in the bunk asleep, I heard a sound from his bed and waited—at last!—for my best friend to console me, to cheer me up.

"Hey, Davis," he said.

I stopped sobbing and waited with my eyes closed and head still buried in my pillow for his expression of solace.

"Two words," he said.

I waited some more. No sound.

"What?" I finally asked him.

"You suck!" he said.

A week later we played the Inters in a rematch. This time no one came to watch. We played them in the afternoon. We won 11–0. I went four for five, Cantor hit two home runs, and Singer hit one. Although we were vindicated, it was like the proverbial tree falling in the forest, with no one there to hear it.

Yet to this day, more than sixty years later, as I write this chapter, I will never forget that ground ball that went through my legs, nor the ironic words of comfort from my best friend, Richie Singer.

■ ■ ■

I was hired as a counselor at Camp Equinunk in 1964 after my freshman year at Yale. I had met a young woman at a party weeks before, and at the time I still had no plans for the summer. She told me about Camp Equinunk. (She was a veteran of the affiliated girls' camp across Union Lake, Camp Blue Ridge.)

On the spot I decided to call the owner of Equinunk to see if he had a last-minute opening. As luck would have it, he did. And influenced, I believe, by my years at Camp Echo Lark, he hired me to be a counselor in the senior bunks. There might have been another factor too. "We've never had a Yale student as a counselor at our camp," he said.

Like Camp Echo Lark, at Equinunk each age group performs a short version of a Broadway musical show every Saturday night in front of the rest of the camp. My ability to play music by ear came in handy. After the first show, I told the dramatics counselor, Jeffrey Laffel, a camp veteran whose family were part owners of Equinunk, that the piano player was playing in too high a key for the kids to sing because he was reading the music in the key written for professional performers. Laffel was puzzled. He asked what else he could do. "Well," I said, "if he played it by ear, he could adjust the key down, which would allow the kids to make the high notes." Laffel looked at me in surprise and asked me if I knew how to do that. I said yes but added that I came to Equinunk to be a senior counselor on the ball fields. Period. But the next morning, I heard my name announced over the intercom by head counselor Henry "Henny" Goldman: "Lanny Davis, come to the HQ!"

Arriving at the cabin on the lower side of the campus, I found Henny with Jeff Laffel, who seemed to be holding his breath with his head down.

"You are now the music counselor," Henny told me abruptly.

"No, I am not," I protested. "I came here to be a senior counselor on the ball field with teenagers." Henny, famous for not taking no for an answer, waved me off. "Davis, it's either you say yes and play the piano for our weekly musicals while you stay as a counselor in the senior group, or you are assigned to the freshman group worrying about bed-wetting all summer."

That settled matters. I remained as a senior counselor, and I also played the piano for rehearsals in the afternoons and for the weekly shows throughout the rest of the summer.

A couple of weeks later, Jeff told me we had to put on a full-length counselor show for "Parents' Weekend," which would also be attended by all the girls' camp, in addition to the boys. Earlier in the summer, he heard me playing a ballad I had written for my first girlfriend crush the summer before, Babs Shapiro. He told me he loved the song, and I heard him humming it as he walked out to go back to the bunks. *Success!* I thought. I had always wanted to write songs that people could easily remember and hum. That was what my dad had taught me.

The day after Henny had announced I was the new music counselor, Jeff Laffel came into my bunk and threw on my bed the script of a famous 1939 play called *The Man Who Came to Dinner*, which was a Broadway hit for two years before being made into a movie in 1942. Written by the legendary duo George S. Kaufman and Moss Heart, the comedy features a pompous fictional radio personality named Sheridan Whiteside, who visits a small Ohio town for a publicity stunt in the middle of winter. On his way up the steps of the home of a family called the Stanleys, Whiteside slips on a patch of ice, falls, and breaks his hip. Whiteside is carried into the home of the Stanleys, where they are forced to put up for the next several weeks with the chaos of Hollywood celebrities flying in from California to visit Whiteside.

"Why did you give me this play?" I asked Jeff.

He answered, "I want you to read it, and let's write music to it and put on a musical for the Parents' Weekend counselor show. I will revise the script to make it into a musical."

I thought that was utterly impossible. We could not write the music and lyrics, and he would have to rewrite the play and then cast, rehearse, and put on a full-length musical in three weeks. It was crazy. But we decided to try it.

That night we wrote our first song. I thought of a song about Whiteside's fall. I sat at the piano in the social hall and wrote a melody with the notes fitting the title of the song: "A Little Bit of Ice." It would be sung by Mrs. Stanley, complaining to her neighbor about that ice patch causing her the loss of her privacy and the chaos of housing Whiteside—an unwelcome, injured guest—who has taken over her house and disrupted her family's peace.

The next night Jeff asked me to play the melody he loved that I had written for my girlfriend Babs, which had a first line (and title): "When this summer I met you . . ." As I played he scribbled away. The new first line and the title of the song fit the syllables of my title, "When This Summer I Met You." Except he wrote the perfect title for the love scene it would fit into—"Keep Your Eyes on Tomorrow."

That song turned out to be the favorite of our musical, *Whiteside!* The parents in the audience were singing it and humming it when the show was over—I could hear them as they were leaving. And it was probably the best song I ever wrote among more than one hundred over a lifetime. Sixty years later, at a New York City party we attended in the summer of 2024, I played "Keep Your Eyes on Tomorrow" to a group of guests at the party. When I was done, I could hear people leaving the piano humming the melody. And I still got the same surge of joy about writing a memorable melody that my dad had told me so long ago was the purpose of writing music.

But let's return to the 1960s for a moment.

One of the parents in the audience who was involved in the music and record business approached us and told us he wanted to introduce us to a serious Broadway show producer who was a friend of his. By mid-October (this was 1964) we were in the producer's living room. I was at the piano, and Jeff was ready to sing each of the songs after first setting up the plot and context for each one. We were excited. I am not a professional popular music accompanist, and Jeff had a good but not professional singing voice, but we agreed to meet the producer at his New York City apartment to go through the musical, with Jeff explaining the setting for each song in *Whiteside!*

I am not making up what happened next.

We played all the songs in the first act and kept looking for a reaction, good or bad. We got none. Not a word. Not a good sign. But not a bad one. He got up and excused himself, seeming to head for the restroom. Jeff and I were hopeful. We knew the second act was better, and we had not yet played the most memorable song of the show, "Keep Your Eyes on Tomorrow."

We waited for him to return. And waited. And waited.

Finally, after twenty minutes, Jeff looked at me and stated the obvious. "I don't think he's coming back." I responded that he would have told us that and not just walked out of his apartment, leaving us there unattended.

Then someone who seemed to be a domestic servant entered the room, explained that our presentation was over, and told us we could leave. And that was that—until three years later. In January or February

1967, while I was a senior in my last semester at Yale, Jeff called me with the stunning news that a new show was about to be produced on Broadway based on *The Man Who Came to Dinner.* The title was *Sherry!*—suspiciously similar to our title, *Whiteside!*—including the exclamation mark.

The show opened on March 28, 1967. Jeff and I decided we could not bear to go see it, but we asked a few Equinunk parents who called us and had tickets to see it to let us know what they thought. The reports back were heartening: All said that the songs in our show were better and our plot more entertaining. We both had to admit that we were happy to hear that—no reason other than stupid jealousy. But then we heard that the show had closed after two months, on May 27. There was no pleasure in that. Broadway is tough.

Through the decades, I often wondered how my life would have changed had that producer not walked out on us with no interest but rather had decided to produce the show. Would I have been a long-term composer of musicals? What would my life have been like?

I sometimes asked myself that question during some of my difficult days more than thirty years later, defending President Clinton on television against Republicans hell-bent on impeaching him.

■ ■ ■

Color War at summer camps is not, as someone unfamiliar with such might assume, about racial conflict. It is a three- to four-day competition across all age groups in the last week before the end of the eight-week camp season in July and August. (In the last two decades, most camps have reduced the season to seven weeks.) The word "color" comes from the two colors of the camp, standing for the two teams that will compete on the playing fields. Echo Lark's colors were green and gold, and Equinunk's colors were red and gray. The Equinunk team is led by a counselor "chief" (or "general" at Echo Lark) and several assistants or "boosters."

One reason I decided to go to Camp Equinunk as a counselor rather than Echo Lark was that I had heard Equinunk's Color War was the more intense, with a culture and history going back to the 1920s. And it sure was.

From the first day, most campers are thinking about and looking forward to "the war," as it is called. There is intense competition from the youngest freshman group, ages seven or eight, to the oldest, seniors, who are fourteen- and fifteen-year-old teens. At Equinunk, the politics of who gets to be chosen "Color War chief" is intense from almost day one. Contenders for the coming summer chief designation by camp management start campaigning almost from the first day. Another major incentive to campaign to be Color War chief or one of the deputies is to be painted onto the yearly "plaques" displayed on the walls of the social hall / basketball court. The plaques go back to the founding of Equinunk in the early 1920s. So being listed on these plaques means feeling a part of history, a source of lasting pride. (I was listed on two plaques when I was a counselor in 1964 and 1966 at Equinunk, albeit in the lowest category, a booster.)

Most importantly, once you are a chief, you are invited to come back to the senior's Color War basketball game on the last night before the last day of the war, meaning you get your name called, and you bounce a basketball into the darkened hall with a spotlight on you while both teams and all the parents scream your team name when you were chief. (Some former chiefs in the 1970s, who were chiefs in the 1930s and 1940s, have appeared at the senior game for their moment in the spotlight—some using wheelchairs, but still, they come.)

The first symbolic event of the Equinunk war is the "unburying of the axes" ceremony. The Color War has been "broken" by some dramatic event—such as an airplane pilot hired from a nearby local community airport flying over the camp and dropping "sheets"—which contain the names of all campers, divided into teams for each age group that counselors attempt to make approximately even in as many sports as possible.

Just before the break, the Color War hatchets (colored red and gray for the two teams) are secretly reburied in a hole near the central camp flagpole, with everyone supposed to believe they have remained buried since the end of the previous summer's Color War.

On the first morning of Color War, the two newly anointed counselor chiefs of the red and gray teams go to a spot next to the camp's central flagpole and take a shovel and "dig up" the red and gray axes from the ground. These axes are then plowed into a wooden column that is attached vertically to the flagpole, with numbers from zero to one thousand or more painted on the column. For the next three to four days, before lunch and dinner, the relative points of each team will be tracked by the hatchet being smashed into the wood column next to the appropriate point total for each team.

The tension builds as the points accumulate and teams go up or down depending on the outcome of the various games—on the ball fields, at the lake for the swimming meet, and on the track field for the team track meet.

And then comes the big event at Equinunk—on the last night before the final day: the upper senior basketball competition, known simply as "the game."

The social hall is filled with parents, along with the boys' and girls' camps, while the seniors compete in a game they have anticipated since they were freshman campers ten years earlier. Each of the incoming senior group campers usually buys high-priced, famous-brand sneakers before they come to camp, wears them at the game, and, allegedly, never wears them again. (When my oldest son, Seth, was a senior and played in the game, he took the first shot for his gray team from the arc beyond the foul line. He was not a great basketball player, but the shot went in, although it was the type of shot pejoratively referred to by basketball players as a "brick"—a near line drive that miraculously hits the backboard and ricochets back into the net. The game was videotaped, and

Seth, at age fifteen, can be seen jumping up and down and high-fiving his teammates, deliriously happy.*)

On the last evening, when the final scores are announced at the flagpole, parents of the seniors, who are allowed to attend the entire war to watch their sons, bring their cars to the road near the flagpole and turn on bright lights to flood the area where the closing ceremonies take place—to "bury the red and gray hatchets," allegedly for another year before the next summer's Color War.

For many campers and counselors, Color War competition is intense, even bitter sometimes. Winning (and losing) can threaten friendships during the games when competition becomes physical. Sometimes things get so bad that longtime friends stop talking to each other—even past the end of camp. That happened to me when I was a camper at Camp Echo Lark, when during Color War, my best friend, Richie Singer, elbowed me during the senior basketball game and gave me a bloody nose. At the time I was convinced he did it intentionally, which I realized later wasn't true. The intensity of Equinunk's Color War is even greater than at Echo Lark—among counselors on opposite teams too. Anger and personalizing what happened on the ball fields are common. But then comes the burying-the-hatchets ceremony on that final Color War night. With both teams hearing the final results and still separated and staring at each other, with the winning team cheering and high-fiving and the losing team with sounds of sobs or downcast heads, the war is over. Now it is time to bury the actual hatchets in the wooden board attached to the flagpole.

---

* Some thirty years later, Seth has made a name for himself as an on-air analyst for the NCAA college basketball tournament and has worked alongside famous former professional stars such as Charles Barkley and Clark Kellogg. Once, one of Seth's best friends, Jeremy Kalina, secretly arranged for the tape of Seth making the shot and jumping up and down in celebration to be sent to CBS to be shown during the halftime show of one of the games. Barkley, Kellogg, and others on the set chortled at Seth's celebration, with Seth embarrassed that an audience in the tens of millions was watching "the brick," as it came to be known.

That's when the magic begins and the true purpose of the whole exercise is revealed. Each team chief comes forward and hugs the other, and both take the hatchets from the pole, redig the hole where the hatchets had been three days before, and return the red and gray axes back to the ground. Then leaders of the counselors for each team come forward to add more dirt on top of the hatchets. Then the leaders of each camper team from the seniors to the freshmen come forward and do the same. And then the two teams face each other and mingle, and the hugs begin as the tears start to flow. And then from the headquarters' public address system, the haunting sound of the recorded horn playing the military melody "Taps" fills the air. And as the two teams now become one camp again, all link arms, put arms around each other, and sing the words to "Taps":

*Day is done,*
*Gone the sun,*
*From the lake,*
*From the hills,*
*From the skies.*
*All is well,*
*Safely rest,*
*God is nigh.*

Somehow all the anger at flung elbows and bitter losses and failures on the ball fields melts away. Memories of anger are replaced by feelings of friendship and the sudden ability to view the emotions through the eyes of the other person or the other team, as Atticus Finch had urged Scout.

But here I was at the Equinunk closing ceremony, and I learned a different lesson as I watched the bury-the-hatchets ceremony. Back at Echo Lark, I could never imagine my arms around members of the other team and singing these words together—at least for a while. Somehow the tradition at Equinunk—*the expectation*—of civility was part of the ethos of the camp. It infected all campers and even the most competitive counselors. And the singing of "Taps" together taught me a lesson. When there is an expectation—a *culture* of civility—finding common ground is possible even in the most intense rivalries.

Was this experience at the bury-the-hatchet ceremony at Camp Equinunk a metaphor for what could occur in other intensely competitive and emotionally charged environments? I asked myself this question years ago when I experienced it and over the years since. And yes, more than once, I recognized that it is not a stretch to apply these lessons of the end of Color War at Camp Equinunk as applicable to other experiences in years hence—in business, politics, and life.

## CHAPTER 6

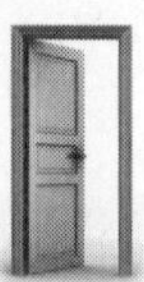

# TUNNEL VISION

I was so excited about going to Yale University for my freshman year that I could barely sleep as I counted the days in August 1963, the summer after my graduation from Newark Academy. As young people will do, I already found myself constantly daydreaming about the future beyond college. What did I want to be when I grew up?

In the last summer of John F. Kennedy's presidency, government service—perhaps even running for public office—seemed a noble calling and a possibility. More accessible to seventeen-year-old me, though, was journalism. I also followed *The New York Times* columnist James "Scotty" Reston, the dean of all political columnists in the early sixties, and found him an inspiring role model. I would start at the *Yale Daily News* and work my way up the ladder.

I realized that as a journalist, I would have to be politically neutral, focusing on documented facts and not innuendo to meet the highest journalistic standards—at least that was the standard then. Yet I also knew that columnists, such as Reston (or my other hero liberal columnists

James Wechsler and Murray Kempton of the *New York Post*), could advocate strong opinions. Might that be a transition to my running for office? What did I know? I was still four months shy of my eighteenth birthday. However, I wasn't only focused on politics, journalism, and other serious stuff that summer of 1963.

Like most young men my age, my mind was often dominated by another part of my body, sometimes to the point of obsession. This preoccupation was reinforced by my trips to the Jersey Shore with one of my best friends at Newark Academy, Steve Lozowick, otherwise known as "Lozzy Loz."

Loz had it all—good looks, blondish hair, and a muscular football player's build, complemented by a dazzling smile and an easy charm that could melt even the frostiest girls. When I compared myself with Loz, I tended to focus on the skinny legs I inherited from my father. (How skinny? So much so that my friends called me "Spider Legs," and my mother sewed up my basketball shorts so they wouldn't look so baggy.) Around Loz, though, I wasn't as self-conscious on the beach. I knew he could attract girls who would circle around, smiling with beckoning looks. The rest would be up to me, irrespective of any perceived physical shortcomings. It turned out that I had a superpower too.

Loz was not only attractive, but he also had the gift of gab. I possessed a trait that turned out to be even more advantageous.

"How do you do it?" he would ask in wonderment. "I can't understand why girls put out for you and not for me. What's your secret?"

My secret was simple: When around girls, I listened more than I talked.

In those days our destination was usually Bradley Beach or Belmar, which was known for attracting a faster crowd—and young women who were more world-wise. Our favorite place on the shore was Asbury Park. Nearly a decade before Bruce Springsteen would make it famous, Asbury Park was known for its boardwalk, iconic Ferris wheel, and overall amusement park atmosphere. The best attraction was the "Tunnel of

Love." This was a three-to-four-minute ride in a two-seated car on rails that went through double doors into darkness, with ghosts and goblins appearing from nowhere supposedly to frighten young children. But for us hormonal teenage males, it gave us a line to use when we saw an attractive teenage female. We'd ask, "Wanna go on a ride with me?"

Any willing girl who said yes was guided to the Tunnel of Love. We would then stand in line, praying and hoping she wouldn't change her mind and walk away. This was a rare event, as they knew perfectly well when we headed for the Tunnel of Love what was on our minds. I came to realize that teenage girls had the same needs I did; they just hid them better.

Within seconds of the car banging through the double doors from sunlight into darkness, the make-out session began. It often progressed into a lot of what is called in genteel circles "petting." Then suddenly, all too suddenly, came the double doors opening into the blinding sunlight. It happened so abruptly and without warning that we were not able to finish kissing or whatever we were doing.

Then, rather remarkably, two young people who had just been intimate parted ways seconds later, sometimes even without a goodbye.

Despite this 1963 summer of love and fun, I never forgot that I was headed in September for my freshman year at Yale. I had followed politics, especially the Civil Rights Movement, since the day in the 1950s when my father identified for me a young pastor who led the inspiring and momentous Birmingham bus boycott. His name was Martin Luther King Jr.

When I read in the newspaper that there would be a historic march for civil rights legislation in Washington, D.C., on August 27, a week before my first day at Yale, and that the Reverend King would be the final speaker, I knew I had to go. I decided to attend as a budding journalist, with a reporter's notebook, and write a personal report of my experience at what I anticipated would be a watershed moment in U.S. history. My ambition was to get the article published in the *Yale Daily News*, which I knew was the oldest college daily newspaper in the United States. I hoped to join the paper as a reporter as one of my main activities at Yale.

I arrived by train from New York City and followed the crowd moving up Constitution Avenue to the Washington Monument. Seeing the beautiful National Mall and the statue of Abraham Lincoln sitting on his marble chair at the end of the reflecting pool gave me a chill. The crowd at the monument started to walk around midday toward the Lincoln Memorial, which was about a mile away and where the podium and all the speakers would be. Something magical happened to me during that walk on Constitution Avenue. I found myself linking arms with strangers, and everyone was singing a song that was easy to sing and immediately memorable.

"We shall overcome . . . God is on our side . . . We shall overcome today-ay-ay-ay."

I tried to interview people, remembering I had come to report on the event as well as attend. I took down their quotations in my little notebook, asking them why they came and what they wanted to accomplish. The comments were friendly but not very revealing. A few comments about "civil rights" and "It's about time," but not much more than that. It was more "I had to be here"—something like my own feelings, actually.

We moved toward the Lincoln Memorial, and I edged my way through the crowd to get as near to the speakers' stage as I could. I found a square block column on top of the steps to the left of the podium and scrambled to stand on top.

At that moment a young man named John Lewis was speaking. He was the third of ten children born in Alabama to sharecroppers and, as a boy, had wanted to be a preacher. A student at Fisk University in Nashville, Lewis had been tapped only weeks before as the official leader of a group of mostly Black students named the "Student Nonviolent Coordinating Committee" or "SNCC" (pronounced "SNICK"). Nine months later, Yale Law School Professor Allard K. Lowenstein would give a name to their efforts: the "Mississippi Summer Project." (I am using the expression "Black" here. But in those days, the word we used was "Negro." John Lewis was one of those who ushered in that social change. He was the first person I heard call himself "Black." He referred to that word over and over again, rejecting the word "Negro" as too much an accommodation to the white *and* Black establishments.)

Two months before the March on Washington, Lewis was among a group of thirty civil rights leaders who met with President John F. Kennedy in the White House Cabinet Room. Kennedy's initial impulse was to dissuade them from marching at all. When it was made clear to the president that the march was happening, JFK used the rest of the meeting to develop a strategy to use it to build support for his administration's civil rights legislation.

Befitting their tender years, SNCC college-age activists were considered more radical than the older leaders of the civil rights establishment. For one thing, they thought the Kennedy administration's proposed bill was too tepid. Consequently, the initial draft of Lewis's speech—written by committee—expressed SNCC's opposition to the legislation. The story of how John Lewis was pressured to tone down that speech has been told many times, but the notion of Lewis as an intemperate firebrand is not accurate. A Lewis biographer, David Greenberg, noted that SNCC's Nashville chapter was the one most faithful to the Gandhian doctrine of nonviolent resistance embraced by Martin Luther King. "After the Nashville movement forced the city to thoroughly integrate its public facilities in May 1963, Lewis—with his earnest, gentle demeanor and unimpeachable devotion to peaceful methods—was a natural choice to become SNCC's public face," Greenberg would write later. Yet twenty-three-year-old John Lewis took seriously his role as the leader of an organization that would stand no longer for marching in place.

I knew none of this backstory at the time, but I knew greatness when I saw it up close.

The passage of his speech that seared itself into my impressionable mind was this: "To those who have said, 'Be patient and wait,' we have long said that we cannot be patient. We do not want our freedom gradually, but we want to be free now!" There were not as many cheers as I thought there should be. I found the speech electrifying. This eloquent and accomplished young man was only six years older than me. I stared at him. Something about him made me think he was special. *He is going to be a great leader someday*, I thought.

He certainly fulfilled that promise. Little could I imagine that forty-four years later, John Lewis—by then a longtime member of Congress—would call to ask my advice on how he should explain to my old law school friend Hillary Clinton, whom he'd publicly endorsed for president early in 2007, that he was going to rescind that support and come out in favor of Barack Obama. John and I had come to know each other in 1998 when I was defending Bill Clinton during impeachment. And he and the Clintons had grown close over the years. He told me often how much he loved the Clintons and how much he admired them for their unwavering support of civil rights since their own college years. But everything changed for John in a profound way on January 3, 2008, and not because of anything either Clinton did. On that date a charismatic junior senator from Illinois—an African American candidate—won the nearly all-white Iowa Democratic presidential caucuses. The implications were immediate and profound. A Black man might well be president of the United States. Soon thereafter John took a phone call from Senator Obama, one he had expected would be coming. As John told me, his head said no, but his heart said yes. He followed his heart.

"History and my life's cause call me to help Barack," he told me. "I hope you will help explain to my dear friend Hillary—to help her understand." I assured him that she would understand, which she did, and with graciousness and class. It was pure Hillary.

All that lay in the future. On this warm August afternoon in 1963, as I stood there, I saw the Reverend King walking to the podium. Up close, he looked small, almost frail. And then he began to speak. And when he spoke, the deepness of his voice and the poetry of his words made it clear to me why he had such a large following and why he inspired so many Americans, Black and white.

Somewhere toward the end of his speech, for the first time, I heard him say, "I have a dream," and then he repeated it again and again. I stopped taking notes, and I forgot about trying to be an objective facts-first reporter. I listened and looked at the crowd, starting to react the first time he said, "I have a dream." Hundreds of thousands of people, all the way down the mall around the reflecting pool back to the Washington Monument, seemed to move back and forth, like an organic wave. I moved too. And here is the ending that we all know so well:

"I have a dream that one day this nation will rise up and live out the true meaning of its creed: 'We hold these truths to be self-evident, that all men are created equal!'"

The Reverend King continued,

> *I have a dream that my four little children will one day live in a nation where they will not be judged by the color of their skin but by the content of their character.*
>
> *I have a dream today . . .*
>
> *Let freedom ring from every hill and molehill of Mississippi. From every mountainside, let freedom ring.*
>
> *And when this happens, and when we allow freedom ring, when we let it ring from every village and every hamlet, from every state and every city, we will be able to speed up that day when all of God's children, Black men and white men, Jews and gentiles, Protestants and Catholics, will be able to join hands and sing in the words of the old Negro spiritual, "Free at last! Free at last! Thank God Almighty, we are free at last!"*

The story of the March on Washington and Martin Luther King's incandescent "I Have a Dream" speech is a familiar one, but it bears reprising in a political memoir by an eyewitness for this reason: Those who weren't there or were not yet born cannot truly fathom the sense of hope and optimism—of possibility—present in the air that day. At the steps of the monument to the martyred president who urged Americans to embrace "the better angels of our nature," the National Mall was filled with men and women who were doing just that. But it's a bittersweet memory. John F. Kennedy never got to sign the Civil Rights Act. By November he, too, had been martyred. Five years later gunmen with twisted politics and hate in their hearts took Martin Luther King and Bobby Kennedy within two months of each other. Then it was onto Vietnam and Watergate. Camelot was done in only a thousand days.

But on this day, August 27, 1963, everything seemed possible.

I was seventeen, and the roar of the crowd, rippling like ocean waves to the Washington Monument and back again, was like a physical force on me. I roared too. Screamed. I was frozen. I literally found it difficult to breathe. I will never forget that moment. I made up my mind I wanted to be part of this movement, somehow.

CHAPTER 7

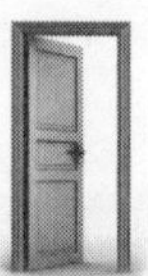

# 1360 DAVENPORT: HOW FRIENDSHIPS FORGED COMMON GROUND

*"For me, there is no question that our nightly 1360 Davenport debates were the peak of my political science education at Yale."*

**DAVID "DA BEAR" FOSTER,** March 7, 2025

What it all comes down to is friends and family—and friends that are like family.

Through the turmoil and amid all the forces of polarization and violence and political, cultural, and generational divides occurring at Yale and across the country in the middle of the historic decade of the 1960s, somehow in one dormitory suite, 1360 Davenport College, in one academic year (1964–65), four roommates overcame their differences and found common ground in friendship. This friendship continues six-plus decades later.

At Yale, since you got there by busting your ass to get good grades, you remember the challenging courses. You remember the professors, famous and charismatic, such as Vincent Scully, who taught a course called the History of Art, which was attended by hundreds of students in standing-room-only lectures. You recall John Morton Blum, the famous liberal historian and author of award-winning books on Theodore Roosevelt, Franklin Roosevelt, and the New Deal. Also Erich Segal, who taught literary arts and writing and became famous for the novel *Love Story.*[*]

You remember, of course, the weekends when the "girls" were bused in on Saturday nights, mostly from the all-women Seven Sisters schools (such as Smith, Wellesley, Vassar, and Mount Holyoke), to attend organized parties called mixers at one of the residential colleges or fraternities. You never forget the intense school spirit at the Saturday afternoon football games at the Yale Bowl. It was not just the intensity of the competition, especially against Princeton or Harvard, but also the excitement of the halftime show and the Yale "marching" band,[†] of which we were so proud.

At those football games, you remember singing the Yale celebratory song every time our team scored. At first it was hard to believe anyone from Yale had actually written the words to this song. Even more incredible was the Yale graduate who wrote them in the 1920s—the legendary Cole Porter. Here are the lyrics:

*Bulldog! Bulldog!*
*Bow, wow, wow*
*Eli Yale*
*Bulldog! Bulldog!*
*Bow, wow, wow*

---

* *Love Story* was set at Harvard, which Segal attended as an undergrad and graduate student. Segal wrote *Love Story* while on sabbatical at Harvard, basing the lead character on two roommates he met at Dunster House, Albert Gore Jr. and Tommy Lee Jones, who was given a role in the Hollywood film of the same name. Yalies claim Segal anyway—we know that while in New Haven, he cowrote the screenplay to the Beatles film *Yellow Submarine.*

† The word "marching" is put in quotes here because there was no marching. It was instead choreographed chaos, as the band ran out onto the field with no particular appearance of a plan, and then when they started to "march," the lines were as crooked as crossing circles, making it clear that they were really not marching lines. It was an intentional mocking of organized college marching bands.

*Our team can never fail*
*When the sons of Eli*
*Break through the line*
*That is the sign we hail*
*Bulldog! Bulldog!*
*Bow, wow, wow*
*Eli Yale!*

All of it was great and unforgettable, but what really lasts are the friendships made.

At Yale, it starts the first year, when all freshmen live on the same large, grassy quadrangle called the "Old Campus," which dates back to 1718. In the 1960s all freshmen were randomly assigned to live in Old Campus dormitories and were assigned, starting sophomore year, to live the last three years in one of twelve (there are fourteen now) separately named "residential colleges." Each college was self-contained, with its own campus, dining room, intramural athletic teams, and traditions.

I was assigned as a freshman to 37 Vanderbilt Hall, which had its own courtyard, giving it a self-identity and separateness from the rest of the Old Campus.

On spring nights windows would be open, and students would sit in the window wells with their legs hanging out and Beatles music blaring. Yale's residential college system helped us forge close friendships, especially starting sophomore year when all of us in Vanderbilt Hall were assigned to Davenport College. At your college, with about 300–350 students, you felt like you knew everyone. You dined together, hung out together, and played touch football on the lawn. The intramural athletic competition between the colleges could be as intense as Ivy League varsity play. Pierson College, located next to Davenport on York Street, had developed a competitive rivalry with Davenport over many years, especially in tackle football. On weekends the colleges would host their own social events. We also had small seminars of ten to fifteen students or fewer that you could opt to attend, often with celebrity teachers, some of whom lived on campus.‡

When I first arrived at Yale in September 1963, nervous and not sure of myself, I knocked on the door of my assigned room on the Old Campus, 37 Vanderbilt Hall. I was greeted by a stocky Midwesterner named David J. Foster. He gave me a big smile, stuck his hand out, and said, "Hi, I'm David Foster from Rockford, Illinois. (We quickly called him "DJ.") He was friends with a fellow member of the freshman football team, Robert Kenney, whose roommate on the top floor at Vanderbilt was Andris "Andy" (or "AB") Baltins. The two of them began hanging out in our room. Robert and David were teammates on the freshman and varsity football team, and, as it turned out, Andy and I both played classical piano and loved to play for each other on the big Steinway baby grand in the common room at Davenport. In late spring it was time to decide on roommates for sophomore year. Over lunch with the four of us, DJ just said, "Let's room together at Davenport."

Robert and Andy agreed.

"Sounds like a plan," I said. We put our hands together on the table and high-fived. And so began the saga of the "1360 Group" (named after our suite number), which we assumed would be a one-year deal. Little did we know that the 1360 Group would continue for six decades—and counting.

DJ Foster was a true student-athlete. As a two-way starter in high school at linebacker and running back, he'd had offers to play in the Big Ten. He chose Yale instead, where during the off-season, he learned lacrosse to stay in shape and ended up being named first-team All-Ivy. He was also a hilarious cutup and great listener. He became the closest kind of friend,

‡ During the three years I lived at Davenport, writer John Hersey—legendary for his thirty-one-thousand-word *New Yorker* article, "Hiroshima," published in a single issue on August 3, 1946, and later published as a book—taught a course in creative writing at Davenport. So did Robert Penn Warren, famous author of the novel describing the life of Huey Long, *All the King's Men*. Sadly, I was so preoccupied with working on the *Yale Daily News* I never took advantage of taking either course, but I got a chance to know and socialize over dinner with both men.

a soulmate really, who helped me through personal crises at Yale and years after. DJ had a mathematical mind (engineering was his future) and was the first person I knew who carried around a slide rule—and knew how to use it. Before the age of commonly available calculators and computers, we did computations ourselves. David was also a voracious reader and seemed to know more about books than anyone I ever knew.

DJ was big and could be physically intimidating until you got to know him. Then you discovered that he was lovable and teddy-bear-like, especially when he assumed his favorite position on a big old easy chair we had picked up for five dollars in the used student market when seniors were moving out and begging people to buy their furniture. This huge intellectual and athletic talent would plant himself in that chair in his boxer shorts and T-shirt at the end of a night studying, when we were gathered round in 1360 for the nightly bull session.

David's sweetheart was Joanne Junor, who'd been the valedictorian at a rival Rockford high school. They remained a couple for most of our four years at Yale and subsequently married.

Robert Kenney came from Newton, Massachusetts, where he was also a star football player, as well as one of the greatest pitchers in Massachusetts high school baseball history. When I once asked him how great a pitcher he had been at Newton High, he matter-of-factly told me about a game in which he struck out every batter through the eighth inning, but then, apologetically, only one in the ninth. This meant he had struck out twenty-seven of the twenty-nine batters he faced. He explained that he failed to strike out the other two batters because he had raced around the bases in the eighth inning for an inside-the-park home run, so he was tired. After his senior year in high school, the New York Yankees invited him to a tryout. When he threw, Bill "Moose" Skowron, the Yanks' power-hitting first baseman, was impressed.

"You've got the heat, kid," Skowron said. "They're going to make you an offer." And they did: New York offered him a contract with a $65,000 bonus, which was a lot of money in those days.

The money paid to Major League Baseball players today—even unproven rookies—is life-changing. It wasn't then. Robert's family figured that a Yale degree was a surer thing. Robert could keep pitching at Yale, and if he were still top-level (or even improved), the Yankees or another Major League club would still be an option. But Robert could not be sure of admission to Yale, so he decided to attend Choate, a top Connecticut prep school, for an extra year. It amazed us. Not only did he turn down the Yankees and their $65,000, but he also did so without even being certain of his admission to Yale the following year.

"How could you turn down the Yankees?" we asked him.

And so he told us the story of his dad, Frank Kenney.

Frank was a traveling salesman who earned little money, certainly not enough to afford to pay for Yale's tuition for one son, much less four (Robert had three brothers). But his oldest son, Brian, got into Yale on a scholarship, starred on the varsity football team, and graduated in 1961. Mr. Kenney got a special Massachusetts license plate that read, "Yale-1."

Then his second son, Jerry, got into Yale and played football too. He graduated in 1963, and Frank got a new license plate: Yale-2.

So naturally the third son, Robert, had to go to Yale, and Mr. Kenney eventually got a new license plate: Yale-3.

Then the youngest son, Richard, entered Yale in 1967 and graduated in 1971, and yes, he got the new license plate: Yale-4.

The Yankees' loss was Yale's gain. And it is easy to forget that, with all those jock sons, Frank and his wife, Madeline, also had a beautiful daughter, Maureen.

During that post–high school year at Choate, Robert joined the wrestling team to keep in shape over the winter. It was a fateful choice. He injured his right shoulder while wrestling. He still played on the Yale varsity baseball team and pitched and hit well, but he was never the same player again. I used to swing by the field when he was pitching and loved to hang out with one of my fraternity brothers who was also a pitcher, albeit (by his own description) a mediocre one. His name was George W. Bush.

But back to Robert Kenney. Baseball took a back seat to football, which he found more exciting. In three years as a wide receiver on Yale's varsity team, he was named All-Ivy League. His size and speed made him attractive to pro football scouts—he was invited to camp by the New York Giants. But I found early on he was even more attractive to women. I recall a lot of the girls I dated made positive comments about Robert, but Robert did not take note. He had been in love—and I mean totally smitten—since high school with a "nice Jewish girl" (as my mom would have called her back then) named Lynne Friedman. And she was clearly in love with him—a classic high school romance (she was naturally the cheerleader assigned to cheer for the star of the Newton High School football team, Robert Kenney). They are still married and in love nearly sixty years later as this page is being written.

So I would tell my dates who asked about Robert: "Forget it. He's taken."

Then there was Andris "Andy" Baltins, always called "AB." He was a tall, fair-haired Minnesotan. We had classical piano playing in common, but when I heard and watched him play, I quickly determined he was the better pianist. Andy had a spiritual, philosophic side that drew me to him. He was more introspective than the rest of us. Even before "meditation" became a word that any of us had ever heard of, AB knew the art of mindfulness and quietude. My polar opposite, I thought, but a great influence on me from the moment we met. Often, when I was overly emotional, he would have this soothing effect on me. AB would quietly approach me when my passions were running a little too high (like always) and whisper in my ear, "It's okay, Lanny." It would have its immediate calming effect. As an attorney in a major Minneapolis law firm, Andy went on to become a nationally regarded expert on mergers and acquisitions and high-level strategic advice to major corporate boards and directors and CEOs.

AB also had a high school sweetheart he loved madly. Her name was Nancy Solstad, and she attended Smith College.

The four of us in 1360 Davenport only roomed together for a single school year, but it was enough. We became like brothers. Today, no matter how long it has been between conversations, when we talk or meet again, it is as if we are always in the middle of the same paragraph that we started the last time we spoke. But brothers sometimes push each other too far. We did that to Robert one night and lived to tell the tale—although we were not sure it would turn out that way.

We had a laundry rotation system in our room. There was limited capacity in the Davenport laundry room of washing machines and dryers. So to be sure of availability, each room signed up for a particular date and evening—usually about every four weeks. In other words, if you missed your night, it would be another four weeks before you could clean your dirty laundry. That would be a problem. Missing your turn in the rotation was a big deal.

One late night after dinner, DJ, Andy, and I returned to the room to discover that Robert had forgotten that it was his turn to take our sheets and dirty clothes to the laundry for cleaning and drying. We looked at the dirty sheets, underwear, and shirts piled up and decided to teach him a lesson. So we took the dirty laundry to the laundry room, and by midnight, when Robert still had not returned, we finished executing the plan. It was not easy. We were on the third floor of the dorm, with stairs leading down to the grassy quad of Davenport campus.

First we disconnected the lower bunk bed from the upper one, where I slept, and carried the four iron pieces down the three flights and reconnected the bed in the middle of the Davenport courtyard. Then came the mattress, then his heavy desk and standing lamp, then his pillow and blankets (and dirty sheets, of course). We neatly made the bed. Then we even found a few books, pens, and pencils to place on the desk. In short, Robert Kenney now had a new, furnished bedroom—but it was in the middle of the Davenport campus, outside, under the stars. We turned and viewed the scene happily. It was done. We high-fived—and waited.

"He might even like it so much he will decide to sleep here for the rest of the year," I said aloud, and we all burst out laughing. That turned out not to be the case. Robert finally returned at about 2:30 a.m., with heavy notebooks and textbooks under his arm, reminding us that he must have been out doing what was fairly unusual for him—studying. He was not amused. We had forgotten that he had an early morning exam and a football practice to go to, and the sun was about to come up.

At first we laughed, then we started to realize Robert had a right to be upset. The three of us systematically began to carry up the bedroom we had carefully created and put it all back into room 1360. Finally, out of sheer exhaustion, Robert lay down and fell asleep. Despite being the skinniest, smallest guy among us, I was left with the assignment of sleeping in the same room in the bunk bed above and with the even worse assignment of waking him up in a few hours to be sure he got to the exam on time. Fortunately, he fell asleep right away, and I went to sleep unharmed.

We all got something out of it in the end: a memory that never left us. Ask our wives. Sixty years later, we still repeat this story often, always with laughter and a bit of guilt as we recall the basic unfairness of what we did to our buddy the night before an exam, just for the sin of forgetting to do the laundry.

■ ■ ■

We all took some classes together. We loved a course on the French Revolution and sat next to one another, fascinated by the thought that from "liberty, equality, fraternity" came a sadistic lawyer-turned-terrorist and mass murderer named Robespierre. Go figure.

We also took a course from a visiting professor and renowned biblical scholar, Rabbi Judah Goldin. It was titled "A Literary Study of the Old Testament." How could we resist taking such a course? Robert, the nice Catholic boy dating a Jewish girl, and me, a nice Jewish boy who rarely went to synagogue after my bar mitzvah. So we immersed ourselves in a small class of about fifteen students, listening to Rabbi Goldin, who had a wry sense of humor. He not only loved analyzing the poetry and spiritual beauty of key passages in the five books of Moses, but he also had a habit of giving weekly quizzes of the most arcane and detailed minutiae of a biblical passage, such as who begat whom in the twentieth generation after Adam and Eve.

I was such an obsessive overachiever that I—may God forgive me—underlined passages in the Bible. Oy vey! I also memorized all the names in the twenty generations after Adam and Eve—couples who begat children, who begat grandchildren and great-great-great-great-great-grandchildren of Adam and Eve. All that begetting interested me for some reason.

On one occasion I finished a twenty-five-question quiz asking such specific questions. Robert was sitting next to me. I looked at his quiz sheet. It was blank. I knew his grades were already on the low side, and I feared he might risk his eligibility for varsity football if they got any worse. So I gave him a gentle nudge with my elbow and turned my test sheet toward him so he could see my twenty-five answers. At the next class, Rabbi Goldin asked Robert and me to stay afterward. We looked at each other with alarm, especially when we saw him holding our two completed quizzes from the previous class.

"You both know the story of Solomon when he solved the problem of the two mothers who claimed to be mothers of the same baby, don't you?" he said.

Frozen in fear, we nodded solemnly. We knew that cheating at Yale could result in expulsion.

The rabbi continued, "King Solomon produced a solution that did not result in one mother being favored over the other, since he could never know who the real mother was. Instead, he said he would split the baby in half and give half to each mother. He lifted his sword, and the real mother cried, 'Don't, don't. I am not the real mother. She is.' And that proved to Solomon who the real mother was, and he gave the baby to her."

Then he looked at us soberly, putting his hands on our shoulders.

"So here is my King Solomonic solution: Since I cannot kill anything that is near and dear to either of you, that is not a solution. And I will not allow this one mistake to cause you to be expelled from Yale."

He added, "But I can do a fifty-fifty split. Not of a human being but of Mr. Davis's 100 percent grade compared to the zero grade that you would have received, Mr. Kenney. So each of you gets a 50 percent grade."

We sighed with relief. From that moment on, Robert and I studied the Bible together. I helped him underline with me, and he managed to pass the course, and I managed to recover from my 50 percent grade to earn a good mark and keep my grade point average high. Robert and I often recall those moments of terror with Rabbi Goldin, and we are both sure he is in heaven and hope he will help us get through the pearly gates by not telling God about the Solomonic solution he had to apply to two sinners cheating on a Bible test.

At some point in the spring of our sophomore year, Andy and I decided to learn how to play a four-handed version of Beethoven's Fifth Symphony on the piano. We practiced separately and together virtually every night. Then early one afternoon, on a spring social weekend, we performed among most of Davenport's three hundred students and their dates in the common room in front of the dining room. It was a moving experience for the two of us. Four hands meant we sat on the same piano bench together, playing from two musical scores—AB the base notes and me the higher notes. We ended with a flourish, as only Beethoven could write it. The entire room gave us a standing ovation, and we took a bow.

I mention this scene because six decades later, Americans old enough to remember feel as though they are reliving the sixties. This is particularly true among us Democrats, who still shudder when we think of 1968: the Tet Offensive that altered the course of the war in Vietnam; the assassinations, first of Martin Luther King Jr. and then of Robert Kennedy; the race riots that left so many American cities in flames; the police-instigated violence at the Democratic National Convention in Chicago;

and finally the election of Richard Nixon over civil rights hero Hubert Humphrey.

Yes, there are echoes of that unsettling time in the spring of 2025, when I am completing this memoir—though Donald Trump seems at times to me to be a far greater threat than Nixon ever was—but I am making a different point. Our time as Yale undergraduates predated most of that. It was the sixties, but we were children of the forties, with an innocence we didn't realize and perhaps didn't deserve. It seemed a good time to be alive, a good time to be an American, and a good time to be at Yale.

The four roommates and our girlfriends had a tradition of hanging out together during weekend parties and dances in the cleaned-out Davenport dining room. Then, at about 10:00 p.m., they would push me toward the Steinway baby grand piano in the common room in front of the dining hall. I would play popular sing-along tunes that most people knew: from Broadway show tunes, such as "Oklahoma!" or George M. Cohan's "Over There," to patriotic songs such as "God Bless America."

Inevitably dozens of Davenport students and their dates gathered around the piano, singing the songs and calling out others for me to play. I had no sheet music, of course, but played by ear and filled in the chords underneath for songs I had heard and knew and some I did not know but could play if someone could sing the first few lines.

The bonding process that occurred from a group of diverse people singing together was inspiring, especially for me, playing the piano in the center of several hundred Yale men and their dates, often with arms around each other, singing and swaying together. Inevitably, at some point during the evening, I would be asked (or I would do it anyway) to play the chorus number from the then-famous Rogers and Hammerstein title song to the popular 1940s musical *Oklahoma!* How could I ever forget my increased pulse when a room full of several hundred Yale men and their dates—usually by then with arms around each other—singing out the last word of the song, with emphasis and exclamation marks,

"Oklahoma!!!" (No, thank goodness, in that era, I did not automatically associate that state as a deep Republican red bastion.)

Invariably, as she stood next to me at the piano for the last song, AB's girlfriend, Nancy Solstad, would ask me to play her favorite, "Danny Boy." An Irish tenor who was a student at Davenport would often come over as I started to play the opening chords. Everyone would listen, mesmerized by our rendition of this haunting ballad.

*Oh, Danny boy, the pipes, the pipes are calling*
*From glen to glen, and down the mountain side.*
*The summer's gone, and all the roses falling,*
*It's you, it's you must go and I must bide.*
*And I shall hear, though soft you tread above me,*
*And all my grave will warmer, sweeter be,*
*For you will bend and tell me that you love me,*
*And I shall sleep in peace until you come to me.*

And there always would be Nancy, tears rolling down her face as the Irish tenor sang out that last mournful line, hugging me and saying: "Thank you, Lanny, for making me so happy!"

Nancy and Andy had known each other since they were eight years old at Kenwood Elementary School in Minneapolis. Nancy claimed that she knew from the third grade that she and Andy were destined to be together. After Yale, they returned home, and Andy went to law school at the University of Minnesota, while Nancy earned a master's degree in social work and then another advanced degree from Union Theological Seminary. They married and had two children: an academically gifted daughter and a much-loved son. They pursued their careers—Andy as a successful corporate lawyer, and Nancy as a social worker and therapist. But she left us too young. It was late spring of 1996 when I heard from Andy that Nancy was losing her battle with ovarian cancer. I immediately booked a plane to Minneapolis. Once I arrived, in coordination with Andy, I entered their house and sat at the baby grand piano in the living room. Andy, who had not told Nancy I was coming, cracked open their bedroom door so Nancy could hear as I started playing "Danny Boy."

When the song was over, I climbed the stairs slowly and entered the bedroom. There was Nancy, propped up on a pillow, tearful but with a big smile.

"Thank you, Lanny," she said, just as she had so many times at Yale thirty years earlier. "You have made me so happy."

She passed a few weeks later, on June 30, 1996. I learned later that Minnesota Senator Paul Wellstone visited her the day before she died.

■ ■ ■

*The seasons come, the seasons go,*
*The earth is green or white with snow,*
*But time and change shall naught avail*
*To break the friendships formed at Yale.*

**"BRIGHT COLLEGE YEARS,"** Yale alma mater

Even though the four of us were roommates for only one year—sophomores at Davenport College—we forged a friendship that time apart could not erode. In the years since our graduation in 1967, we stayed in touch, sometimes sporadically, through our Yale reunions, phone conversations, personal visits, and in later years, emails and texts. Our college girlfriends became our wives, and except for Andy and Nancy, who waited nine years, we all had children within a short time after graduation. It was natural in those days to leave school, start working, get married, and have children. We continued the friendship from a distance, got together regularly, and wrote and phoned. Except now it was with wives, making a group of eight rather than four.

In my own case, I brought *two* wives into the 1360 Group. Robert Kenney and I both got married in our senior years at Yale. I wed Elaine Charney, my girlfriend from my Camp Equinunk days, in 1966. Bob married Lynne Friedman two months later. DJ married Joanne Junor six months after that, while AB and Nancy Solstad tied the knot in 1968.

Elaine and I separated in 1982, when Marlo and Seth were young. She was and remains a good person and a great mother, and will always be remembered as a legendary Color War chief at Camp Blue Ridge (the sister camp to Equinunk, where we first met in 1962). When marriages end up in divorce, there are almost always two sides of responsibilities and regrets. That was the case for me and Elaine.

During the latter years of our marriage in the 1970s and early 1980s, Elaine was active in Hexagon, an amateur theatrical group. The cast included politicians, lawyers, lobbyists, and others who loved center stage—meaning there was no shortage of volunteers in Washington, D.C. Elaine was a choreographer and sometime participant in the Hexagon chorus and in the politics-themed satiric skits. She got me involved playing the piano during rehearsals and often writing music, most frequently the opening or closing chorus numbers.

Hexagon was the place where I first learned that Washington could be bipartisan and that opportunities existed to rise above politics for the common good—in the case of Hexagon, to raise money for important charitable organizations that were not high-profile. Once upon a time in the capital city, Republicans and Democrats fought it out on the floor of the House or Senate but then came together in the evenings for social get-togethers. Politics was better for it. Once a year, for "Congressional Night," members of Capitol Hill attended the Hexagon show and a dinner gala afterward. It was always a good time, but one particular dinner reminds those who were there of what we are missing in our current age of polarization, vitriol, and dysfunction.

One year, Rhoda Glickman, the wife of two-term Kansas Democratic Congressman Dan Glickman, came to me with the lyrics to a song she had written called "Raising Hell in Heaven for Hexagon." She asked me to put them to music. Dan Glickman's idea was that he and four Democratic House colleagues—and one Republican, Dan Quayle—would sing the number. Its gist was that if we members are nice to one another in Congress, when the time came, we'd be more likely to be admitted through the pearly gates.

The number would be capped by an appearance by the inimitable House Speaker Tip O'Neill, who would make a surprise entrance on stage in an angelic white gown, playing Saint Peter judging at the pearly gates. He wore a golden halo over his head, and his role was to bless the six singing congressmen, invite them into heaven, and then tell a joke—that is to say, *one* joke.

But Tip wasn't known for brevity, and so on performance night, March 22, 1979, Dan Glickman and I were backstage with the director, who reminded the Speaker before he walked onto the stage, "We are running late, Mr. Speaker, so just one joke. And then the curtain falls."

O'Neill smiled and nodded his understanding. When he walked out onto the stage in that white gown with that golden halo, however, the ovation and uproar went on for several minutes. Of course, Tip didn't do much to quiet the audience so he could tell his joke. But finally, he did.

He told a clever gag in an Irish brogue, and the audience laughed and clapped. That was supposed to be it. But the Speaker didn't leave the stage. Surprise! He loved the laughter and applause, so he told another joke. Laughter and applause again. And then again, surprise! He told another joke. And another.

And another.

Backstage, Dan and I didn't know what to do. The director left us, quickly came back, and handed Dan a long stick with a curved hook at the end—called a "burlesque hook" (used in the olden days to get a comedian off the stage who, like the Speaker, couldn't resist extending his time for a few more jokes).

With trepidation, Democratic Congressman Glickman stepped cautiously onto the stage when the Democratic Speaker of the House was too enthralled with the audience's applause to see him coming. Dan carefully put the hook around the Speaker's neck, and with uproarious laughter from the audience (and some boos from those who wanted more), Dan gently tugged him off the stage. At the last moment before being pulled offstage, the Speaker stopped, waved to the audience, and bellowed, "To all you House Republicans, I'll be there before you, and I will do my best to get you into heaven—but no guarantees!"

The audience roared with laughter, both Republicans and Democrats alike—it didn't matter. Their cheers continued on and on.[§]

I love Hexagon for another reason, though: It's how I met my current wife of forty-one years (and best friend and adviser), Carolyn.

Together, over more than four decades of marriage, we have shared our love for music, books, family, and cats and dogs and all stray animals, and we've found common ground from an abiding and deep love and mutual respect.

I first met her one night when I was backstage tinkering at the piano, playing some classic Broadway show tunes from the 1950s. A young woman from the cast approached the piano. She asked me if I could play "Summertime," one of George Gershwin's most famous, beautiful ballads from his 1935 now legendary musical *Porgy and Bess*. I nodded my head and started to play it, but she asked me if I could lower the key slightly. I nodded my head again and dropped the key by one-third. I could tell she was impressed. I was even more impressed as I heard her sing: A beautiful natural, rich vibrato—she was clearly a talented singer. I asked her if she ever sang professionally, and she just shrugged, displaying what I came to realize was a sincere (if misplaced) modesty about her musical talents. She merely mentioned she had been in musicals in high school and had gone

§ A *Washington Post* story capturing the moment appeared the next day, March 23, with the headline, "The Speaker Brings Down the House."

to Western Michigan University in Kalamazoo, where she had been active in musical theater.

Months later, after Elaine and I had officially separated, my first cousin Ted, who was like a brother to me and had experienced a divorce too, called to see how I was doing. He advised me to find a beautiful woman immediately and ask her out for dinner. I protested I couldn't think of any, but he pushed me.

Then I recalled the young woman who had sung Gershwin's "Summertime" backstage so beautifully. But I couldn't remember her last name. I was pretty sure it was Carolyn Atwater. And I thought she lived in Northern Virginia. So with no internet to help in the search, I took out the huge Washington, D.C., Metro Area telephone book (including Maryland and Virginia) and looked under the heading "Atwater." I found about thirty names. By now I was stubborn and refused to give up. I called every "Atwater" listed with a Northern Virginia address, asking each person who answered if I could talk to "Carolyn." Each time the answer was the same: There was no Carolyn at the number.

About an hour later, disappointed and frustrated, I called a friend from the Hexagon cast. I described Carolyn and asked him whether he knew her and possibly her address or phone number. But when I kept repeating the name "Atwater," he interrupted me.

"Oh, you must mean Carolyn *Atwell*—not Atwater."

Encouraged, I hung up the phone and looked up all the "Atwells" in Northern Virginia. There were about twenty. About a dozen calls into my mission, a female voice answered. "This is Carolyn," she said. "Who is this?"

I took a deep breath, introduced myself, and reminded her we had met at Hexagon.

"Oh, I know who you are," she said. "You're the piano player."

I was happy and relieved. But I still had to cross the Rubicon and ask her the important question. "Would you have lunch with me sometime?"

She agreed. She worked at a law firm near where I worked in downtown D.C. I picked her up, and we drove to a nice restaurant on the Potomac River waterfront called The Gangplank. We spent the lunch talking about a variety of topics, from music to legal issues she had learned about as part of her administrative work at the firm. When I heard her discussing legal cases and dissecting the written decisions of some of them, I heard a future lawyer—although I didn't mention that for the moment.

What especially impressed me was her closeness with her father and how she'd spend time with him in his basement workshop, where they would do everything together from building furniture to electrical repairs. This impressed me more than her many diverse talents for the simple reason that my handyman skills started and stopped at changing light bulbs.

As we got to know each other better, Carolyn and I would sometimes go for an early dinner in a nice restaurant along the Potomac, a few miles south of what was then called National Airport. At times a piano player played quiet music in the background, which gave me an idea. I had previously substituted for a piano player during some trips to the Maryland seashore, with Carolyn standing by and listening and sometimes singing a song or two.

So I asked Carolyn if she would like to try to sing at this restaurant while I played as a substitute when the piano player had a night off. Hesitant at first, she warmed to the idea, and we rehearsed some classic standards from the 1940s and 1950s—songs sung by Frank Sinatra and Tony Bennett—as well as the famous Broadway musical songs from the same era.

One night, I asked the manager of the restaurant whether he would allow me to substitute for the piano player on his night off. He knew me from my political activities and was a little dubious, but I mentioned that Carolyn was a talented singer and she could sing soft ballads, so he agreed to let us give it a try.

The first night was a success, as we noticed (and so did the manager) diners nodding and smiling. We returned several times and provided some enjoyment for diners, which pleased the manager. It pleased us too. Just for kicks, we put a tip bowl on the piano, and sure enough, we were collecting a few dollars a night in the jar. It was fun, and we did this for several months. As music had done so often in my life, I noticed that it brought us closer.

I continued to enjoy our lunches and dinners, especially the lively conversations we had about almost every subject. I knew politics, of course, but Carolyn also had diverse interests ranging from U.S. history, which we both loved, to legal issues, music, theater, books, and sometimes contemporary culture. She was then, as I immediately recognized during our lunches, a voracious reader and remains so to this day.

The intellectual stimulation was constant. While talking with this beautiful and intellectually captivating woman, I would simply lose track of time. Looking back, I think any man would have fallen in love with her. I certainly did. And the love is deeper now, after four decades together.

Over many months we grew closer, and I introduced her to my two children, my daughter, Marlo, and son, Seth. It was not easy for her or for them. Carolyn is fourteen years younger than me, meaning she was closer in age to my teenage daughter than to me. However, both Marlo and Seth came to understand that she made their dad very happy—and that realization made them happy. They grew to appreciate Carolyn's love for me, her love for music and our pets, and her work and interest in them and their lives—and over time we all adjusted to a new life together.

Carolyn and I were married on December 22, 1984, in Bethesda, Maryland.

Several years into our marriage, I convinced Carolyn to think about law school.

"After all these years, I have never won an argument with you," I told her. "You should become a lawyer."

I said this lightheartedly, in case she wasn't interested, but I was serious. Carolyn is so smart and has such an analytical mind that I thought she'd be a natural. It turned out to be true. She applied and was admitted to one of the top law schools in the country, Georgetown University.

Carolyn got some early experience as a federal criminal prosecutor during one of her Georgetown Law summers, when she obtained a coveted position in the U.S. Attorney's office for the Eastern District of Virginia. I recall her telling me at the time the important lesson she learned from one of the leaders of that office: to always be aware of the power of a prosecutor—the power to do good enforcing the criminal laws of the nation as well as the potential power to do harm by abusing that power. She saw years before I did that this power to do good is often underappreciated by the public (or by those accused of crimes). Prosecutors have the obligation to prosecute and obtain guilty verdicts after due process and trial of those alleged to have committed crimes. But as Carolyn often reminded me then and through the years when I encountered prosecutors at the federal and state levels in my law practice, the ultimate duty of all prosecutors is to do "justice"—not to obtain convictions. Her wisdom on this issue, as on so many others, made a lasting impression on me with regard to the present and recent experiences I have had with federal and state prosecutors.

After clerking for a federal judge, Carolyn became assistant to the president of the National Center for Missing & Exploited Children (NCMEC).

NCMEC is one of the leading organizations in the world dedicated to preventing and finding those responsible for child abduction and sexual exploitation. NCMEC provides training and tools to law enforcement, including the CyberTipline for reporting child sexual abuse material on the Internet. They are also know for the AMBER (America's Missing Broadcast Emergency Response) Alert program, which uses television, radio, and the internet to publicize information about child abductions.

Amber Hagerman was the inspiration for the program. She was kidnapped when she was nine years old on January 13, 1996, near her home in Arlington, Texas, while riding her bike in a parking lot. Her body was found four days later. Although her killer was never caught, the little girl's death created a public groundswell of concern. Police in Dallas and Fort Worth started a program with local media to broadcast missing children alerts in real time. George W. Bush, who was then in his first term as Texas's governor, supported formalizing the program. NCMEC worked with law enforcement and broadcasters in other states to create their own programs.

Seven years later, at a somber White House ceremony attended by Amber's mother, my old Yale fraternity brother signed the PROTECT Act of 2003, throwing federal resources into the fight.

"No child should ever have to experience the terror of abduction, or worse," said President Bush. "No family should ever have to endure the nightmare of losing a child . . . And our nation will fight threats against our children."

I was proud of Bush that day, and I've been proud of Carolyn every day since the first day I met her and to this day.

She became an authority through experience and studying federal and state laws regarding child abduction and sexual exploitation. She was a key person assisting NCMEC President Ernie Allen, who turned NCMEC into the leading agency helping local law enforcement and the Justice Department find abducted children and inform parents about precautions to take to protect their children from the monsters who would often grab them when a mom or dad was looking away at a shopping center or supermarket. Allen, who had started his career working with future Senator Mitch McConnell when he was a county official, would often tell me he was amazed at what a quick study Carolyn was and how so many members of Congress and their staffs mentioned to him that they depended on Carolyn to answer their questions and give them advice.

Carolyn also helped draft Allen's testimony before congressional committees. One senator who prioritized child protection issues was the former chairman of the Senate Judiciary Committee, Senator Joseph R. Biden of Delaware. As chairman of the Senate Foreign Relations Committee, he continued his concern for the international aspects of the issues through his then-committee staff director, Antony Blinken. Years later, I visited then-Deputy Secretary of State Blinken on a client matter. As I began the meeting in his large office on an upper floor in the State Department building, Blinken began with the question: "How is your wife, Carolyn? Senator Biden and I were grateful for her help on protecting children."

■ ■ ■

Carolyn and I had our first son, Joshua Benjamin, in 1998, shortly after I left my position at the White House as President Clinton's special counsel.

As of this writing, Josh is studying law at a paralegal school—often helping me write legal memos at my practice—and is a loving father, husband, and son.

Our youngest son, Jeremy, is twenty years old. In high school, he was a skilled varsity baseball player who helped his team win the local regional championship and played a key role in its rise to the quarterfinals of the Maryland state tournament. He is now a student at Coastal Carolina University.

Marlo, my first child (with my first wife, Elaine Charney), graduated from Tulane University and married David Sims, then a young business entrepreneur and now a technical job placement expert. They are the proud parents of three children—Jake, Sydney, and Devon. Very early in her life, Marlo showed a natural talent for organization, management capabilities, and people skills. At eight years old, she worked in my father's dental office during summer breaks, helping my mother organize the appointment books and making follow-up calls to confirm appointments.

My mother often said that Marlo was a natural office leader with an outgoing personality who charmed patients with her smile. "Someday she will lead any office she is working for and will be impossible to say no to," my mom would say. "And she will be a natural success in sales and marketing." That prediction turned out to be true in all of her future jobs. Marlo is now a successful part of a real-estate buying and investing organization.

My oldest son (also with Elaine), Seth Lewis Davis, graduated from Duke University in 1992, where he wrote about sports for the *Chronicle*, the student newspaper. Seth also started his own TV show on the campus channel. He called the show "Cameron Corner" (after the school's famous basketball stadium), and—amazingly—his first guest was famous head men's basketball coach Mike Krzyzewski.

After leaving school, Seth went on to write about college basketball for *Sports Illustrated* and became a well-known TV analyst for the NCAA basketball tournament, first on CBS for many years and recently for Turner Broadcasting and other stations. In 2024, he started his own website, "Hoops HQ," and (discounting the fatherly exaggeration) remains one of the most respected college basketball reporters, writers, and TV analysts in the nation. He has also authored and coauthored several books, including the definitive biography of legendary UCLA coach John Wooden. His most recent "as told to" book is the story of basketball star Rex Chapman, with the honest and compelling title *It's Hard for Me to Live with Me: A Memoir.*

I remember when Seth was much younger and I was on national TV a lot regarding my White House work for President Clinton, young Seth would sometimes tell me he was known as "Lanny Davis's son." Now I remind Seth that, given his national reputation, I am proud to be known as "Seth Davis's father."

Seth and his wife, Melissa Cohen Davis—a graduate of the University of Connecticut, a brilliant student and partner to Seth, and a great mom—have three sons: Zachary and Noah, who are both students at the University of Texas, Austin, and Gabriel (a skilled high school baseball player).

I realize this has been a long digression from my storyline of the four friends who roomed together at Yale and extended that year into a lifetime of friendship.

My motivation here is twofold. First, this memoir would be a distorted accounting of the adventures (and pratfalls) of Lanny Davis if I didn't take the time to conscientiously introduce the reader to the most important people in my life.

Second, my marriage to Carolyn helped me learn that finding common ground is as important in our personal relationships as it is in politics. Carolyn and I have learned how to do it, as have all members of the 1360 Group—and every successful couple or collection of friends.

"Home," Robert Frost wrote in an evocative poem about death and friendship, "is the place where, when you have to go there, they have to take you in." I have felt at home with the 1360 Group since the first year I met them at Yale University.

■ ■ ■

Thinking about the challenges of finding common ground—this is in the category of too-good-to-be-true—one comic episode occurred shortly after 1360 Davenport roommate Robert Kenney and his new wife, Lynne Friedman, were married.

Robert and Lynne fell in love in high school, at a time when such a relationship was seen as dual rebellion: Jewish girls, as my own sister, Tama, experienced, were strongly dissuaded (usually most vehemently by Jewish mothers) from even dating non-Jewish boys (let alone marrying them). And Robert's devout Catholic mother made it clear that although she liked Lynne a great deal, Lynne and Robert, if they married, had to do so in a church by a priest.

And so in high school and on into college, they knew they had to be discreet, at least until they had time to charm their mutual future in-laws, mostly the two moms. But they met considerable resistance from both of them. Yet Robert and Lynne, who are admirable and appealing people to this day, evoked the old adage that "love conquers all." Eventually, they put their feet down.

"We are getting married with or without your blessing," they told their mothers. "We prefer your blessing." And that was that.

As it turned out, the wedding was neither in a Catholic church nor a synagogue but instead in the living room of Lynne's parents. The officiant was a civil judge. It was one of the most inspiring weddings anyone could remember because the love between Lynne and Robert was simply infectious. More than sixty years later, they seem more in love than when I first met them during freshman year at Yale in 1963. And as far as I know, the only trouble they encountered because of their "mixed marriage" was an Irish American cop with a puckish sense of humor. The result of this encounter was a memorable story for any Jewish–Irish Catholic couple.

Not too long after they were married, Robert was driving Lynne's car in downtown New York City and made a U-turn that he quickly realized was illegal—and then noticed an NYC patrolman motioning him to pull over.

"License and registration," the cop said, and Robert opened the window. As Robert tells the story, when he heard those three words, he heard a faint Irish brogue. The police officer looked at Robert's driver's license.

"Robert Kenney," he read out loud. Then he looked at the car registration. "Lynne Friedman."

The patrolman looked closely at Robert, perhaps a little sympathetically, Robert thought.

"'Kenney'?" he asked. "You Irish, lad?" he asked.

"Yes, sir," Robert answered.

He pondered the registration, seeing the name "Friedman."

"Who is this Friedman?"

"Oh, that's my wife," said Robert. "She owns this car, and we were recently married, so she hasn't had time to change the name on her registration."

The cop looked at him skeptically.

"You Catholic?" he asked.

Robert hesitated, wondering why he was being asked such a question and what it had to do with his U-turn infraction. He answered anyway.

"Yes, sir, I am."

The officer looked at the registration again. "Friedman. Your wife's last name. She's Jewish, right?"

Robert hesitated again, wondering where this inquisition was going. "Yes, sir, she is."

Now it was the cop who skipped a beat. Then with perfect timing, he deadpanned, "I cannot give you a ticket. You have enough problems."

We all have problems in life, but for Robert and Lynne, the difference in their faith traditions was not one of them. After their marriage shortly after graduation, they parented two sons, both of whom went to Yale and played football. Lynne became a respected psychologist and therapist, including family counseling. On Martha's Vineyard, she led many public interest organizations supporting the arts and helping the elderly. Robert was a Big Brother to inner-city boys. Both became "support parents" for a young girl from the inner city, and the miracle of their sponsorship and love for this now-grown woman is an amazing thing to see.

Religious differences were never an issue for Carolyn and me, either. Carolyn made her own decision to convert to Judaism, influenced in large part by traveling with me on a business trip to Israel, which she found inspiring. After we were married, we organized the bar mitzvahs for our boys, and in most substantive theological ways, she practices Judaism and writes her own special "Haggadah" telling the story of Passover and dedicating each Seder to a special person with great impact on the world in the previous year. Our Seders were attended by a range of non-Jewish special guests, from the head of a local Palestinian support group to Jack Kemp, a former Republican congressman, cabinet secretary, and famous Buffalo Bills quarterback.

After graduating and marrying Joanne Junor, DJ Foster attended Harvard Business School and went into the U.S. Navy under an officer training program during the Vietnam War. Upon completing his military service, he became an engineer and senior official for a multinational engineering company, and Joanne got her master's degree in gerontology.

After spending many years abroad, they came home, and then their true missionary Christian good works began. Both DJ and Joanne became active in the church, and David spent decades working in prisons ministering to inmates. I always knew that he would get to the pearly gates much easier than I. And I know that if need him and Joanne to lobby Saint Peter on my behalf, all I have to do is ask. That is what the 1360 Davenport group does for one another.

Our friendship post-Yale strengthened even more because of visits to one another's summer getaway homes. Ours was a small house in western Maryland overlooking Deep Creek Lake, and the Kenneys' was in Martha's Vineyard. During one biking journey, I hit the wrong brake—the front rather than the back—and hurtled over the front wheel, landing on my forehead. Somehow I was not badly injured. No matter how many years passed, no matter whose home we visited, at night we would still sit around and retell our old room 1360 stories, and we never got tired of repeating them. Miraculously, our wives did not either.

One of my most vivid post-Yale memories occurred at the now legendary Harvard-Yale football game in September 1968, when I wasn't looking to find any common ground with Yale's archrivals from the "H" school in Cambridge, Massachusetts. Both teams were undefeated, but Yale had two future NFL players in its backfield and was leading, 29–13, with forty-two seconds left. It was too much time.

Harvard scored a touchdown and a two-point conversion, then recovered an onside kick and did it again—a touchdown with no time left on the clock and another two-point conversion that ended the game in a tie at 29 (back then, college football games could end in a tie).

Robert, Lynne, Elaine, and I were frozen in the stands, in disbelief at what we had just witnessed. Seconds before, we had been waving our white handkerchiefs at Harvard fans across the field, mocking them for losing to Yale with the Ivy League championship on the line.

As I finished this chapter more than half a century later, I exchanged emails with an old friend and one of America's greatest journalists and writers, James Fallows, who unfortunately is a Harvard man. I mentioned the game and asked Jim, who was working for the *Harvard Crimson* at the time, whether he was responsible for one of the greatest sports headlines ever written: "Harvard Defeats Yale 29–29."

I thought I had seen that headline as we walked out of the stadium within thirty minutes of the stunning ending. Here is what Fallows wrote back: "I was the night editor at the *Crimson* on Sunday night after the [Saturday] game when we put out the Monday edition with the immortal . . . headline. We did not think of that in time for the game-day extra, which came out a few minutes after the score."

I asked Jim if he came up with it. He credited a photographer named Timothy Carlson, class of 1971, who went on to a successful journalism career in California.

■ ■ ■

In 2020 the lockdowns of the coronavirus pandemic upended nearly everything in American life. But not the 1360 Group. If anything, it made us closer. I think it was David who came up with the idea of scheduling monthly Zoom calls with all eight of us. After about a half-dozen sessions, Andy, always the most philosophical of the original Yale group, came up with the idea that we should focus on one theme for each conversation. We started with the "13 Virtues" that the legendary founder of our republic, Benjamin Franklin, created in the late 1760s that helped make him famous.

These sessions helped give new momentum to old friendships. For one thing, the four women on the Zoom calls claimed an equal footing and no longer had to listen to the men's endlessly repetitive (and inevitably embellished) stories. They contributed their own insights and intellectual analyses when they were the presenters of one of the virtues during the monthly Zoom calls. David took the first assignment and set the precedent by doing a lot of research. We had fun each month and, more than that, found them mentally stimulating. We were pleasantly surprised at how much we enjoyed the intellectual exercise of analyzing the meaning and history—especially with Andy's future wife, Lynne McGuire, the most recent member of the group. She was quiet and sometimes seemed bashful, but when she spoke, as the famous investment bank commercial put it, we all listened.

The group proceeded to analyze all of Franklin's virtues. The personal comments sometimes were amazingly honest and self-critical. It brought us closer than ever before.

When we were done with Franklin's virtues in mid-2021, we looked for another source of topics. I suggested we explore poetry, with each of us leading the discussion by selecting our favorite poem. Since it was my idea, I went first, and I chose my favorite poem, "The Road Not Taken," by Robert Frost, and we spent two hours analyzing its meaning: the contradictory message of wondering about life choices and the "road not taken"—yet Frost ended the poem by telling us he was happy he chose his own road.

Since I was in the middle of writing this book at the time of the discussion, I wondered whether, in looking back at my various choices and then in retelling them "years hence," I had done the same thing as Frost predicted. Would I look back and find a way to remember my choices as the right ones?

Whatever our choices or regrets, life goes on, speeding up, it seems, as we enter our seventies. For example, here was the email the 1360 Group (men and women) received from David Foster at 4:45 a.m., Tuesday, December 28, 2021:

> *Yesterday was a day of diagnostic tests at Riverside Hospital after a mild cardiac event on Sunday. Because we found a serious and complex blockage in my heart arteries, I will have cardiac bypass surgery starting at 7:30 this morning. I ask for your prayers for me, the surgery team, Joanne, and our family as we go through this hard day.*
>
> *I am calm and optimistic about tomorrow, and the three months of healing and rehab that will follow. This is because,*

*"Even though I walk through the valley of the shadow of death, I will fear no evil, for my God is with me."*

*I love you, my 1360 brothers and sisters,*

*David*

At 7:06 a.m. on the morning of December 29, an email arrived in the email accounts of the 1360 Davenport Group from DJ:

***From:*** *DAVID FOSTER*
***Sent:*** *Wednesday, December 29, 2021*
***To:*** *Carolyn Atwell-Davis, Andris A. Baltins, Lynne McGuire, Lanny J. Davis, Robert Kenney, Lynne Kenney, Joanne Foster*

*A good time recovering with great nurses in the ICU! No complications as of now. The surgeon said that all went as planned. Pain is under control and vitals are all good. Going into the step-down unit today.*

*I am so grateful to my loving God, for Joanne, and for the prayers and support of you, and others who found out by email, or word of mouth.*

*David*

We were all relieved and rejoiced.

The 1360 Group lives on . . . just as close friends as ever, maybe closer, more than sixty years later.

*Left to right around the table: Robert Kenney, Nancy Solstad Baltins, Carolyn Atwell-Davis, Lanny Davis, David "DJ" Foster, Joanne Foster, Lynne Kenney, and Andris "Andy/AB" Baltins in 1988 at the Baltins' Wisconsin cabin, "The Hermitage."*

CHAPTER 8

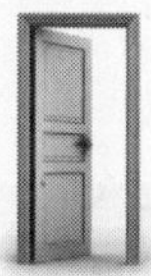

# *YALE DAILY NEWS*

The diploma on the wall in my law office notes that I graduated from Yale College in the class of 1967. At the time, however, it felt like I graduated from the *Yale Daily News*—and attended classes at the college part-time.

My ambition then was to be a journalist, not a lawyer. A *New York Times* columnist, to be specific. I would make my dad proud by replacing legendary *Times* man James "Scotty" Reston. At ten years old, I wanted to grow up and be the next Willie Mays, an ambition I later learned was shared by my Yale fraternity brother George W. Bush.* By the time I got to Yale and decided I wanted to become "chairman" of the oldest college daily in the United States, I had new idols—and more realistic ambitions than patrolling center field in the Polo Grounds.

* In October 2000, as Bush was about to go on stage for his first debate with Vice President Al Gore—a candidate I was helping—Bush adviser Mark McKinnon helped George focus by whispering a calming mantra in his ear: "Willie Mays, Willie Mays."

My pathway to becoming chairman was dependent on the Yale freshmen basketball coach's decision to cut me from the frosh team. As a former player for Newark Academy, I had a high regard for my basketball abilities. And why not? I was a starting guard for a team that won a state championship (as recounted in chapter 4). Yes, it was in New Jersey's small-school division. Yes, the star of our team wasn't Lanny Davis—it was an inner-city transfer student named Fran Pinchot. Still, Fran needed someone to pass him the ball, right? I could be a point guard at Yale. Or so I thought.

It seemed to me I had done well in tryouts, but when I saw the list of players who made the roster without my name on it, I went to the coach's office and protested that there must have been a mistake. He smiled but kindly said, "No, Lanny, no mistake. But good luck."

Chagrined at what I considered a gross injustice (okay, a minor injustice), I headed back to campus. In those days all freshmen lived in the Old Campus quadrangle.[†]

As I walked down York Street to make a left to High Street and the entryway to the freshman campus, I saw a sign that read, "Yale Daily News." I was enticed. I had been the editor of the Newark Academy paper, the *Minuteman*, and I loved to write, especially news stories.

I walked into the building and asked an older-looking man in the front office where the office of the chairman was located and whether the chairman, whom I knew to be Joe Lieberman, was there. I was directed up the stairs and down the hall. So off I went and saw a closed door at the end of the hallway. After seeing Lieberman (which I describe in the preface of this book), I went upstairs to the third floor, where I knew the famous, historic *Yale Daily News* boardroom was located. As I walked in, I saw an elongated dark wood conference table with plush leather chairs on both sides. On the wall, from top to bottom and to the left and

† The first building in the original Yale campus, the Old Campus, was built in 1718. In 1933, seven residential colleges were built for upperclassmen, so only freshman lived on the Old Campus. Then the number of colleges expanded to twelve in 1963, and then another two new ones, expanding the number to fourteen, were built in 2017.

*The 1967* Yale Daily News *board. I'm in the front row, third from left.*

right, were black-and-white photos of each of the "boards" of the *News*, going back to the nineteenth century—meaning the top managers with titles, with the chairman sitting in the front row.

As I walked around the room, I saw the names of young men and the images of them in shirts and ties with serious looks on their faces. It was an illustrious group. Some had become famous journalists. Others had gone into public service, including Peace Corps Director Sargent Shriver; Supreme Court Justice Potter Stewart; Yale's newly named president, Kingman Brewster Jr.; and the famous "Mr. Conservative" and author of *God and Man at Yale*, William F. Buckley Jr. himself.

A few months later, I tried out for the school paper in a competition with about one hundred other freshmen. This time I made the cut. From my earliest days as a *Yale Daily News* writer, I knew I wanted to "run" for chairman of the *News* someday.

From an early age, I had this desire to be challenged, to lead, to change things—change them for the better. These feelings were nurtured at the dinner table where my dad talked about the great presidents (all of them Democrats in his telling, from FDR onward) and the importance of social justice. Many young people my age were inspired to get into politics by John F. Kennedy, and some, including Bill Clinton, felt the spark of running for high office, even president, thanks to JFK.

My ambition was not always well received by my contemporaries. Maybe I wore it too much on my sleeve. It was a word applied to me negatively when I was running for Congress in the 1970s. And it seemed to track me in many other periods of my life. Knowing some people saw it as a problem, I tried to control it. But I like to think it comes from a good place, a place of optimism, and a desire to do good in the world.

The Kennedys put the best face on this durable human trait. As they would often say (paraphrasing George Bernard Shaw), "Some [people] see things as they are and ask, 'Why?' I dream things that never were and ask, 'Why not?'"

That became a mantra of our generation. But making a difference doesn't come easy. Once I started working on the *Yale Daily News*, I was determined to work harder than everyone. By autumn of my junior year, 1965, I was earnestly running for chairman of the paper. I knew that the most important qualification was writing a lot—on serious subjects. My best friend on the staff, John Rothchild, a brilliant writer, agreed to co-byline several portraits of leading Yale leaders, starting with Kingman Brewster Jr., who had become president in the first few months of our freshman year, shortly before JFK's assassination.

With the help of Brewster's young personal adviser, Henry "Sam" Chauncey Jr., we got the interview with "the King." It took place at the Yale eating club, Mory's, made famous by popular singer and saxophonist Rudy Vallée, who opened his nationally broadcast 1940s radio show by singing the "Whiffenpoof Song" (named after Yale's famous multiharmonizing a cappella group), with the first line: "To the tables down at Mory's, to the place where Louis dwells . . ."

The story we wrote, however, turned out to be boring. I recognized that when barely anyone mentioned it to us. It could have been highly newsworthy except that Brewster made a passing reference to Yale's all-male status that he quickly insisted was "off the record." What he said was that he might just consider taking steps that could lead Yale to adopt "some form of coeducation." We couldn't write it, but I made a mental note of it.

I wrote often, showing up every morning to get an assignment from the editor on duty so that my byline would appear nearly every day, hopefully on the front page.

As Woody Allen said, 80 percent of success in life is showing up, so being on the constant lookout for interesting stories paid off. One day, while leaving an exercise class at Yale's Payne Whitney Gym, I saw a familiar small food cart and heard the familiar man who went with it, standing in front and shouting in his familiar thick Italian accent known around New Haven. It was part of a ritual where the vendor, whom we knew only as "Chris," would hawk his food while spicing his pitch with various shouted curses.

The custom was to curse back at him or answer his wave by walking over and buying something as he called out for people to purchase a "hotta dogga" or "getta your candy."

What many of us didn't see at the time was that most people didn't seem to see him at all, at least not as a human being. This particular day, for whatever reason, after I purchased a "hotta dog," I wondered, *Who is this guy? How did he get here? What's his story?*

I started asking him questions. It took a lot to get him to talk about himself, especially after I took out my reporter's notebook (by then always in my back pocket) and began taking notes. I came back a couple more times. This was not the kind of "serious" journalism that would get me votes for chairman of the *Yale Daily News*. Still, I found Chris interesting and decided I wanted to explain to our readers who he was and where he came from. So I did what any reporter would do. I started out by asking his full name.

"Hey, Chris, what is your last name?"

He replied with a profanity.

"No, really," I asked. "Please."

"Columbo," he said after a pause.

"What?" I asked. "Do you mean Columbus?"

"Columbo," he repeated and spelled it out.

That simple question broke the ice. He began telling me his life story.

All these years later, the details of that story are not what gave this episode importance in my life—and they weren't at the time either. What was significant about the story I ended up writing was that, like my fellow students and faculty members at Yale, I had been content with the caricature of Chris, the hot dog vendor. Behind the expletives and central casting accent, however, was an interesting person—and his very name was the tip-off. Christopher Columbus, sailor and explorer, had gone in search of the Indies and found America. Nearly five centuries later, Chris Columbo had come here in search of the American Dream. He was finding it, too, and I decided to tell that to the readers of the *Yale Daily News*.

I went back to my room, read over my pages of notes, and wrote through the night and into the wee hours. I loved writing, and still do. I especially loved writing this story. In the morning I arrived at the *News* building on York Street and found the editor on duty. I handed him the story and saw him peruse the first few paragraphs. This was autumn of 1965. Serious events were taking place all around us. The Civil Rights Movement had gained momentum, galvanizing many students. Joe Lieberman was among those who'd gone to Mississippi to register voters. Growing student unrest was forming over the Vietnam War.

Glancing at the top of my story, the editor seemed unimpressed. I asked him to read it to the end, saying that I would abide by his judgment, and walked outside his office. Soon, I heard the sound of laughter. Then more. Apparently, I had captured Chris Columbo's wit and charm. I realized my story was going to be published. Late that night, after the editing process was over, a copy editor asked me, "So what's the headline?"

At the *Yale Daily News*, reporters were supposed to propose a headline first. I hadn't given it any thought—I hadn't really believed they would publish it—so I came up with the first thing that popped into my head. Inspired by *Will Success Spoil Rock Hunter?*, a 1957 Hollywood comedy starring Tony Randall and a new beautiful blond actress named Jayne Mansfield, I wrote it down on a piece of paper and handed it to the editor: "Will Success Spoil Chris Columbo?"

"Perfect!" the editor said.

The next day, as I walked to my morning classes, I saw a lot of Yale students with their morning copies of the *Yale Daily News* standing in groups, laughing and reading things aloud. When I got closer to one group, I realized they were reading my piece about Chris.

When I went to the newsroom later that day to get another story assignment, everyone I passed by in the hallways, including Francis Donahue, our omnipresent business manager who had been with the *Yale Daily News* since the 1930s, complimented me on the story. I went upstairs to check out the "comment book," where the paper was pasted up story by story to allow staff and editors to write comments. Usually my stories attracted few comments, good or bad. But this day was different. There were scrawled comments throughout the page on top of the story. All were positive. Many with exclamation points.

Most journalists and writers have had this experience: the rush of people reading and liking your work. Had it been the age of the internet some five decades later, we would say this story went "viral" across the Yale campus and beyond. In the process I learned an important lesson: I had followed the traditional pathway of running for chairman of the *News* by writing a lot of "serious" articles, but it was my feature story about Chris that had struck a chord with our readers. Others on campus experienced the curiosity I had when I decided to write the story: "How come I never knew anything about Chris until now?"

So I learned the importance of making a human impact and connection. This is a lesson not only about good journalism but also about being effective in business, politics, and life. I also knew I had to develop a "platform" as a candidate for chairman and decided that the chief issue

I would promise to promote as chairman was the need to admit women at Yale.

I'd found out that the chief rival of the Yale student newspaper, the *Harvard Crimson*, had an outgoing president who had made money for his classmates. I wanted to see if I could do the same at Yale. I decided to pick his brains (without anyone at Yale knowing), so I enlisted one of my Yale pals, Richard Van Wagenen, to make the introduction. Richard was from Washington and had gone to high school with the *Harvard Crimson* president, whose name was Donald Graham. So through Richard, who was sworn to secrecy, I made an appointment to visit Graham at his Washington, D.C., home on a Saturday in August 1965.

We spent a day with Don at his beautiful Georgetown mansion and met his mom, Katharine Graham, who smiled when Don kidded us about the supersecrecy of our mission. Mrs. Graham, who was widowed two years earlier, had essentially inherited ownership of *The Washington Post*. I wonder if the sight of two guys from the *Yale Daily News* collaborating with the president of the archrival *Harvard Crimson* struck Kay Graham as something akin to *Washington Post* and *New York Times* editors sitting down and helping each other.

Don explained his idea of publishing career supplements about working in particular industries, writing stories about the companies and the CEOs in those industries, promising them free distribution on Ivy League campuses, and then hitting them up for ads, which, of course, they could not refuse, knowing articles would be written about them and their companies.

I put that idea in my platform when I ran for *Yale Daily News* chairman. It was a hit—as was my vision of a coeducational campus—and after I was elected, we did publish several profitable "career supplements," which made money. Until now no one other than Richard and I knew about my consulting with Don.

Through the many years since that summer of 1965 and our first meeting, Don and I crossed paths many times after I came to D.C. to work after my law school graduation. He ultimately became publisher and owner of *The Washington Post*, succeeding his mother. Almost every time we met, Don reminded me good-naturedly that I owed him because he imparted the secret that helped me get elected chairman of the "*Yalie Daily*," as he called it. But he always promised, with a smile, that he would keep his oath of secrecy.

The third element of my strategy for winning the chairman election was simple. I decided to meet in person with every eligible voter, get their ideas for improving the paper, and then write a platform that incorporated their ideas. This entailed meeting some seventy fellow students, ten of whom were seniors in the class above us who held the management positions.

I noticed that a lot of people I called were surprised to hear from me and even more surprised to hear me ask to meet with them. (There were no emails or text messages back then, so reaching people by phone usually required multiple tries during the days and evenings.) I discovered quickly no one else seeking the position was making such efforts and certainly not talking to people in one-on-one sessions, with follow-ups. After a second or sometimes a third visit, I asked my classmates if they would be able to make a "commitment" to vote for me so I could keep a count. Most agreed, and by early October (the vote was in November of my junior year) I had reached the needed number of thirty-six.

Late one night, however, there was a knock on my door in Davenport College. I opened it to find my friend John Rothchild, whom I figured would be my managing editor if I were elected chairman. John, who seemed slightly inebriated, had other ideas. Before I could say anything, he told me he was running for chairman against me and wished me luck.

I was stunned and felt betrayed. Within five minutes my phone was ringing. The word was already out. Knowing who John's close friends were, I did an immediate count on my list of how many votes committed to me would likely switch to John. I counted about twenty. I also sensed that the seniors in charge of the paper were unenthusiastic about me. I heard from one of them (after the Rothchild October surprise) that I was too "unpolished." I had a hard time grasping that term, but it was one of my first lessons that optics and perceptions matter.

Thirty minutes later there was a knock on my door.

It was Boris Baczynskyj, a six-foot-three-inch, 270-pound Ukrainian. He was only marginally active on the newspaper staff, but he had called immediately after the Chris Columbo profile and pledged his support to me. He said he "identified" with Chris and liked that I made him into a real human being in my story. I didn't know Boris well. But I knew about his strong feelings for Ukraine and hatred of Soviet Russia's domination of his country and culture. In a conversation that seems contemporary today, we talked about his country. I expressed awe and said maybe after he graduated Yale, he would go home and help Ukraine someday become free of Russia. In response, he gave me a big hug.

Now he was at my door expressing fury at Rothchild's "treachery." I tried to talk him out of his anger, but he wasn't easily mollified.

"Rothchild reminds me of Brutus—or Khrushchev," he sputtered. I laughed. *I am no Julius Caesar,* I thought. Then Boris hugged me again and left. The election was now scheduled for the evening of November 22, 1965, the two-year anniversary of President Kennedy's assassination. Boris vowed he would talk to every one of the seventy or so potential voters and report to me on whether I could include them in my "hard" count.

Another touching example of loyalty came from a high-profile conservative leader in the Yale Political Union, someone already known in Tennessee politics. His name was Victor H. Ashe. Victor went on to become mayor of Knoxville and later served as U.S. ambassador to Poland, appointed by his friend from Yale who was a year behind him, George W. Bush. Ashe told me that Rothchild had offered him a weekly column in return for his vote. In response Victor told Rothchild that where he came from, a commitment was a commitment. Then he added, "Besides, Lanny already promised me a column, and he is going to win." (It was true. Victor already had proven himself to be a talented columnist with a flair for entertaining writing—albeit he was a strong Republican who had supported Barry Goldwater for president in 1964.)

I cherished such loyalty and character. Above all, I will never forget how hard Boris worked for me, and I never quite understood why. We hadn't spent that much time together. One night, shortly before election night, I mentioned my gratitude to several former roommates.

Robert Kenney, a perceptive judge of human nature, said something interesting. "I'll bet when this is all over, and you've won the chairmanship, you will end up spending more time with John Rothchild than Boris."

"I won't let that happen," I protested to Robert.

Sadly, it turned out to be true. Another lesson learned. The sixty members of the *Yale Daily News* class of 1967 and the senior managers eligible to vote gathered about 7:00 p.m. in the historic boardroom. Rothchild and I were invited to leave while the vote took place.

As I left, I looked at the walls filled with the black-and-white photos of prior board members going back to before Henry Luce's time in 1920. I couldn't help but remember the first time I had seen these pictures—the day I was cut from the Yale frosh basketball team and first met Joe Lieberman. *Just maybe,* I thought. Then we walked into another room where Rothchild and I awkwardly tried to make small talk.

A little while later, we were called in to hear the results. To cheers from most parts of the room, it was announced I had won two-thirds of the vote and was the new chairman of the *Yalie Daily.* Boris was standing in the back of the room with his fists in the air, pumping them. I shook Rothchild's hand, and when the applause died down, on sudden impulse, I held up my hand and asked for unanimous support for John to serve as managing editor, which immediately was ratified.

Then I realized, in the back of the room, Boris was not shouting, "Aye."

I circled the long conference table. He hugged me, and I hugged him. I whispered that I had made the decision on the spur of the moment to ensure unity. Boris nodded and gave me a sad but understanding look. Then he hugged me again.

Later that night I returned to Davenport College and ran into Robert Kenney. He congratulated me, and I told him about my quick decision to support Rothchild for managing editor. He said it was the right decision and reminded me of his prediction: "You are going to end up spending more time and being closer friends with Rothchild than Boris."

Again, I protested. "That won't be true," I said. But it was. Boris did not accept my invitation to become a columnist. I knew his mind was on troubles in his homeland in Ukraine. Of course, I owed him so much and always told him how grateful I was. But after graduation I seldom talked to or saw Boris. I don't think he came to any of the post-1967 five-year class reunions. I learned he went back to Ukraine after the breakup of the Soviet Union. In the early years of the twenty-first century, I heard he had passed away.

Decades later an ache about whether I had done right by Boris remains.

The following January I walked into the chairman's office and sat down at the big desk for the first time. I recalled again the day I first met Joe Lieberman and asked him how to become chairman. My thought at that moment: *I should thank the Yale freshman basketball coach for cutting me.* I saw on my desk a three-by-five-inch file card, with all lowercase words typed à la poet e. e. cummings. I expected it. All the previous chairmen who had called to congratulate me told me to expect it. It was from Francis Donahue. He was the older man I first met on my way up to introduce myself to Lieberman. All the chairmen of the *News* preceding me since the late 1930s, I was told, considered Francis like an uncle, or even a father. They all reminded me to look forward to Francis's hand-typed notes of wisdom and advice on those three-by-five cards.

But we all knew there was one chairman he loved more than any other and by a large margin. A man who loved him back. I read the card he had left on my desk.

> *Tough job never forget [to] be fair i'm your friend pick up the phone for bill*
>
> *(signed) Francis*

As I read these words, the phone rang. I picked it up.

"Hello, Mr. Davis. It's Bill Buckley."

There it was, as all the prior chairmen had predicted: The traditional first call on the first day always came from William F. Buckley Jr. Buckley had led the paper in 1949–50.

"Hello, Mr. Davis," he said again. "This is Bill."

I couldn't resist. "Bill who?"

He ignored my puckish humor. He wished me well, gave me his home and office numbers, and issued two sentences of advice: First, don't forget to take care of Francis—he's the "connecting tissue of us all." Second, "You can argue your convictions while still being civil with others who differ from you."

I learned over time, consistent with Buckley's advice, that the famous Mr. Conservative maintained close friendships with nationally renowned liberals, as I have done with many conservatives.

My first editorial had the traditional headline—counting from the years since the oldest college daily was founded on January 28, 1878. So the headline this time was "Enter the 88th." The editorial began as follows:

> *Every incoming NEWS board for the 87 previous years has probably felt that it would do things in a new and better way than its predecessor. This one is no different.*
>
> *Most NEWS boards have also taken themselves and their opinions far too seriously, believing in their sublimely vain state of mind that their visions and expectations for Yale would in some way be realized. Here too this board is no different.*

> *. . . [W]hat affects all Yale students . . . is the unrealistic, artificial and stifling social environment of all-male Yale.*
>
> *Coeducation at Yale should not be beyond argument . . . The question is no longer whether, but when and how, Yale should become coeducational. And it is about time for all concerned—students, faculty, alumni and administration—to face this question head on.*

A couple of weeks later, Sam Chauncey, the young aide to Kingman Brewster who also lived in Davenport College, mentioned to me that President Brewster wanted to see me in his office. I asked him what about. He said, "Your favorite subject."

I arrived the next morning at Woodbridge Hall, the small square building that had been the location of the Yale president's office since 1901. He didn't waste any time, aside from making a joke that he hoped I would be a less controversial chairman than he had been in 1940, when he editorialized in support of the "America First" movement as a way of trying to keep the United States out of the Second World War raging in Europe.

Brewster knew I had promised to put a coeducated Yale at the top of my agenda. He was familiar with the arguments in favor, which ranged from simple fairness to the basic dangers associated with an all-male campus: Many Yale students had been injured and died in auto accidents caused by sleepy drivers on the way home in the middle of the night from faraway girls' colleges such as Vassar in Poughkeepsie or Wellesley outside of Boston—both more than four hours away by car.

"I intend to begin the process of coeducating Yale," Brewster said bluntly. "And you can help."

We discussed using the editorial page with guest columns from experts and educators about the value of a coeducated environment. I suggested we get the Harvard football coach to write a column admitting to recruiting advantages, as Harvard had a "coordination" relationship with nearby all-women Radcliffe College, allowing women to attend classes at Harvard and get credits.

I asked him whether he was going to go "all the way," which when said aloud had an obvious double entendre. Brewster, Chauncey, and I all laughed.

"We are going to do it step-by-step," he replied. "I can't explain more. But at some point, you will think we have failed, and you will be wrong. Someday women will be Yale students and graduates, I promise you. And you will help us get there."

I was excited. I was a little confused at how he could succeed by failing first, but I didn't argue. I called someone I knew would be perfect to head the coeducation campaign for the newspaper, a classmate who joined the *Yale Daily News* as a freshman with me. His name was Rick Taft, and he was a great-grandson of President William Howard Taft and son of Republican Mayor of Cleveland Seth Taft. Rick said yes immediately. It was Rick who came up with the name "Coeducation Forum," the masthead logo of regular columns on the topic of coeducation in undergraduate education—both its pros and cons. We published two to three columns a week for five months in the winter and spring of 1966.

One source of opposition surprised us. It came from Princeton University's president, Robert F. Goheen, who agreed to write a column.

"There are many young men who at this stage of their lives do not want daily, close association with young women," he wrote.

This struck me as far-fetched, and we had no shortage of voices willing to write rebuttals. We published a counterpoint from famous sociologist and author David Reisman of Harvard.

"Yale will cut itself off from some of the more gifted young men whom it might like to have as students if it remains a non-coeducational place," he wrote.

In April 1966 we polled 100 faculty members and 800 Yale undergraduates. The results were even stronger in favor than Rick and I expected. A total of 80 percent of the 640 undergraduates who responded and 89 percent of the 83 faculty members who responded supported "some form of undergraduate education for women at Yale if adequate financial backing were available."

As Brewster and Chauncey had correctly predicted, we saw significant positive feedback from Old Blue alumni when we published columns by other Ivy League football coaches with "coordinated" coeducation as Harvard and Cambridge had, such as Brown and Pembroke or Columbia and Barnard, boasting the coeducated environment as an advantage in recruiting top players. Perhaps not surprisingly, even the oldest and most conservative of Old Blues preferred to beat Harvard than keep Yale all male the way they remembered it.

On December 16, 1966, with just a month left in our class of 1967's tenure as leaders of the *Yale Daily News*, Yale's and Vassar's boards of trustees announced a plan to "merge"—with Vassar closing down (and presumably selling) its Poughkeepsie campus, and over time Vassar women would attend Yale in New Haven but maintain their identity as Vassar women. Brewster, we learned, had held secret meetings with his friend who was president of Vassar. The coordinated approach seemed to be a politically wise first step toward women at Yale. Brewster and Chauncey tipped off Rick Taft and me a week before the announcement—just before our tenure at the *Yale Daily News* would end in January 1967.

"You and the 1967 *Yale News* board deserve this before you guys leave," Sam told me, reiterating that Brewster had said the same thing.

But the coordination idea did not work, as Vassar was several hours away. It simply wasn't equivalent to the deal Harvard struck with Radcliffe. Those two campuses were so close that women could attend Harvard classes and still live in Radcliffe dorms. Brewster surely realized this: This was what he'd hinted at during our meeting. And so after a year of experimenting with coordination, Brewster announced that Vassar and Yale would merge—meaning Yale students could live on the Vassar campus at Poughkeepsie and Vassar women could live on the Yale campus.

That concept inevitably failed as well: Few Yale men wanted to go to Poughkeepsie, and many more Vassar women and alumni did not want to give up earning a Vassar degree. So less than one year later, on November 27, 1967, the Vassar Board of Trustees announced a reversal of its merger decision and decided instead to take steps to coeducate Vassar on the Vassar campus and not have ties to Yale in that process.

Less than two years later, while I was still in New Haven (at Yale Law School), I got a call from Brewster. He reminded me how he had urged me to be patient, explaining that by failing Yale would ultimately succeed in "going all the way." He remembered that phrase and repeated it with a laugh. In September 1969 the Yale Corporation announced it would take steps to admit women as undergraduates—creating a fully coeducated Yale. Brewster invited me over to Woodbridge Hall to tip a brandy glass with him and Sam Chauncey.

Kingman Brewster died in 1988, at the young age of sixty-nine. I never reminded the many women who went to Yale, or parents with daughters who went to Yale, that Rick Taft and I had collaborated with the great Yale president and his brilliant young aide, Sam Chauncey, to help begin the path to coeducation at Yale. Then a half century passed, and Sam Chauncey decided it was time to tell all. In October 2017, at the fiftieth reunion of the class of 1967, I arrived a day late. Many of my classmates, and many of my fellow *Yale Daily News* alumni, greeted me with unusual enthusiasm and congratulations. As it turned out, Sam had spoken at the class dinner the night before our arrival and told the story for the first time.

It was an early lesson that being patient in politics can have dividends and that following a strategy to success is not always a straight line. It took time to persuade resistant conservative Yale alumni and not clobber them with arguments. Kingman Brewster taught me that.

In the fall of 1966, I was invited by the Yale Political Union to introduce Bill Buckley at a debate scheduled with famous liberal Yale University chaplain William Sloane Coffin Jr. The topic of the debate was "Resolved: That Government Has a Duty to Promote Liberty as Well as to Protect Equality." It was scheduled for November 17 in the Yale Law School auditorium. I gladly agreed.

I had come to know and admire the Reverend Coffin for his national liberal activism on social and civil rights issues and his early opposition to the Vietnam War. My first contact with Coffin was in my freshman year in September 1963. After lunch in an eating hall, I realized I had inadvertently left the only manuscript of my article about the historic March on Washington, which I had attended just a week before, in the hall. I was in a panic. In those days before computers, no electronic backup existed. I had also neglected to make a carbon copy. But someone had found the manuscript and turned it over to Coffin. He sent me a note and asked me to come by to meet him.

By then Coffin had already become a famous civil rights activist. In May 1961 a young interracial group of students and volunteers was viciously beaten up when they exited Freedom Ride buses in Montgomery, Alabama, to support civil rights for Blacks. Weeks later Coffin and other northern faculty members organized their own Freedom Ride in support of the students, and their arrests in Montgomery, Alabama, received national media attention. Coffin was featured in a May 25, 1961, *New York Times* article headlined "Bus Riding Chaplain."

Coffin greeted me warmly and said he loved my firsthand report on the march and my description of being in proximity to Dr. King when he delivered his historic "I Have a Dream" speech. He suggested I submit it for publication in the *Yale Daily News*. I told him I had already done so, but it had been rejected on the grounds that it violated their policy not to publish "guest" news articles (I wasn't on staff yet). Coffin immediately volunteered to help me get it published elsewhere. He did just that, and in the autumn of 1963, it appeared in a new Yale literary magazine called *Criterion*.‡

---

‡ *Criterion* lasted only a few years, and I searched for copies of my article but could never locate that edition of the magazine. And none could be found in the Yale library archives.

That was actually my second interaction with Reverend Coffin. And before the Buckley-Coffin debate, I couldn't resist asking Reverend Coffin about our first meeting, which I remembered but assumed (and hoped) he did not. No such luck.

In the late spring of 1962, a few members of the Newark Academy cum laude society attended a speech in New York City featuring the Reverend Coffin as the speaker. This was after his national media attention for his Freedom Rides arrest and other activities. Unfortunately, two of my cutup friends and I couldn't resist conspicuously flirting with nearby coeds during the speech. As high school boys, we weren't all that smooth, which is another way of saying we were noisy about it—to the point that Coffin had to stop his speech briefly, waiting as we were escorted out of the room by the supervisor of the lunch and our embarrassed faculty adviser.

The next day the Newark Academy assistant headmaster brought us in, scolded us, and required us each to write a letter of apology to Coffin. The administrator said that if Coffin was offended, we were in peril of being expelled. This was the ignominious episode I asked Coffin if he remembered.

"Of course," he said with a laugh.

He added that he had written back to the school headmaster and told him he had not noticed anything, and there was nothing to apologize for. He said he did that to make the point—that he didn't care for "classic BS by pompous prep school headmasters."

"After all, you and your friends were guilty only of being teenagers—a condition," he reminded me with a smile, "I once had." We both laughed.[§]

§ George W. Bush had an initial encounter with Coffin that was much different. Dubya's father had just lost a 1964 congressional race in Texas to Ralph Yarborough, a liberal Democrat. In George's telling he introduced himself to Coffin, who replied, "I know your father . . . He lost to a better man." It was a gratuitous shot at the Bush family, which understandably offended George, and frankly an ugly thing for a faculty member to say to a college underclassman. For his part, Coffin disputed the account. When I heard it myself, I was torn. Not only did I personally like both men, but I also knew that

Coffin also talked to me about a Yale Law School graduate who was involved in a national student recruitment effort to find northern student volunteers to go to Mississippi in the summer of '64 to help register Blacks to vote. He wanted me to meet this young man, whom he called "very charismatic." His name was Al Lowenstein.

On the morning of the Coffin-Buckley debate, November 17, 1966, I wrote a *Yale Daily News* editorial reflecting my personal and ideological conflict, which I would feel even as I introduced my famous predecessor as *Yale Daily News* chairman, Mr. Buckley. I ended the short editorial as follows:

> *As for us [the editorial board of the Yale Daily News], we are quite sure that our heads, at least, will be for Mr. Coffin. But our hearts, we are hesitant to admit, will be with Mr. Buckley. After all, once a News chairman, always a News chairman.*

That night, after I introduced Mr. Buckley, he couldn't resist an affectionate jab at my ambiguous editorial. "Regarding Mr. Davis's acknowledging a conflict between my having Mr. Davis's heart and Mr. Coffin having his head, having read Mr. Davis's editorial since his election, I must say I am happy to have his heart and for Mr. Coffin to have his head."

The audience rewarded this gentle zinger with a roar of laughter and applause. The Political Union members' vote on the resolution after the debate reflected the same conflict that I had confessed myself. The final vote on the resolution was slightly in favor of Coffin's "liberal" yes position: 143 in support of the resolution and 131 against.

---

each of them was sincere when recounting their divergent recollections of the exchange. This long-ago incident was reprised when George ran for president in 1999. That year Bush revealed that Coffin had written him a letter, saying, "If I did this, I apologize." Bush showed grace too. Regarding Coffin's letter, he told *The Washington Post*, "I was most grateful."

During the debate, Buckley himself showed some ambiguity, surprising all (but me) by praising Reverend Coffin's "intelligence" and "mental gifts" and calling him a friend, which, he hastened to add, was "remarkable," as Coffin was "almost entirely wrong." This gentle remonstrance by Buckley reminded me of his last advice to me during our brief conversation on the first morning of my chairmanship of the *News*, reminding me of the importance of being able to "disagree agreeably." They are words to live by.

Buckley and Coffin maintained their friendship through the years. Both Lowenstein and Coffin were frequent guests on Buckley's popular nationally televised debate show *Firing Line*. In 1974 Buckley scheduled me for an appearance on *Firing Line* to discuss my first book, *The Emerging Democratic Majority: Lessons and Legacies from the New Politics*. The theme of the book and of my interview with Buckley was about the need for the Democratic Party to build coalitions and to seek common ground with people from differing political outlooks. The evidence for my pragmatism was pretty stark: The year before my book came out, "purists" of the left insisted on backing George McGovern over Ed Muskie in 1972. In the ensuing election, the Democratic ticket lost forty-nine states to Richard Nixon, with the result being an escalation of the Vietnam War.

Our term as leaders of the *Yale Daily News* was due to end in mid-January 1967, but I always remember the fitting conclusion of that experience, thanks to Kingman Brewster deciding to attend my wedding to Elaine on December 18, 1966. I know that sounds strange to generations in the 2000s—married while still in college and in our early twenties? Looking back, we *were* young. And today's younger generation probably has it right: Wait a while to mature and be ready to find professional achievement for both parties before making final marriage commitments.

Our wedding that night was held at the historic Essex House hotel on Central Park South. Word spread that Yale's president would be attending. Brewster had become famous even this early in his tenure, so there was excitement among the guests about his being there. Altogether, more than two dozen Yale friends were in attendance.

At the end of the wedding, the master of ceremonies asked all the Yale students to come to the center of the ballroom and asked Brewster and Sam Chauncey to lead us in singing Yale's classic alma mater, "Bright College Years," based on a nineteenth-century German anthem.

So there he was, the president of Yale, with a few glasses of champagne under his belt, leading us in the middle of the ballroom in the alma mater, with the famous last line:

*Bright college years, with pleasure rife,*
*The shortest, gladdest years of life.*
*The shortest, gladdest years of life.*
*Where'er upon life's sea we sail.*

And out of our pockets came the white napkins, with President Brewster holding his high as we waved them back and forth in rhythm with the words.

*For God, for Country, and for Yale!*

## CHAPTER 9

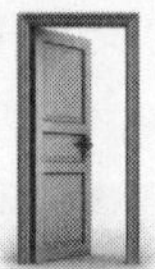

# DUBYA: FROM FRAT BROTHER TO POTUS

I looked down at a white-hot iron brand with three letters—"DKE"—standing for "Delta Kappa Epsilon." I was in the final stages of the initiation ritual to be invited to join my preferred fraternity.

I felt the heat on my stomach through the pillowcase over my head. I had the pillowcase on, with smothering hot air within, for about five hours while I sat on the floor in the DKE party room with my legs straight. I had been doing nothing but listening to a very loud vinyl record (the only kind that existed in those days) playing two notes back and forth due to a crack in the record. After the first hour, I had decided I couldn't take it anymore. Four hours later I was mentally unraveled.

But that was easy compared to the large, white-hot DKE brand I was looking at. I was now disoriented enough to actually believe they were going through with it and stick that brand on my back, leaving me in pain and with a scar for life.

Someone whispered loudly in my ear. I immediately recognized his voice.

"Get ready, you butthole! This scar is going onto your back forever!"

Then I felt the intense heat waves move from my stomach to my side to my back. My shirt was then pulled out and up, baring my back, and I felt my skin getting hotter and hotter as the brand approached it. Trying to keep calm, I thought that these intelligent Yale students from fine families would never ever actually brand me. But then, as my back burned with the heat waves, and the brand seemed about to touch my skin, I thought, *Holy shit! These assholes are actually going to do it!*

"Ahhhhhhhg!" I screamed. "Don't you dare!"

And then . . . a shock.

A burn.

The skin on my back sizzled, but it seemed to be something hot with a point, not the whole red-hot DKE brand I had just looked at. They pulled the pillowcase off my head. There was applause and cheering as I reached to rub the burn on my back. It turned out to be from just a cigarette burn, thank goodness.

I looked into the face of the young man whose whisper I had initially recognized.

"Congratulations," George W. Bush said. "You are now my brother."

Later I would vote for this man for president—of my fraternity.

■ ■ ■

In 1967, my senior year at Yale, one year after my initiation into DKE, I found myself in the position of the anointed "big brother" to a sophomore "pledge" enduring the preliminary period of initiation into the fraternity. George Bush had asked me to take on the assignment, even though this "little" brother would actually be much bigger than his "big" brother. The pledge's name was Calvin Hill, the famous All-American football star.

During the final ritual ceremony, I monitored the hours Calvin was sitting on the floor with the pillowcase over his head, as I painfully remembered what I had experienced the year before. Then came the final horrific moment—the fake branding. But what I most remember with Calvin, which I also went through, was known as the "fake pool ball humiliation." The shtick was that as Calvin was led toward the backyard with the branding iron awaiting him, he, like everyone else, was led past a pool table, and I held the white cue ball in my hand below the pillowcase so he could see it.

"Now, Calvin," I whispered to him, still with the pillowcase over his head, "I am here to protect you. I will ask you to give me back this white cue ball. The fraternity's president, George Bush, will order you not to give it to me. You must ignore Bush and give the cue ball to me, and you will be fine. If you listen to Bush and don't give it to me, you will be skunked out" (meaning rejected from admission to DKE).

"Do you understand?" I asked Calvin.

He nodded under the pillowcase.

"Promise me you will give me the ball and ignore Bush's instructions not to."

"I promise," he whispered.

And so the time came. I took the white cue ball and said to Cal, "Here, Cal, take this ball from me."

Bush was standing next to me. He screamed at Calvin.

"Don't you dare take that ball from Davis, you asshole, or you will be skunked out immediately!"

I said quietly, "Cal, I am your big brother. Don't listen to Bush, trust me—give me the pool ball."

Bush screamed even louder.

"Don't you dare, Hill! I don't care how great a football star you are! If you give Davis that ball, you are skunked out of DKE!"

Hill hesitated.

"Calvin," I said quietly. "Listen to me and do as I told you to do—give me the ball, and you will be fine."

And so after some hesitation, Hill gave me the ball.

I screamed, "You butthole!" as Bush and virtually the entire room of DKE men joined him, shouting along with me. "Didn't you hear our DKE president tell you not to give it to me? Now you are skunked out!"

I won't describe in detail Calvin's reaction to this moment. I don't wish to embarrass him any more than telling this story already will. All I can tell you is when this same stunt was done to me the previous year, I started to cry. (And I am told, so did many other Yale students under the same battered-human-being mentality we were all in at that point in the initiation.)

I felt guilty, sure. But I also felt pleasure. It was done to me—so now the great and famous Calvin Hill had to suffer the same! This rationalization is not original to me, nor to those who participate in college campus Greek life. (Although the first known complaint about hazing in the academy came from Plato in 387 BC, so maybe Greeks are to blame.) At their most benign, fraternity rituals are a form of bonding. At their worst, especially when they involve the forced consumption of alcohol, such practices can be deadly. So what's the appeal? To answer that question, let's fast-forward twenty-four years to Durham, North Carolina.

It was February 1990. I was in Cameron Indoor Stadium, the famous Duke University basketball arena, where Coach Mike Krzyzewski and his superb basketball team were about to play a game in front of the packed "Cameron Crazies," as Duke's fans are called. My son Seth was then a senior at Duke and a sports columnist for the *Chronicle*, the student newspaper.

Seth had gotten me a coveted ticket to go to a Duke home game. I walked into the arena early so I could watch the team warm-ups before the sellout crowd arrived. About an hour before tip-off, with the arena still almost empty, I looked across the floor to the Duke bench. And there was Seth sitting with Duke's freshman superstar, Grant Hill. Yes, Grant Hill—Calvin's son. The son of my "little" fraternity brother who pledged twenty years ago. If you're not a sports fan, allow me a brief digression into what Calvin had accomplished in his athletic career.

A star quarterback in high school, he was a halfback on some of the best Yale teams in modern times. They were the best because of Calvin and our quarterback, Brian Dowling. Brian, also a DKE, was an all-around athlete who dabbled on the margins of professional football but was a superb college quarterback. Brian Dowling inspired us all, but none more than Garry Trudeau (class of 1970), a cartoonist with the *Yale Daily News* who went on to international fame as the creator of *Doonesbury*. Brian is the inspiration for the "B. D." character in that strip. With Brian and Calvin in the backfield, Yale went 16–1–1, winning two Ivy League championships. A first-round draft pick of the Dallas Cowboys, Calvin Hill played in the NFL for twelve seasons, rushing for more than six thousand yards and forty-two touchdowns while playing in four Pro Bowls and winning a Super Bowl ring. This was the man whom, years before, I had urged to give up the pool ball during the final pledge ritual and then screamed at him for doing so. His son Grant (whose mother attended Wellesley College, where she was friends with Hillary Rodham) was too slight for football. But he was one of the most sought-after high school basketball players in the country and ended up, as his father had, at a top-notch academic school.

I felt momentarily stuck in a time warp. The years had flown by, and so much had changed. Yet there were Calvin's son and my son with their arms around each other. I looked for a telephone booth nearby, as in those days, there were no cell phones. I pushed in multiple quarters to get through to Calvin in Reston, Virginia.

I told him where I was and whom I was watching.

"Calvin, if I had told you in college that twenty-four years later, I'd be looking at your son and my son with their arms around each other at Cameron Indoor Stadium, sitting on the Duke bench, what would you have said?"

Calvin's response was a laugh.

"I'm still pissed at you for convincing me to give up that pool ball and then screaming at me," he replied, remarkably still remembering the moment.

We then reminisced about how amazing life is, that one generation later, our sons were together on a national stage—one a basketball All-American, the other a college journalist (like his old man), writing a story about him. To this day they remain friends. Seth became a star CBS broadcaster and analyst for CBS's TV coverage of the NCAA college basketball tournament. Grant, after finishing his own career as an NBA superstar, joined him in the CBS TV sports booth. At one Final Four, it was just the two of them sitting on chairs at halftime between the games, doing analysis on what to expect in the second half. Is all of that because of our long-ago shenanigans at the DKE house? Obviously not, but our fraternity years are why Calvin and I take the time to savor it together.

So much had changed over more than two decades. Yet the new generations continue to connect us with the past.

■ ■ ■

Three decades after leaving New Haven, a moment occurred when I forgot myself and got carried away and said something personal in anger about my old friend and fraternity brother George. And I did so on national and international live television. It was August 17, 1998. President Clinton had agreed to testify before a federal grand jury investigating the Monica Lewinsky matter.

Earlier in the day, I heard a news report that George, serving his second term as Texas governor and everyone's most likely front-runner for the 2000 Republican presidential nomination, had called the scandal a "national embarrassment." I was in the MSNBC cable TV studio on Nebraska Avenue in D.C., doing analysis, when I heard about the criticism. It upset me.

Just after President Clinton finished his testimony, I heard a familiar voice in my earpiece. It was Tom Brokaw, the famous NBC news anchor, speaking from network headquarters in New York.

"Lanny, we are coming to you in seconds for first reactions to President Clinton's testimony."

My heart skipped a beat, and I felt as if I could barely breathe. I had no time to think or prepare.

I will delve into this period and these interviews more in a later chapter, but when Brokaw cued to me, I found myself thinking of all those DKE fraternity parties and college-age hijinks.

"I was in college with George Bush Jr.," I said. "And if we start seeing smug, sanctimonious comments from political officials, especially Governor Bush, throwing stones in glass houses . . ."

My voice trailed off. After I made a few more comments about Clinton holding up under the questioning and taking responsibility, there was a brief break. I heard a voice in my ear again. It was Brokaw.

"Lanny, you're going to have to explain your 'people in glass houses' comment," he said. "You must have more to tell about George Bush."

I was stunned and nearly panicked. What the hell had I just said? I hadn't intended to harm George Bush—and certainly not over our time at Yale. Not when I had participated in similar conduct as my old friend in those years (and later). And I certainly hadn't meant to imply that George had compromised himself during his marriage to Laura.

I made a quick decision to backpedal. Without any delay. Thank goodness, as I look back.

When Brokaw came back live, he asked me to explain my last comment.

I answered something like, "Governor Bush and I were friends in college. That comment was a mistake. I regret I said that. I have nothing to say on that."

Later—I forget exactly when—I apologized to Governor Bush during a phone call when I was at the White House as President Clinton's special counsel. Not surprisingly, he was gracious about it.

"Not to worry," Bush said. "I understood."

After the Supreme Court's 5–4 decision in *Bush v. Gore*, ruling that the Florida recount could not legally continue and making George W. Bush the president-elect, I heard from many Democratic friends who told me how much they "hated" Bush and disrespected him.

I decided to speak up to describe the man I knew—to try to set the record straight from my personal experience with him as friends at Davenport College and fraternity brothers at DKE. I wanted to remind everyone that, irrespective of our political differences, I knew George W. Bush to be a good man with a good heart.

I wrote an op-ed published in *The New York Times* on December 16, 2000.* I began by describing a time—I thought it was 1967 (when I was a senior and George was a junior), and it was after dinner, and a bunch of us were sitting in Yale's Davenport College common room.

A student from my graduating class walked by our group—a student believed to be gay (although that word wasn't yet in vogue). Someone in the group called him a "faggot." (In the actual op-ed the *Times* editor thought it best not to use that word, changing it to "nerd.")

When I heard the word, instead of speaking up and objecting, I remained silent. I was ashamed of my cowardice. I am still. Then someone broke the silence.

"Hey, it's not so easy for him. He's a good guy. Leave him alone."

It was George W. Bush.

My reaction seemed similar to others: We were stunned. I remember looking at George as if seeing him for the first time. *Whoa,* I thought.

---

* Lanny J. Davis, "The George Bush I Knew," *The New York Times*, December 16, 2000.

*This guy is deeper than I had perceived him to be. I want to get to know him better.*

I also wrote in the *Times* column that George was smart—maybe a "coaster" academically but "street smart, quick-witted, savvy, common sense smart, and, especially, smart about judging and understanding people."

Would I have known in college that these same qualities would at least contribute to his being elected and reelected governor of Texas and elected and reelected president of the United States? In a word, no.

Certainly, none of us back then at Yale or in DKE, including, I am pretty sure, George W. Bush himself. But maybe I'm still selling him short. George was always the master of reducing people's expectations of him. Some misjudged him for lacking intelligence. They were wrong. From personal experience I knew that he was not only smart—he was also brilliant at convincing others that he wasn't. The master of setting low expectations, I thought in later years.

Fast-forward about thirty-four years. It was May 2001, four months after Bush took the oath of office as the forty-third U.S. president, and the spring of our pre-9/11 innocence. I heard that he was giving the commencement speech at Yale to the class of 2001. I called his top political adviser, Karl Rove, to ask if my wife, Carolyn, and I and our young son Josh, then three years old, could hitch a ride home on Air Force One if we rode up to Yale by train to hear Bush's commencement speech.

Rove talked to the "boss" and called me back and said that President Bush wanted me to hear his speech and that, yes, we could ride back from Yale on Air Force One with him afterward. (As it turned out, my logistics were faulty. In order to make it to Hartford's Air National Guard base, where Air Force One was parked for the flight back to Washington, we had to leave New Haven before the commencement address. So we missed the speech.)

We made the flight, however, and shortly after taking off, President Bush came down the aisle to greet us in the back of the plane. Carolyn and I were still feeling starstruck being on Air Force One. Despite working in the Clinton White House, I had never been aboard the presidential jet. Bush greeted us in his shirtsleeves. He smiled, and we hugged. The traveling White House press corps, sitting in the back section of the plane, stared, I imagined, in shock. What's Lanny Davis, a liberal Democrat—and Clinton lawyer, no less—doing on Air Force One hugging it out with George W. Bush? Neither of us felt obliged to explain it.

Bush first asked me about Robert Kenney. The two of them had briefly played on the Yale baseball team together. I knew that Bush greatly admired Bob.

"How's Kenney doing? Is he still with Lynne?"

I was impressed that he not only thought of Robert as his first question to me but that he also remembered his girlfriend's name. This reminded me of yet another reason why he was president and not I. (It also reminded me that almost every male who saw and met the brilliant and gorgeous Lynne Friedman immediately had a crush on her, including possibly the future president of the United States.)

Bush asked me if I liked his commencement speech. It was an awkward moment. I admitted, with some embarrassment, that I hadn't heard him deliver it. I explained that the Secret Service had approached us just before the speech and told us we had to get to Hartford ahead of time by car if we wanted to be there in time for Bush's arrival on the presidential helicopter, Marine One.

So Bush leaned over to Karen Hughes, his senior adviser and communications director, and asked her, "Do you have a copy of my speech to give to Lanny?" She handed him the copy. He took it, opened it up, and handed it to me with a clearly underlined section that he wanted me to read.

"Just read it—because I had you in mind when we wrote it," he said. "Remember the History 35 exam?"

I couldn't believe he still remembered that moment and that exam.

I flashed back to that moment thirty-four years before.

It was the spring of 1967, my senior year and George's junior year. The course, History 35, was a review of the Populist, Progressive, and New Deal eras. One of the most popular classes at Yale, it was taught by one of the school's best-liked and most charismatic professors, John Morton Blum.

The final exam was open-book, so you had to read the huge U.S. history textbook's relevant sections on these three eras and use them to answer the questions in essay form. That meant reading, underlining, and—for me—outlining in the margins of the text to be ready to quickly locate the section where the answer(s) could be found.

I was studying in the Davenport library on the second floor, where the large dining room was situated, when Bush sauntered in about midnight and asked me if he could borrow my notes.

"My notes are virtually worthless," I explained. "This is an open-book exam!"

"Don't worry, Lanny," he said. "Your notes are great, and that's all I need."

"No, George. You have to focus on the textbook and bring it to the exam with you."

He shrugged and seemed to wave me off.

I handed him my notes.

The next morning I was rushing to get to the exam on time, and I heard Bush's voice behind me.

"Hold up, Lanny. I'll walk over to the exam with you."

So he caught up with me, and I saw he had the textbook under his arm. I eyed it suspiciously.

"George, did you read and underline and outline the text?" I asked him.

He shrugged and didn't really answer. He hugged the text under his arm even more tightly.

"George, give me that textbook. I want to see it."

He kept walking while making no movement to let me take the book from him. I reached over and grabbed it from him, overcoming his resistance.

Then I opened it to see if he had at least underlined the important sections that would likely be covered on the exam.

As soon as I opened the book, I heard a loud sound: *crack!*

That book had *never* been opened.

"George!" I exclaimed, a mixture of delight at my suspicions being proven and chagrin about his poor prospects of passing the test. "You haven't even opened the damn book for the whole semester, much less last night to study for the exam!"

Bush gave his usual disarming smile and relaxed shrug.

"Not to worry, Lanny," he said. "It'll be fine."

Later I learned, to my consternation, that Bush had gotten a C+ on the exam. And me, with all my diligent studying and outlining, had gotten a B+. It pissed me off. It also reminded me how truly smart Bush was—he just loved to hide it from everyone else.

So with that memory flooding back to me, I sat next to the president of the United States, who was smiling smugly, waiting for me to read his commencement speech, which was—he said—written with me in mind. It began, after the normal salutations, with a typically irreverent Bush quip.

"I congratulate all the parents who are here," he said. "It's a glorious day when your child graduates from college. It's a great day for you; it's a great day for your wallet."

The speech continued, this time with Bush's signature self-deprecating wit. "Congratulations to the class of 2001," Bush said. "To those of you who received honors, awards, and distinctions, I say, 'Well done.' And to the C students, I say: *You, too, can be president of the United States.*"

This was vintage George Bush. I laughed aloud, with delight. My wife and Karen Hughes asked me to read it aloud. After doing so, I told them a brief version of the story of the History 35 exam, the sound of the "crack" of the book, and my consternation at his C+ grade.

Now it was Bush's turn to laugh, joined by Carolyn and Karen. Bush clapped with delight as we hugged again.

*Yup,* I thought, *George Bush got the last laugh.* And he deserved it.

■ ■ ■

President George W. Bush's father, President George H. W. Bush, also had a great sense of humor about his "number one" son (called by the media "Bush 43" to distinguish him from his dad, "Bush 41").

I wrote a White House memoir in 1999 about my fourteen months as President Clinton's special counsel, defending him to the press corps on the various "scandals" regarding alleged 1996 campaign finance violations.† My book concluded that not one of these scandals involved illegal activity, and all of them were driven by partisan opponents who tried to claim, without much credibility, that Republicans were pure when it came to political fundraising, while the Clinton campaign was not.

In the book, I had written some sympathetic words about unfair media treatment on various occasions of Clinton's predecessor, Bush 41. Ron Kaufman, a friend of mine who had served as the elder Bush's White House political director, sent him a copy of my book, pointing out the pages where I had mentioned him favorably and sympathetically.

Although Bush knew about my friendship with his son at Yale and specifically at DKE, I was surprised (and delighted) to receive a personal letter from him, dated July 17, 1999, with the top-quality stationery imprinted simply with "GEORGE BUSH." Here is how he began the letter:

> *Dear Lanny,*
>
> *Your new book having been handed to me by your friend and mine Ron Kaufman yesterday, I immediately read pages*

† Lanny Davis, *Truth to Tell: Tell It Early, Tell It All, Tell It Yourself: Notes from My White House Education* (New York: Free Press, 1999).

*250–56. All of us in public life should (should have) come as clean with some chapters in our own lives as you did on those seven very readable pages . . .*

(This was a reference to my ending my book by owning up, at times, to having not-so-clean hands in being overly partisan in my role during and after my White House special counsel's position as one of President Clinton's chief media defenders.)

Then I got to his last paragraph, which referred to the alleged existence of an embarrassing photograph of his "number-one son" toasting his fraternity brothers, who were partying that Saturday night with girlfriends and various women who had come in on buses from Vassar or one of the other Seven Sisters schools.

I was sometimes asked about this photo by the media. I had no knowledge of it and believed it to be apocryphal. But the rumor persisted, so much so that it reached the ears of Bush 41.

I wrote another book[‡] in 2006 expressing sympathy for Bush 43 about what I thought was unfair treatment of him by the White House press corps and sent a copy to a friend of mine who worked in the White House. I was delighted to receive a personal note from Bush 41 thanking me for the sympathetic reference to him.

I framed the letter, and it remains on my wall at home.

*[T]hanks for not producing that infamous picture of your classmate dancing nude on the DKE bar. Actually I don't see how there can be such a picture because I know that our number one son had no time to dance on the bar, for he was usually in the Yale Library at his special quiet place in the*

‡ Lanny Davis, *Scandal: How "Gotcha" Politics Is Destroying America* (New York: Palgrave, 2006).

*reference stacks doing his basic scholarly research on Homer, or was it Larry Flynt.*[§]

Years later, I gave him a copy of the letter. He read it, laughed, and said affectionately, "My dad—he's something else!"

■ ■ ■

One day in early spring of 2006, I received a phone call from Karl Rove, Bush's top White House political operative, with an opening statement that surprised me.

"You're not going to believe this," Rove said. "President Bush just suggested we appoint you as a member of the Privacy and Civil Liberties Oversight Board. When your name came up, we all just about fell off our chairs."

I had to look up that agency to figure out what it did, as I had never heard of it. The Privacy and Civil Liberties Oversight Board was established by Congress in 2004 on the recommendation of the 9/11 Commission and as part of the Intelligence Reform Act. Members of the board were appointed by and reported to the president and the Executive Office of the President. It comprised five members, and at least one had to be a member of the opposition party.

Its mandate was to attempt independent "citizen" oversight of the intelligence community, which was mandated by Congress and the American people to get to the bottom of the global terrorism movement and specifically groups such as al-Qaeda, which carried out the 9/11 attacks.

In December 2005, *The New York Times* and other news organizations broke the story that the National Security Agency (NSA), the government's primary surveillance intelligence agency, was engaging in

§ Flynt was the flamboyant publisher of *Hustler*, an extremely graphic pornographic magazine.

telephone intercepts in search of terrorists planning attacks on the United States and, in doing so, sometimes listened in on conversations with American citizens. Such telephone surveillance was illegal without a specific warrant obtained from a special court established in 1978 called the Foreign Intelligence Surveillance Act (FISA) Court. Surveillance of foreign citizens alone did not require such a warrant, but a warrant was required if a U.S. citizen was involved, and it was for potential terrorist threats without probable cause of a crime.

As the *Times* and other papers reported, the NSA had allowed such intercepts without always going through the cumbersome and often time-consuming process of obtaining a warrant. The NSA's reasoning was that after 9/11, intercepting and anticipating another 9/11-type attack was too time-sensitive to go through the FISA court process. NSA personnel believed that so long as the U.S. citizen side of the conversation was only "incidental" to the purpose of listening in on a known or likely foreign terrorist, the surveillance was legal.

They were wrong. Ultimately, Congress intervened to allow such surveillance, and necessary changes in the law were required to catch up with technology and vocabulary changes since the 1978 pre-internet era. New authority was granted by Congress but not until 2015, nearly ten years later.

Meanwhile, I found myself on the frontlines of the issue when I accepted the appointment. I was the only Democrat out of the five members, but it didn't matter. One of the appointments was Theodore "Ted" Olson, an accomplished Republican lawyer who had participated in the effort to impeach President Clinton.[¶] Nonetheless, we found we had a lot in common and became friends, as I did with the other members of the board.

---

¶ Clinton was ultimately acquitted by the Senate in a bipartisan vote. More on this in a later chapter.

I found myself enjoying visits to the Bush White House and having access to, as well as interviews with, the leaders of the U.S. intelligence community, including the CIA, NSA, and FBI. After visiting the NSA and seeing the surveillance program in real time, I came to appreciate the care NSA senior agents took in avoiding any civil liberties violations of American citizens. I was even a bit concerned at the extra layers of checkpoints that NSA lawyers, led by the agency's inspector general, Joel Brenner, and the NSA director, General Michael Hayden, imposed on those performing the intercepts. The extra layers were intended to minimize intrusion on the privacy rights of U.S. citizens who happened to be on the telephone with a suspected terrorist. I became concerned that these young NSA specialists were being so careful to stop and get further clearances that we might miss interrupting a 9/11-type terrorist mission. I mentioned these concerns in a private conversation I had with IG Brenner and General Hayden as I was leaving.

I was surprised when both men reminded me that no matter how urgent the antiterrorist goals, the Constitution and the rule of law had to be respected. My impression was that both and others in the intelligence community were uncomfortable with the pressure from the White House (primarily from Vice President Dick Cheney's office) to ignore the law and the hard work of making a legislative fix. I was delighted that Olson and Hayden agreed that the program was close to the line between legal and illegal, and there needed to be a congressional fix for it to continue. And I came to respect Olson's willingness to say so, even in the face of friends he knew well and who worked in Cheney's office.

That was the beginning of a long friendship with Olson, which blossomed into even greater admiration after his victory on June 26, 2013, in the landmark Supreme Court case ruling any state law discriminating against gay marriage to be unconstitutional.

In the spring of 2007, I made the agonizing decision to resign from the oversight board because the vice president's office had attempted to edit and censor part of our annual report. I had drafted a small section calling on further oversight of antiterrorism programs to be sure federal laws were updated and the FISA court given greater scrutiny for allowing intrusions on privacy and telephone intercepts involving U.S. citizens. The language I used was moderate and prudent, and other members of the board, including Olson, agreed. But then we received back a redline-edited version of our report, with the entire section I helped draft on greater oversight deleted.

I objected, taking my concerns to the Office of the President, the White House counsel, the chief of staff, and ultimately—I believed but was never certain—to President Bush himself. In my view the vice president's legal staff had no business interfering with the independence and oversight responsibilities of the board. Yet I also recognized that the board was not a quasi-independent agency in the executive branch, comparable to the Federal Trade Commission or the Federal Communications Commission.

So while most of the board members objected, as I did, to the vice president's office redlining of our annual report, which Congress required us to write, this was in fact the way Congress enacted the legislation. The executive branch had the legal right to edit our report, and Cheney's office had apparently been given that portfolio by the West Wing.

So I called Karl Rove and told him I was going to resign. I told him I did not want to do so as part of an attack on President Bush or in any way make the president look bad. Rove understood exactly why I was resigning, and he promised me, "We will have your back on this."

And they did. My resignation was not criticized by the White House press secretary, and indeed a White House spokesman thanked me for my service, and that was that.

Somewhere I had the feeling that my old friend George Bush, whom I knew had stuck his neck out to appoint me in the face of what I imagined was a lot of grief from White House conservatives and partisans, understood what I had done and didn't hold it against me. I sent him a note, thanking him for the appointment.

■ ■ ■

Then it was 2008, President Bush's last year in office. In the spring of that year, my then ten-year-old son Josh asked me if it was true that I knew President Bush and President Clinton and liked them both. I said yes. He seemed surprised. He said something like, "But one is a Republican, and the other is a Democrat. Isn't that right, Dad?" as if that was a reason not to be friends with both.

The next day I called the White House and finally got through to President Bush's personal secretary. I asked her to give the president a message. I asked her to tell him about my exchange with Josh and ask him if it would be possible, perhaps in the last weeks of his presidency, when there wasn't much to do and the boxes were all packed up, if I could bring Josh by to visit the Oval Office. I wanted to let Bush explain why it is possible to be friends while still having serious political differences.

It was a lesson I had learned over the years, and the fact that my own son questioned it was a reminder of how ubiquitous the prevailing pressure is on the other side and how important it is to constantly harp on the need for civility in politics and mutual respect. I wanted my son to learn this as well—in person. And also to meet a real president of the United States and see the Oval Office.

Carolyn and I came in the very next day. That was how quickly President Bush responded. We sat in the lobby of the West Wing when a Secret Service agent came out, pointed to Josh, and asked, "Are you Josh Davis?"

Josh nodded yes, a little nervously.

"Come with me," the agent said, and Josh followed him down the hall.

I saw President Bush with his head out of the Oval Office, waving to me and holding the door open for Josh to enter.

Fifteen or twenty minutes later, the agent came out and motioned for me and Carolyn to follow him down the hall. As we walked into the Oval Office, there was our son with President Bush's arm around him.

"So what question did you ask me, Josh?" Bush said. "Tell your mom and dad."

Josh said, "What was your scariest moment as president?"

President Bush said, "First I told him right after 9/11. Then I told him about when I was asked to throw the first pitch out at Yankee Stadium and was waiting in the passageway under the stands leading to the field. I told Josh I was worried about embarrassing myself if I spiked the ball in the dirt or threw it way over the catcher's head."

Then Bush said, "I told Josh I noticed someone walking toward me in the underground tunnel heading toward the field, and it was none other than Derek Jeter! Who wished me good luck."

Bush said that Josh said, with great excitement, "You mean you met Derek Jeter?"

We all laughed. Josh seemed more excited about the president meeting Derek Jeter than his own meeting with the president.

But then Bush told us that Jeter stopped and asked him if he wanted to throw a few pitches to him to warm up. After they threw a few back and forth, Bush said Jeter commented that he had thrown fine and turned to head onto the field.

As we left the Oval Office and Josh and Carolyn were walking down the hall, the president pulled me aside and whispered in my ear, "I didn't tell this to Josh, but what Jeter actually said to me was, 'Mr. President, you'll be fine. But don't fuck up.'"

Although Jeter was kidding around, Bush said it made him even more nervous.

But as most people watching remember clearly, Bush took the mound and in front of an overflow stadium threw a good fastball strike. The crowd, and the country, cheered. It was symbolic at a time when America needed good omens. The commander in chief had stood up and thrown that strike. He was ready to lead the country against terrorism and the murderers responsible for 9/11.

As we left, Josh watched as President Bush and I hugged. I told my son as we left the White House complex what I wanted him to remember most about that experience with President Bush: "You can strongly disagree in politics, but that doesn't mean you can't respect the other person and still be friends."

I recalled then a moment some seven years before, which I wrote about it in a book published in 2006 called *Scandal: How "Gotcha" Politics Is Destroying America.*

I wrote in the book's prologue about the occasion on June 14, 2004, when President Bush invited former President Clinton and former First Lady (and at the time a U.S. senator from New York) Hillary Clinton back to the White House for the presentation of their official White House portraits.

The room was filled with former Clinton White House aides, and I remembered the hateful words from so many of my friends who strongly opposed Bush's military intervention in Iraq and much more about his persona and policies. There was an atmosphere of tension, and some whispered about booing Bush when he entered the room.

When George and his wife, Laura, took the podium in a sun-filled and audience-packed East Room, the tension was still palpable. But Bush made it all evaporate in seconds. He looked down at the Clintons and their daughter, Chelsea, sitting in the first row, and said, "President Clinton and Senator Clinton, welcome home . . . Over eight years, [you] filled this house with energy and joy . . . My congratulations to you both."

The reaction was instantaneous. An immediate standing ovation, to my great relief. In the remarks that followed his welcoming opening salvo, Bush praised the Clintons with his patented irreverent style.

"You've got to be optimistic to give six months of your life to running the McGovern campaign in Texas," he said, referring to George McGovern's lopsided loss in the 1972 campaign. The entire room erupted in laughter.

Then it was President Clinton's turn. I will never forget his words:

> *The president, by his generous words to Hillary and me today, has proved once again that, in the end, we are held together by the grand system of ours that permits us to debate and struggle and fight for what we believe is right . . . You know, most of the people I've known in this business, Republicans and Democrats, conservatives and liberals, were good people, honest people, and they did what they thought was right. And I hope I'll live long enough to see American politics return to the vigorous debates where we argue who's right and wrong, not who's good and bad.*

As I wrote in *Scandal*, "There was a thunderous standing ovation. It grew even louder as President Bush nodded and pointed toward President Clinton with a gesture of affirmation and Clinton pointed back at him."

This would later be called a virtual friendship fist bump.

I thought of Al Lowenstein at that moment—and the lessons he had taught me in the trenches of the civil rights and anti–Vietnam War movements, as described in the next two chapters.

I remembered Lowenstein's funeral, when the ultimate conservative, William F. Buckley Jr., and the ultimate liberal, Massachusetts Senator Edward Kennedy, spoke of their mutual love and friendship for Lowenstein. This was the same spirit and understanding about the larger public purpose of politics as Clinton and Bush embraced when they uttered their mutual words of affection a quarter-century later.

I write these words as the 2024 presidential campaign season gets underway—and as American politics has devolved into a spectacle that is very nearly the opposite of the graciousness and mutual respect displayed in the East Room that day in 2004.

Can anyone say with a straight face that things are better today?

## CHAPTER 10

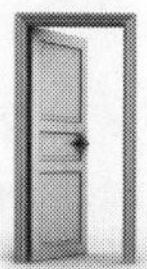

# AL LOWENSTEIN AND THE POLITICS OF PERSUASION

*It is beyond dispute that [Al Lowenstein] brought more young people into American politics than any individual of our time.*

**DAVID BRODER,** Pulitzer Prize–winning *Washington Post* reporter and columnist

"You have to reject the voices of bullshit violence and radical confrontations that just frighten the very people we need to persuade," the intense young man said passionately. He was pointing his finger at a group of people in the corner of the room who had interrupted him with taunts and sarcastic comments, such as "Sellout!"

"Get over your own anger and ask yourself: What is the best way to persuade people who disagree with you to agree with you and get what we want?" he said. "It's not to bully people with your righteousness."

That was my first personal exposure to Allard K. Lowenstein. He came across as idealistic but frustrated: a teacher trying to educate students who just didn't get it. We were in a stuffy classroom building of Yale's Old Campus, about fifty of us crammed into a small, seminarlike room.

Lowenstein was recruiting students for the Mississippi Summer Project. This was one of hundreds of meetings he and others had organized on campuses across the nation to recruit college students to go to the Deep South in the summer of 1964 to register Black people to vote. Although this was the first time I had heard him speak in person, I felt like I already knew him. In the first few months of my freshman year in the fall of 1963, I had read his name in the *Yale Daily News* so many times that I thought he was a professor, or at least an older graduate student. When I looked up his bio, I was surprised to realize he had graduated from the University of North Carolina in Chapel Hill in 1949; attended law school in New Haven, graduating in 1954; and then served a two-year stint in the U.S. Army. Now Lowenstein was trying to do his part to help the United States live up to the noble words in the Declaration of Independence and U.S. Constitution, which Martin Luther King Jr. had described the year before at the Lincoln Memorial as "promissory notes" to Black Americans.

In my four years at Yale and in the thirteen years from my graduation in 1967 to Lowenstein's assassination in 1980, he was the most important political influence in my life. Tens of thousands of 1960s college students would say the same thing. If you want to achieve change, Al said, you must do it through politics. And politics meant persuading those who don't agree with you to open their minds. And that meant listening and respecting them.

Lowenstein's refusal to demonize those with political opinions different from his own put him at odds with the leading progressive activists of the sixties, just as it would today. He had little use for those on the "New Left" who saw confrontation, even violence, as the only means to achieve change. The irony—and, for many of us, the tragedy—is that the activists who hated Lowenstein the most were not the extremists of the political right but those on the left, who felt threatened by the legions of young people who accepted Al's message of the politics of persuasion and rejected the politics of political destruction.

The list of Al Lowenstein acolytes just on the Yale campus in the 1960s included multiple future national, state, and local elected leaders and at least one future president of the United States, Bill Clinton.

Although Lowenstein played a historic role in leading the anti–Vietnam War political movement within the Democratic Party, the cause that meant the most to him was civil rights—fighting to end discrimination against Black people.

He was imploring us to help him in that cause in the spring of 1964, my freshman year, while trying to enlist volunteers to go to Mississippi that summer. His appeal immediately reminded me of how inspired I'd been by Dr. King the previous summer, but as he spoke, I realized that I already had summer plans and couldn't go.

I had signed a contract to become a counselor for eight weeks at Camp Equinunk, and I was looking forward to returning. I also had the sense that Lowenstein would not be impressed by my reason for not signing up.

Still, I wanted to meet him and tell him I wanted to be involved in the Civil Rights Movement and how much his idea of how to conduct politics resonated with me. The essence of Lowenstein's message reminded me of Atticus Finch's advice to see the world through other people's eyes.

Doing so, Lowenstein maintained, was the best way to find common ground, even between liberals and conservatives, Democrats and Republicans. Finding that common ground, he argued, didn't mean being part of a squishy "center" with no convictions. He was an unapologetic FDR-style New Deal liberal who believed government was more often than not the best mechanism to achieve social justice and equal opportunity.

The conservative approach—of relying on private enterprise and free markets and viewing government (as Ronald Reagan was saying, even then) as the problem, not the solution—was an insufficient response at a time of huge racial and social injustices. But Lowenstein argued that somewhere between those two approaches, there was common ground to be found. But you can't find that ground without listening—or by simply assuming that conservatives are hard-hearted and evil. Many also want to help the poor and create equal opportunity for all. They just disagreed on the best means of achieving that common goal—government versus private, federal power versus state power.

This was the core of the debate from 1787 through 1789, when the U.S. Constitution was written and adopted, he pointed out. The compromises that resulted included a House reflecting all voters and a Senate equalizing voting power between big and small states, that is, respecting states as possessing their own sovereign power within a federal system. In reality, Lowenstein said, we liberals had to persuade Southern conservatives in Congress to find a way to compromise on what they thought they could not politically or personally accept: ending Jim Crow and treating Black people as equals.

Young white kids from elite schools, Lowenstein argued, had an obligation—a *moral* obligation—to go to the South or elsewhere into the front lines of the political arena to reach out to those less fortunate than us, including working-class whites who saw liberated Blacks as competitors for their jobs.

This is what I heard from Lowenstein, and it stuck.

From that moment his influence remained with me for the rest of my life.

As Lowenstein was leaving, I sought him out to introduce myself. His face was flushed from the insults and badgering by the New Left group in the back of the room. I told him I agreed with his approach and belief in politics to persuade people, and I wanted to work with him and asked him to help me be more involved in politics.

Then he asked me the question I was embarrassed to answer.

"So are you going to Mississippi to help us?"

I hesitated. "No," I said, "I can't."

"Why?"

I mentioned I had a contract to be a summer camp counselor (emphasizing the word *contract* as if that mattered).

He saw through it immediately.

"Bad answer, Lanny. You're not worried about being sued for breach of contract. You just want to go to summer camp."

I was silent.

He added, but not harshly—instead quietly, with amazing (to me) empathy and understanding that surprised me: "You need to think about what's truly important compared to other things."

And that was that. He walked away.

About two months later, in late June 1964, I read the horrifying news that three young men involved in the Mississippi Summer Project—two from New York City, Andrew Goodman and Michael Schwerner, and a young Black man from Meridian, Mississippi, James Chaney—had been murdered near Philadelphia, Mississippi. Their bodies were found in an earthen dam in Meridian weeks later.

I shuddered at the thought that I could have been one of those three civil rights workers, killed in the dead of night. I don't recall experiencing what we now call survivor's guilt. But I do remember feeling admiration for them. I thought then, and think now, that those who gave the last full measure of devotion to the Civil Rights Movement are owed as much admiration, or more, as the war heroes at Arlington Cemetery, the place where Al Lowenstein is buried.

The next time I crossed paths with Lowenstein was a night in the autumn, probably of 1967, during my first semester in law school. Since I first met him as a freshman, Al had been back to Yale dozens of times to speak and meet with students, but I didn't see him. My excuse was that my work for the *Yale Daily News* was all-consuming, which was true. I think my real reason was that I was still embarrassed that I had responded to his call to work for civil rights in Mississippi by telling him I was going to summer camp instead.

When I went to hear him speak at the law school in the fall of 1967, my position on the Vietnam War had evolved from ambiguity to strong opposition. I'll concede that my opposition was incentivized by the loss of my undergraduate student deferment from the draft. But a fear of combat wasn't the only concern for me or my generation. Was stopping the spread of Communism in Southeast Asia enough justification for the frightful cost in human lives, especially among Vietnamese civilians? We didn't think so. Fear of being drafted may have been the factor that focused our attention on Vietnam, but our views that the United States had stumbled into an immoral and unwinnable war were genuine and deeply felt.

That night Lowenstein was back doing what he did best: imploring students and young people to get involved in traditional politics, to persuade rather than to polarize—this time in the effort to get America out of Vietnam. He urged us to go to New Hampshire to knock on doors for Eugene McCarthy, the Minnesota senator who was the only one willing to challenge President Lyndon Johnson in the Democratic Party primary. Al urged us to shave our beards, forget about drugs and "turning on and tuning out," and get "clean for Gene."

"We can't end the war by getting high," he said, "or by demonizing anyone who supports the war because they, like millions of Americans, believe the lies by the Johnson administration. We have to *persuade* voters to vote against Johnson to get out of Vietnam—not demonize and confront them, as the far left claims is the only way."

After the speech was over in the law school auditorium, I summoned up the courage to reintroduce myself to him. He amazed me not only with a warm hello, hug, and congratulations on my election as chairman of the *Yale Daily News* but also by recalling the last time we had spoken more than three years earlier: "So how was summer camp? Probably a lot more fun than spending the summer in Mississippi."

So when he said, "When can you go to New Hampshire? I will call the McCarthy campaign and tell them to put you to work," I told him I was ready.

In February 1968 I did go to New Hampshire with a friend for a long weekend, with the primary scheduled for March 12, 1968. Elaine was pregnant with our first child, due in the summer, so I couldn't stay long.

We arrived late Friday night and stayed at the home of one of the McCarthy campaign supporters. We went to McCarthy headquarters in Manchester early the next morning. This was my first experience working in any political campaign, much less one so momentous on the front lines of trying to stop Lyndon Johnson's renomination and add momentum to ending U.S. involvement in Vietnam.

Even early in the morning on a bitter-cold New Hampshire day, hundreds of students and older people were standing in line, waiting to be given three-by-five cards with names, addresses of voters, and street maps. There was no GPS back then, so we were given local street maps of Manchester neighborhoods to tell us where to go and what doors to knock on—in search of Democrats most likely to vote in the March primary.

The instructions on what to say and how to say it were handed to us as well, along with a rating system from "1" to "5" to assess likely voter preference, with "1" being definite McCarthy voter and "5" being definite Johnson voter. Some of the people who opened their doors to me were downright hostile, accusing me of being a "Communist" or "anti-American" for opposing "our president and our troops" and slamming the door in my face. But most, even pro-war Johnson voters, were friendly, and some even invited me in to have a "cup of cocoa" and "a chat."

I remember one particular voter to this day. She was an elderly lady and started out quite angry that I was working against a Democratic president. She was clearly a party loyalist who supported Johnson not because she liked him personally. She warned that if you defeated an incumbent president for the nomination, that meant the election would go to "that terrible Nixon fellow."

Still, I wanted to talk to her and test out what might persuade her to vote for McCarthy, especially how she felt about the Vietnam War. So I asked her the one question I thought might move her: If I got drafted and had to go to Vietnam and was killed, what did she think was the reason for my death? What would my parents think?

She hesitated. "I guess to defeat the Communists," she answered.

But I asked, "Do you think those Vietnamese Communists, most of them peasants living in little villages that we are burning down, are really a risk to the United States? To you? To me?"

I tried not to argue, just to ask and wait for her to answer.

She hesitated again. "I guess, honestly, I don't know, but I don't think they are."

"So why are we there killing them?" I asked her. "And risking getting killed ourselves?"

"I guess I don't really know," she answered.

So I asked, "Would you consider voting for McCarthy to remind President Johnson there should be a strong reason why old men send young men to war and risk their lives? To send him a message?" I reminded her that in World War II, there was no doubt about the reason it was worth fighting and dying for.

She paused. "You have a point I didn't think of. Maybe Johnson will pay more attention to the problems you raised about the Vietnam War if McCarthy does well here in New Hampshire."

As I thanked her and started to walk away from her front door, she said, "Thank you for being so civil. That isn't what I see on TV among these long-haired, shouting anti-Vietnam protesters. You have made me wonder."

And that was enough.

I thought I had done my job to raise doubts without humiliating her. As I walked away, I wrote a "3" for undecided on her card. Then I thought again, crossed it out, and changed it to a "2." I was guessing she should be recalled on Election Day, reminded to vote, and might vote for McCarthy just to send Johnson a message that he needed to change his policies.

As I reflect on that first experience going door-to-door talking to everyday Americans and not political activists or fellow antiwar liberals, I learned that the lesson Lowenstein had tried to teach us about bringing about racial justice in the Mississippi Summer Project four years before—the one he preached that night in his speech at Yale Law School—was literally and demonstrably true.

It was the ultimate Al Lowenstein lesson to me, to all of us, our sixties generation of liberal kids: If we wanted to end the war, to achieve social justice for our country, the best path was through politics, specifically the politics of persuasion, not bullying or demonization.

After that I kept in regular touch with Lowenstein. I knew his first choice for taking on President Lyndon Johnson had been Senator Robert F. Kennedy, but Kennedy balked at running against his old adversary. RFK told Lowenstein he was afraid that the race would be depicted as a personal feud between himself and Johnson.

But after McCarthy exceeded expectations in New Hampshire, winning 42 percent of the vote, with Johnson under 50 percent, the pressure on Bobby Kennedy to get in the race was overwhelming. He announced a couple of weeks later, embittering McCarthy and many of his idealistic young supporters. But not me. I found McCarthy's coolness almost patronizing. And I admired Kennedy. I heard that Lowenstein would not switch, however. He felt McCarthy was owed his continued support, at least for a while. Lowenstein finally switched to Kennedy just before the June 6 California primary. The turning point, Al told me, was when McCarthy declined to campaign in Black neighborhoods of Milwaukee before the Wisconsin primary.

After Robert Kennedy's assassination the night of his victory in the California primary over both McCarthy and Humphrey, I tried to reach Lowenstein (along with probably thousands of other Lowenstein followers) to see what we should do. Should we support McCarthy? Or give up and support Humphrey, the inevitable nominee—or what?

I heard that Lowenstein had called a national conference of supporters of McCarthy and RFK to come to Chicago at the end of June to decide what to do. When I finally got through to him on the phone, he urged me to come to Chicago, which was hosting the Democratic convention that year. He said he was organizing a "Coalition for an Open Convention"—meaning trying to get enough delegates for McCarthy, especially those formerly for RFK, and those supporting Senator George McGovern of South Dakota to work together to deprive Humphrey of a first ballot victory at the national convention at the end of August.

At the Chicago conference, the big debate was, as usual, between the "political process" liberals such as Lowenstein (and me) and those on the more radical left who wanted to reject participating in the election and take to the streets in demonstrations and confrontation with the "old politics." Lowenstein's impatient response during the debate was basic: "If you engage in violence and hate-Humphrey rallies, you will end up with Richard Nixon—escalating the war and harming poor people. Is that okay with you?"

I stood up and agreed with him.

On the last day of the conference, Lowenstein surprised me by asking me to make the closing speech on "staying in the political process and fighting." I tried to oblige, though my speech was drowned out by boos from the anti-Lowenstein left, so I cut it short and sat down. The last speaker was a handsome young pastor, introduced by Lowenstein as a close aide to the Reverend Martin Luther King Jr., who had been killed a few months earlier.

This charismatic young man spoke about the need to build coalitions of the pragmatic, not of the pure—a Lowenstein phrase. He ended his speech by calling for a new rainbow coalition for progressive change—white, black, brown, blue-collar workers and affluent progressives, East, West, North, and South—to keep King's hope and dream alive.

He received a standing ovation.

His name was Jesse Jackson. I introduced myself to him after the speech. That was the beginning of a friendship that has lasted to this day and was especially important to me exactly thirty years later when I reached out to Reverend Jackson to minister to a hurting friend—Bill Clinton.

## CHAPTER 11

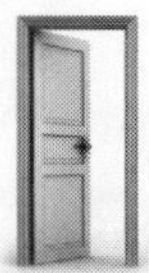

# ABRAHAM, MARTIN, AND JOHN . . . AND AL

*Has anybody here seen my old friend Bobby?*
*Can you tell me where he's gone?*
*I thought I saw him walkin'*
*Up over the hill*
*With Abraham, Martin, and John.*

**DICK HOLLER,** "Abraham, Martin, and John,"
first sung by Dion

Late that night in Chicago, well after midnight, several dozen of us who were close to Al Lowenstein gathered in his large hotel room suite. He invited me to join, which made me believe I had made it at least to the outer edges of the inner circle.

The subject: "Where do we go from here?"

With the death of Robert Kennedy still uppermost on our minds, Lowenstein pulled out his overstuffed wallet and showed us a scrap of paper we had all read about but had not seen. It contained a scribbled note from the late Senator Kennedy.

Lowenstein reminded us that a Kennedy aide had handed him the note in early May, the month before Bobby's assassination, when Lowenstein was sitting in the back of a bus late one night on a trip from a New York state Democratic Convention to New York City. RFK was sitting in the front of the bus and had seen Al walk by with only a nod.

At that point Lowenstein had still refused to switch his support to Kennedy from McCarthy.

So Kennedy had sent him the note, which Al proceeded to read to us in a quiet, anguished whisper. I remember all of us peering over his shoulder, fascinated to see RFK's actual handwriting and the scribbled message as Lowenstein read.

> *To Al, who taught us—who knew the lesson of Emerson, and taught it to the rest of us—they did not see, nor did thousands of young men pressing to the barriers of their careers yet see, that if a single man plant himself on his convictions and there abide, the huge world will come round to him.*

And then below, "From your friend Bob Kennedy."

I remember repeating that phrase to myself that Lowenstein had said: *"If a single man plant himself . . . the huge world will come round to him."*

That was Al Lowenstein.

Notwithstanding Lowenstein's prescience about what would happen if violent leftists took to the streets at the Democrats' 1968 convention—and how the ensuing riots drowned out the party's message and set the stage for Richard Nixon to win in November—there were other elections that year and other campaigns. One of them was Al's own.

Lowenstein used his own national fame as the antiwar "coalition" liberal who led the "Dump Johnson" movement to run for Congress that November in the Fifth Congressional District of New York. Located in the south shore area of Long Island, it was an ideal seat for Lowenstein—home of the heavily Jewish, liberal "Five Towns" area: Lawrence, Cedarhurst, Woodmere, Hewlett, and Inwood—adjoining villages and communities of Hempstead, Long Island, in Nassau County.

The fact that Lowenstein had moved there only so he could run for Congress didn't seem to matter. Some critics called him a carpetbagger, but his response was disarmingly simple: "I know the issues that matter to this district and to the American people," he would say, "and I will work hard to represent this district." His street-to-street, door-to-door campaign convinced enough voters of his sincerity. Lowenstein won the seat by a narrow margin, despite the fact that the Fifth District had more registered Republicans than Democrats (by a 3–2 margin).

Two years later, in the fall of 1970, after I had graduated from Yale Law School but was still living in New Haven, I received a call from Congressman Lowenstein. I thought he was asking me to help him in what I knew would be a tough reelection bid. The New York State Republican legislature had redrawn his district to defeat him—carving out the liberal Democratic Five Towns and substituting for them the large conservative Republican town of Massapequa.

Instead, Al asked me if I could rally some Yale students to help campaign for a Republican member of the New York congressional delegation, a U.S. senator who hailed from upstate New York named Charles Goodell. Lowenstein had gotten to know Goodell when he served in the House of Representatives. (Congress had numerous liberal Republicans at that time, just as it had many conservative Democrats.) Lowenstein had come to like Goodell, who shared his opposition to escalating the war in Vietnam. After Bobby Kennedy's death, Goodell had been appointed by Governor Nelson Rockefeller to fill Kennedy's Senate seat.

Naturally, President Nixon was furious at Goodell's outspoken criticism of the administration's escalating bombing campaign in North Vietnam. Nixon behaved in his typically vindictive way, endorsing the New York Conservative Party nominee who was running against Goodell in a three-way race with Democratic nominee Richard Ottinger. The Conservative Party nominee was James Buckley, brother of—yes, small world—William F. Buckley Jr., the former *Yale Daily News* chairman who had mentored me.

So I asked several friends from Yale Law School to accompany me to New York City to hand out literature for Goodell. One of those I called was Hillary Rodham. Hillary couldn't go to New York, but I got a half-dozen law and undergraduate students from the Young Democrats to take the train to New York City on an October morning to help Goodell.

We took an early Amtrak from New Haven to Grand Central Station and found Goodell at a nearby subway stop. As we handed out his campaign brochures and brought commuters over to meet him and shake his hand, I noticed an eleven-year-old boy with blondish hair also handing out the literature enthusiastically.

He looked a lot like the senator. I asked him what his name was.

"Roger," he said.

Some forty years later, I got to know this young man after he had grown up and become the commissioner of the National Football League. Roger Goodell and I remain friends to this day.

■ ■ ■

The next month Goodell lost his race, with the antiwar vote divided between himself and Ottinger, allowing Buckley to win with a plurality of the vote. Out on Long Island, Lowenstein also lost by a narrow margin.

Many months later, I think it was the fall of 1971, sometime after midnight I received a call from Lowenstein. I was living in a D.C. suburb in Prince George's County, Maryland. My wife and our two little children had moved there in December 1970. I had signed up as a speechwriter to work for the presidential campaign of Maine Senator Edmund S. Muskie, who was expected to announce his candidacy for the 1972 Democratic nomination.

The phone woke my wife and me up. Al didn't say hello. That was his custom. He just made a statement: "I am in town visiting some friends. Come pick me up in D.C. I want to introduce you to one of them whom you need to get to know." He gave me a corner in Washington, D.C., where I would find him.

I protested that it was too late and that I couldn't just pick up and leave at that time of night. His response was something like, "See you soon," and he hung up.

Of course, I got out of bed and went to pick him up. Why? I was, I realized, as did many other Lowenstein followers, irrational—almost possessed by him. My wife correctly described me as such. Yet there I was, forty-five minutes later, pulling up to a dark corner in D.C. where Lowenstein stood, surrounded—don't ask me how or why—by more than a dozen people of various ages as he held forth.

Al barely said hello when he got into the car. He just directed me to a small townhouse in Georgetown. It was now close to 2:00 a.m. *Who the heck is going to answer the door at this hour*, I wondered, *much less welcome us in for a visit?*

As if reading my thoughts, Lowenstein said, "Don't ask. This is a friend I met in the House gym after he left to work for Nixon. We are still friends."

A few minutes later, Lowenstein knocked on the door, and there stood a youngish man, wearing his bathrobe, with a big smile. He hugged Lowenstein and then turned to me, not seeming at all surprised that Lowenstein had brought along with him a new young man to be introduced to him.

Al said, "Hi, Don. I wanted you to meet my friend Lanny Davis."

"Hi, Lanny. I'm Don Rumsfeld. Nice to meet you. Come in for a cup of coffee. I'm a Republican, but don't worry—I won't tell on you."

The three of us laughed as we entered to sit at his kitchen table. Lowenstein and Rumsfeld talked politics, Nixon, the war, and stories they seemed to find funny. I listened, amazed but also very sleepy.

When I got home, it was almost dawn—just in time to give my baby son Seth his early morning bottle.

Little did I know that about four years or so from that night in 1971, Rumsfeld would be named secretary of defense under Gerald Ford, who became president after Nixon resigned on August 8, 1974. At age forty-three, Rumsfeld was the youngest defense secretary in U.S. history. Even less did I know that about twenty-six years later, that same Lowenstein friend would be appointed secretary of defense for the second time—this time by my friend George W. Bush.

Bush, in turn, would choose as his vice president another Yale man—albeit a dropout—named Dick Cheney, who earned his spurs in the Nixon White House as Rumsfeld's deputy. (Cheney would also come in for some good-natured ribbing in that Yale commencement speech Bush delivered in 2001. "A Yale degree is worth a lot, as I often remind Dick Cheney, who studied here but left a little early," Bush said to general laughter. "So now we know: If you graduate from Yale, you become president. If you drop out, you get to be vice president.")

■ ■ ■

The long and extremely painful memory of being cut off by Al Lowenstein from all contact and friendship—the modern term would be "ghosted"—is too difficult to relate in full, even now, more than four decades later. The bottom line is that I worked for Lowenstein when he sought election to Congress from Brooklyn's Fourteenth District in 1972. Once again, the allegations that Al was a carpetbagger were raised, although this time they were raised not by the media but by the local Democratic Party machine. It was led by an old-style political boss named Meade Esposito, who was backing a conservative, pro–Vietnam War Democratic candidate, Congressman John J. Rooney.

Defying the advice of his senior campaign advisers and activists close to him, including me, Lowenstein spent a lot of time trying to win over the more conservative, Rooney-supporting white working-class neighborhoods. We argued that he—and we—should concentrate our efforts on increasing turnout in the more liberal and minority areas, where he could expect the most support.

Lowenstein lost the June 1972 primary by a narrow margin. As we feared, the more liberal areas had not turned out in the numbers we had targeted, but the turnout in the old-line white working-class neighborhoods was larger than expected, energized by opposition to Lowenstein's liberalism and the old-line Brooklyn Democratic Party organization's strength. The margin of loss was about eight hundred votes. There was plenty of anecdotal evidence of voters in the more liberal Lowenstein neighborhoods being denied the right to vote for arbitrary reasons by the precinct officials controlled by the Esposito organization. For the rest of the summer, volunteers gathered affidavits to seek a court-ordered new election.

I couldn't stay. It was time for me to go home to my family and begin the prospect of looking for a job at a law firm. In the meantime I wrote an article analyzing why Lowenstein lost. It was ultimately published by *Washington Monthly*, a cutting-edge new liberal political magazine founded by the iconoclastic journalist Charles Peters. The editor of my piece was none other than John Rothchild, my erstwhile last-minute opponent for the *Yale Daily News* chairmanship.

The thesis of my *Washington Monthly* article was that Lowenstein lost because he stuck to a campaign strategy of trying to rebuild the Robert Kennedy coalition of working-class whites, liberals, and minorities. I thought the article was positive in its praise of Lowenstein's principled (though I used the word "stubborn") decision, even at the risk of losing the primary.

When I heard that Lowenstein had won the court case, I immediately jumped on a train to go to Brooklyn to help in the revote, which was scheduled for just a week or so after the decision.

When I arrived, however, I discovered I was persona non grata. Lowenstein saw me and refused to say hello or shake my hand. I was told that Al was "livid" over my criticism of his campaign strategy in the

*Washington Monthly* article. "What?" I asked. I praised his courage for trying to rebuild the RFK coalition, even at the expense of winning. But they still said he thought I betrayed him by writing that piece.

I was stunned but picked up the pile of three-by-five voter cards for a particular precinct and went to knock on doors for the next week. The night before the second primary election, all the campaign workers gathered for a final inspiration and thank-you talk by Lowenstein. He asked everyone in the room to introduce themselves. When it came my turn, he interrupted and asked the person sitting next to me to introduce himself.

Everyone in the room realized what had just happened. I had a hard time breathing. I still worked for him the next day, getting the vote out. He lost this time by a much larger margin. The night of his defeat, when it looked like his political career was over, he walked around the room and gave everyone a hug and thanks.

When he got to me, he hesitated. I said, "Sorry, Al."

He might have interpreted that to mean "sorry" for writing the *Washington Monthly* story. I really meant "Sorry for your loss." But whatever, he hugged me, thanked me, and asked me to stay in touch. That was the last time I saw Al Lowenstein alive.

On Friday, March 15, 1980, I received a call from a mutual friend of Lowenstein with the news that Al had been murdered by a mentally unbalanced former student protégé from Stanford, who claimed to police that he was ordered to do so by voices in his teeth. He shot Al in the chest while he was in his law office, trying to calm the disturbed young man down.

A week later I attended the memorial service at New York City's famous Central Synagogue at East Fifty-Fifth and Lexington Avenue. I wasn't surprised at the size of the crowd—exceeding three thousand people—or the breadth of political celebrities from both the left and right, as well as national celebrities from Hollywood and the arts.

Nor was I surprised that the two people leading the memorial service would be the hero of the liberal movement, Massachusetts Senator Edward Kennedy, and "Mr. Conservative," William F. Buckley Jr.

Buckley and Lowenstein had become friends after Lowenstein was a regular guest on his much-watched public television program, *Firing Line.* Ted Kennedy and Lowenstein had been through many elections and tragedies together. At the time Al was campaigning for Ted (along with me, as a volunteer in Iowa) in his primary challenge against President Jimmy Carter, which in my mind harkened back to our New Hampshire days challenging LBJ.

"Who but Al could have as friends Bill Buckley and Bobby Kennedy?" Ted Kennedy said at the service. "For me and for so many others, he was our brother." There were moments of laughter when Al was eulogized by Indiana Congressman Andy Jacobs as "a gentle tornado." Some of the speakers remembered the after-midnight telephone calls, like the one I had received, from Al to "pick me up now." His nephew Douglas Lowenstein induced knowing chuckles when he quipped, "Al always set aside time for his family. Unfortunately for us, it was usually between midnight and three a.m."

Famous 1960s liberal movement folk singers Peter Yarrow and Mary Travers sang a song with the lines reflecting Lowenstein's legacy: "Weave me the sunshine out of the falling rain. Weave me the hope of a new tomorrow."

*Washington Post* reporter Lee Lescaze, who was covering the service, wrote, "Lowenstein pallbearers wheeled his oak coffin out of the synagogue, and his friends filed slowly out to contemplate that never again will they get an improbable call at an unlikely time from someone who introduces himself and says: 'Al Lowenstein told me to call this number.'"

For purposes of this memoir, after some effort, I located the full text of Bill Buckley's comments on Lowenstein in a book he published in the 1980s of his various speeches. The following is the portion which had the greatest impact on my politics and my life:

> *Perhaps my own experience with him was unique in that we conservatives did not generally endorse his political prescriptions.*

> *So that we were, presumptively, opponents of Al Lowenstein, in those chambers in which we spend, and misspend, so much of our lives. It was his genius that so many of those he touched—typically arriving a half hour late—discovered intuitively the underlying communion . . .*
>
> *Although Allard Lowenstein was at home with collectivist formulations, one had the impression that he might be late in aborting a third world war because of his absorption of the problems of one sophomore. Oh, they followed him everywhere; because they experienced in him, as we all did, the essence of an entirely personal dedication . . .*
>
> *A poet might be tempted to say, "If only the Lord had granted us that Allard should have arrived late at his own assassination."*

As we walked out of the service, many of us were thinking how happy Lowenstein would have been knowing that both Kennedy and Buckley were there. Their presence proved, once again, the enduring lesson he never tired of imparting to us.

Fight on issues, but it doesn't have to be personal. If you want to get progressive change, you must reach out to the middle and, especially if you are in Congress, across the aisle. Most importantly, Lowenstein helped me learn to persuade voters—as I tried to do when I knocked on the door of the elderly woman in New Hampshire to convince her to vote for Gene McCarthy. You can't force people to agree with you.

These lessons stayed with me for the rest of my life and attracted me to work for Democrats who were more than simply liberal on the issues. They were willing to build broad coalitions and compromise to win change.

But I had one more thing to learn from this man.

Allard Kenneth Lowenstein engendered great loyalty among those who believed in him—as I discovered joyously. He also demanded great loyalty and could be quick to judge you for falling short in his eyes, as I learned painfully. In the end I was enriched by this experience too. Our friends will let us down occasionally, as will our political allies and even our role models. They are only human. And yes, it is indeed divine to forgive.

I'm confident that Al would have granted me absolution for what he considered my transgression—as he did Bobby Kennedy—and that we would have resumed one of the most rewarding friendships of my life. We never got the chance, however. I sometimes think of this when people I love fall short in my eyes. I try not to be too harsh in judging them and to be quick to forgive. Sometimes, when I hear that Dion song from the sixties, I add one more name to the litany of the fallen.

*Anybody here seen my old friend Al?*
*Can you tell me where he's gone?*
*He freed a lot of people, but it seems the good they die young.*
*I just looked around, and he's gone . . .*

CHAPTER 12

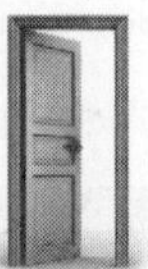

# YALE LAW SCHOOL: WHAT'S A LIBERAL? WHAT'S A CONSERVATIVE?

*You are in Property I class. From this moment on, such words as "fee simple" are banned in this classroom. You can buy a hornbook to pass my final exam. This is Yale Law School, not Harvard. From now on, we will be discussing the moral, ethical, and political implications of private property ownership.*

**CHARLES REICH,** Yale law professor and author of *The Greening of America*

When Professor Reich began property class with that quote, most of the class and I thought he was kidding. This was before Reich became a national progressive cultural icon. He seemed to be serious.

One obvious point he was making was that lawyers use opaque words, such as "fee simple," when they could just as well say, "property owned free and clear." And he didn't want to waste time on teaching us concepts that could be memorized from the "hornbook," the law school version of "CliffsNotes," which allowed generations of high school and college students to complete their summer reading or essay assignments of lengthy novels by reading compact summaries and not the actual works.

Reich quoted one of his favorite law school faculty members, Professor Fred Rodell, an outspoken, self-described "liberal" and leader of that majority wing of the Yale Law School faculty in those days. Rodell had once famously said, "There are two things wrong with almost all legal writing. One is its style. The other is its content. That, I think, about covers the ground."

Reich's condescending reference to Harvard was also typical of what I learned early on, really from my first day in early September 1967: the smug attitude of Yale faculty and students toward their chief rival. Two snarky quips I heard in my first week at the law school emblemized that mentality.

The first was that "Harvard Law School trains you to be president of a large corporation. But Yale Law trains you to be president of the United States or members of the Supreme Court." (Clever but untrue: Two U.S. presidents attended Yale Law, Gerald Ford and Bill Clinton. Harvard has the same number, Rutherford B. Hayes and Barack Obama. And on the current Supreme Court, the two schools are tied.*)

Another witticism was to compare the different titles of the bankruptcy law course taught at Yale Law with Harvard. At Harvard Law, so the saying went, the bankruptcy law course was titled "Creditors' Rights." At Yale, the same course was titled "Debtor's Estates."

*Oh,* I thought at the time. *Okay I get it: We at liberal, socially conscious Yale are more sympathetic to the poor debtor than to the wealthy creditor.* Looking back more than a half century later, I have a different reaction. Is there something inherently better, that is, more "liberal," about someone who borrows money and stiffs the lender than the lender

* On the current high court, Justices Thomas, Alito, Sotomayor, and Kavanaugh attended Yale. Chief Justice Roberts and Justices Kagan, Gorsuch, and Jackson went to Harvard. The ninth and most recently confirmed justice, Amy Coney Barrett, is a graduate of Notre Dame Law School.

who loans the money and gets stiffed? I don't necessarily think so. It was obvious that Yale Law liked to put down "corporate" Harvard, however inaccurate those caricatures were. Now I wonder whether those gags and stereotypes possibly reflected some type of inferiority complex at Yale.

In truth, both law schools in the 1960s were largely "liberal" in both students and faculty in their view of seeing the law as an instrument to promote liberal causes and political candidates. Both were staunchly anti–Vietnam War, pro–civil rights, and pro–New Deal and welfare state—meaning that they were largely in sync with the Democratic Party. And both schools took pride in pushing students to go beyond "what" the law says in hornbooks, summarizing statutes, and precedents going back to the English common law cases.

Yale, Harvard, and other "liberal" competitive law schools, from the Ivy Leagues on the East Coast to the University of Chicago, Stanford, Cal, and UCLA on the West Coast, largely promoted themselves by pushing students to ask the why and what underpinning the law. *Why* did the words or precedents say what they said? *What* were the underlying policies, moral values, and, yes, political considerations that played into the court's decisions?

This is why orientation at more liberal law schools often morphed into an ideological argument familiar today: Should the United States Supreme Court and other federal and state judges read a statute or the Constitution strictly the way it was written at the time or interpret the law to reflect contemporary values?

We didn't use the terms "broad" versus "strict" construction way back then, which came to be in vogue in the 1980s and 1990s as a way to describe an allegedly "liberal" versus "conservative" split. But that's what it came down to. Only later in my second year at Yale Law School and much later in the twenty-first century did I come to learn the nuances, ambiguities, and ultimately the inaccuracy of those oversimplified labels and distinctions.

Professor Rodell, quoted by Professor Reich on that first day of class, was seen as one of the leaders of the Yale Law majority liberal wing in the late 1960s. Rodell was known to be a close friend of Justice William O. Douglas, the liberal hero on the Supreme Court at the time. Appointed to the Supreme Court by FDR in 1939, Douglas led what was seen as the "liberal" wing of the court for thirty-six years until he retired in 1974.

Rodell did not mince words about negativity toward Justice Felix Frankfurter, Douglas's conservative counterpart. Nor did he hide his disdain for one of Frankfurter's acolytes on the Yale Law faculty, Professor Alexander M. Bickel. Both Frankfurter and Bickel attended Harvard Law, and Bickel had clerked for Frankfurter after graduating. (Rodell's comment about Bickel's attendance at Harvard was, "It figures.")

Justice Frankfurter was appointed to the court the same year as Justice Douglas, although he retired earlier, in 1962. Frankfurter's opinions and speeches reflected a more "conservative" approach regarding the need for federal judges to exercise "judicial restraint." Naturally Professor Bickel promoted that philosophy in his constitutional law teaching.

But as I came to discover when I got to know Professor Bickel much better in my second year at the law school, these distinctions between "liberal" and "conservative" and "strict" and "broad" constructionism were not so clear in practice. Both sides seemed willing to use the approach of the other when it was convenient or reinforced, whether consciously or not, their moral, social, and political values.

A classic example is the historic case that brought Justices Frankfurter and Douglas together in 1954. The decision by the high court in *Brown v. Board of Education* overturned a longstanding Supreme Court precedent established in the now-notorious 1896 *Plessy v. Ferguson* case. This decision held that racial segregation in public schools did not violate the Fourteenth Amendment's "equal protection" clause. The *Plessy* court found that separate railway cars for white and Black passengers were "separate but equal" and thus could not be overturned on constitutional grounds, a precedent that was used to legalize segregation under the Constitution.

Fifty-eight years later, the *Brown* decision reversed *Plessy*. It did so by unanimous vote, bringing Justices Frankfurter and Douglas together and every justice who was in between. This was thanks to the hard work of Chief Justice Earl Warren. The former California governor was appointed to the court as chief justice in 1953 by Republican President Dwight Eisenhower.

The court's liberal wing might have been ready to address the social injustice of "separate" but obviously unequal segregated schools simply to undermine Jim Crow–style discrimination, but Warren wanted a united front. In a line of reasoning tailored to the conservative faction, Warren argued that there was a different factual record in 1954 than there had been in 1896.

The evidence at trial showed that racially segregated schools were "inherently unequal." For example, the data showed all-Black public schools consistently received less funding and inferior teachers and classrooms while ending up with lower educational results. Sociological evidence also showed that Black children were taught they were inferior to white children because they needed to be "segregated" in public schools.

The result that Chief Justice Warren sought was driven by his notion, shared by so many Americans, that almost ninety years after the end of the Civil War, it was high time to end racial segregation in public schools. The conservatives on the court, including Justice Frankfurter, also had to ignore the conservative doctrine of "stare decisis"—a barrier to the Supreme Court directly reversing a prior precedent just because the times had changed. The doctrine of "judicial restraint" just didn't work when the political arena was still locked in segregationist U.S. senators from the Deep South (almost all of whom were Democrats). In reality only the "unelected" judges had the ability and the will to rectify this national moral stain on the nation since slavery was introduced in the early seventeenth century.

My sense of the artificiality of the "liberal" versus "conservative" labeling, at least within the legal community, was proven when I got to know the allegedly "conservative" Professor Bickel much better in my second year at the law school.

When I obliquely referred to him in conversation as a "conservative," he suggested that I read his widely regarded book, *The Least Dangerous*

*Branch: The Supreme Court at the Bar of Politics*, which was published in 1962.

Reading it, I found myself confused about Bickel being labeled "conservative." The thesis of his book, mirroring Justice Frankfurter's philosophy, was that the federal judiciary (with particular focus on the Supreme Court) is unelected and has life tenure. It could only be "the least dangerous branch" if it exercised self-restraint in the cases it chose and in applying the law as strictly as possible based on the words of the statutes or the Constitution.

In our current vocabulary, Bickel's definition might be deemed "conservative" and "strict constructionist," but as *Brown* and other cases showed, these distinctions were not always that clear. I was even more confused about the appropriate way to "label" Professor Bickel when I got to know his personal political views. He was a liberal Democrat by any normal definition. He voted for Adlai Stevenson and John F. Kennedy for president and loved Harry Truman and FDR. He was a social and cultural liberal on all the issues, as far as I could tell. He was a strong First Amendment civil libertarian.

If that wasn't a liberal, then what was?†

Moreover, in the ensuing years, law review articles and other research delving into the *Brown v. Board* backstory have revealed a more interesting—and much more "activist"—role on the part of both Frankfurter and Bickel.

It's largely forgotten now, except by constitutional scholars, but *Brown* was argued twice before the court. The first time, in 1952, National Association for the Advancement of Colored People lawyer (and future Supreme Court justice) Thurgood Marshall's presentation didn't

† Bickel's political liberalism was subsequently proven before a national audience in his celebrated defense of *The New York Times* and *The Washington Post* against the Nixon administration in the famous 1971 Pentagon Papers case. Bickel's defense of the First Amendment and argument against any "prior restraint," even when the publication of classified information was not in dispute, won plaudits from ACLU liberals.

seem persuasive to the court's majority. Douglas and the other three liberal justices were inclined to strike down school segregation. Playing to the other five justices, famed lawyer John W. Davis, the lead counsel for the school boards, presented a detailed and sweeping history of the Fourteenth Amendment, as well as the intervening judicial review of the doctrine of "separate but equal." Davis had the scholarly literature on his side.

In response, the court did . . . nothing. Oral arguments having been concluded and legal briefs submitted, the Warren Court delayed its ruling. We learned later that Frankfurter spent the year maneuvering behind the scenes to have the case reargued. Meanwhile, he tasked Bickel with preparing a memo marshaling arguments to counter Davis's impressive presentation. While conceding that the Fourteenth Amendment was never intended to end school segregation, Bickel's memo argued that when the amendment was ratified in 1867, public education was a trivial governmental endeavor compared with its outsized role in American society in the 1950s. This was the hook Earl Warren used to hang his hat on.

■ ■ ■

Over the years this confusion about the most accurate "label" to describe Professor Bickel or others taught me an important lesson. The answer, I eventually concluded, is that it's better to avoid all labels if possible and instead to rely on facts. It also follows that steering clear of simplistic labels is the first step toward avoiding absolutist judgments about which side is "good" and which side is "evil." A more than respectful and productive way to conduct public discourse is to embark on a dialogue to try and determine which side of the political divide is "right" on any given question versus who is "wrong."

And maybe, God forbid, to admit to ambiguities and conflicts between two reasonable positions.

I got to know Professor Bickel well as a result of my participation during my second year at the law school in the competition to win the Thurman Arnold‡ Moot Court Prize.

Moot court is a competitive appellate argument. Contestants are given hypothetical facts. The panel of judges then determines who has made the best oral argument, largely in response to tough, adversarial questions from the bench.

I was fortunate to make it through various preliminary rounds among a large number of second-year and third-year students (first-year students were not allowed to compete) and then to the "final four."

The judging panel for these finals was led by U.S. Supreme Court Justice Potter Stewart. The others included Harvard Law Professor Archibald Cox (who, just four years later, was appointed as special prosecutor for the Watergate investigation and then was fired by Nixon after Cox demanded access to White House tape recordings, leading to the historic "Saturday Night Massacre" on October 20, 1973); Arthur Dean, the Kennedy administration attorney who led the successful negotiation of the Nuclear Test Ban treaty with the Soviet Union in 1963; and Edward Weinfeld, a U.S. district court judge from New York.

The four finalists were given a hypothetical case, with two assigned to defend the plaintiff's right to sue, or their "standing," and two others (me included) challenging their right to sue. Our hypothetical case concerned whether the chaplain of the U.S. Senate, whose salary was paid by taxpayers, had consistently included in his opening morning prayer to the Senate an assertion that all should believe in the divinity of Jesus Christ. The hypothetical stipulated that such a sectarian prayer, excluding Jews, Muslims, and many other religions, was a violation of the First

‡ Thurman Arnold was a renowned Washington, D.C., lawyer and the founder in 1946 of the now prestigious law firm Arnold & Porter (now called Arnold & Porter Kaye Scholer after the latter merged with A&P in 2017). Arnold was a Yale Law graduate, taught in the law school for several years, and served as an assistant attorney general for antitrust under Franklin Roosevelt and then as a federal judge on the prestigious D.C. Circuit Court of Appeals for two years before founding his law firm.

Amendment's prohibition on government establishing a religion—the so-called "Establishment Clause."

I was assigned the position that the taxpayers' plaintiffs had no constitutional "standing" to be heard by any federal court, let alone the Supreme Court. Under Article III of the Constitution, federal courts could only hear "cases and controversies." That phrase meant only parties with "standing" could obtain federal jurisdiction to decide a case. "Standing" meant the plaintiffs had to show that they could prove a "concrete, particularized and actual or imminent [injury], fairly traceable to the challenged action and redressable by a favorable ruling."[§]

The quantity of monetary loss suffered by taxpayers paying for the chaplain's salary was obviously minuscule. But they were nonetheless seeking a remedy in the courts to preclude an obviously unconstitutional prayer by the Senate chaplain.

Personally, I was aghast when I realized I had to argue something contrary to my own political and personal beliefs—that there was no judicial remedy for such egregious behavior. A few nights before the final argument, we had a chance to do a "stress test" dress rehearsal before three members of the Yale Law faculty who taught constitutional law.

When it was my turn, Bickel played the primary role in questioning my argument that the taxpayers had no standing as taxpayers and thus the Supreme Court could not even hear the case. Sensing my ideological discomfort with the position I had to take, Bickel began with a question that, it seemed to me, he asked a little too gleefully: "Mr. Davis, suppose a group of taxpayers could prove that, collectively, they had been forced to pay hundreds of thousands of tax dollars every year to pay for the chaplain's salary. This is serious monetary injury supporting a patently unconstitutional prayer by the Senate chaplain. Are you really saying these plaintiffs have no remedy?"

I hesitated, sensing a minefield, but forged ahead. "Professor Bickel," I replied, "there is no way that the particular impact on these taxpayers

§ *Monsanto v. Geertson Seed Farms*, 561 US 139 (201).

is anything more than pennies, and probably less than that. That is not enough to satisfy the requirement of a true 'case and controversy' and standing to sue."

I saw him smile. I had the feeling I had walked into a trap.

"But just suppose, hypothetically, they could prove the impact on them was as high a quantity of dollars that you deem sufficient to qualify for judicial standing, say millions or billions of dollars. What is your answer then?"

I hesitated again. Now I saw the slippery slope he had me on. I couldn't figure out how to get off. So I changed the subject.

"I believe, Professor Bickel, that was exactly your point in your book, *The Least Dangerous Branch*—that unelected judges needed to exercise self-restraint. Here that means federal courts declining to hear the case because of the lack of a 'case or controversy' under Article III."

He smiled again, this time saying, "Good try, Mr. Davis. Always a good idea to quote a judge's book with approval when responding to a question."

Then he continued, "But you didn't answer my question: How much financial impact would be enough to allow taxpayers as taxpayers to have standing to challenge in federal court unconstitutional conduct of a government official?"

I was silent. I hated to give the answer.

"I can't say an exact financial impact sufficient to establish standing, Professor Bickel. It's like Justice Potter Stewart once said when he had to come up with the definition of obscenity or hardcore pornography in a 1964 Supreme Court case,[¶] when he said something like: 'I don't know the exact definition, but I would know it when I see it.'"

"Another good try, Mr. Davis, especially since Justice Stewart is going to be the chief judge on your competition panel," Professor Bickel said. "But I don't think that will do."

---

¶ *Jacobellis v. Ohio*, 378 US 184 (11964).

He paused. "Let's hold it for now. See me in my office after this rehearsal is over."

Deflated and dispirited, I showed up in Professor Bickel's office an hour later to face the music. I knew that I had been terrible, almost frivolous, in quoting Justice Stewart's definition of pornography.

"So what is your true and honest answer, Mr. Davis? You said you read my book. But you forgot to mention what the ultimate message of the book would be when applied to your position in this moot court competition."

I was still stumped.

"The simple answer is *no remedy.* Courts are not meant to remedy everything. That is what my book explained and demonstrated under the Constitution."

"So I am supposed to say, 'There is no remedy.'"

"No," Bickel responded. "Think again. That is not what my book says. My book says no remedy *in the courts*—where there are unelected judges. You, of all people, given your political interests and activities, should know what the real answer is."

I started to see where he was headed.

"Do you mean 'politics,' Professor Bickel?" I said. "The word everyone thinks is so tainted? The remedy is in the political arena, in Congress passing a bill regulating an acceptable nonsectarian prayer? And the president signing it?"

I realized as I spoke that I had indeed ignored the real lesson of his book. Judicial restraint under Article III meant relying on democratic (small "d") institutions to effect changes. *Right out of Al Lowenstein's playbook,* I thought.

He nodded.

I thanked Professor Bickel and said good night. As I drove home, I thought, *So the lesson is, once you take a position, stick to the principle—and accept the consequences.*

■ ■ ■

The finals took place a couple of nights later. The auditorium was packed, and the upper balcony was filled, as well as the full auditorium. I even saw Yale President Kingman Brewster Jr. there, along with Sam Chauncey, my old Davenport College friend and conspirator on the "coeducation plot."

I was nervous as I looked at the all-star panel, led by a real Supreme Court justice. I tried to calm myself by remembering that Potter Stewart was a former chairman of the *Yale Daily News*. Maybe he would know that I was too. Of course, that wouldn't help in the judging of my performance, but maybe it would make him more friendly.

Each law student was supposed to have fifteen minutes, but we all ran a bit long—the exercise took about two hours. When it was my turn, Justice Stewart took the lead, beginning by asking me to define standing and explain why I argued there was none here if the parties were acting only as taxpayers.

Archibald Cox asked my personal opinion on whether the chaplain should be allowed to preach in such a sectarian way, and I said my personal opinion should not enter into my answer—nor should a judge's. The law said there was no standing, and unelected judges had to show self-restraint intended by the Framers as they wrote Article III.

While my back was to the audience when I stood at the podium, I thought that Professor Bickel, whom I had seen sitting in the back row, must have liked that answer. Toward the end of my argument, Justice Stewart came in for what turned out to be the final question of the night.

"Mr. Davis, I know you wouldn't answer Judge Cox's question about your personal opinion of the prayer, and I understand that, but could you explain whether you are arguing that there is no remedy at all to stop the chaplain from engaging in a clearly unconstitutional violation of the First Amendment's Establishment Clause?"

"I am not saying *no remedy at all*, Justice Stewart. I am saying under Article III, a taxpayer has no *legal* standing in a federal court, and thus the court has no jurisdiction."

"So is there any remedy?" Justice Stewart asked.

"Yes, there is, Justice Stewart. But not a legal one. The remedy is called democracy. It's called politics. It's up to Congress to regulate the chaplain's prayer and the president to sign a law passed by Congress if necessary. And the people get to tell Congress what to do."

I continued (and I am paraphrasing my closing; my memory is less than perfect after more than fifty years):

> *In other words, we don't look to unelected judges to solve our problems—to legislate their policy preferences from the bench. No, they must abide by the limits placed on them under Article III. But we can ask our elected representatives to remedy this unconstitutional action and fire the chaplain if necessary.*
>
> *The preamble to our Constitution rests ultimate legal authority not in the states or in the courts—it begins, "We the people . . ." and ends "do ordain and establish this Constitution for the United States of America."*
>
> *Thus, it is up to us, the people, to be active in politics, to vote, and then insist that our elected representatives respond to our concerns to ensure the Constitution's separation of church and state. If we don't do that, then that is on us, not the courts. But we must.*

When I sat down, I heard one clap, which quickly stopped. I didn't have to wonder who it was. The abortive applause violated a protocol announced by Justice Stewart at the very beginning of the argument warning against any applause. But I didn't need to turn around. I knew who was responsible for that clap. My mother.

After twenty minutes that seemed like twenty hours, Justice Stewart led the panel back in to announce the winner of the Thurman Arnold Moot Court Prize for 1969. When I heard my name announced, I was somewhat surprised and obviously happy. There seemed to be a gasp before applause. I know a lot of the audience, especially third-year students, thought the winner was a member of their class. (I agreed. I thought he had been better.)

Afterward, the contestants were invited into the faculty lounge to talk to the panel and mingle with the faculty. Professor Bickel was there. He smiled and nodded. *He deserved credit for the victory,* I thought.

Confirming that impression was Justice Stewart, who shook hands with me and tipped his wineglass toward me as he congratulated me. I thanked him. He then asked me whether I had enjoyed my year as chairman of the *Yale Daily News*. I nodded. "Definitely," I said. He said he understood because he actually enjoyed being chairman in many ways more than serving on the Supreme Court.

"I could write editorials without asking a majority to agree with me," he said with a laugh.

As I turned to leave, he added, "I was impressed when I asked you what remedy was left if the courts couldn't address the problem, and you said the word 'politics.' I was glad you had the guts to use that word. A lot of young people today think it's a dirty word. I hope you and others like you stay with it and get into politics to make this country and the world better."

Again, I can't say he used exactly those words, but that is close.

I was proud that was the message I left him and others with. I also remember being proud that I followed Professor Bickel's advice—to defend a principle of judicial restraint by the unelected judges, a liberal principle that also meant relying on democracy and politics to make change possible.

I now believed in that position and didn't care if I was labeled a conservative for taking it—or a liberal for that matter. It was a lesson I remembered and tried to apply in the years ahead.

■ ■ ■

It was the evening of April 4, 1968. For the last few days, several dozen members of the Corporate Law class (involving a mix of second- and third-year law students) had been involved in a mock negotiation of a "buy-sell" agreement over the sale of a fictional business.

The professor, Jan Deutsch, set up the hypothetical. He designated me as the "seller" of the company. I leaned on my former Yale college roommate from 1360 Davenport, David Foster, who was at Harvard Business School, to help me understand the strengths and weaknesses of the balance sheet and the price I should be asking for (teaching me the difference between actual "cash flow" and listed "profits," which included noncash expenses, such as depreciation).

It should have been a fun exercise, involving theoretical money and a learning experience about how to negotiate business terms and then write down the legal provisions to govern all aspects and possible risks of the sale. Instead the experience was a nightmare, mainly due to my own stubbornness. To this day I shudder in embarrassment when I think about it. It's an intricate and tedious story, but suffice to say that early in the negotiations, as the owner and seller of the family company, I got annoyed at what I thought was overly cute "lowballing" and legal trickery by the buyer and his team of attorneys.

The absolute deadline for concluding the negotiations and signing a written agreement—no extensions, Professor Deutsch told us many times—was precisely at 8:00 p.m. on Friday, April 4, 1968. Professor Deutsch reminded us, perhaps mistakenly in retrospect, that he would not grade us on whether we actually completed a deal. So that left a thought in the back of my mind: I always had the option of saying no.

The negotiations began officially on Monday, March 31, and took hours each day.

Unfortunately I allowed my personal pride to get in the way of good judgment. I started to resent what I thought was bad faith by the buyer and his team—specifically last-minute changes to terms I thought had been settled.

On Thursday evening, April 3, we agreed we had made enough progress that we needed to complete final drafts of the detailed legal terms and conditions of the final "buy-sell agreement." The two legal teams were up all night drafting.

The next morning I was told by the head of my legal team that the buyer had changed his position on several issues, including a significant reduction in the sales price. I lost my temper and accused the student playing the role of "buyer" of acting in bad faith.

At about 6:00 p.m. on April 4, I went off to another room with my legal team to read the agreement and to be ready to counter with a final sales price. I was tired. I was irritated. I saw the lower price and didn't consider the additional risks the buyer had absorbed in return. I was just pissed off. Not over facts. Or substance. Or money. (It wasn't real money anyway.) No, it was about pride.

Then at about 7:05 p.m., I heard a lot of noise—moaning and screams that seemed more in agony than anything else.

I came out of the room and saw most of the student body crowded into the student dining room, where there was a television set. I raced down the hall and heard *CBS News*' Walter Cronkite saying the words, "Dr. Martin Luther King has been shot, and he is dead."

Dr. King, we had learned from the first announcement, had been assassinated on the balcony of his small hotel, the Lorraine, in Memphis, Tennessee. Standing next to him and holding him in his arms as King lay dying was a young minister, the Reverend Jesse Jackson.

I couldn't breathe. I felt dizzy. Some students were tearful. I saw my fellow players in the negotiations exercise around the television set. The lead attorney on my team, a close friend, asked me if I was ready to sign. In light of the horrible tragedy of Dr. King's assassination, he said, "Why not forget about the differences and your anger and just sign the damn agreement so we could focus on the King tragedy?"

I don't know why I was so focused on my anger at what seemed to be disrespect. I can't imagine any reason why to this day. But I said no, I was not ready to sign. When the word among our buyer and seller teams spread that I was still not ready to sign, most of us walked down the hall, away from the TV set reporting on the King murder, and continued to argue about the terms of the written agreement and who was, or was not, acting in bad faith.

Instead of focusing on what was truly important—Martin Luther King's martyrdom—we were arguing about various legal terms or minor differences *over the sale price of a company that didn't actually exist.*

As the clock approached 8:00 p.m., almost an hour after the news of Dr. King's death was announced, someone thought about asking Professor Deutsch for an extension. But he could not be found. It was one minute to 8:00 p.m. It was now clear to me and everyone the time had come: Either I agree to sign, or all the work and effort goes down the drain. Once again, my lead lawyer and friend pulled me to the side and said, with intensity, "Sign the damn agreement."

But I took it all too personally. I lost all sense of perspective. And so I turned to the group and, to their disbelief, said, "No." Then I turned and walked out of the room. It was over.

■ ■ ■

The next morning Professor Deutsch heard different versions of the failure to reach an agreement, but all sides agreed on one thing: I acted like a jerk. He was too decent a person and too talented an educator to say anything unkind. I think he saw the painful experience as a "teachable moment."

"Remember, Lanny, the point of this exercise was to learn about the negotiation process, and especially for you to learn about yourselves and how you would react to the other party disappointing you or frustrating you at various times," he said. "You will someday learn lessons from what happened to you, and I assure you that you will be better off after you reflect on those lessons."

Despite the passage of so many years as these words are written, the poor behavior I exhibited, driven by ego and a lack of empathy for those who had participated in the exercise—especially my own "lawyers"—is painful.

I did learn lessons, as Professor Deutsch predicted. Not that I didn't make the same mistakes in business, politics, and life again because of anger and personalization of a bad moment or not following Atticus Finch's advice to put myself in other people's shoes.

Decades later, one of the top lawyers on the buyer's team, who had been most angry with me, passed me on a street in Washington, D.C. I said hello, and he walked by me. Maybe he didn't recognize me. Maybe he did and was still mad.

I wasn't angry with him. I was angry with myself—still, after all these years.

CHAPTER 13

# "HE WILL BE OUR GENERATION'S FIRST PRESIDENT. NO, SHE WILL BE."

In the autumn of 1970, after my Yale Law School graduation in May, I first heard the name Bill Clinton. I had decided to stay in New Haven until December, when my job as a speechwriter for the pending presidential campaign of Maine Senator Edmund Muskie would begin.

From the very start—literally before I met him—there was this buzz about Clinton as a "political comer" from Arkansas who just started law school after returning from the prestigious Rhodes Scholarship, two years at Oxford in the UK. I kept hearing his name during various visits with faculty at Yale College or hanging out at the *Yale Daily News*. I heard he had been freshman and sophomore class president at Georgetown University, with aspirations to return to his home state to run for governor someday. His name seemed to pop up whenever anyone was talking about politics, which was often in those days at Yale.

While waiting to start the Muskie job, I was also helping my old friend Joe Lieberman in his race in New Haven for the Democratic state senate nomination against an incumbent who had backed Lyndon

Johnson and supported the Vietnam War. One evening, I was told to expect a visit from Clinton at our local headquarters.

Joe had told me that Clinton aspired to be the first future president from our generation. I recall saying to myself, "Not likely." That distinction would go to someone else I had met the previous year. And it wasn't a "he." It was a "she."

Her name, of course: Hillary Rodham.

More than five decades later, my memory of meeting her for the first time (as I briefly described in the preface of this book already) in September 1969 is still vivid. I was standing in line to register for my last year at Yale Law when I turned around and recognized her.

I had read in a magazine about her commencement address at Wellesley College and seen the accompanying photograph. She had been selected to make the speech by her senior class. The speech was a brilliant analysis of the tumultuous and historic decade of the 1960s—with the assassinations of John F. Kennedy, the Reverend Martin Luther King Jr., and Robert F. Kennedy; urban riots; the counterculture and drugs; and the Vietnam War. These were the words I recall reading:

> *We arrived not yet knowing what was not possible. Consequently, we expected a lot. Our attitudes are easily understood having grown up, having come to consciousness in the first five years of this decade—years dominated by men with dreams, men in the Civil Rights Movement, the Peace Corps, the space program—so we arrived at Wellesley and we found, as all of us have found, that there was a gap between expectation and realities.*
>
> *But it wasn't a discouraging gap and it didn't turn us into cynical, bitter old women at the age of eighteen. It just inspired us to do something about that gap. What we did is often difficult for some people to understand. They ask us quite often: "Why, if you're dissatisfied, do you stay in a place?" Well, if you didn't*

> *care a lot about it, you wouldn't stay. It's almost as though my mother used to say, "You know I'll always love you, but there are times when I certainly won't like you." Our love for this place, this particular place, Wellesley College, coupled with our freedom from the burden of an inauthentic reality, allowed us to question basic assumptions underlying our education.*

*Wow,* I thought. *I have to meet this girl.*

And there she was, providentially, it seemed, standing behind me as we were waiting to register for classes. I introduced myself and asked her if she was Hillary Rodham. She seemed startled that I knew her name, so I told her, "I read your commencement speech last night, and it really spoke to me—and to all of our generation who experienced the last seven years. I think it is the best contemporaneous history of what we all went through that I have yet read."

She thanked me. I asked her if there was any advice I could give her about getting through her first semester—professors, academic pressures, reading cases, and so on. She thanked me again, said, "No, thank you," but added that she was interested in volunteering for legal services (an LBJ-era "Great Society" program setting up law offices where the poor could find a pro bono attorney).

"Do you know where the nearest clinic is?" she asked.

I was astonished. I did know where it was and had done some work there, but I immediately told her she needed to learn how to survive in law school, at least in her first semester, before doing volunteer work. She demurred. She said something like, "Oh, I will figure that out. But I came to law school because I want to do public service and am ready to get started."

I was struck by her passion. And sincerity. She wasn't trying to impress me—or anyone else. She meant it.

I told her where the clinic was and reoffered to help her if she needed my advice and expressed hope we could spend some time together talking about politics and the future. She nodded and thanked me again, and I turned to register. When I was done and walked away, I turned, and she looked up as she was beginning to register. I waved, and she waved back. I walked away and then looked back at her again.

I thought, *I have just probably met the first likely president of the United States from our 1960s generation. Also, the likely first female president.*

■ ■ ■

I was on the phone when Clinton first appeared at Lieberman headquarters and introduced himself by saying "Hi, y'all" in a soft Southern drawl. I shook his hand and waved to him to sit at a table with about a dozen volunteers and help stuff envelopes for a mailing to primary voters.

My first impression of him was that he didn't look like a future president: He was tall, bearded, and somewhat long-haired. When I finished my phone conversation, I turned around to talk to him.

Instead of sitting at the table, there he was, standing and surrounded by all the volunteers, talking. No one was stuffing envelopes! All these young people were looking up at him, literally, men and women alike. All of them were—I swear it seemed to me at first glance—leaning into him. It was as if they were mesmerized—that was the word that occurred to me. I also noticed that he would slowly stop and talk to one person at a time, then move to talk to another. As he talked to that person, it seemed that he made them feel like they were the only person in the room. I thought, *No doubt, this is a special talent.*

When I stood up, he noticed and broke off, appearing a little embarrassed at distracting everyone from their envelope stuffing. We chatted a little about his early experiences in law school and his political interests. He told me about his time at Georgetown University, and when I asked him if he had been politically active, I had to pull it out of him that he had been elected class president.

Fast-forward about four years, and I heard he was running for Congress—the same year I first ran for a congressional seat myself in Montgomery County, Maryland, a suburb of Washington, D.C.

We both lost, but instead of running for Congress again as I did, Clinton ran for Arkansas attorney general in 1976, won the Democratic primary, and then was unopposed in the general election. He was only thirty years old at the time and a statewide officeholder. He won his first term as governor of Arkansas in 1978 and lost reelection in 1980.

In 1990 Alvin "Al" From, a friend of mine from the Muskie campaign days and someone who helped me in my congressional campaign, called to tell me that Clinton had accepted the position, while serving as governor, to chair the Democratic Leadership Council (DLC). The DLC was a centrist group Al and some others had formed to bolster the moderate Democrats in the Senate and House worried about the Democratic Party's overshift to the left.

That drift, which progressives tended to ignore, deny, or attribute unconvincingly to "messaging" problems, had resulted in landslide presidential campaign losses in 1972, 1980, 1984, and 1988. Those were the headwinds any Democrat would face in 1992, and I thought the DLC was a perfect fit for Clinton. Before he was formally a candidate, the DLC post would afford him a platform to travel and speak throughout the country and present his special blend of progressive views on issues while reaching out to Republicans and moderates as he had done as governor.

Clinton called to tell me he was about to announce that he was running for president and invited me to come to Little Rock for the announcement, but I couldn't make it. Then I heard from Hillary. I told her I would certainly support Bill when the time came, but I wanted to hold off on any official endorsement or involvement for a while since I was an automatic voting delegate as a DNC member (sometimes called a "superdelegate").

In the early fall of 1991, I attended a "coffee klatch" (a morning get-together for coffee and pastries in which a candidate or their surrogates would speak about the issues) in Bethesda, Maryland, with Hillary as a guest speaking on behalf of her husband's presidential candidacy. After a great hug and hello, I introduced her to Carolyn. I worried a bit when I saw them huddled off by themselves, talking and laughing, and I remembered worrying, *Were they exchanging "Lanny stories" and discussing the challenges of being married to me?* As we left, Hillary asked me if I was ready to "commit" to Bill with my automatic delegate vote, which would be helpful for them to tout. I told her I would be there at some point but would probably wait for the convention the following summer.

On December 15, 1991, that changed. I attended a debate of all the Democratic candidates on the stage at the Kennedy Center theater. The place was packed. The other candidates on the stage were all excellent, and I could have supported any of them: Nebraska Senator Bob Kerrey, a friend of the now-deceased Al Lowenstein; Iowa Senator Tom Harkin, whom I admired for his steadfast concern for working people and the less fortunate;* and former Massachusetts Senator Paul Tsongas, decidedly moderate to conservative in his economic policy views, which I appreciated.

But I was simply dazzled by Bill Clinton that night. This was the first time I had really seen him as a candidate—at work, so to speak. I decided, then and there, that there was no reason to delay supporting him and, moreover, that I wanted to work to get him elected president. His answers to questions were simple but also subtle. He could explain an issue without talking down to people. The charisma and personal warmth I had seen that night at Lieberman headquarters translated to the big stage. It was clear to me that he was a star in the making, the best our party had to offer—and the candidate who offered the strongest chance for Democrats to capture the White House.

As I left the Kennedy Center, I literally bumped into a young Democratic Party aide whom I had known for several years who had signed

* On July 13, 1990, Harkin made history by introducing the Americans with Disabilities Act in a floor speech in which he employed American Sign Language—as a gesture of solicitude for his deaf brother.

onto the Clinton campaign. His name was George Stephanopoulos. I told George to tell Clinton I had decided to work for him. I asked George where Clinton was staying, and George told me. I phoned when I got home and left a message with the hotel operator.

At about midnight the phone rang. Carolyn picked up, annoyed, and heard someone say, "Sorry it's so late. This is Bill Clinton. May I speak to Lanny?"

As she handed me the phone, thinking it was someone else joking with us, she said to me loud enough for the person on the phone to hear, "Some asshole who claims to be Bill Clinton is on the phone. Tell him not to call so late."

As it turned out, of course, it *was* Bill Clinton. He apologized for calling so late but was responding to my message. We talked for a few minutes, and I told him how impressed I was with his performance at the debate that night and that I was ready to commit my superdelegate vote as a DNC member and automatic delegate to the convention that summer. He was happy and invited me to attend a Q and A session at the Mayflower Hotel the next day, which would be attended by members of Congress and other think tank leaders.

I went and was once again taken with the combination of his brilliant command of the issues and his ability to translate them into simple, easily understood facts and reasoning. He could appeal to centrists and even conservatives—just what I knew the party needed.

Fast-forward again to 1993 or 1994. Clinton was now president of the United States. Carolyn and I attended our first-ever reception at the White House for a "music" event in the East Room.

As Carolyn and I went through the receiving line, I realized this would be the first time she would have a chance to meet Clinton in person and the first time they'd spoken since the midnight phone call. Carolyn wondered whether Clinton would mention what she had said when she handed me the phone. I didn't think so, but I was wrong.

When I introduced him to Carolyn, he smiled, shook her hand, and asked, "Aren't you the one who called me an asshole?"

She laughed, the president laughed, and I was relieved. I thought, *Who else but Bill Clinton could have gotten through this moment this effortlessly? Who could so easily charm a person who had called him an asshole?*

Little did I know that about five years later, I would be on television and on the phone from early morning into the wee hours virtually non-stop for almost eleven months trying to help Bill Clinton avoid impeachment. But that is a story for another chapter.

CHAPTER 14

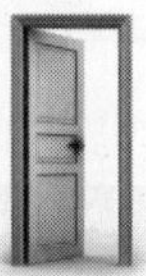

# EDMUND MUSKIE PAYS THE PRICE DEMANDED BY PURISTS

On the eve of the 1970 midterm elections, the senior staff of Connecticut Democratic U.S. Senate nominee Joe Duffey gathered in a Hartford hotel room.

The Duffey campaign became a lightning rod, a magnet for antiwar "politico" liberal activists in the Al Lowenstein mold. He rejected the politics of confrontation and alienation and was a great supporter of Lowenstein's approach. Duffey was a congregationalist minister who seemed to have broad appeal even in centrist political circles with his quiet, moral-based, eloquent opposition to the Vietnam War. Born in a small working-class town in West Virginia, he also seemed better able to connect with moderate or conservative working-class voters than most liberals.

These were the kind of voters we hoped, as in 1968 in the Robert Kennedy campaign, would be supportive of opposition to the Vietnam War while still voting for someone who understood their conservative instincts on cultural and religious issues.

We and much of the rest of the country were concerned that the overt demagoguery of the incumbent president, Richard Nixon, might be working, using the slogan "law and order" as code words for urban crime and fear. Nixon was following the playbook of Alabama Governor George Wallace's 1968 presidential campaign, using the same racist dog whistles to frighten middle-of-the-road voters from both parties.

The television was on, and a close-up shot revealed a face that evoked Abraham Lincoln. He was the U.S. senator from Maine, Edmund S. Muskie. When he started speaking, the room suddenly quieted. His eyes were steady, and his voice was deep and resonant.

In 1968 Muskie had run as the vice presidential candidate to the Democratic nominee, then Vice President Hubert H. Humphrey. Humphrey was often interrupted and prevented from speaking by anti–Vietnam War protests (since Humphrey, as Lyndon Johnson's vice president, was naturally associated with Johnson's unpopular Vietnam War policies). Muskie caught national attention when he invited a representative of the antiwar protesters to come to the stage to speak in return for their allowing him to speak.

Those of us in the "political process" wing of the anti–Vietnam War movement took notice. It was consistent with what we'd learned from Lowenstein—the only way we were going to take back the government and end the war was by civility toward middle America, not disruption and confrontation. Muskie seemed to be a liberal-centrist but was also willing to listen to dissenters on the left. Here was a Democratic Party voice who was reassuring, steady, and articulate.

The "Muskie election eve speech" became part of our generation's political lexicon. It was written by Richard Goodwin, one of President Kennedy's speechwriters. Here is its most memorable passage, which propelled Muskie into front-runner status for the 1972 Democratic nomination against Nixon:

> *[T]here are those who seek to turn our common distress [of crime and violence] to partisan advantage—not by offering better solutions, but with empty threats and malicious slander.*

> *They imply that Democratic candidates for high office in Texas and California, in Illinois and Tennessee, in Utah and Maryland, and among my New England neighbors from Vermont and Connecticut—men who have courageously pursued their convictions in the service of the Republic in war and in peace—that these men actually favor violence . . . and champion the wrongdoer.*
>
> *That is a lie.*
>
> *And the American people know it is a lie.*

My immediate thought was, *This is the liberal-leaning centrist who can beat Richard Nixon. This is who we need in 1972, not a candidate who will appeal to the purists in the left-wing base of our party but will end up losing to Nixon in a landslide.* Sadly, I was right.

The split in the liberal movement that Lowenstein first described and was exemplified in the 1968 McCarthy-Kennedy campaigns and anti–Vietnam War movements also evolved in the Muskie-McGovern contest for the 1972 Democratic nomination.

The "purists" who most opposed Lowenstein's approach were students and liberal activists supporting South Dakota Senator George McGovern. McGovern defined himself more clearly than any other Democrat as favoring an immediate withdrawal from Vietnam and speaking of the war in moral and political terms. On the other side, there were those who also opposed the war but followed the Lowenstein approach of looking for support in the center-left and center-right.

The people working for Muskie weren't well known at the time, but they later became a huge force in Democratic Party politics. The roster included Joe Lieberman; the Podesta brothers, Tony and Joe, both destined to play prominent roles in the Clinton White House and future Clinton campaigns (for both Bill and Hillary); Michael Medved, who became one of the leading conservative talk show hosts in the 2000s; and Larry Kudlow, who served as President Trump's chairman of economic advisers.

My children used to get sick of my saying to them over the years, "I met him/her in the Muskie campaign." They would often sarcastically respond, "Dad, is there anyone on the entire planet who did *not* work on the Muskie campaign?" (Two of my friends did not: Bill and Hillary decided to support McGovern instead.)

The morning after the Muskie election eve speech, I called Don Nicoll, Muskie's top aide, whom I had first talked to in the spring of 1970. I had written an anti–Vietnam War speech for then New Haven Mayor Dick Lee for the New Haven Vietnam "Moratorium" demonstration on the New Haven Green. Nicoll had told me he liked the speech and wondered if I was interested in coming to Washington, D.C., to be a speechwriter for Muskie.

I said yes on the spot, turning down several other offers to work for Wall Street, law firms, a local New Haven U.S. District Court judge, or as a lawyer for the D.C.-based U.S. Civil Rights Commission. All I wanted was to be part of a presidential campaign that stood a chance of ousting Richard Nixon and ending the war. In my opinion Muskie was the most "electable" candidate in our party, a man who could appeal to the center.

My ultimate dream was to work in the White House for a Democratic president, at the center of American history and policy. I was ecstatic. The salary Nicoll offered me was, I think, about $9,000 per year—far less than the Wall Street law firm offers I had received. Nonetheless, within weeks, in early December, my wife and I and our two young children, Marlo and Seth, were driving to Washington, D.C.

■ ■ ■

Muskie had problems as a candidate, for sure. Most importantly, he needed a clear and concise message establishing him as a critic of the Vietnam War and supporting a negotiated withdrawal. He feared a "unilateral" withdrawal, to use the vernacular back then in the mainstream media to indicate an extreme position by the Democratic left. Although

Muskie had come to believe that U.S. military involvement in Vietnam was a terrible mistake—both morally and practically, because the war could not be won—he also believed it would not be easy to get out of Vietnam quickly. At the very least, there needed to be a negotiated exit ensuring that U.S. soldiers would be able to leave without risking their lives as their numbers dwindled. He also often pointed out in speeches and in private that, as a point of honor, the United States owed those South Vietnamese who had put themselves at risk by aligning with or helping the United States, even just as translators, the opportunity to escape before the North Vietnamese took over.

Finally, there was the difficult matter of American prisoners of war being held in barbaric conditions in North Vietnam.

Muskie's thoughtful approach had no appeal for the antiwar base of the Democratic Party. McGovern cosponsored a resolution with Republican Senator Mark Hatfield, setting a hard deadline of the end of 1971 for total withdrawal of all U.S. forces. Muskie's position made him a stronger general election candidate against Nixon for the same reason it weakened him in his bid to capture the nomination.

A campaign slogan that emerged on bumper stickers and in the media—"Trust Muskie," a result of the November 1970 election eve speech and the frequent references to his "Lincolnesque" appearance—only highlighted the fuzziness of his message as contrasted with McGovern's.

When I arrived in Washington in December 1970, I saw my role in the campaign as trying to bridge the gap between Muskie's centrist support and the primary voters on the left who were for McGovern. When Lowenstein asked me to invite Muskie to attend an April 1971 "Dump Nixon" rally (one of many Lowenstein planned), I went to the campaign leadership with the argument that this would be a high-profile way of proving that he cared about the antiwar base of the Democratic Party, even if they did not prefer him over McGovern. They agreed. I called Lowenstein to tell him the answer was yes, and he put out a press release that Muskie had agreed to attend.

A couple of weeks later, I was horrified to learn that Muskie had vetoed the decision. He told his campaign staff he did not want to attend, predicting the audience would not possibly be positive and the appearance might alienate his more conservative, prowar supporters in organized labor and elected officials still loyal to President Johnson.

I asked for a chance to talk to Muskie myself in his Senate office to persuade him to attend the rally. He was gracious and listened to my arguments that he needed to show the young antiwar students that he was against the war and cared about them. Finally, he agreed. I called Lowenstein back and got his commitment that Muskie would be the first speaker at the rally and that he could leave early. I sent Muskie that message and was told he was happy to hear that would be the case. As it turned out, Muskie's instinct not to go to the Lowenstein rally was vindicated, and I turned out to be wrong on three counts.

For starters, I could not keep my promise to Muskie that he would get to speak first at the rally and then be able to leave. The night before the rally, I was informed that the advance man for one of Muskie's other Democratic opponents for the nomination, Indiana Senator Birch Bayh, had secretly gone to the printer where the program was being printed and changed the order of speaking, putting Bayh first and Muskie second.

When I saw the program, I was outraged. I went to Lowenstein to protest and threatened to call Muskie and tell him not to show up. Al convinced me that it would become a big media story if Muskie canceled at the last minute and that it wouldn't be a big deal if he spoke second. I swallowed hard and acquiesced.

When Muskie arrived the next day and I told him the unhappy news that he would be speaking after Bayh, he growled at me but seemed okay when I assured him that he would speak second and then could still leave early. It didn't make my situation any better when I learned later that Bayh, after his speech, walked by Muskie and whispered something to the effect of "Gotcha on that one—we got the order of speaking changed last night."

Even worse was Bayh's vow at the end of his speech before Muskie was introduced. He promised to support the Hatfield-McGovern resolution to withdraw from Vietnam completely by year's end. It earned him a rousing ovation.

Second, Muskie's comments about a scheduled withdrawal fell flat with the audience. He reminded the crowd of young people who despised Lyndon Johnson, whom they openly called a war criminal, that he came "to challenge policies, not personalities." He praised the "brave men" killed in the war, and apparently referring to the danger of a hasty withdrawal, he warned, "We cannot add to the honor we do them by risking other lives in their names." While he added his opposition to increasing the "tonnage" of the bombing of North Vietnam or "widening the war into other countries," he was greeted by silence in some places and boos in others.

After Muskie left, casting a dark look at me, indicating how unhappy he was that I had persuaded him to come, I then made a third mistake. This one I had great difficulty living down and almost cost me my job in the Muskie campaign. I was supposed to be in New Hampshire the next day to debate a McGovern supporter at the University of New Hampshire in Durham. R. W. "Johnny" Apple Jr., a famous *New York Times* political reporter who had covered the Providence rally, offered to give me a ride to New Hampshire. I was happy to accept. Not only was I a great admirer of Apple, but I also thought it would be interesting to talk with him during the two-hour drive. I fancied that I could help shape his story about Muskie's speech in a more positive direction.

Not yet sophisticated enough to set ground rules with Apple, I never even raised the issue that our conversation should be off the record. I just hoped he would write a story about Muskie's courage to appear in front of an audience that he knew was not favorable to him and that he had shown he cared about young people and their concerns about the war. But when I read his story in the *Times* the next day, I was horrified.

He referred to the negative reaction of some in the crowd, including a sign held up by one young spectator, "The Nixons and Muskies are all alike." Apple also wrote that "younger members of the Muskie staff" had "persuaded the Senator that he must come" to the Providence rally or write off any possibility of support from the young, and they were worried that "Mr. Lowenstein, who travels widely on college campuses, would 'bad-mouth' Mr. Muskie if he failed to appear."

The story made it sound as if young campaign staffers were taking credit for changing Muskie's mind rather than crediting Muskie for the courage to appear at the rally. I knew that the plural "members" was not accurate and that everyone would know I was the source of Apple's reference. When the campaign manager called me that morning and asked me if I was the source, I said yes.

He surprised me when he said that he understood that my intentions were right and that the idea was good.

I felt a bit better after Tony Podesta, Muskie's New Hampshire campaign manager, cheered me up by telling me he thought the story was helpful since it reminded New Hampshire primary voters, who were substantially opposed to the Vietnam War, that Muskie cared about going to an antiwar rally even though he expected a nonpositive response.

Yet as the perceived "front-runner" for the party nomination, Muskie was a sitting duck for negative media. Without a crisp message, it was inevitable that the "Trust Muskie" slogan was going to be mocked in the press. But more serious were the frequent stories from anonymous sources that Muskie had a "temper" problem. One story, which made the rounds quickly, was that he had gotten so mad one day that he had torn the telephone out of the wall and thrown it across the room. (There were no cell phones to toss in those days.)

The temper issue morphed into broader concerns "about temperament" in many analytical pieces in the newspapers. That may be one of the several reasons why the infamous "crying incident" became so pivotal in changing Muskie's fortunes, leading to the downward spiral that ended his candidacy in the late spring of 1972. All this seems quaint in the time of Trump, but it was quite real at the time and quite significant.

For most of the 1971 campaign, the *Manchester Union Leader*, New Hampshire's largest newspaper and the mouthpiece of notorious right-wing publisher William Loeb, had filled its front pages with blaring anti-Muskie headlines about almost everything. That is why an incident on February 26, 1972, in which Muskie appeared to choke up with tears, got so blown up by the media. Loeb had referred to Muskie's wife, Jane, as a "lush," which inflamed Muskie—as it should have. He insisted on confronting Loeb publicly at a live press event outside the offices of the *Union Leader.*

David Broder of *The Washington Post*, one of the leading political reporters of the time, set the press narrative.

> *MANCHESTER, N.H.—With tears streaming down his face and his voice choked with emotion, Senator Edmund Muskie (D., Maine) stood in the snow outside the Manchester Union Leader this morning and accused its publisher of making vicious attacks on him and his wife, Jane.*

Other news outlets covered it similarly. And though I understand the challenges of doing consummate political writing on deadline, and specifically held Broder in high regard, in this case, the press got it wrong. I was there and was within ten feet of Muskie in front of the flatbed truck where he stood. Muskie was certainly angry, denouncing Loeb's cowardice for attacking his wife. And it was true that, at times, his anger seemed to cause him to halt—some would say "choke"—on his words. But he was not crying. Even Broder subsequently admitted that what he saw as tears might have been snowflakes melting down Muskie's cheeks, as the television network shots clearly showed he was speaking in blizzardlike conditions.

But once the "tears streaming down his face" phrase spread across the nation's three main TV news networks, which influenced about 90 percent of the viewing public each night, the term "crying incident" became the phrase that repeatedly harmed Muskie. It crystallized the preexisting perception among the media cognoscenti regarding his problems with temper and temperament.

A more graphic lesson for me about how media spin can sometimes be more determinative of political fortunes than facts was the reaction of the national political media after the 1972 New Hampshire presidential primary. Any candidate who wins a multicandidate primary with five candidates by a nine-point margin (in this case, Muskie defeated McGovern 46 percent–37 percent) would have the right to claim a major victory, and the media could have treated it that way.

Instead, the media emphasized the fact that Muskie came from a nearby New England state and inflated the expectations for him. They had been writing a narrative of Muskie's "weakness" or "slippage" compared with McGovern, so the fact that Muskie won by such a solid margin was completely lost. A visitor from Mars would have read the media reports and concluded that Muskie had *lost* the primary, not won.

Of course, it didn't help when Muskie's New Hampshire campaign chairman stated ahead of time that she would "kill herself" if Muskie did not win more than 50 percent of the vote. I was with Maria Carrier, the lady who uttered that quote, the night Muskie beat McGovern by nine percentage points and the media headlined the win as a loss. Thankfully, Maria did not keep her promise. She did blame herself for the media's curious spin.

Everything went downhill after New Hampshire. When McGovern won Wisconsin decisively, that was just about it for Muskie. A few months later, after Muskie lost in Pennsylvania, the campaign was over. McGovern went on to win the nomination, delighting the antiwar base of the Democratic Party. They stayed delighted all the way through the general election until the last few days when they realized that Nixon was about to win in a landslide.

Not only did Nixon win with a historic 23.2 percent margin—60.7 percent to McGovern's 37.5 percent—but he also won the popular vote by over eighteen million votes and carried forty-nine out of fifty states. I went home and decided to write a book to try to understand a mainstream media press corps that depicted winning as losing if their "expectations" (or predisposed narratives) were not met.

I worried about my fellow liberals who shared 99 percent of my views on the issues choosing ideological purism over coalition-building compromises. It also worried me that there was a lack of regrets or second thoughts among my liberal friends who chose McGovern over Muskie. Whether Muskie would have defeated Nixon is doubtful. But at the very least, there is little doubt that Muskie would have won more votes and states than McGovern. How could he not?

My book was submitted to the publisher with the title *Lessons and Legacies from the New Politics*. But the editors changed the title to *The Emerging Democratic Majority* because, in my last chapter, I pointed to encouraging signs of liberal wins at the state and local level beneath Nixon's landslide victory. The marketing department also wanted me to take advantage of *The Emerging Republican Majority*, a big seller from the conservative side, written after the 1968 campaign by Nixon staffer Kevin Phillips.*

It was Phillips's thesis that, with George Wallace's votes combined with the Nixon Republican vote, the Republicans would have an enduring "conservative" majority. It certainly seemed that way after the results of the 1972 election. But I wrote my book to challenge that thesis—on the naive belief that the Republican suburbs would become increasingly liberal, as seen in the election of progressive Democrats in the 1972 congressional, state, and local elections.

* Phillips dedicated the book to the "two principal architects" of the majority he predicted: Nixon and Attorney General John M. Mitchell.

There was some evidence I would have been proven right but for the setbacks of Jimmy Carter after his narrow post-Watergate victory in 1976 over Gerald Ford. But President Carter suffered the misfortune of the Iran hostage crisis and an economy featuring double-digit inflation and unemployment. And after the landslide victories of Ronald Reagan in 1980 and 1984 and the comfortable win by George H. W. Bush in 1988, it certainly seemed that my original thesis about the Muskie versus McGovern split in the Democratic Party—with purists on the left causing the Democrats to lose touch with the great center that wins general elections—was borne out.

Until Bill Clinton embraced a "New Democrat" philosophy of the center-left and center-right to win the 1992 election, the Democrats certainly seemed to be facing a wasteland of an enduring Republican conservative majority. Although not many people read *The Emerging Democratic Majority* and it became a punch line in my marital saga, it was my first book, and I was proud of it.

As I write my last book fifty years later, I have reread the introduction to that first book by Iowa Senator Harold Hughes, an early Muskie supporter. His words are relevant to today's progressive base of the Democratic Party, which often prefers to lose while fighting with moderates and conservatives rather than accept something less than perfect. And I think of Al Lowenstein and the lessons he taught me. Here is what Hughes wrote:

> *Coalition-building is the imperative of the American political process. America is a nation of widely diverse people from different backgrounds and perspectives. The political coalition is the best—perhaps the only—instrument available in a democracy to unite people who disagree on some issues but are willing to work together nonetheless on others . . .*
>
> *Underlying all of what Lanny Davis has written is a wholesome faith in the decency of the electorate and in the capacity*

> *of the American people to change and grow and work together despite their differences.*

I have been through some political wars myself, and some of the stars of yesteryear have faded from my eyes, but I share this view wholeheartedly.

CHAPTER 15

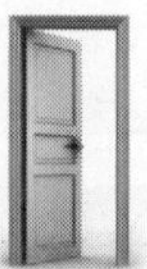

# A FUNNY THING HAPPENED ON MY WAY TO CONGRESS

In late 1972 I overcame my resistance to beginning a career as a lawyer in a large Washington, D.C., law firm. With four-year-old Marlo and two-year-old Seth in tow, Elaine and I moved from Prince George's County, Maryland, to a small house in Montgomery County—a place with good schools but high real estate prices. With help from my parents and Elaine's (and from the government in the form of an FHA loan requiring only a 10 percent down payment), we moved in the spring of 1973 into a small house just outside Silver Spring.

As it turned out, I wasn't done with politics.

Shortly after we moved to Montgomery County, a friend of mine from the Muskie campaign—a young attorney named Michael Barnes—called me. He was a prominent Maryland Democrat (and a future five-term congressman). Mike knew of my political ambitions and my desire to get involved in local county politics. He introduced me to many elected and Democratic Party officials at various social occasions. He got me appointed to a "party reform" committee, where I met other leaders and helped forge a compromise on the presidential delegate selection process between the "reformer" and "party regular" factions.

Mike told me the "buzz" was that I was a "good compromiser" (when that was still considered a virtue in American politics) and that I was being referred to by some as "future comer." But it was also true that I had just moved into the county, and no one knew me other than a handful of Democrats and a few neighbors.

Being relatively anonymous changed instantly on August 2, 1973, when I was mentioned by name in a *Washington Post* article written by the famed Watergate reporting duo Bob Woodward and Carl Bernstein. They wrote that I had been included on the White House "enemies list" presumably assembled by Charles "Chuck" Colson, Richard Nixon's notorious political hatchet man.

It made me a minor celebrity in my family and circle of friends. "Mazel tov!" my mother shouted over the phone. "We're so proud of you," added my father. "You made the list!"

Family acclaim is one thing. But it helped me professionally too.

I was amazed at how much a single news article identifying me as a Nixon adversary elevated me in the eyes of the Montgomery County Democratic Party leadership. I was immediately offered up as a sacrificial lamb to run against Representative Gilbert Gude, the popular liberal Republican incumbent. Republicans abided Gude, and local Democrats loved to vote for a liberal Republican to show their presumed political independence.

Gude seemed virtually unbeatable. He had won his previous six elections by double-digit margins, despite the Democrats having a two-to-one party registration advantage, and the gap between him and the hapless Democratic challenger grew larger each time he ran. (His opponent two years before, in 1970, was none other than my future law partner, Thomas Hale Boggs Jr., son of the Democratic House majority leader at the time.)

A member of the Democratic Central Committee named A. Wesley Barthelmes Jr. also urged me to run.* Wes said to me, "If you think you can't win, you have to meet my new boss, Joe Biden, the new senator from Delaware." (Wes had recently been hired to serve as Biden's "administrative assistant"—the functional equivalent in today's parlance of chief of staff.)

Biden, too, Wes told me, was told by everyone he couldn't beat the venerable Republican incumbent, J. Caleb Boggs. No Democrat wanted to run against Boggs. So Biden, a twenty-nine-year-old councilman from the small town of New Castle, Delaware, was—like me—asked to be the sacrificial lamb.

He was more than thirty points behind in the summer before the November 1972 election, with no money—just energy. No one thought he had a chance, except for his wife and indefatigable sister Val, who was running his campaign. Joe won by fewer than four thousand votes on election day, Nov. 7, 1972. He wouldn't turn thirty, the constitutional required age to be a U.S. senator, until November 20.

About a month after Joe's amazing victory, his wife, Neilia, and thirteen-month-old daughter, Naomi, were killed in a terrible car accident while Christmas shopping. So, when I walked into his office with Wes to meet Biden, I think in October 1973, I felt awkward about talking about my political campaign when I knew he was still deep in grief.

Joe was excited to give advice to someone else about politics. He knew all about my "hopeless" campaign and immediately told me to ignore all the pessimists the way he did. He reached into his desk and showed me his "key" to the upset victory: a huge tabloid-sized newspaper, about eight pages in length, with a big picture of the handsome young Biden on the front page. I don't remember the exact language of the headline, but it

---

* Barthelmes, who had been a Washington newspaperman for fourteen years before entering politics, also died before his time. Although he'd survived being dropped behind enemy lines as a U.S. Army paratrooper on D-Day, Wes couldn't beat the brain tumor doctors found in 1976. He was fifty-four years old, and his passing was a great loss to this nation.

was something like: "Time for new energy and change in Washington" (I am making that up, but it was pretty close to that).

"You see, Lanny," Joe said. "People throw away fancy campaign brochures. But they like to read newspapers. I used to love looking back and seeing people turning the pages and actually reading." His enthusiasm was infectious.

With Joe's example as inspiration, I agreed to do it but only after being assured there would be no real opposition in the primary. If I was going to be a sacrificial lamb, I didn't want to run in an expensive and divisive primary on my way to the slaughterhouse. Also, although I knew I would lose, I thought it would be helpful in the future to have run.

While working on the Muskie campaign, I'd always thought, *If I ran, I would learn from their mistakes.* If I lost, I couldn't blame them, only myself. In short, I had to get this out of my system—and in a race where no one, including myself, expected me to win. Instead, my decision to run would put me in a competitive primary where I would make enemies and where the negative perception of me as "overambitious" took root.

■ ■ ■

For starters, I underestimated the fallout from being labeled as a "carpetbagger" who ran for Congress from a district I'd lived in for less than a year. Members of the local media kidded me that I didn't even know where Gaithersburg was, and they were sort of right. Although I had already committed to running a serious campaign and not embarrassing the county officials, I still had to answer a big question: How do I begin when I knew fewer than a dozen people in the entire county?

I began by making a list of ten or so names that were familiar and called and asked each one to hold a coffee klatch for me. The average turnout of each of these was five to ten people. I would have been discouraged, but Joe Biden had told me that if I could get one person or a couple of folks among those attendees to hold another coffee klatch and keep repeating that pattern for a few months, do the math: ten-by-ten-by-ten and so on. The numbers would start to build up.

Following Al Lowenstein's practice when he ran for Congress, I found a few high school teachers who attended these small events and asked if they would invite me to speak to their classes. Maybe the principal would allow me to give a nonpolitical speech at a student assembly on the importance of getting involved in politics. Eventually I made that speech many times to many student assemblies. My favorite line, which was borrowed from Lowenstein, was after asking the assembled students to raise their hands if they were interested in pursuing a career in politics.

I received the expected no response or even laughter. Then I delivered the punch line, which almost always received applause.

"So if the best and brightest people of your generation ridicule anyone who decides to get into politics and run for office, when you become adults, who will be left to run your lives?"

After a month or so, I found that I had gone from ten friends to some one thousand volunteers dropping our campaign's tabloid newspaper on doorsteps every weekend, à la Joe Biden, with a huge photo of me on the cover and a large bold headline:

"Lanny Davis: New Energy, New Leadership for Montgomery County."

Everyone in the local party was pleased I was running and expanding the number of people involved in politics. No one criticized me, and the media ignored me. I was happy. But then came a surprise.

Just before the filing deadline in May 1974, my phone rang. It was Marvin Mandel, the governor of Maryland and a fellow Democrat. He cut the pleasantries short and got right to the point.

"Lanny, we have decided that Sidney Kramer will be our congressional nominee in Montgomery County to avoid his taking on an incumbent state senator," Mandel said. "He has agreed. So you need to drop out, and I will name you as chairman of my reelection campaign in the county."

I didn't know who Sid Kramer was. I checked him out, and he seemed to be widely respected as a businessman and loyal Democrat who served on the county council. His wife, Betty Mae, was a beloved longtime Democratic precinct official. He had agreed not to challenge their area's incumbent state senator in the Maryland legislature only after Governor Mandel had promised he would have no opposition to become the party's nominee to run against Congressman Gude.

Of course, Mandel made that promise before talking to me.

Instead of being a loyal soldier and recognizing that I was a newcomer and should not challenge the governor or run in a primary against his chosen candidate, I was not ready to roll over—at least not that easily. I surprised the governor by saying I needed time to think about it.

I called a meeting of all my volunteers to ask what they thought. I was shocked that more than five hundred people turned out, most of them high school students who had been going door-to-door for me. Many stood up and asked me if I was going to "sell out" after all the promises I had made about the need to create a "new generation of leadership."

Then one of my key supporters, an older lady and veteran of Montgomery County politics named Rita Federman, stood up at the end of the painful meeting and summed up the feeling in the room: "You are betraying all of us by doing this deal."

*Betraying us*. That was it for me.

The next day I called the governor back. His assistant said she would take a message. I told her to tell the governor, "Thank you, but no, thank you—I intend to continue to run in the primary." Just like that, I went from being a sacrificial lamb giving myself up for the team to a local pariah. The same party leaders who pleaded with me to run against Gilbert Gude now described me as being "too ambitious" and "not a team player." The governor, party leaders and officials, and Councilman Kramer were all against me now.

I ended up losing the primary to Sid Kramer by a narrow margin, but that narrow margin was not a good thing for me. I was told that Sid was humiliated because he hadn't won by a substantial margin over a virtually unknown carpetbagger. Moreover, during one of our debates in the closing days of the campaign, I'd alienated Sid on a personal level. When he was hesitant while answering a question on a complicated foreign policy issue, I jumped in and gave a better answer. (I had studied the issue during the Muskie campaign.) But then I couldn't resist adding, "Maybe Mr. Kramer isn't ready to run for Congress and to address national issues."

It came out harsher than I intended, and I noticed that the dig stung his wife and three children, who were in the audience. After the debate, Sid said to me quietly, "You didn't need to do that in front of my family."

He was right.

Two years later I paid the price when I ran again. I knew I had to eventually bring closure to the wounds I had caused Sid. I didn't know that it would take another ten years for that to happen.

■ ■ ■

I decided to run again in 1976. This time I assumed no one would run against me for the Democratic Party nomination. Who else would want it? Gude had defeated Kramer in a landslide, and I had a grassroots organization of volunteers left over from the 1974 primary that was ready to be reactivated. I had continued going to every high school and class that would have me. By late 1975 I had hundreds of high school teachers working for me, as well as hundreds of their students. Just as importantly, the students' parents thought favorably of me because I had motivated their children to work on a political campaign rather than getting into trouble.

Again following the advice of Joe Biden, I created a new series of tabloids, with each focused on different issues, but all of them had two things in common: The first was the huge front-page photo and headline about "New Energy, New Leadership." The second was photos of me and important national elected officials such as Muskie and Senator Abraham Ribicoff, with quotes describing me and my work for them in positive terms. I was careful not to change the quotes, and I never used the word "endorse." I didn't think of calling Ribicoff at the time to get permission to use the photo again. I didn't think there was any need. The personal comments about me were true in 1974 and were still applicable in 1976.

Or so I thought. Anyway, I was having fun, making speeches, talking about issues, and meeting new people, and no one seemed angry with me. Everything was going well. The May 4, 1976, primary was about two months away, and we were already planning our general election campaign.

One of my favorite Broadway musicals was titled *A Funny Thing Happened on the Way to the [Roman] Forum*. In my case a not-so-funny thing happened on the way to my unopposed Democratic primary. I was in Miami Beach, Florida, visiting my retired parents when the telephone rang. It was my campaign manager, Rita Federman.

"Hello, Congressman Davis," she said.

"Very funny," I remember saying. "And a little optimistic."

"What, you haven't heard the news?"

"What news? I am in Miami Beach, remember? You just called me here."

"The news is that Gilbert Gude just announced he is not running again. And you are going to be our nominee and our next congressman!"

It took me a minute or two to digest that sentence.

"Are you serious? I mean, about Gude dropping out? Why did he?"

"He offered no explanation. What he didn't say is that 'I am dropping out because I know I can't beat Lanny Davis.'"

But not so fast. Within a week four Democrats who served in the Maryland legislature declared their candidacies, along with one very famous national political celebrity: Frank Mankiewicz, who had been Robert Kennedy's press secretary during the senator's tragic presidential campaign. Mankiewicz was seared into the consciousness of Democratic Party activists when he announced on live television the death of Senator Kennedy twenty-six hours after he was shot on June 4, 1968, after winning the California Democratic primary.

Sid Kramer immediately announced his support for Mankiewicz. I knew that was my fault. Kramer's endorsement established at least the perception that Mankiewicz was the front-runner. I was initially somewhat starstruck myself. During our first debate with all the candidates on the stage, after Mankiewicz answered a question on any given issue, I kept repeating, "I agree with Mr. Mankiewicz."†

I noticed Rita pacing back and forth at the back of the room. She seemed upset. Afterward, she grabbed my lapels and said, in the sweet, gentle, loving way that only Rita could when she didn't like something I had said or done, "Either you decide you want to run for Congress and will beat this arrogant guy Mankiewicz, or you can go find another campaign manager!"

I had to admit he did seem a bit full of himself. His campaign slogan reinforced that perception: "Frank Mankiewicz will be more than just a freshman congressman."

Then came two moments that convinced me I could beat him in the primary. The first was a meeting of my campaign volunteers Rita organized immediately after the first debate. We had a small, inexpensive headquarters in "downtown" Wheaton in a strip mall. It held fewer than one hundred people comfortably, but when I arrived, there were probably five hundred people filling the room and spilling out onto the sidewalk. Often described in the local press as "mostly students and housewives,"

† In other circumstances I might have been among Mankiewicz's supporters. When he died in 2014, the *New York Times* obituary perfectly captured Frank's charisma—and disillusioned destiny. "He became a journalist and lawyer and, inspired by the Kennedys, went to Washington at the dawn of the New Frontier and took an executive position at the Peace Corps, full of idealistic hopes," the obit noted. "What he encountered were assassinations, the Vietnam War, and the Watergate scandals."

my army of volunteers burst into thunderous applause when I arrived. I started to speak halfway in the door, but Rita interrupted me.

"Why don't you ask everyone what they think before you start giving your usual speech?"

And so I did. Their comments repeated the same theme: "You had the guts to run against Gude when no one else would, and we're glad you didn't let them push you aside. You will win the primary."

That was my first wake-up call. Then came the decisive moment that convinced me I could beat Mankiewicz. It happened at the annual Montgomery County Democratic Party's 1976 spring party, a small-donor event at Indian Springs Country Club in Silver Spring, attended by about one thousand people.

I saw Frank standing in a corner as I walked in. He was surrounded by people asking for his autograph or listening rapturously to his deep, gravelly voice opining on various national and international issues. Meanwhile, I decided to circulate throughout the party and, one at a time, introduce myself to everyone in the room, many of whom I did not know, and ask for their support. After several hours, as the ballroom was emptying out, I headed for the exit and saw, to my disbelief, that Mankiewicz had not moved at all. He was still standing in the corner, as if he were holding court. It suddenly hit me.

"I can beat this guy," I told Rita. "I want it more than he does."

She nodded and said, "Now you get the picture. Prove it to me. No more 'I agree with Mr. Mankiewicz' every time you answer a question at a debate."

"Got it," I said.

"Good," she replied. "At six o'clock tomorrow morning, your driver will be in front of your house. You're heading for the intersection of Jones Mill Road and Connecticut Avenue, where the cars will be backed up three stoplights during rush-hour traffic. Sleep well. Sleep fast."

Rita was referring to a technique a friend of mine used to win the county executive race in Baltimore County, Maryland. He went to median strips in the early mornings and evenings, where traffic piled up behind traffic lights. With a volunteer by my side, I walked down the strip and invited the commuters to open their windows for a quick handshake and handed them our tabloid newspaper through the window—if they opened it.

We'd asked the friendlier commuters if we could put an "easily removable" bumper sticker on the back of their car. About one in ten, I'd estimate, would agree, and the volunteer quickly affixed the bumper sticker before the red light turned green. Bumper stickers are by far the best way to increase name recognition in local politics and convert the perception of grassroots support into a reality.

I was walking down the strip at about six thirty one morning, repeating my usual repetitive mantra to each driver who would open the window, like a broken record.

"Hello, I'm Lanny Davis, running for Congress. May I give you my newspaper campaign brochure?"

"Hello, I'm Lanny Davis, running for Congress . . ."

"Hello, I'm Lanny Davis, running for Congress . . ."

Then came a lady in a small Volkswagen who opened her window with a smile. Except when I started to say my mantra, I looked into her car and saw that she was naked from the waist up because she was nursing her baby.

At a loss for words, I blurted out, "Hello, I'm Congress, running for Lanny Davis."

It just so happened that on this particular morning, a young newspaper reporter named Gloria Borger, working for *The Washington Evening Star*, had shown up to write a story about my median-strip campaigning. (She later became a prominent political writer and CNN commentator.)

She had her notebook in hand as I walked down the median and saw the lady with the baby. She witnessed my shocked reaction and my flustered gaffe. Her account of the vignette left an impression of an energetic candidate with a sense of humor—a nice combination in politics, though sadly one largely missing from twenty-first-century American civic life.

Our goal was to contact all the core primary voters in the eighth congressional district and evaluate which ones were "definite" ("1's") or "very likely" ("2's")—voters who would turn out to vote for me in the primary on May 4.

Sometimes I would get a call from Rita and be told to call a particular voter who our precinct neighborhood captain said was particularly influential but still just a "2."

In those days, of course, there were no cell phones. So I would call Rita at headquarters from various phone booths, usually in gas stations, with a pocket full of quarters ready for use. She would give me a name and number, and there I was, in a phone booth at a gas station, introducing myself to strangers—not even knowing their names but asking them for support and offering to answer any questions.

One of our mathematical whiz kid volunteers did the simple math of the number of votes, or voters identified as "1's," it would take to be pretty confident of my winning the primary. There were five serious candidates in the primary, including me. Frank Mankiewicz was the clear front-runner in all the internal polls we were taking—until the last week. That was when our data showed that my campaign's diligence (and Frank's complacency) caught up with him.

There was a total of eleven candidates, so the math was that getting 25 percent to 30 percent of the vote would likely be enough.

Our calculation was pretty basic: Among the district's 180,000 registered Democrats, we wanted to identify at least 30,000 or more "1's" (dependable Lanny Davis voters) and be sure they turned out to vote. As we approached May 4, all our precinct captains tallied up the numbers. They had about 25,000 "1's" and about 15,000 "2's." That meant if we turned out nearly all the "1's" and just one-third of the "2's," I would win.

As the votes started to come in at about 8:00 p.m., we were way ahead of the "official" count on TV and radio because we were getting calls into headquarters from our precinct captains when the machines were opened and the tallies were announced.

After about thirty minutes, the pattern was impossible to deny: We were running at or ahead of our projected winning number in all the precincts reporting in. By 9:00 p.m. there was no doubt that I had won. Here were the final totals for the top five of us:

| | VOTES | PERCENTAGE |
|---|---|---|
| Lanny Davis | 24,336 | 27% |
| Frank Mankiewicz | 19,229 | 22% |
| Idamae Garrott | 16,126 | 18% |
| Charles A. Doctor | 13,874 | 16% |
| Lucille Maurer | 11,717 | 13% |
| Total turnout (including the other six candidates): 90,133 | | |

Our grassroots organization was so precise that we knew I was going to win before the final count was in and before the media announced the winner. The only thing on my mind, and Rita's, was that this was the beginning of our campaign against the Republican nominee, State Senator Newton Steers. With the local press gathered at the Democratic Central Committee headquarters, our first (and unfortunately, in retrospect, only) thought was to get over to the headquarters as quickly as possible to get a boost from all the live (and free) media there.

Our efficiency in knowing the results ahead of the media and our opponents, however, turned out to be a disadvantage. It encouraged a serious misjudgment by me. I forgot I needed to wait, at least, for my opponents to catch up and get their own numbers in to determine they had lost. That is the decent and gracious thing to do, as I should have known.

Instead, we opted to get me in front of the media before 11:00 p.m. evening news broadcasts so I could begin to set out our general election campaign themes.

So even though the final results were not in by about 10:00 p.m., we headed to the County Democratic Central Committee headquarters to congratulate my opponents and to deliver some opening themes to the assembled media. It was a rookie mistake.

When I walked in to shake hands with county party leaders, I was surprised at the shock on the faces of everyone there. I heard several people say, in apparent anger, "What's Davis doing here? The votes haven't even been counted." Others said disgustedly, "Couldn't he wait a little while just out of decency until his opponents concede?"

I was surrounded by media, so I made my speech, thanked my opponents, and said that I hoped we would unite as a party to recapture this congressional seat that had been held by Republicans for twenty-four out of the previous twenty-six years.

Even as I spoke, I sensed a negative energy in the room. It was the opposite of what I expected. I just didn't get it. I was so focused on beginning the general election campaign and taking advantage of the free media moment that I missed the big picture.

The underlying negative perception of me that I had overcome to win the primary was that I was too ambitious and insensitive. In one instant I had solidified that perception.

So instead of taking a victory lap armed with momentum to win the general election and garnering goodwill from my defeated Democratic opponents, the moment of joy and triumph became the moment when I planted the seeds of doubt and division that led to my defeat.

■ ■ ■

Bad news, it is often said, comes in threes. I don't know about that, but I do attribute my subsequent defeat as a congressional candidate to three factors: (1) my own hubris, which manifested itself as hyper-partisanship—despite my knowing better; (2) an honest (and minor) mistake on my bio that was exploited skillfully by one of my opponents; and (3) pushback from the local media, one outlet in particular. But let's start at the beginning . . .

■ ■ ■

I was initially described in the press as "young, fresh, dynamic." A few months later, in the homestretch of the November general election, I was deemed "inexperienced," "overambitious," and "aggressive." Jumping the gun on primary night was not a good look, but that was a single misstep that could have been easily overcome. But it wasn't the only one.

It started with the decision to trumpet a purist liberal Democratic Party message.

Flush with overconfidence after the primary, my campaign advisers and I came up with exactly the wrong platform for my general election campaign. Montgomery County is reliably Democratic today, as are the other D.C. suburbs in Northern Virginia, as well as Maryland. But in 1976 Montgomery County had been regularly electing Republicans for years. In those days I came to understand that most federal employees saw themselves as being politically "independent." Ticket-splitting was common.

So what did we decide to emphasize? *Vote for Lanny Davis because he is a Democrat.* If you thought closely about the headline we put out on our campaign tabloid newspaper, it argued with itself: "For 24 out of the last 26 years, Montgomery County has elected a Republican congressman," we wrote. "Isn't it time for our county to have a Democrat in a Democratic Congress?"

Worse, I compounded the problem by chasing my primary opponents to the left to be sure there was no space between them and me, especially the man I thought would most likely beat me, Frank Mankiewicz.

It didn't position me very well for the general election. Newton Steers was a fellow New Jersey native (and fellow Yale undergraduate and law school alum) who was both wealthy and well connected. After serving as a pilot in the U.S. Army Air Corps during World War II, he made a fortune as the head of an investment company. And though he was a Republican, Steers was related by marriage to the Kennedys—John F. Kennedy was a groomsman at his 1956 wedding, and Jacqueline Kennedy was the matron of honor. As I headed for my first public debate with Steers, I winced as I recalled my experience during my primary debates with fellow Democrats. For every question on new social spending or federal programs, my answer was yes—yes on a single-payer "socialized" health-care system, yes on more money for free college education, yes on free childcare, yes on more welfare, and yes on increasing taxes on the wealthy.

I'd never exactly defined what I meant by wealthy, meaning that it could be plausibly said that I'd called for raising the income taxes of upper-middle-class voters who constituted a large chunk of Montgomery County voters, including Democrats.

When asked what government programs I would trim to pay for the difference, I only had one example: Cut spending on the much-maligned new Air Force bomber, the B-1. (I couldn't ever answer the question of how just getting rid of the B-1 bomber could possibly pay for all these new spending programs. Short answer: It couldn't.)

Again, the reason I had taken these stances was no mystery: To win the primary, and especially to defeat Mankiewicz, I sought to avoid allowing anyone to outflank me on the left, which is where the Democratic liberal primary voters resided, then as now. So I just kept throwing red meat to the base.

In other words I fell into the very same trap I had warned our party about in *The Emerging Democratic Majority.*

To be fair to myself, on one occasion I decided to resist the temptation to just mouth the unthinking knee-jerk liberal answer to every question—and it did not go well.

"I don't need to go to these coffee klatches," I told my best friend, Sheldon Hochberg, who often drove me to events. "You could go for me and just say yes to every question asked about every new government program, regardless of how expensive they are and whether they work."

Sheldon had been thinking the same thing. Encouraged, I said, "Tonight I am going to suggest that government isn't the answer to every social program. I am going to suggest that we should use the private market and business to help us solve problems too." Sheldon was enthusiastic.

As it happened, the audience that I was facing that night was in a neighborhood near the National Institutes of Health (NIH) in Bethesda. It didn't dawn on me until too late that most of the audience were NIH workers (or that about half of Montgomery County's working population were either federal employees or government contractors).

When I suggested gingerly that government regulation and rules are not always the best answer to all problems and that maybe we should turn to the private sector on some occasions, I was met with an eruption of hostile questions.

"I work for the federal government and have all my life," one man said. "We do a great job. Are you saying you want to replace me with a private, for-profit business' employee? Why are you bashing government workers like right-wing Republicans do?"

Before I could answer, someone else stood up.

"You mention government bureaucracy as if it's a bad thing. What makes you think I am less efficient than someone who works for a private business?"

"Well, I wasn't exactly intending to criticize you or any government worker personally," I struggled to say. But then there were more interruptions, and it was all downhill from there.

"Well, that was a great experience," I said to Sheldon as we drove home. "Have any other 'new ideas'?"

That was the first strike against me.

■ ■ ■

Strike two wasn't entirely my fault. In American politics there is a phenomenon I call the "crystallizing negative event," which can undermine a candidate in far greater proportion to the supposed offense—particularly if it reinforces a vulnerability or previously perceived flaw.

The examples are numerous, but I'll cite two: In 1967 Michigan Governor George Romney (father of the future GOP star Mitt Romney) embarked on a tour of Vietnam months before officially launching a presidential campaign. Before the trip Romney had acquired an image among the political media as an intellectual lightweight. This was absurd. As chairman of American Motors, George Romney had not only been an executive venerated by his workers and Wall Street; he was also a visionary who foresaw the rise of smaller automobiles. Under his tenure AMC's stock rose from seven dollars a share to ninety dollars, making him a very rich man. Yet this unwarranted reputation followed him into politics—and it solidified when he went to Vietnam.

Accompanied by generals and upper military brass in the early days of his much-publicized tour, Romney said he supported the war. On his return home, he said he had changed his mind. He explained his flip-flop by saying he'd been "brainwashed" by the generals who insisted the war was worth fighting and claimed America was winning.

Boom! Repeated over and over again in the media, the "brainwashed" line, which was an imprecise slip of the tongue, doomed George Romney's presidential candidacy before it got off the ground.

A less fraught example occurred more than two decades later when President George H. W. Bush visited the National Grocers Association convention in Orlando in 1992. Working off a two-paragraph "pool report,"‡ *New York Times* correspondent Andy Rosenthal wrote that Bush was amazed by a supermarket grocery scanner. The story was bogus

‡ Since Dwight Eisenhower's time in office, a select cross section of White House correspondents accompanies the president on all trips outside the compound, whether it's one block away or to a foreign country. Their report, "the pool report," is distributed to all beat reporters—and beyond.

("fake news," we'd call it today). Rosenthal, who wasn't even present at the Orlando event, mischaracterized the pool report. Nonetheless, the anecdote took on a life of its own. It became a convenient, if inaccurate, metaphor for an upper-crust president perceived to be out of touch with the economic realities of everyday American life.

My own negative crystallizing event was a bit different: The pivotal factoid was technically true but just as trivial as the Bush grocery scanner example.

But as I learned the hard way, perception is sometimes all that counts. Here's what happened: In my campaign literature in 1974, I had listed among my various background facts my academic record at Yale.

After I won the 1976 primary, Robin Ficker, a perennial candidate who stayed in the race as an independent, decided to fact-check my claims about my background in my campaign literature. A stubborn gadfly in Maryland politics who was still seeking office as recently as 2024, Ficker stumbled upon something.

My 1976 campaign literature listed me as having graduated "cum laude, Yale College, Yale Law School." Cum laude means "with honors," which would have meant a "B+" average. But when Ficker called the law school, he was told *no one* was awarded "cum laude" or "magna cum laude" in my graduating class of 1970 or any year thereafter because in my last year, 1969–70, the letter grading system was abolished.

When a *Washington Post* reporter called asking me to respond to Ficker's assertion that I had "lied" and "inflated" my academic record, I stumbled because I couldn't remember what I had included in that brochure. It was written in 1974, when I first started to run, and we just kept repeating it in all subsequent iterations. I went back to read what we had written, and it said, *graduated cum laude, Yale College, Yale Law School.* I certainly thought that was true. I hadn't remembered the change in the grading system. I called Yale Law School, and they confirmed that in my last year, 1970, they had stopped designating students as "cum laude" because of the use of "pass-fail" in the third year.

It was an honest mistake, and a minor one at that, but it ended up playing into a larger narrative. It was also said, for example, that I'd exaggerated the Nixon "enemies list" angle on the basis of a single Chuck Colson memo. In addition, a local newspaper noted that I had listed my membership in a local Rotary Club when I hadn't attended many meetings and that I had claimed to have organized a local citizens consumer organization when others were more involved in establishing the group.

Yes, these were nitpicks, but the reason they stuck was that they played into the narrative of Lanny Davis being "overly ambitious"—the kind of guy who would show up in a congressional district and immediately start running for Congress. Or show up prematurely at party headquarters the night of the primary.

And in the heat of a political campaign, the expression "honest mistake" is an oxymoron anyway. Especially if it feeds into a prior negative perception. My true failure was ignoring Atticus Finch's advice. I had neglected to see myself through other people's eyes.

■ ■ ■

Strike three, the final blow to my 1976 general election campaign, was something I had no control over. In those days Democrats in Montgomery County still liked the idea of voting for a liberal or moderate Republican. Many still do, which is why Larry Hogan remains so popular in Maryland, which Kamala Harris carried 2–1 over Donald Trump in 2024.[§]

The 1970s versions of Larry Hogan were Gilbert Gude, who remained highly popular even after stepping down, and another widely admired Republican, Charles "Mac" Mathias, then the senior U.S. senator from

§ In the end Hogan's personal popularity wasn't enough: Although the former governor ran far ahead of Trump, he still ended up losing the 2024 Senate race to Angela Alsobrooks, a Democrat from Prince George's County. In January 2025 she became Maryland's first Black senator.

Maryland. Despite their looming presence, until the final ten days of the campaign, our internal polling showed we had a steady lead. Then we were hit with a slew of television ads featuring Mathias and Gude endorsing Steers—a direct appeal to liberal Republicans, Democrats, and independents.

This barrage hit home. Until then, our polls showed me garnering the support of nearly 90 percent of Democrats while splitting the independents (and winning 10 percent of the Republicans). This would have been a winning formula. But the wind shifted quickly.

When you are a candidate on the streets every day shaking hands, it doesn't take long to sense the mood of voters—whether there is a positive or a negative shift going on. During the closing days of my successful primary campaign, it felt like a warm and steady breeze was at my back. When things turn negative from one or more crystallizing events, it feels like a gale-force wind in your face. After Steers's Mathias-Gude endorsement ads hit the airwaves in the closing days, I could sense immediately something had changed among voters.

As I reached out to shake many voters' hands, I noticed, in contrast to the days before the primary, when I would get a big smile and pat on the shoulder, many would look down, reluctant to make eye contact. Some even refused to shake my hand. Our nightly polling calls to a sample of one hundred random voters started to shift, heading to fifty-fifty on individual nights and, over five nights, a slight lead for Steers. I had a strong feeling that it was slipping away. The coup de grâce came the Saturday before the election.

As it happens, good-government Democrats aren't the only ones who like to show their independent streak by occasionally voting for a (palatable) Republican. The same dynamic exists in the media, or at least it did then. My second congressional campaign came only two years after *The Washington Post* helped usher Nixon out of the White House with its Watergate reporting. In 1976 the *Post* editorial page surprised no one by endorsing Jimmy Carter for president. In the ensuing years, it has never endorsed a

Republican presidential nominee—and rarely backs Republican candidates for any office. But it endorsed Steers in 1976. I knew then I was going to lose.

Although it initially felt like friendly fire, after reading the *Post* editorial, even I had to admit that there was not a serious reason to endorse me over a popular state senator with legislative experience who was cast in the liberal Republican Mathias–Gude tradition.

Despite the sinking feeling in my gut, I had to keep cheerful and find the will, inside my largely empty stomach and aching heart, to keep going all the way through Election Day. Only Rita Federman, my campaign manager, and my wife knew how bad things were looking.

I remember feeling so hopeless yet desperate that on Monday, November 1, the night before the election, I stood on the street corner near our small Silver Spring home, at the corner of Connecticut Avenue and Veirs Mill Road. It was dusk. I stood waving to cars passing me by, as if I could win any votes this way. Instead of the encouraging honks and thumbs-up signs I had seen and heard on the last day before the May primary, most cars passed without any sign they noticed me—and the ones who did gave thumbs-down signals.

On Election Night, here were the final results:

| | TOTAL VOTES | PERCENTAGE |
|---|---|---|
| **Steers** | 111,274 | 46.8% |
| **Davis** | 100,343 | 42.2% |
| **Ficker** | 26,035 | 11% |

I was actually surprised it was that close. I won over one hundred thousand votes and lost by less than 5 percent. Ficker's 11 percent of the vote and his fact-checking my bio formed a one-two punch I couldn't overcome. After the first hour, when we saw the smaller percentage of Democrats I had received and the higher number coming in for Ficker, I was able to prepare myself for the trip to headquarters to console my supporters and to give what I hoped would be a dignified concession speech acknowledging Steers's victory.

I didn't think I would ever run again—and I was right. But I wanted to go out with grace. Maybe in the back of my mind, I was trying to prove to myself and everyone else that the harsh, negative personal image of me that I had ended up projecting was not really me.

So after spending time at headquarters consoling a lot of crying people, men and women, I decided to go to the Republican headquarters and shake Steers's hand in person.

On my way out the door, a local *Washington Post* columnist named Richard Cohen—who went on to become a widely read and popular national political columnist for many years—heard I was going to Steers's headquarters and asked if he could drive over with me.

I said yes, and we talked on the way over. Mostly, I tried to prepare myself for my entrance into Steers's headquarters. I entered with a smile, nodding to people as I walked and even shaking a hand or two. Then Steers appeared at the end of the open lane. He looked somewhat shocked but still, after some hesitation, offered an outstretched hand. We shook, and there was thunderous applause—kind of out of relief but also in acknowledgment of an unusual moment where partisan politics ended and people could connect as real human beings again. I said a few words to the crowd, congratulating Steers for his "impressive victory," and then left.

Cohen was scribbling away as I tried to continue bantering with him. But I was ready to go home. I was driven to our small house, said good night to Cohen, and walked in, with my two young children, Marlo and Seth, standing at the door. It was after 10:00 p.m., but they were still up waiting for me.

I kneeled down, hugged them, and thought, *This is why I should be happy and get over the pain of all the work and all the effort ending up in defeat.* Then after I put Marlo and Seth to sleep, I went into the living room on the first floor. Elaine tried to console me. I tried to console her too.

Eight years later we would go through a sad divorce, but on this night—and countless other nights during that campaign—Elaine was there for me. In the long run of time, and after we both moved on and remarried, I have never forgotten what she did for me: the great mom and wife she was for so many years and, especially, how she stood by me during the highs and the very lows of that election night.

■ ■ ■

After Walter Mondale lost the 1984 presidential election in a forty-nine-state landslide to Ronald Reagan, he called fellow Democrat George McGovern, who lost the 1972 race to Nixon in a similar blowout. Mondale asked McGovern how long it took for the pain to subside.

"I'll call you when it happens," McGovern quipped.

I wasn't running for president (and didn't lose overwhelmingly like Mondale and McGovern), but the pain of losing a political election is quite real. In my case two footnotes to the campaign helped me heal. One of them came the very next day. The other took nearly thirty-five years.

When I woke up the morning after my defeat, the phone kept ringing with friends calling to ask if I had read Cohen's *Washington Post* column. I hadn't. I was told that it summed me up best, and it would cheer me up. I doubted that was possible, but I was wrong.

The headline was "**The Hardest Part of Losing Is Doing It Graciously.**"

Forty years later it *still* cheers me up to read it.

"On paper it looked so good. On paper there was a mammoth registration edge, an opponent who for once was not an incumbent, a primary victory in the spring, an appeal to youth, the right stands on the right issues, more than enough for Lanny Davis to win." That was how it began. Cohen continued,

*But on Tuesday night Davis stood with the losers. He stood on a Wheaton sidewalk, hollow-eyed, hugging some campaign workers, walking one of them to the curb for a quick bucking up, looking into the eyes red from tears, trying to cheer everyone up when he himself looked for all the world as if someone had kicked him in the stomach.*

*It could not have been easy. In fact, he said it wasn't. After four years of campaigning, three campaigns and a personal debt that could buy someone a nice house, he had gotten creamed.*

*He lost well, he lost graciously, but he lost. It was interesting to watch. Few people lose as total as politicians do . . . .*

*So I went off to Montgomery County to see Davis lose his congressional race. I went because here was a man who took it all so seriously, who tried so hard, who went out early in the morning waving at commuter traffic and campaigned late into the night. He was so ambitious, everyone said. He wore it on his sleeve, which may be why he lost. He would not be a good loser.*

*But he was. Before he arrived at his campaign headquarters, the place was like a wake. There was a woman there named Carol who had worked for Davis for two years . . . She looked up, big tears rolling down a freckled face and asked me to account for this newspaper's endorsement of Newton Steers, Davis's Republican opponent. I begged off . . .*

*Davis arrived. Here was the guy who some said was out for himself, always on the make. He would be bitter, some people told me earlier in the day.*

*There would be recriminations. There was nothing of the sort. Instead, Lanny Davis went to work . . . He hugged some and touched others and talked to anyone needing talking to.*

*How do you feel? I asked. He looked at me, smiled, and then the smile quickly faded. "Awful," he said. Then he turned back to talk to some campaign workers, trying to cheer them up . . .*

*He piled into a car for the short drive to see Steers for the traditional handshake . . . He talked about how important it was to keep your sense of humor, to see the absurdity of it all and how the worst part of campaigning was having to listen to the sound of your own voice all the time—wondering along with everyone else if you were about to launch into the same old pitch.*

*A Steers aide was waiting where the Davis car arrived. The aide opened the door, smiled, introduced himself, and said he would show him inside . . . [Someone with him said]: "You know the hardest part? This is the hardest part."*

*None of it looked easy to me.*

■ ■ ■

The other event that gave me solace wasn't immediate. Actually, it didn't come for more than three decades. Long after I was criticized for "inflating" my anti-Nixon bona fides, a book was published in 1989 that vindicated me. It was called *From: The President—Richard Nixon's Secret Files*.¶

A friend of mine involved in my congressional campaign sent me a copy, pointing me to the page number that bolstered the claim I made while running for Congress. The page reprinted a memo written by White House lawyer Charles "Chuck" Colson—infamous as Nixon's political hatchet man, with the title of "special counsel" to the president.

The memo read as follows:

---

¶ Bruce Oudes, ed., *From: The President: Richard Nixon's Secret Files* (New York: Paddington Press, 1974).

*EYES ONLY*
*March 24, 1971*
*TO: John Dean*
*FROM: Charles W. Colson*

*A person by the name of Lenny [sic] Davis is in charge of the youth section of the Muskie headquarters. I am told that he had a long record of involvement with Communist Party affairs in New Haven. Would you please have an FBI check run on him? Be certain that they do a thorough one and let me know as soon as we have the result.*

*Tickler—April 24.*

This was the first time I saw the actual memo. Woodward never shared it with me and perhaps never had a copy. Delighted, I immediately called my mom, and she celebrated once again. Then she asked me: "Were you really head of the New Haven Communist Party?" I hated to disappoint her. "No, Mom," I said.

But that's not the sense of vindication I'm talking about. Those feelings came when I finally met Colson in person. It was an unexpected thrill. I was attending a dinner preceding the National Prayer Breakfast in Washington, D.C., when George W. Bush was president. When he worked for Nixon, Colson, a tough former Marine, had posted on the wall of his Virginia home an old Green Beret slogan: "When you've got 'em by the balls, their hearts and minds will follow."

While serving prison for his Watergate crimes, Colson embraced an entirely different philosophy, one informed by his profound religious conversion to Christianity. This deep faith manifested itself not only in an utterly transfigured persona but also in the vast prison ministry Colson spent the rest of his life leading.

On this evening conservative columnist Cal Thomas, the host of the dinner, invited me to be his guest. "There is someone I want you to meet," Cal told me. "You must come."

When I arrived, Cal steered me over to a vaguely familiar face.

"Hi, I'm Chuck Colson," the man said as he stuck his hand out. I shook it, amazed. I became even more amazed when he said, "I admired your work for President Clinton—and I had the same title as you, 'special counsel.' I've wanted for a very long time to say something to you: I am sorry. May God forgive me."

I looked at him, stunned.

"You know, I'm the guy who put you on the 'enemies list.' That was wrong. Please forgive me."

I looked into his eyes and felt a strange peace. It was eerie. I also saw a profound goodness and spirituality.

I thought of my dad, who had passed away in 1996 and had used the words "hate" and "evil" to describe this man. My eyes teared up. I wished my father were alive to hear me say the words that came next.

"Of course, I forgive you, Mr. Colson," I said. "And please forgive me and my late dad, for we used to use the word 'hate' about you."

Chuck Colson immediately hugged me, whispering in my ear, "I know your dad is in heaven, and he is smiling right now at the both of us loving God and forgiving each other."

I learned an important lesson that night: I vowed that I would never use the word "hate" about people in politics with whom I disagreed. It's a promise I believe I have kept.

## CHAPTER 16

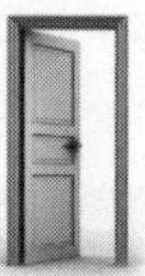

# BECOMING A D.C. LAWYER—AND LEARNING FROM THE BEST

In the summer of 1972, after Ed Muskie's campaign ended and Al Lowenstein's loss to John Rooney in the Brooklyn primary, I'd tried to delay the inevitable moment I knew was coming: to work as a lawyer in a Washington, D.C., firm. Before beginning such a terrible life, which is how I imagined it, I decided to complete an article for a magazine to explain why Lowenstein had lost and what it portended for the future of the Democratic Party.

The article was published in *Washington Monthly* in August 1972.* (As noted earlier, the editor who worked on the story was John Rothchild,

---

* The founder and editor of *Washington Monthly* was a journalistic icon, Charles Peters. One of the original group of Kennedy administration officials who started the Peace Corps, Peters became a journalistic legend not only for challenging liberal orthodoxy but also by hiring a future generation of journalistic stars to work for little pay at his small start-up. The roster of alums included Jon Meacham, James Fallows, David Ignatius, Joe Nocera, Katherine Boo, Nicholas Lemann, Michelle Cottle, Jonathan Alter, Gregg Easterbrook, and Stephanie Mencimer. One author characterized Peters and his publication as reflecting "radical centrist" political thought, which is why I found him and his magazine so appealing.

the same guy who had given me the "October surprise" when he suddenly went from supporting my run for chairman of the *Yale Daily News* in the fall of 1965 to running against me.) Rothchild said the article needed more "edge," so I acquiesced to edits that injected more snark than necessary.†

But I had other, more pressing problems. When I returned from the second Lowenstein primary, I had little choice but to try to earn a living, as Elaine and I had virtually no money in the bank and two kids to feed. While writing the article, I was so desperate for rent money I took unemployment compensation, to which I was entitled for working in the Muskie campaign for over a year.

In mid-September I again tried to postpone applying to law firms. My excuse this time was another writing project—the book explaining the lessons of the 1968 and 1972 election debacles to my fellow Democrats.‡ But we were literally out of money and knew we couldn't survive on unemployment checks while I took several months to write a book. So after a lot of soul-searching and seeing no alternative, I decided to try to practice law.

I wrote a dozen or so letters and mailed them to the managing partners of the major D.C. firms. My first job interview came at the invitation of famed Washington lawyer Edward Bennett Williams, the founder of Williams & Connolly. Although it would become a legal powerhouse, in those days it was a small firm that had just recruited Joseph A. Califano

---

† This was the same article that triggered Al Lowenstein's refusal to talk to me when I returned to Brooklyn to work in his court-mandated second primary campaign.

‡ *The Emerging Democratic Majority*: *Lessons and Legacies from the New Politics* was written and researched on nights and weekends while I worked full-time at a new job at a respected Washington law firm. It was released in late 1973 by Stein and Day, a boutique New York publishing house. Its founder, Sol Stein, served in the infantry during World War II before becoming an accomplished playwright, author, and editor who wrote scripts for Voice of America before going into publishing. Among the books he edited were *Notes of a Native Son,* by James Baldwin, and Elia Kazan's *America America*. When Stein and Day folded in 1989, Sol wrote a devastating exposé of the nation's bankruptcy system called *Feast for Lawyers*. I didn't take it personally.

Jr., a highly respected former cabinet official and Lyndon Johnson confidant.

I first met Ed Williams on the Muskie campaign. Ed seemed impressed with the "young people" in our corner of the campaign headquarters. We called ourselves the Youth Coalition for Muskie, phrasing I chose because the word "coalition" was what Lowenstein had taught me about how progressives could win general elections while attracting more moderate or conservative voters. While talking to our "Youth Coalition" one day, Ed said he appreciated that I was willing to "go into the headwinds rather than tailwinds," meaning while most of my law school friends and associates had gone to work for McGovern, I had chosen Muskie. (I told Ed about Lowenstein's influence on me. He loved Lowenstein too.)

One of the original so-called "superlawyers" whose expertise and influence went far beyond the courtroom, Ed was a legendary trial attorney and a larger-than-life figure in U.S. politics, the Washington social scene, and professional sports. He was the controlling partner of the Washington Redskins and majority owner of the Baltimore Orioles. He was also charismatic, dapper, charming, and utterly loyal.

Although Ed had become a Democrat a decade before I knew him, he still had many Republican friends—and several high-profile Republican clients. I didn't set out consciously to emulate him, but he was an inspiration to an entire generation of young lawyers in many ways. Fifty years after we met, the media would find it strange that the man who defended Bill and Hillary Clinton so ardently would take on Donald Trump fixer Michael Cohen as a client. It wouldn't have surprised Ed in the slightest.

His roster of clients from the left side of the aisle included Lyndon Johnson protégé Bobby Baker and New York Congressman Adam Clayton Powell. Among those on the right were Nixon cabinet official John Connally and fugitive financier Robert Vesco. Ed represented notorious Teamsters President Jimmy Hoffa, who was murdered in a presumed Mob hit. Ed also represented men who ordered hits, ranging from Mafia boss

Frank Costello to CIA Director Richard Helms. At one point Ed represented blacklisted Hollywood screenwriters Robert Rossen and Sidney Buchman, who were cited for contempt of Congress for refusing to testify about their Communist activities. That same year he advised Senator Joseph McCarthy, the champion Red-baiter of the era, who was being censured by Congress for his excesses in going after people such as Rossen and Buchman.

Opposing lawyers (who almost always lost when they went to trial against Ed) marveled at the mesmerizing effect he had on juries. A big part of his magic wasn't magic at all. Ed liked to recite the adage, "Never ask a witness a question to which you don't already know the answer," and he put this into practice with extensive pretrial preparation. He did his homework in other ways too. Observers of Jimmy Hoffa's 1957 bribery trial in Detroit were initially perplexed when Hoffa's defense team selected a jury with only four whites. A big clue came when former heavyweight champion Joe Louis, a hometown hero, approached Hoffa during a recess and gave the Teamsters boss a warm hug in sight of the predominantly Black jury.

As *The New York Times* noted in its 1988 obituary of Williams, he specialized in using character witnesses to maximum effect. In another bribery case, he summoned a who's who of political heavyweights to attest to John Connally's many good deeds. Among them were Lady Bird Johnson, former Secretary of State Dean Rusk, Democratic Party éminence grise Robert Strauss, and evangelist Billy Graham.

When Ed asked the world-famous preacher what his profession was, Reverend Graham answered, "I teach the gospel of Jesus Christ across the face of the earth."

Almost on cue, one juror exclaimed, "Amen!"

As the *Times* noted when retelling this story, "Mr. Williams said he thought that was a good harbinger of the acquittal that was to follow."

The obituary also quoted Muskie as saying, "Anyone who is fortunate enough to get close to Ed Williams is well served."

To that assertion, like the John Connally juror, I say, "Amen!"

■ ■ ■

Ed gave me an immediate offer to join the firm, but he said he couldn't make it official until I had met with the newly named partner, the aforementioned Joe Califano, who was out of town.

In the meantime I interviewed at Arnold & Porter, a much larger and more famous Washington, D.C., firm. For me, it was love at first sight. For one thing the very name of the firm gave me a good feeling. One of its original partners was Thurman Arnold, an esteemed former appellate court judge—and Yale man. You may recall that the moot court award I won in my second year of law school was the *Thurman Arnold* Moot Court Prize.

The A&P office was located in a spacious, four-story mansion at 1229 Nineteenth Street, one block south of Dupont Circle. Built in the 1880s, one of its early residents was future U.S. President Theodore Roosevelt. The mansion originally had eleven bedrooms and three bathrooms before it was converted into a law office. Paul Porter, then in his late sixties, greeted me at the door himself and took me around for interviews with attorneys whose workspaces were more like living rooms than law offices. Little did I know that when I was taken to my new "office" after saying yes to A&P, I would take a rickety little elevator to the third floor of the mansion and then walk up narrow, winding stairs to a tiny attic with a desk in the middle of it, barely able to stand up without hitting my head. (To this day, when I walk down Nineteenth Street, I always look up at the little triangular attic window on the top floor with nostalgia for the room where I began my legal career.)

When I called Ed to tell him I had made up my mind to go to A&P, he was unhappy but understood.

"I should have given you the offer right then and not waited for Joe [Califano] to get back into town," he said.

Ed more than forgave me. He became a friend and an ally. In my first congressional campaign, he and his wife sponsored an event in their spacious home that attracted ten times the normal crowd. His bright and lovely teenage daughter, Ellen, became a volunteer in my campaign. (When given the chance to reciprocate, I didn't rise to the occasion.[§])

The only case I worked on during my first (and, as it turned out, only) year at Arnold & Porter was litigated in front of what was then called an "administrative law judge."

The case required defending the maker of a pesticide (called "Aldrin" or "Dieldrin") used by corn farmers to control or kill corn worms, which, when active, could destroy virtually an entire season's corn crop. But this pesticide, which corn farmers said they needed to earn a profit, was also "persistent," which means that it didn't naturally break down as organic substances do and thus persisted not only in the ground but also in the corn that people ate and digested.

We knew traces of this pesticide had been found in human blood banks across the country. We also knew of evidence that this compound, in high concentrations, had caused cancer in mice. I resisted taking this case, but in my status as a first-year associate (and also dead broke), I didn't have the leverage or perhaps the fortitude to turn it down. As it played out, the administrative law judge decided against us, ruling that the recently created Environmental Protection Agency was well within its purview to ban the pesticide. Lawyers don't like to lose cases, but in this instance, I was relieved by the verdict—it eased my conscience.

Unfortunately, over all my years as a litigator, I never once got to argue a case before a jury. It seemed that whenever I was representing either a plaintiff or defendant in a private suit, I found the "sweet spot" of compromise between the two opposing positions in a lawsuit (or between a government agency and my client it was suing). I knew it was more lucrative for my law practice to

§ It's still painful to recall, but in 1973, after I was selected as a delegate to the Democratic Party's midterm statewide convention, Ed asked me if I would stand aside so his daughter could go. Although I doubted the Montgomery County Democratic Central Committee would have accepted Ellen (rather than name one of their own), I should have graciously done as Ed asked.

litigate in a courtroom to pile up huge legal fees. But I discovered that in the long run, clients would be happier with me if we avoided litigation, as we knew the usual victor in a lawsuit is neither the plaintiff nor the defendant but the lawyers. So instead of growing up to be like the ever-victorious television trial lawyers I'd idolized when I was young, such as Perry Mason (or Edward Bennett Williams), I ended up settling virtually all my cases.

I learned that the most important lesson is not only to settle cases but also, in a broader sense, to find "solutions" for clients, whatever their problem. The man who really taught me this great lesson was the legendary face of Patton Boggs, the iconic Washington law firm that was my next port of call.

■ ■ ■

Thomas Hale Boggs Jr. was already well known in Washington by the time I got to know him. His father and namesake, Thomas Hale Boggs Sr., had been House majority leader. The family came from New Orleans, and Hale Boggs, which was how he was known professionally, was a close confidant of President Lyndon Johnson.

His son was called "Tommy" Boggs in D.C., but by the time I met him in the winter of 1971, the junior Boggs was a serious Washington player, even at age thirty-one. He was also five years older than me, and I wasn't in the habit of calling my elders by their boyhood names: I addressed him as "Tom."

Tom and I first met at his parents' annual Christmas party at their home in Chevy Chase, Maryland. It was a coveted invitation by anyone in politics (Republicans and Democrats), law, or journalism. How I came to be invited is another one of those "It's a small world" stories that happened so many times in my life and fit one of my mother's favorite Yiddish expressions: "It's bashert!" Roughly translated, it means something between "kismet," destiny, or, as my mom would say it when a nice Jewish girl met a nice Jewish boy and they ended up getting married, "meant to be."

I was on my way to Muskie headquarters on L Street in December 1970 when I literally bumped into someone named Steven Roberts, a twenty-eight-year-old *New York Times* reporter. I'd first met Steve at Yale Law School earlier that year, shortly after the gunning down of four students at Kent State by the Ohio National Guard during an antiwar protest. Steve was interviewing Yale "student moderates" on their reaction to the killings. I gave him a quote about why we needed to defeat Richard Nixon at the polls the same way we had stopped Lyndon Johnson from running again in 1968—through the politics of persuasion, not confrontation.

We had gone "clean for Gene" in New Hampshire's Democratic primary, I told him—a reference to scraggly college students shaving and getting haircuts while canvassing for Senator Eugene McCarthy, whose strong showing in the New Hampshire primary had helped push Johnson out of the 1968 race. After reading Roberts's story in the *Times*, my father asked me to find out whether he was related to someone named Willie Rogow, a guy with whom my dad had gone to elementary and high school in Bayonne. Dad said he had heard his best friend, Willie, had changed his last name to be "less Jewish-sounding."

I called Steve from New Haven and thanked him for the story he wrote, and he confirmed his dad was indeed my dad's Willie Rogow. He gave me his dad's phone number, which I gave to my dad, and the two of them renewed their friendship after more than thirty years. So when Steve and I crossed paths that December in front of Muskie headquarters, he impulsively invited me to attend what he called "*the* Washington Christmas party" at the home of his father-in-law, Congressman Hale Boggs, and his mother-in-law, Hale's beautiful wife, Lindy.

I asked him if he was sure it was okay.

"Listen," he replied, "if my wife, Cokie, could convince my father-in-law to accept a Jewish boy for a son-in-law, I can convince him to let you, the son of my dad's best friend in grade school, attend the Christmas party as my guest."

When Elaine and I got there, Steve introduced us to Cokie, who was already a well-respected National Public Radio correspondent (who would soon become a national media star when she took over as the host of the ABC Sunday morning news show *This Week*). Steve then introduced us to Cokie's sister, Barbara Sigmund, who was mayor of Princeton, New Jersey. Barbara surprised me by saying she had heard a lot about me from Al Lowenstein.

"How do you know Al?" I asked her. I assumed that, like me, she had met Lowenstein at some Democratic event or antiwar rally or at Princeton, where he often gave speeches. But no.

"Actually," Barbara said, "I was engaged to Al. Didn't you know?"

No, I didn't.

So my political hero was once engaged to the sister-in-law of the son of my dad's best friend and sister of Tom Boggs, my future law partner for more than a quarter century. "Bashert" indeed.

Then Steve brought me over to meet his brother-in-law. I shook hands and looked at that round, friendly face and smile and instantly liked him.

"Welcome to Washington," said Tom Boggs.

"Too bad Muskie lost," he added. "He might have won if most of your friends hadn't worked for McGovern."

It was a nice quip, reflective of either political insight (he sized me up as a liberal—and most of my liberal friends *had* worked for McGovern) or a guy who did his homework ahead of time. Either way, I was impressed and also pleasantly surprised that one of Washington's most astute Democratic movers and shakers saw things the way I did: Liberal purists win primaries but then lose general elections.

The next time I crossed paths with Tom was when I was approached to run for Congress against Gilbert Gude, as he had done himself in 1970 (he also came up short). I asked him if I should run.

Tom answered without hesitation. "Of course, you should," he told me. "You will learn more about politics and especially about yourself while running for office, whether you win or lose. Perhaps even more if you lose."

When he asked me what Arnold & Porter would say, I grimaced and told him I didn't think they would take it well. Big firms prefer their young associates to put in maximum billable hours and not gallivant off seeking political office. He nodded, understanding. Then he said, "Come work for us."

Today, Squire Patton Boggs is a global law practice with fifteen hundred lawyers in more than forty offices spanning four continents. At the time the firm employed about seventeen attorneys with a half-dozen partners. It was started in 1962 by James R. Patton Jr., a North Carolinian who went to Yale for graduate school—in forestry. He left after one semester for Harvard Law School (which I never held against him), and after five years at the prestigious establishment law firm Covington & Burling, he hung out his own shingle in 1962. The following year he was joined by George Blow, a Covington & Burling colleague, and a couple of years later by Tom Boggs, whose offer to me seemed almost impetuous.

"Are you sure your partners won't mind paying me while I am out campaigning, at least part-time?" I asked him.

Typical of Tom, he shrugged, as if it didn't matter whether they minded or not. "Don't worry about it," he said. "I'll take care of that."

■ ■ ■

I arrived at Patton Boggs & Blow in early January 1974 to discover that Tom's confidence that Jim Patton would approve of my hire was somewhat exaggerated. I ended up being given a small empty office next to Patton's palatial corner office. So when I arrived each morning, I couldn't avoid passing him in the hallway. Each morning I would say, "Good morning, Mr. Patton," and each time I did, he would walk by me without replying and stride into his office.

Over time Patton started being civil, and then we became close. He eventually became like a second father to me. Ultimately, Tom's faith that I'd fit in at the firm was borne out. After a year or so, Jim put me on the firm's biggest account: Mars Inc., maker of M&M's, Snickers, and other snack foods. I ended up spending about 75 percent of my time for the next twenty years working for Mars, traveling around the world, visiting Mars plants, and advising the company on contract disputes, employment litigation, and a variety of policy and legal issues. After my 1974 congressional campaign, the general counsel of Mars invited me to leave Patton Boggs and become associate general counsel of Mars Inc., with an eye to promoting me to U.S. general counsel within a couple of years.

I almost said yes. I liked the client and couldn't help but daydream about how much larger my bankbook would be. But I wasn't yet a partner at Patton Boggs and decided if I were to leave the firm to go to work for a large company such as Mars and things didn't work out, I wanted it to be on my résumé that I had made partner at Patton Boggs before I left. Do I regret it? Not really. The money would have been nice, but I've had an eventful and rewarding life in the law and politics. Moreover, Tom Boggs became my senior counselor, personal counselor, law partner, mentor, and dear friend for the rest of my life.

In my early days at Patton Boggs, I asked Tom the most important lesson I needed to learn to be successful as a Washington lawyer. He took out a pencil and drew three lines, intersecting at a single point.

One line was marked by the word "law." Another line was marked by the word "media." A third line was marked "politics." The three crossed. Boggs took his pencil and put the point on the page where the three lines crossed.

"Here is how you practice law—not just in D.C. but anywhere. But perhaps in D.C. most effectively," he said, looking at the diagram. "Right here."

He tapped the pencil point to where the lines marked law, media, and politics intersected.

"Few people have all three talents. Some have one or two of the three. Hardly anyone is really good at all three."

Then he looked at me and imparted wisdom I clearly remember fifty years later.

"You," he said, "are three for three."

He added, "Your only job to be a successful lawyer in this town, or anywhere, is to solve your clients' problems. And frequently you can't only solve them in a court of law. In D.C., usually you can't. You need to use politics and sometimes media too."

Many years later I got the chance to test the three-part strategy exactly as Tom had recommended. In 1986 I received a call from the owner of a small North Carolina company called Irvin Industries, which was a subcontractor supplying to Goodyear Aerospace a small parachute designed to be attached to a bomb dropped by low-flying aircraft. The purpose of the "ballute," as it was called, was to slow down the rate of descent to allow the pilot to escape the force of the detonation. Goodyear charged a high price for the ballute, marking up Irvin's price quite a lot and reaping a big profit.

Apparently, this wasn't enough for Goodyear, which decided to cut out the middleman and produce the ballute itself. The United States Air Force went along, eliminating the subcontractor and awarding Irvin's contract to Goodyear—which would have most likely put Irvin out of business.

Goodyear won the contract as a sole source at a high price, as there was no competition. The following year, however, Irvin submitted a bid to the Air Force that was almost one-third the price Goodyear was charging the Pentagon. But Goodyear, intent on blocking Irvin from winning, dropped its price to below cost, meaning it would lose money on the contract. Apparently, the plan was to drive Irvin into bankruptcy and then jack up its price again. The taxpayers would get fleeced—and a small company would go out of business.

This seemed a perfect opportunity to apply the Tom Boggs three-pronged law-media-political strategy. I convinced the client, Irvin's owner, to let me try it. First, we filed a lawsuit against the Air Force for violating the "Competition in Contracting Act," which required the government to allow competition if there was a viable competitor to a prior "sole source" supplier.

Then I went to Tom, who telephoned (who else?) the author of the Competition in Contracting Act, powerful Texas Democrat Jack Brooks. Boggs predicted that Brooks, a committee chairman famous for straight talk, would not be happy with the Air Force if the facts checked out, and he would call the secretary of the Air Force to demand an explanation. Which he did.

Then I applied media pressure to add to the legal and political pressure. I started by making cold calls to *Washington Post* reporters I thought might be interested in a story about an unknown little North Carolina company getting steamrolled by a behemoth defense contractor. Then I got lucky. One young reporter immediately saw the embarrassing contradiction between Goodyear's high price when it was sole source and the below-cost price when it had to compete.

The reporter's name was Michael Isikoff. Yes, the same reporter who, for both the *Post* and *Newsweek*, would break many Bill Clinton–Monica Lewinsky stories in 1998. But that was in the future. Under the headline "Goodyear Accused of Contract Ploy," Isikoff nailed the story. Here was the money shot in his November 4, 1986, piece:

> *As the executive supplier of bomb parachutes for the U.S. military, Goodyear Aerospace Corp. overcharged the government $46 million the past three years and then dramatically dropped its price two months ago to shut out a fledgling competitor, the competitor alleged in a lawsuit made public yesterday.*

Once I prompted media interest—but before the *Post* story ran—I scheduled a press conference. I didn't know if anyone would show up other than Mike Isikoff, but it didn't matter. What mattered was what appeared in his newspaper:

> *"We allege that Goodyear has demonstrated in the classic pattern of the monopolist's pricing strategy—excess profits and inflated prices when there is no competition, below-cost pricing when a competitor attempts to enter the market, and once that competitor has been eliminated, a return to monopoly prices and profits," Irvin's lawyer, Lanny J. Davis of the Washington law firm of Patton Boggs and Blow, said at a press conference yesterday.*

Weeks later the assistant U.S. attorney responsible for handling the matter told the Justice Department lawyer defending the Air Force to settle the case. Irvin agreed to withdraw its lawsuit in return for being able to bid fairly—and won the competition the next year. When Goodyear subsequently tried to underbid to defeat Irvin's price, we filed another case under the False Claims Act for contract fraud.

Voilà! That case was settled too—with the Justice Department collecting money from Goodyear and Irvin piggybacked to get a percentage of the DOJ's recovery under the False Claims Act. My client was, to say the least, pleased. We won. The public won. And Tom Boggs's use of all three disciplines to create a solution for the client also won. I also learned an important lesson for the future.

■ ■ ■

On September 14, 2015, seemingly in good health at the age of seventy-three, Tom died. He was sitting on his couch late at night, probably smoking a cigar and watching television alone. A severe heart attack appeared to have killed him instantly.

I last talked to him in the spring of 2014. He told me about the crisis Patton Boggs faced because it had taken on an Ecuadorian case involving local residents' claims against Chevron Corp. His firm, he said, had allied with a New York lawyer seeking a multibillion-dollar judgment against

Chevron. Tom asked for my legal and crisis management advice. (By then I had become a combination of lawyer and media/crisis manager, and he took some pride, as he said, whenever we crossed paths, that I had "remembered where the lines crossed at the pencil point.")

He told me the firm he had spent his life creating—"my life and my soul," as he described it—was in danger and probably wouldn't survive. I was shocked. Then he told me the whole gruesome story of how this truly great and innovative law firm had put itself at risk in the now-infamous Chevron case.

Typical of Tom, he blamed himself more than others and asked me whether there was any media strategy to tell the truth, someday, about what really happened. In my last call with him, he'd resigned himself to defeat. "It's time to move on," Tom told me. "I've lost my firm and will never forgive myself—nor will Jim Patton."[¶]

It was the only time I ever heard him become tearful—incongruous for tough, placid, stoical Tom Boggs. I promised him I would be there to get the truth out someday. Shortly after that call, on May 7, 2014, a $15 million settlement with Chevron was announced, and Patton Boggs was acquired by Squire Sanders, a global powerhouse founded in Cleveland, Ohio, in 1890. The new name of the firm would be Squire Patton Boggs.

After the public announcement, Tom called me again to ask what I thought of the media coverage. He told me to give him some time, but then we'd get together for lunch at The Palm restaurant and plan his comeback. The walls of The Palm are lined with comical caricatures of the famous lawyers, lobbyists, journalists, pols, and other celebrities who dine there regularly. One of the most noticeable was the likeness of Tom over his regular table.

To my regret we never had that lunch at the Tom Boggs Table. Sixteen months later I received a phone call from Cokie Roberts telling me her brother had died the night before. I sobbed, and so did she. I told her how

¶ Jim Patton passed away at the age of ninety-one on October 18, 2020.

much I loved Tom, how much I owed him, and how much he had taught me. She said the same.

Several days later I went to The Palm for lunch to have a chance to see the Boggs Table, the candle, and the portrait on the wall of Tom and his big smile. I stood by the table, said a silent prayer, and focused on specific memories I had of Tom and his impact on my life.

Aside from learning how to combine my skills at law, media, and politics into a winning solution for my law clients, Tom taught me some lasting lessons about business, politics, and life. Here are three:

- **Disbelieve liberal sanctimony that broadly labels all "lobbyists" as evil or "lobbying" activity as antidemocratic.** Tom Boggs not only consistently made substantial personal financial contributions to liberal Democrats and to liberal causes, but he also helped the workingman just by being in the room. He saw no inconsistency between his progressive views and commitments and representing big corporations and special interests as a lobbyist. I don't either. "When I am in the room," he would say, "the outcome is going to be better for liberals than when I am not in the room."
- **Always keep a sense of humor in politics.** Take the issues, but not yourself, seriously. Who could forget Tom's great belly laugh when he saw a political irony or hypocrisy on either side of the aisle? "Don't tax you, don't tax me, tax the other guy behind the tree," he used to needle Republicans who were busy carving out fancy loopholes that always seemed to help their wealthy donors the most. He was always pro-choice on abortion, even though he came from a strict Catholic family. Yet he sometimes tweaked me about pro-choice women who opposed government dictating what they could do with their own bodies while calling for prohibitions on firearms and

strict regulation of guns and hunting.** I defended these two positions as not being inconsistent, but all he would do was smile and use that same line that he thought epitomized the double standard: "Don't tax you, don't tax me, tax the other guy behind the tree."

- **At client or strategy meetings, listen more than you speak.** This is familiar advice, but there was an important Tom Boggs codicil: If possible, try to be the final speaker in the discussion. I would watch Tom during a meeting with clients or fellow lawyers or political strategists. He would sit there like a wise Buddha, always with a cigar in his hand or puffing quietly. Every so often, he would grunt. We were never sure whether that was a grunt of assent or dissent. Yet afterward, clients would invariably say, "Wasn't Boggs amazing? He really is wise."

** Tom was a hunter and owned a retreat on Maryland's Eastern Shore specially configured with a lake that lured Eastern Shore geese to fly into the area. An invitation to the all-male gatherings was prized by countless politicians, congressional leaders, corporate executives, and top D.C. lobbyists. I turned down Tom's invitations because I have never been able to shoot animals for pleasure. (Tom would smirk as he watched me eating a steak at The Palm, asking me whether my conscience was stricken for the poor cattle who lost their lives for my benefit.) After Thanksgiving in 1993, he called from his hunting retreat. He needed some crisis management help. He and his guests had been charged with illegal hunting on his duck preserve. It seemed that among the hundreds of ducks shot by guests that morning, one was a federally protected mallard. This allowed federal agents, hiding in the tall grass, to cite all the hunters, including Tom. So when he called and asked for my advice—he told me he wanted to save his guests from embarrassment, especially a Michigan congressman known for sponsoring federal legislation to curb hunting on duck preserves—I recommended he enter a guilty plea, and perhaps the federal prosecutors would charge just him and not the other guests. He did just that and paid a $4,000 fine. I also asked him if he could find something positive to do to show his contrition. He did that too: He paid to have the dead ducks picked and cleaned and donated to the Jesuit Community of Georgetown, a group that helps feed the city's needy.

When I asked Tom whether his grunts every so often meant anything, he only smiled at me, knowingly, and said, "Keep them guessing." Then he added, "Including you." Yet I noticed there was always a smile shortly before or shortly after that sagacious last statement—as if to assure everyone that while he took what he said seriously, he did not take himself so seriously.

In truth I rarely could follow Tom's advice about staying silent during a meeting or waiting to be the last person to speak. Sometimes I irritated people in the White House by speaking up too much at meetings about the need to be proactive with the media. Nonetheless, I learned how to be an effective Washington lawyer, and I owe much of it to Tom Boggs.

I also learned to be a better friend and learned the word "loyalty" as the most important value in relationships—in business, politics, and life—from Thomas Hale Boggs Jr. And yes, sometimes I even called him "Tommy."

I still miss him.

# CHAPTER 17

# THE MIRACLE OF CHILDREN AND OUR CONSTITUTION

I am sitting in a small library room in the grand Daughters of the American Revolution Constitution Hall, not far from the White House. As I later learned, this room was chosen to look like the small White House library, located on the ground floor of the main residence where the president and the First Lady live. It is midwinter 2002.

I had been seated in front of a camera, with microphones hanging over my head and a half-dozen production staff surrounding me, the cameras ready to roll for a special documentary episode of the popular TV show *The West Wing*, created and produced by the brilliant Aaron Sorkin.*

The idea was to interview prior U.S. presidents and their aides, interspersed with scenes from Sorkin's hit show, which ran in prime time on

* A few years ago, Aaron Sorkin was involved in an adaptation of *To Kill a Mockingbird*. The stage production opened in December 2018, starring Jeff Daniels as Atticus Finch. I went to the play wondering whether Sorkin had kept my favorite line about considering things from another point of view. I was not disappointed. Daniels repeated the line almost word for word.

NBC from September 1999 to May 2006—mixing reality with fiction to convey the magic of working in the White House.

The invitation was thanks to Dee Dee Myers, who had served as President Clinton's first press secretary in the first term. After her White House service, Dee Dee had become one of several political consultants to Sorkin on scripts and story ideas. Sometime in autumn 2001, Dee Dee asked if I would be willing to be interviewed for this special segment. She said Sorkin was interested in some of my stories about crisis management in the White House when I worked for President Clinton as his special counsel from 1996 to 1998. They wanted me to think of uplifting, inspirational stories, which was the overall theme of the special.

Of course I said yes.

So there I was in front of the cameras, trying my best to tell stories that would interest the audience and hoping to impress Sorkin and his producers enough that they would include one of my tales in the final version that would air on NBC.

I picked a few yarns I thought were most entertaining. For example, I told them about when I leaked to the Associated Press that President Clinton allowed big donors to stay overnight in the Lincoln Bedroom. My purpose in preemptively leaking the "bad story," I explained, was to take the steam out of the Republicans' plan to make nasty headlines about this and other Clinton campaign fundraising practices during what we expected would be nationally televised hearings the coming summer.

When I was done with my behind-the-curtain reveal to the group of producers and technicians, I looked around to try to assess the reaction. There was silence in the room.

"Well," I asked, "how did I do?"

More silence.

Finally, the producer of my interview said something like, "Honestly, we can't use any of this, Lanny. You see, Mr. Sorkin wants this segment to be uplifting, inspirational. But all your stories are . . . well . . . depressing."

*I don't think we can use any of it* felt like a gut punch. I nearly panicked. I had already called family and friends and told them I might be part of a *West Wing* special episode. Everyone was excited. Now I realized I had struck out.

Minutes passed. I sat and watched the production staff packing up. Suddenly, an idea came to mind. I remembered one inspirational moment involving the White House. Although it was long before I worked there for President Clinton, I decided to pitch it anyway.

I turned to the producer and told him I did have a story about the White House, but it occurred more than twenty years before I worked there for President Clinton. It was quite inspirational and memorable—at least to me. I started to relate it without asking his permission. It occurred on August 9, 1974, the night Nixon resigned from the presidency and left Washington shortly after noon, famously waving goodbye to his supporters as he boarded Marine One.

He was the first president of the United States forced to resign because he was told by Republican leaders he had no chance to avoid impeachment by the House and conviction and removal by the Senate. The producer sat listening to me while others continued packing up.

So I told him that on that night, August 9, I got home about 10:00 p.m. and told Elaine my idea: I wanted to wake the kids (our six-year-old daughter and four-year-old son) and drive them to the White House to be there for this memorable moment in U.S. history. I asked her to come with me.

Naturally, she thought I was crazy. "Don't wake the kids," she said. "You can go if you want to." Naturally I ignored her advice.

I picked up both children, who were sound asleep in their beds, and as they moaned and groaned, carried them to the back seat of the car, where they immediately fell back to sleep.

Thirty minutes later I turned the corner from Seventeenth Street onto Pennsylvania and stopped in front of 1600—the beautiful, brightly lit, white-columned North Portico of the White House. In those days there were no barriers, so you could drive in front and sit in a car at the curb. I was astounded by what I saw. Actually, by what I did not see. I looked around in amazement. I was the only car at the curb.

Suddenly it hit me. There's no one here! And this is what I told the producer:

> *On the day Richard Nixon resigned . . . At ten o'clock at night, I drove [my daughter and son] downtown and parked in front of the White House. And I said to them, "Look, there isn't a solider, there isn't a policeman, and there isn't a gun anywhere to be seen. The most powerful person on the planet left this place on his own . . . because of the rule of law."*
>
> *Now that may be corny, but I said to myself, "God bless America that made a system like this, where there is no military that I can find." And I turned around, proud of my eloquence, and [both kids were] sound asleep!*

I looked at the producer to see what he thought of my story. I hoped that if he found it as inspirational as I remembered it, he would let me repeat it on camera before everyone unplugged everything and went home.

The producer stared at me. Then I noticed, for the first time, everyone in the room, who had been packing up, had stopped to listen.

Then the producer said, "That's a take."

"What?" I asked. "What do you mean, 'a take?' I can repeat it on camera if you want."

For the first time in our session, he smiled. Then he said something like, "The camera was running, Lanny. You were looking at me, but the camera was running. You didn't know. The microphone was kept live above you. Your story is amazing. You don't need to repeat it. It will never be as good the second time as what you just did without knowing we were taping. In fact you were better because you didn't know. I think Aaron will love it."

I was delighted. And hopeful.

■ ■ ■

Several months later, on April 23, 2002, Carolyn and I sat down to watch the special (season 3, episode 19). By then I had been told that my story *might* make the cut.

The entire show, which was another brilliant concept and execution by Aaron Sorkin, was widely watched (and rewatched over the years) and won an Emmy Award. It included interviews of three presidents (Jimmy Carter, Jerry Ford, and Bill Clinton) and others who served as senior staff in the White House, such as Dee Dee Myers; Paul Begala, former Clinton political counselor; Leon Panetta, former Clinton chief of staff (and future CIA director); and David Gergen, who had advised Presidents Nixon, Ford, and Clinton.

I checked my watch. The hour for the segment was almost over. It seemed my story about my crazy trip to the White House with my two young children hadn't made the cut. My heart sank. Then as the background music grew toward what seemed to be an inspirational ending of the episode, suddenly there I was, a close-up shot, telling my story, with the final line: "The most powerful person on the planet left this place on his own . . . because of the rule of law."

For weeks, months, and years, even into the 2020s, I still receive calls from people who have seen the segment, which has become even more widely available through streaming technology. I received a thank-you letter from Sorkin himself and put it on the wall of our home office. I also got a call from my son Seth, now thirty-two years old, who had watched the segment. "Did you like it?" I asked him.

Seth couldn't resist. "Dad, you were great," he deadpanned. Then he added, "You completely made that story up."

"How would you know?" I rejoined. "You were fast asleep!"

He laughed and admitted I had a point.

Little could I ever imagine on that night when I made my speech to my sleeping kids that about fifty years later, a president of the United States would deny the results of an election without evidence and ignore our Constitution and the rule of law. And not leave office quietly or peacefully.

## CHAPTER 18

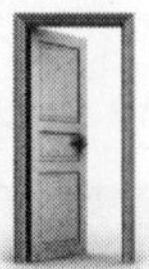

# JOSEPH LIEBERMAN AND PURPLE POLITICS

On April 16, 1970, Elaine gave birth to our second child, Seth Lewis Davis. My mother and father were at Yale New Haven Hospital with me, waiting for his arrival.

When the nurse brought Seth out at about 5:00 a.m., all swaddled in a soft blue flannel blanket, his dark hair was immediately apparent. When I looked down at him in wonder, his eyes were open, and his face seemed untouched by the birthing process. He wasn't even crying, just kind of staring at me in curiosity.

My mother was cooing gibberish to her new grandson. She turned to me and mentioned the eighth day from Seth's birthday as the day for Seth's "bris." That is the Jewish ritual circumcision ceremony mentioned in Genesis in the Old Testament. Even non-Orthodox, not-very-religious Jews, such as my parents, regarded the bris as important. It is a social occasion, too, when family members and close friends are invited into the home. A rabbi, who is medically trained and certified, removes the foreskin of the baby boy with a surgical tool resembling a small razor blade.

The bris ensures connection among all Jews from modern times back to ancient times.

I had thought about the bris ceremony over the years. I had only one experience attending one. I swore I would never let a future son of mine go through it at a house party with people drinking punch just before my baby son cried out in pain. *Ouch!*

So I interrupted my mother. "We're going to do the surgery in the hospital where it is safer, Mom," I said. "And that's it."

She protested that the bris was an important ritual for a newborn Jewish boy. Rather than arguing with her (since I knew we were "reform" Jews who barely attended synagogue except on the high holidays), I just said, "No, Mom. No bris. I will ask to schedule the surgery here in the hospital."

Mom must have sensed it was useless to argue. She just turned and marched down the hallway of the hospital in anger. Ten minutes later a nurse approached me. She told me I had a phone call and to follow her to the nursing station.

A phone call? This early in the morning? Who even knew that Seth had been born besides Elaine's parents, Sid and Jeanette Charney, who were already on their way to New Haven from Queens after we called them with the great news?

I took the phone and heard a familiar voice:

"Lanny, mazel tov on the birth of Seth!"

I immediately recognized the voice of Joe Lieberman. I was stunned. How did he know I had a son that had just been born? How did he know his name was Seth? I quickly put it all together.

"Did my mother just call you?"

He paused briefly and did not answer.

"You're having a bris," he said. "You must. It's one of the holiest of all ceremonies in the Jewish religion."

"It's not safe—I want a professional surgeon to do the cut," I said, somewhat disingenuously.

Joe saw through that answer. "Don't worry, you don't have to be the *sandek*," he said.* "I will hold the baby during the ceremony. You can hide in the bathroom so you don't have to witness it."

So Joe had figured out the real reason I didn't want to have a bris ceremony for Seth. It wasn't about health care and safety. I didn't want to hear and see my little boy cry as the cut was made.

"Okay, Joe," I responded. "I will go along with you and my mom. That's two to one, so I yield. But you have to be more than the sandek. You have to be Seth's godfather too."

"Deal," said Joe.

The bris occurred on April 24, 1970, eight days after the birth, without incident. Seth did very well, despite my fears.†

Fast-forward thirty-six years. The date is November 7, 2006. It was about 10:00 p.m. Seth was no longer an eight-day-old baby who was about to be sliced by a razor blade held by a rabbi (allegedly) with a surgical degree. He was a fully grown man whom any father would be proud of. We arrived together at a hotel suite in Hartford, Connecticut, to join Joe in celebration of his reelection to a fourth term as a U.S. senator from Connecticut. Joe had just won by a double-digit margin, but it had been an eventful campaign. In August he lost in the Democratic primary, which is unusual for a three-term incumbent, because of one issue: his vote in support of the Iraq War Resolution on October 16, 2002.

His opponent, Ned Lamont, had defeated Joe by a narrow margin. Although he would later become a two-term governor who earned high marks from Connecticut voters for his handling of the COVID-19

---

* *Sandek* is the Hebrew word for the person holding the male child during the bris.

† In 1999 I appeared on *The Geraldo Rivera Show* on CNBC during the early days of cable television to answer questions about President Clinton's pending impeachment vote. I had been on a plane a few weeks before when I encountered Geraldo, and while chatting about personal matters, I told him the funny story about Seth and Lieberman. Before the interview started, Geraldo asked me to repeat it on air. So I did. That night I received a call from Seth. "Dad," he asked, "could you please not tell that story about me and the bris and Joe Lieberman on the air in the future?"

pandemic, Lamont campaigned against Joe in a way I found objectionable. If voters listened only to his campaign, they'd think that Lieberman was the only Senate Democrat who voted in favor of the Iraq War resolution. Actually, twenty-eight other Democrats voted to give George W. Bush the authority to invade Iraq, including Charles Schumer, John Kerry, and Hillary Clinton. Many of them, including Kerry and Hillary, opposed the invasion but didn't want to hamstring the commander in chief after a devastating attack against the United States.

They also believed that Saddam Hussein had developed weapons of mass destruction—as did Saddam's own generals. Although I found Lamont's criticism cynical, it certainly was effective. And it would be used a decade later by the Obama campaign against Hillary.‡

In truth it was the broad consensus of the Democratic Party to give President Bush authority to intervene militarily to remove all weapons of mass destruction from Saddam Hussein's control.

For that reason (and because he was a lifelong friend), I supported Joe's running as an independent against a duly nominated Democratic Party nominee. Weeks before primary day, Joe told Democratic primary voters that if he lost, he would run as an independent in the general election. When the polls were closing on primary night, Joe and a group of his closest advisers, including myself, agreed that he could and should continue running as an "independent Democrat" (promising to vote with the Senate Democratic caucus if he won).§

‡ I opposed the October 2002 war resolution because I wanted to give the UN inspectors more time to find affirmative proof that Saddam had weapons of mass destruction. I was suspicious of the weak circumstantial evidence leaked to the press and later provided to the UN. But if there was proof of WMDs, I believed there was no choice but to take them out, as they represented, in the hands of a madman such as Saddam, a genuine threat to U.S. national security.

§ Many years later Rachel Maddow falsely accused Lieberman of hiding the ball and not letting primary voters know ahead of time that he would continue campaigning if he lost running as an independent. That night I texted her producer, Lisa Ferri, who apparently passed along my objection, and—to her credit—Rachel made a correction within a couple of days. I laud her to this day for owning up to her mistake, and we became friendly in later years.

At the time Seth was working for *Sports Illustrated* while living in Ridgefield, Connecticut, with his wife, Melissa, and his young son, Zachary. After the primary loss, Seth volunteered to become a local leader of "Democrats for Lieberman." He knocked on doors and proudly identified himself as "Senator Lieberman's godson."

When the votes were counted in the three-way race, Joe had won in a landslide. Seth and I headed for Hartford, where Lieberman's state headquarters was throwing a victory party. We walked into the hotel suite amid all the noise and jubilation. Joe saw us and held up his hands to quiet down the celebration momentarily.

"Hold on, everyone," he said. "I want to announce the arrival of my godson, Seth Davis—head of Democrats for Lieberman in Ridgefield, who helped us win tonight."

As the packed room watched, Seth slowly walked to the front of the room, leaned over, took Joe's hand, and kissed his ring.

"Thank you, Godfather," he said. "Thank you, Senator Lieberman."

The room shook with shouts and cheers as Joe and Seth hugged and kissed. And of course, I was tearful, remembering that early morning call thirty-six years earlier from Joe with the command, "You're having a bris!"

■ ■ ■

During Joe's first term in the Senate, my mentor and law partner, Tom Boggs, called me about setting up a meeting with Lieberman, whom he knew was one of my best friends, on behalf of a client. I was concerned that Joe would be influenced to vote in favor, even against his better judgment, of the position Tom and I were advocating for on behalf of our clients.

I was also concerned about the optics of my doing so. I did not want Joe to feel compromised if he voted the way I was lobbying him to vote and then word got out that his friend influenced him.

In the book I wrote after leaving the Clinton White House, I noted the failure of many journalists and liberal critics to distinguish correlation from causation when it comes to lobbying. To prove my point, I used the faux syllogism of those who fail to make the distinction: The rooster crows, and then the sun rises. Therefore those given to innuendo will infer: The rooster *causes* the sun to rise.[¶]

Too many journalists and many liberals tend to use the word "lobbyist" by definition as negative, even evil. When Barack Obama was first elected president, he refused to hire any registered lobbyists to work in the White House.

So when I told Tom I would not lobby my close friend, I thought that was that. But that was never the case when it came to Tom challenging the unthinking conventional wisdom that lobbying was some kind of evil.

He said something like this to me, although I can't vouch for these exact words: "You are going to lobby Joe Lieberman unless you have a better reason not to than 'optics.' If you tell me you are going to ask Lieberman to violate his conscience because of your friendship, and you think he might do so, that's not going to happen. But if you are telling me you are worried about irrational people who declare all lobbying to be corrupt, then the hell with them."

Just to be extra safe, I called Lieberman's chief of staff, Clarine Nardi Riddle. I asked Clarine what she thought about my lobbying the senator on behalf of a client on a particular amendment to legislation that would favor my client's interests, as well as the public interest. She asked me to send her the information on the amendment and the arguments I would be making in favor of it.

She called me back and said that Lieberman would see me but couldn't offer me any information on what position he might take on voting yes or no on the amendment. I said fine, and we scheduled the meeting.

---

¶ Lanny Davis, *Truth to Tell: Tell It Early, Tell It All, Tell It Yourself: Notes from My White House Education* (Free Press, 1999), 138–39.

When Tom and I walked into Lieberman's office with a group of representatives from the client, I assumed Joe would be standoffish with me for appearance's sake. Instead, he got up from his chair, came around his desk, and shocked Tom, the clients, and especially me by coming up to me and giving me a big bear hug before turning to Tom and the clients to shake their hands.

Tom proceeded to make the presentation along with the clients. I remained silent.

As we left his office, he again gave me a hug and said I should give his love "to my godson, Seth Davis." And he went on to explain the story about his having to hold Seth during the bris and Seth kissing his ring—like he was Marlon Brando in *The Godfather.*

I was astonished. Joe was unconcerned about letting everyone know not only about our friendship but also the story of the bris! Later on, Clarine called me to say he had studied the amendment and decided, on the merits, that he couldn't support it. I told her I understood. In a way, I was relieved. I thought that he had proven my point and did not agree to do anything just because of friendship. He had acted on principle, even if that meant saying no to me as a lobbyist. How could I have thought otherwise?

One reason I have enjoyed writing this book is that I have learned more about myself as I string together memories from childhood to the present. I have realized that an important theme in my life, once I got involved in politics in the mid-1960s at Yale and thereafter, is how critical it is, while pursuing progressive change, to *persuade* others of the wisdom of Democratic policies—not to coerce them or threaten them. I also learned the importance of finding common ground and how to disagree agreeably. Not only with conservative Republicans but also with the Democratic Party leftists who had made life so difficult for Al Lowenstein.

Joe Lieberman, more than any other political leader other than Lowenstein, also influenced me on the importance of the politics of persuasion—finding a "center" starting with principled liberalism but somewhere between left and right, a Third Way that Bill Clinton embraced in 1992 when he reshaped the Democratic Party and made it competitive again while winning the presidency after three consecutive Republican landslides. I learned from Lieberman (and Clinton) the importance of being able to disagree politically without indulging in demonization of the other side. Lieberman infuriated some liberals with some of the positions he took over the years. These are the individuals whom I label "purists"—defined as people who see anything less than 100 percent what they agree with as evil. With them, any compromise is not only a source of disagreement but also a reason to attack others' motives and character.

Lieberman was, without question, a liberal on all the key issues: pro–federal government business regulation, pro-choice, pro–civil rights, pro–gay rights, pro–gun control, pro-environment, and so on. However, he was also willing to compromise with conservatives, knowing that a middle position was worth accepting if that was the only way to achieve progressive change, even if it was just incremental. For this reason he was popular with Republicans in the Senate—not because he voted with them (he voted with fellow Democrats well over 90 percent of the time) but because he was willing to listen, compromise, and find common ground to pass legislation that he could support.

I also believe that when Senator Lieberman took the Senate floor in mid-September 1998 to criticize President Clinton's conduct on a moral basis but still said he would oppose impeachment because no abuse of presidential power undermining the constitution had occurred, that allowed a lot of Democrats offended by Clinton's personal conduct with Ms. Lewinsky to oppose impeachment.

One of the great thrills of my life was on the night of August 17, 2000, when Lieberman took the podium at the Democratic National Convention to accept the vice presidential nomination. I knew history was taking place: the first Jewish nominee for vice president, with a chance after November to be next in line to be president.

The opening line of his acceptance speech paid homage to his precedent-breaking selection—and he delivered it like a Borscht Belt comedian: "Is America a great country, or what?"

I thought back to our days at Yale, nearly four decades earlier, when Joe encouraged me to work hard toward becoming chairman of the *Yale Daily News*. But for some five hundred or so votes in the state of Florida, or those infamous "hanging chads" not counted as votes, Joe would have been vice president.

That is why I have described Joe Lieberman as a "purple senator." He combined the colors of "Red State" Republicans and "Blue State" Democrats. Joe was truly "purple" in substance and in conduct.

Still, I was often shocked by the vicious personal attacks leveled against Lieberman's character even after he retired in 2013. Aside from his position on the Iraq War, many progressives never forgave Lieberman for his endorsement of GOP presidential nominee John McCain over Barack Obama. Joe appeared at the 2008 Republican convention to speak for McCain, and I was horrified.

First, I knew that he and McCain had become close friends in the Senate. Second, I remember vividly that McCain had campaigned for Joe in the 2006 Connecticut reelection race against the Republican nominee after Joe had to run as an independent.** Those who never forgave Lieberman for that endorsement of McCain forgot that he campaigned for Hillary Clinton in 2016 and Joe Biden in 2020 against Donald Trump.

Joe and I continued to bond through the years over our common "coalitionist-centrist" approach to winning elections and achieving incremental progressive changes. That approach came to be known, thanks to Bill Clinton, as the "New Democrat" philosophy or, as I mentioned earlier, the Third Way—not a mushy center but a willingness to stand on

** In a nonpublic act, which also proved to me his political and personal integrity, Joe's friend and fellow Yale alumnus, then President George W. Bush, quietly put the word out to Republican Connecticut leaders that he supported Lieberman and refused to campaign for the Republican nominee in that 2006 election.

principle from the left or right and still seek common ground, even if that meant compromising a little.

This philosophy was coined to describe a new national Democratic Party organization begun in 1985 called the Democratic Leadership Council, or the DLC (as described in chapter 13).

Bill Clinton has said that very few people in America were more responsible for his winning the presidency than Al From, the DLC's chief organizer and president, and I agree with him. It was From's idea to ask Clinton to become the new chairman of the DLC in 1990. Clinton succeeded the first three chairs and cofounders: Missouri Congressman Dick Gephardt, Virginia Senator Chuck Robb (the son-in-law of President Lyndon Johnson), and Georgia Senator Sam Nunn.

Not surprisingly, Joe became chairman of the DLC in 1995 during Clinton's first term as president. I came to realize later that there was a direct line from Al Lowenstein in the late 1960s to the DLC in the 1980s, Bill Clinton in the 1990s, and even Barack Obama in the new century. Progressives, at least those who were paying attention, came to recognize that the perfect is the enemy of the good, and building coalitions and learning how to reach out to more moderate Democrats, independents, and Republicans—while remembering to disagree civilly—is the only kind of politics that can produce meaningful or lasting change.

Lieberman taught me this lesson perhaps more than any other. And then one day he was gone.

■ ■ ■

Joe died abruptly in the spring of 2024, after most of this chapter was written. One might have thought that the sudden death of this wonderful man and dedicated public servant would have muted the tired old attacks that he and I both regarded as badges of honor. One would have thought wrong.

"Joe Lieberman was more than a friend to me. He was more than a brother. He was my soulmate," I wrote in a sorrowful column at the time.

I also noted that Joe made a lot of Democrats unhappy when he supported McCain for president in 2008 and when he was critical of Obama during the campaign—and it made me unhappy. But that never stopped me from loving and admiring him. I wasn't the only one who felt this way. After he left office, I heard Bill Clinton express that sentiment to George W. Bush at the White House when Bill and Hillary returned for the presentation of their official White House portraits. "Wouldn't it be great if we could say someone is right or wrong," Clinton said, "and not that they are good or evil?"

Lieberman's honorable life and personal integrity always reminded me of how right Clinton was to make that distinction. I listened to many of my fellow Democrats and fellow liberals using awful language about my friend Joe—in fact, telling me they hated him.

I would ask, again and again, how can you hate someone who has voted with his Democratic colleagues in the Senate throughout his career more than 90 percent of the time? Can't you just disagree?

Instead of getting more people like that in American politics, we seem to be getting fewer. For that reason, Joe's passing was a tragic loss for this country. He was irreplaceable. It was also a body blow to me and my family.

On March 27, 2024, I was on an Amtrak train from New York to Washington when my cell phone rang. It was Seth. I heard from the tone of his voice that something was wrong.

"Dad, did you hear the news about Godfather Joe?"

"What news?" I asked with great foreboding.

"Dad, he died after a fall early this morning."

I gasped and started to sob so uncontrollably that passengers on the train turned to look at me with concern. Seth cried with me. Memories. Memories.

When I hung up, I immediately recalled the last time Joe and I had talked. I had phoned him to express my concern about his support for the "No Labels" effort to field a third-party ticket for the 2024 presidential ballot. I told him how concerned I was about Donald Trump's disregard for the rule of law, his threat to suspend the Constitution, and his embrace of Vladimir Putin and autocracy. How can you do this, Joe?

"This is what I feel, Lannyla," he said, in his usual tone of love and respect with a touch of humor. "But I promise you: If I think what we are doing will help elect Trump, I will withdraw."

I expressed skepticism that he could derail that train before the damage was done. He said softly, "I understand how you feel." I tried to say the same words, but I just couldn't. I was too concerned.

Then he said, "I love you, Lannyla."

I said, "I love you, too, Joe."

As I sat on the train crying, I thought: *Now he's gone. Say it ain't so, Joe.*

CHAPTER 19

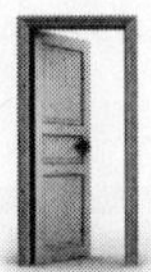

# GOLF AND LIFE

What is it about golf? This isn't a gender thing. Women golfers understand it too.

How do you explain the euphoric sensation from a regular golf foursome over many years? I played with the same three friends virtually every weekend for twenty-five years. It ranks as one of the great pleasures of my life, just behind the love of family.

It's about more than friendship, arising from being together for four to five hours a day on the golf course. It starts with the joy of the early morning tee-offs with three friends who are fierce competitors but as close as brothers; the often cool, sometimes subfreezing, fresh morning air; the quiet; the view down the first fairway; and the smell of freshly mowed fairways and greens.

And then it's time. You stand next to this little white ball sitting nicely on a tee—not rushing at you at ninety miles per hour like a baseball pitch, not twisting away from you with topspin like tennis players see. It's just sitting there, seemingly so easy to hit.

Then whack! The laws of physics seem to be suspended. The ball goes up in the air. Sometimes it goes straight down the fairway. Sometimes. Often, it has a mind of its own and makes a sharp turn to the left (called a "duck hook") or sharply to the right (called a "banana slice"). In either event, too often the little white ball crashes and ricochets into various trees and then lands ignominiously and against all odds exactly behind a tree, utterly unhittable. And that is just the first swing on the first hole.

You might moan, groan, bitch, give excuses, slam your club down, and curse. You stare balefully at your two opponents in the foursome on the other team, even your own partner, daring them to say anything or even to look wrongly at you. Instead, they usually look away. And then you think, I am so glad to be out here playing golf. There is no place I'd rather be.

That's golf.

Sometimes we used to try to explain how we could get such pleasure from such constant misery on the golf course. We couldn't. All we could do was feel joy and mental relief, thankful to have escaped from the reality of the real world into the surreal world of focusing all your attention on hitting a little white ball and sharing the pleasure/pain with your golf mates.

In the late 1970s, Sheldon Hochberg, my fellow Washington lawyer and obsessive golfer who was also my best friend and regular golf partner, went to play one day at the Washingtonian Country Club's National Course in Gaithersburg, Maryland. We did not have a scheduled tee time, but the "starter" in charge of tee times told us there was a twosome on the first hole, and they might be willing to let us join and play as a foursome. We walked to the first hole. The two men about to tee off seemed about our age (mid-thirties or slightly older). They immediately invited us to join them. Their names were Marvin Ben Bassett and Jack Greenspan.

At first glance Marvin looked like his priority was not to play golf but to be the master of golf clothing style. His shirt matched his pants, and his socks matched both. His golf hat had a dash of the same color. His golf shoes were perfect, just the right shade to match his pants, socks, shirt, and

*From left: Marvin, Jack, Sheldon ("The Commissioner"), and me.*

hat. A larger man than us, he outdrove us in distance, his strength evident by the vicious *crack* sound when he struck the tiny, innocent golf ball.

As for Jack, he was a welcoming man with a friendly smile and a warm handshake. I don't recall what Jack was wearing, only that in contrast to the impeccably dressed Marvin, he looked a bit rumpled. He was also a few inches shorter, with a not-exactly-athletic build. But looks can be deceiving. Even his slow backswing was misleading. We assumed Jack would hit the ball short and straight like me. But no. After a slow inside backswing and a lazy downswing, at the last second, Jack squared up his driver clubface, and then we'd hear that sound—*whack!* The ball would go almost as far as Marvin's, and sometimes farther. Always, it seemed, right in the "sweet" spot of the club, adding to his distance. I often thought over the years that Jack always hitting the sweet spot matched the sweetness of the man.

I also learned not to be fooled by Jack's good nature when it came to competitiveness in a match. He was intense. Just when I started to relax, thinking I was ahead of him, he'd go in for the kill and often win. But always with a smile.

We accepted their invitation, a foursome for the first time: Sheldon and me versus Marvin and Jack. We agreed on "match" play, which means that the low score for the twosome won or tied the hole. Sheldon and I sensed these two guys were competitors. That put pressure on us to show them we could beat them. Recognizing that they were about the same skill and handicap as us, we decided to play for money—the traditional "Nassau" golf match: two dollars for the winner of the front nine, two dollars for the back nine, and three dollars for the Nassau bet (the team ahead by total holes over the eighteen holes). Stakes that low mean the pressure to win isn't about the money. It's about pride.

At this first historic match, we were dead even going into the eighth hole—"all square" is the golf expression. It was a relatively short par three, about 160 yards. But the green was tricky, sloping sharply from left to right and surrounded by sand traps with steep banks before the green. Marvin and Jack teed off first, and both of their balls landed softly on the green. I was impressed. Now it was Sheldon's turn. He hit his tee shot to the left of the green, with a tough chip to get on—let alone close enough for a par putt. That put pressure on me to hit onto the green to give us a chance to tie for a par. But I hit short of the green, into a sand trap. A trap (or "bunker") with soft sand is tough enough to get out of; you have to use a sand wedge—a thick-flanged, sharply angled club—and hit into the sand behind the ball so the sand lifts the ball up onto the green. But my ball landed on hard mud, as it had rained earlier in the morning. I chose a less-angled club with a sharp edge, not a thick flange, called a "pitching wedge."

When Marvin saw my choice of clubs, I heard him whisper to Jack, loud enough for me to hear, "This guy has no clue. He isn't using a sand wedge. He is nuts."

But I knew better. I had practiced this "pick" shot using a pitching wedge off hard sand often. The idea is to clip the ball clean without touching the hard surface, lifting it up quickly. If I did it right, the ball would lift quickly in the air onto the green. It worked.

To Jack's (and more so, Marvin's) surprise, the ball came up out of the trap, landed about thirty feet to the left on the slated green, turned right and rolled and rolled to the hole, hit the back of the cup, popped slightly into the air, and plop—into the hole for a birdie! Marvin and Jack missed difficult putts for birdies to tie, so Sheldon and I won the hole to go plus-one. We also won low ball on the par-five ninth hole, so we won the first nine holes, plus two, for two dollars.

They won the second nine by plus one, but we were "one up" on holes for the eighteen-hole Nassau bet, so we ended up winning one dollar. We tried to disguise our happiness. We shook hands with Marvin and Jack and made a date to play the next weekend. And so it began. Little did we know this match would continue weekend after weekend, virtually all year, sometimes through torrential rain, snow, sleet, even a real blizzard, for more than a quarter century.

As we started playing regularly, we realized we needed a way to resolve rule disputes on the golf course. The official rules were contained in a little book Sheldon always carried that was published by the United States Golf Association. Still, there was much to be argued about. Was a ball hit into a "lateral" hazard (which meant the ball could be dropped at the point it crossed the hazard, resulting in a one-shot penalty)? Or was it hit "out of bounds" (resulting in rehitting the ball from the same place and taking a two-shot penalty)? That sort of thing.

Sometimes the arguments were impassioned, with the rule determination sometimes meaning the difference between winning and losing two whole dollars! Since Sheldon carried the United States Golf Association rule book, we agreed he would be named the "commissioner" to decide all rule disputes. However, once he got the title, he announced that all his rule determinations were not appealable. If you tried to argue with him, including me, his partner, he would dismiss your comments by saying, "The commissioner hath ruleth . . . and hath moveth on." And that would be that.

We also started to play multiple bets, monetary rewards for making a birdie or getting on a par three in one and two-putting for a par (or paying money for three-putting for a bogey), and many others. So the commissioner kept track of all the bets, and usually over lunch, he would announce the results of which team owed how much. And his announcement was not subject to appeal.

Ultimately, we decided to open a bank account and deposit all the money won (or lost, as it were). We called it the Players Fund. We distinguished a "golfer," who only played in good weather, from a "player," who hit the links in virtually any weather, no matter what. (We once played on Christmas Day in a real blizzard, dressed in woolen hats and ski coats and using orange balls to find them in the snowdrifts.) Obviously, we were "players," not "golfers." And proud of it.

We even played on December 22, 1984. The weather wasn't an issue: This was a winter's day when the weather was rather mild. But that evening I was getting married for the second time. Marvin insisted we should play just to see whether my wife-to-be, Carolyn Atwell, would object.

"That's a test," he said, referring to Carolyn's reaction.

She passed it and then some. Not only did Carolyn not object, but she was also relieved to get me out of the house. Marvin was impressed. "You married a player's wife," he said. "Good for you."

There was supposedly an annual election for the next year's commissioner. But as Sheldon reminded us, he was always elected unanimously. Actually, he nominated himself, closed the nominations before anyone else could be nominated, and then announced the vote was unanimous. It was all done in good fun, but there was a moment when Sheldon proved he was the right man for the job of commissioner. On one of our annual golf trips to North Carolina, Marvin had teed off and sliced the ball way to the right, well off the golf course a few hundred feet into a large housing construction project next to the course. I declared the ball out of bounds, and therefore Marvin had to hit another ball and take a two-shot penalty.

Sheldon contradicted me. No, he said, the ball had landed in a "lateral hazard," as it was a man-made construction site. That meant Marvin could drop the ball near where the ball had gone off the course and take only a one-shot penalty. I was furious. "You're my damned partner! What kind of ruling was that?" I insisted that we would hold off deciding who won that hole until we asked the local PGA professional at the end of our eighteen-hole match. The pro's name was Stewart. Then Sheldon uttered the expression that became emblematic of his anointment as an absolute dictator: "If Stewart says I am wrong, he is wrong." (To my great irritation, and to add to Sheldon's legend, when we finished the course and consulted Stewart, he agreed with Sheldon's ruling.)*

Over the years I grew accustomed to being mocked by my golf mates, including by my three sons—Seth, Josh, and Jeremy—because I didn't hit the ball very far. I chose to use a shorter-hitting club, a three-wood, off the tee rather than the flatter "driver," which would normally go farther. I also learned to hit a short, stiffer backswing, giving up distance for accuracy. Fellow golfers would walk past my shorter drive, muttering the male chauvinist comment, "Play with your husband much?"

My answer was to make up for my shorter distance with an accurate "chip" shot when I was off but near the green, using my pitching wedge. I got so good at it that I would often par a hole by chipping and one-putting, while the longer hitters would curse as I tied or beat them despite their outdriving me on most holes. I loved picking up the ball out of the hole after a one-putt par and saying, "That's called 'the Davis Chip'—good enough for the par and the win."

A few years after our first match, when the money started to accumulate in the Players Fund, or TPF, we decided to use the fund to finance an annual golf trip for the four of us. We picked the golf mecca of Pinehurst, North Carolina, and specifically, a group of golf courses in and around a golf resort called Whispering Pines.

---

* I asked "Commissioner" Hochberg to review this chapter for accuracy. He said I got this account wrong. In the spirit of full disclosure, here is Sheldon's note correcting my account: "Lateral hazards must be water hazards . . . However, your version makes for great reading."

Hard as it is to believe, we played a five-day team tournament—leaving early Wednesday morning, stopping off to play eighteen holes at a nice course in Henderson, North Carolina, and then completing the five-hour drive to arrive by early evening at Whispering Pines. Then we would play thirty-six holes in the morning and afternoon for the next three days and complete the last and final round on Sunday morning before driving home. That's 144 holes in five days. It's a lot of golf.

We played our usual money game, "match play" (counting holes, not scores), each round. We also kept track of the lowest total scores for all eight rounds among all four of us to see who would win the "TPF Cup" each year, with the winner's name engraved on the cup. The winning twosome would host a dinner with our wives to award the cup and "elect" the commissioner for another year. Emblematic of the sheer joy of our annual trip was one comment made by Jack Greenspan early in the morning on one of our first trips, shortly after we left for our drive south to North Carolina. Jack was not known for a lot of emotion or communication. He was the sweet, silent type, as his wife, Lois, sometimes appreciated. During our second or third trip, as we drove down Interstate 95 South through Virginia, the normally quiet Jack broke the silence.

"It's terrible!" he said suddenly and loudly.

"What's 'terrible,' Jack?" I asked him.

"Oh, this is terrible, terrible," he repeated. "I can't stand the thought of it."

"The thought of what, Jack?" Marvin asked.

"Nothing to look forward to," he said in a sad voice. He paused, then continued, "Nothing to look forward to. Golf in a few hours. Then dinner. Then a putting competition on the putting green next to the Whispering Pines dining room for twenty-five cents a hole before dinner. Then a great dinner. Then playing gin rummy. Drinking whiskey. Then bedtime. Then waking up the next morning for a great breakfast."

He continued in his deadpan monologue, "Then eighteen holes. Then a great lunch. Then another eighteen holes. More putting green competition. A great dinner. Then more poker and Jack Daniels. Only to wake up and start all over again. For three more days.

"And most of all, no wives, no kids, no work. Just golf. Terrible. This is just terrible!"

We all laughed and high-fived.

So every year, on the first morning of our drive to our golf trip, about the same time and place on I-95 heading south, Jack would say, "Terrible!" And repeat the identical words. Every time. For over twenty-five years. Of course, he would.

■ ■ ■

Almost every athlete experiences a moment when the zone sets in, all outside noise and thoughts are lost, and you are having, for no discernible reason, that perfect game that comes and goes so quickly you have a hard time believing it happened. And you rarely experience it again.

It happens to pitchers pitching a no-hitter or perfect game—twenty-seven batters, twenty-seven outs, and nine innings with no one reaching base. It happens to baseball hitters, who go on a streak where the ball looks as big as a softball. My usual golf score was in the low- to mid-eighties. Once in a great while, I would break eighty, but the well-worn expression is so true: the difference between eighty and seventy-nine is more than one shot, meaning when you knew sinking a putt would allow you to get below eighty, the pressure would build.

Then one day, when I was forty-three years old, I experienced the "zone" sensation. It was Saturday, July 9, 1988. I knew I was playing well, and by the last hole, I thought I had a chance to break my personal record of seventy-six. I had gotten a lot of pars and had a lucky birdie on the seventeenth hole after making up for a lousy drive with the Davis Chip and a nice putt. On the eighteenth hole, I should have been allowed the "honor" of hitting first, as I had won the previous hole, with a birdie no less. Instead, Sheldon, Marvin, and Jack raced ahead of me to tee off first.

I was left to hit by myself while they had already driven their carts down the fairway. I was irritated, even more so when I saw Sheldon drop his club next to my ball on the fairway and race ahead with Marvin and Jack to hit their final shots to the green and putt out, waiting for me to finish up by myself.

"What the hell are you guys doing?" I shouted as I approached my third shot, just in front of the green, to use the Davis Chip to try for a final par putt. My shot went past the pin, which sloped steeply from the back to the hole. I noticed that Sheldon, Marvin, and Jack stood behind the green, finished, with a group of people from the nearby lunchroom in the clubhouse. It seemed strange to me. What is going on? I thought again. I got to my putt and saw how downhill and slick the green was, so I wanted to avoid hitting it too far past the hole and three-putting. I tapped it softly and let it roll . . . roll . . . roll . . . and, miraculously, it went into the cup for a par.

Then suddenly I heard a roar behind the green. And applause. Jack and Sheldon were rushing to me before I could reach into the hole to pick up the ball. Sheldon took the ball out of the hole and showed me the scorecard: I had scored a par seventy-two on our Norbeck home course, breaking my record by four shots. They knew I was in the zone and didn't want to do anything to break my concentration. Sheldon, the scorekeeper and commissioner, signed the card with the date, 7/9/88. I had it framed, and it remains on my wall to this day.

So the generations turn, and the next generation—our sons—challenged us to a similar tournament as we had done over the years with Jack and Marvin. Seth Davis and Evan Hochberg grew up close in age in a crib at the same time. Evan had blond hair, and Seth quickly developed dark curls. From their time as baby boys together through adulthood, they became best friends forever, and we called them "Salt" and "Pepper."

They ended up going to archrival colleges (Seth to Duke, Evan to UNC-Chapel Hill) and exchanged calls and trash-talking notes before and after the Duke-UNC basketball games. Inevitably, when they reached their thirties and we were in our sixties, they challenged us to a golf trip match, like the TPF ones had with Marvin and Jack over the many years. And with smart-ass cockiness, they taunted us to say yes, with overconfident predictions of beating their "old guy dads."

The old guys won the first year's tournament. The whippersnappers won the second one with some clutch play at the end. Sheldon and I tried to act as if we were upset that we had lost. But we both knew—and didn't have to say it to each other—that we were proud of our two sons for how they won.

We played a third match several years later in 2015, and we were down to the last hole in the last round, all tied. I stood over a difficult thirty-foot putt that, if I made it, would give Sheldon and me the win. Somewhere in the back of my mind, I felt some guilt that if I made the putt, we would beat our sons, and they would be disappointed. Then I remembered when, at one point, I had told Sheldon I would feel bad if we beat them again. He made me repeat to him the line from *Damn Yankees* spoken by the character playing the devil: "Never feel sorry for anyone! Never feel sorry for anyone!"

So I stepped back to putt the ball in the hole for the win. I tried to feel happy as I accepted their handshakes. But inside, I couldn't help it. I felt bad at the look of disappointment on Seth's and Evan's faces. Then again, I never was a Yankees fan, so I shouldn't have been surprised at my feelings.

■ ■ ■

Marvin left us first, on February 16, 2002, twenty-five years after the first match, when he looked so dapper and I holed out a chip shot out of the bunker. Marvin had always had some kind of problematic heart condition he never would explain. We worried about him from time to time. But I didn't know he was sick enough for his life to be at risk.

Two years before he passed away, I was forced into a terrible dilemma. One that haunts me even as I write these words. Marvin worked for a company whose owner made repeated promises regarding retirement support and other benefits. During many rounds of golf, Marvin told me that the company was reneging on these assurances. It gnawed at him, not just because of the financial hardship but also because he thought it was unjust after all his years working loyally and so productively for the company. I agreed that it was unfair but informed him that unless he had it in writing, it would be difficult to enforce.

As it happened, I was retained by this same company in a commercial dispute that had nothing to do with Marvin. But the company became my client—about the same time Marvin retired and demanded they pay his retirement benefits. The company denied making any promises, so Marvin sued them. Marvin's attorney sought my testimony concerning my advice to him on the golf course. The predicament was that I was now representing this company as a lawyer. And yes, it was true: I had told Marvin on the golf course that, in my opinion, he deserved to receive retirement benefits—a conversation his lawyer wanted to put in evidence.

So now I am under oath during a deposition, with Marvin sitting in the room glowering at me. I had no choice but to tell the truth. Under questioning, I related one fact that didn't necessarily help Marvin's case: that I had advised him to get the promises in writing. But his attorney wanted as part of the record that I told Marvin that I thought he was entitled to the pension and other benefits. But when asked whether I had offered him my view of the dispute, I said yes, but then I declined to say what I had told him. The reason was that my law partners had advised me that my opinion was not a fact, and by stating my opinion, I would be showing disloyalty to my client and could be disbarred or disciplined for doing so. The managing partner at Patton Boggs warned me that I risked my partnership in the firm if I violated a basic rule in the legal Canon of Ethics by offering an opinion detrimental to my client. So I was instructed by him to tell the truth, stick to the facts, and not speculate on what the client "should" have done.

When I followed this instruction during the deposition, Marvin stood up and stormed out of the room. I wanted to cry, which I did on my way home.

Soon afterward I was at a party attended by Marvin. I approached him and told him how sorry I was and tried to explain my dilemma. He walked away from me in midsentence. That was the last time we ever spoke. The result of my approaching him at the party and trying to repair our friendship was his lawyer filing a complaint against me before the D.C. Bar Association for talking to his client without going through his lawyer. After Marvin died a few years later, I went to the funeral and made my "shiva" visit to his home, where family and friends gather after the funeral. When I walked in the door, within minutes both his wife and children asked that I leave, which, of course, I did.

I got into my car and cried, grieving the death of my longtime golfing buddy and dear friend and missing him so—and still doubting myself for not standing up for him even at the risk of angering my law partners. I was in a no-win situation, but I feel guilty about it to this day.

Then it was Jack's time. Starting at age fifty-three, he began showing signs of Parkinson's disease. He deteriorated physically, not mentally, over the years. But it was never enough to discourage him from attempting to hit golf balls at the Norbeck practice range. He insisted on going there to swing even when he could barely move his arms or stand up.

It was a moving sight to see his beautiful and loving wife, Lois, at the practice tee with him, well after his Parkinson's had advanced to the point he was confined to a wheelchair and could barely keep his head up straight. Yet there was Lois, helping him out of his wheelchair and standing behind him, with her arms around him, helping him lift his club and swing through the ball. And yes, as his club approached the ball, even slowly with Lois's help, I could hear the sweet "click" of the ball in the sweet spot of the club. Same Jack.

In early February 2020, he was admitted to a hospice, where he would be made comfortable as his life was inevitably ebbing away. I visited him there almost every night. He was cocooned in feelings of devotion by Lois and their sons—Steve, Ricky, and Brad—along with their wives, grandchildren, friends, and nurses—everyone who worked at the hospice had come to love "Sweet" Jack too.

As the end grew near, his family was kind enough to allow me a few minutes each evening, before I left, to be alone with Jack and to whisper a few words in his ear. Even though he was in a coma, I recounted for him the golf stories and memories of the Players Fund tournaments and our years of friendship.

On the night of February 25, 2020, I sensed that Jack was in a deeper, quieter coma. I had the feeling this might be the last time I would see him. I held his hand in the peaceful room and whispered, "It's *terrible*, Jack. *Terrible.* Nothing to look forward to. Golf, lunch, golf, dinner, Jack Daniels, breakfast, golf. No wives and no kids. Just us. And golf. Forever."

As I said these words and held his hand, I swear I saw a faint smile on Jack's face. At least I think I did. I leaned over to kiss his forehead as a way of saying goodbye to Sweet Jack, the man with the sweetest-looking golf swing of us all. I promised him someday he would have to witness again with irritation the Davis Chip rolling up to the hole for the tap-in par.

And I knew the magic would never end.

## CHAPTER 20

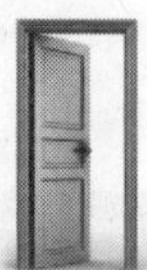

# TELL IT EARLY, TELL IT ALL, TELL IT YOURSELF

Working in the White House was a lifelong dream. I was hardly the only one of my generation who harbored it.

I was fourteen years old when John F. Kennedy became president. It is well documented that his election inspired Roman Catholics, who believed JFK's victory proved that the old chestnut about America being a place where anyone could grow up to be president was really true. For a Jewish teenager who revered Kennedy, the lessons of the 1960 election had a more universal application.

I could grow up to be president too. Why not?

Years later, after losing my 1976 congressional campaign and knowing I couldn't afford to run for elective office again, I gave up on my dream—but not on politics. There were other heroes besides Jack and Jackie Kennedy in "Camelot," as the one-thousand-day presidency of John F. Kennedy came to be called. Some were cabinet members and agency heads. Some were press secretaries or presidential confidants. My dream of working in the White House wasn't abandoned, so much as tailored more realistically to my own political talents. I still wanted to help a president achieve change for the better.

In our family the words "for the better" equated to helping a Democrat achieve liberal social and economic justice, in the tradition of Franklin Roosevelt and Lyndon Johnson. After Bill Clinton's 1996 reelection, I had high hopes Clinton could be that kind of transformational president, governing in the Democratic Leadership Council–New Democrat mode, with a center-left philosophy on most policy issues but a record in Arkansas of fiscal and cultural moderation or conservatism—and of being able to work constructively with Republicans.

Despite Clinton's comfortable margin of victory in 1996, lingering questions arose during the campaign about fundraising practices. For months a series of "no comment" or diversionary but nonresponsive answers by the campaign had only created a greater pressure cooker. Initially fueled by the media, it was kept stoked by Republicans in Congress—and by the Clinton team's inability to get on top of the story.

I figured that any hopes of a historic Clinton second term would depend on the president's ability to relieve that pressure cooker. And I thought I could help.

An early conversation, before I arrived, with White House Press Secretary Michael McCurry (who was on his way to becoming one of the most effective media experts in the history of the presidency) gave me an early glimpse of the counterintuitive strategy for doing just that.

So in the predawn hours of my first days working at the White House in early December 1996, I entered the compound from the Pennsylvania North gate, looking at the brightly lit presidential mansion, walking on the roughed-up bricks that, at some point, might have touched the shoes of Abraham Lincoln, Theodore Roosevelt, and John Kennedy. Still, I often asked myself in those days in some wonderment, "How did I get here?"

■ ■ ■

You could say it all comes down to a wrong turn. When I graduated from Yale College in 1967, I made a left turn out of Davenport College to go to 127 Wall Street in New Haven, the address of the Yale Law School, rather than a right-hand turn. That isn't a metaphor for the political spectrum. It's literally a direction. Turning to the right would have led me in the direction I'd planned since the day I'd become chairman of the *Yale Daily News*: heading to New Haven's Amtrak train station en route to New York City, where I envisioned someday working for *The New York Times* and ultimately becoming a political columnist like my (and my dad's) journalistic hero, James "Scotty" Reston.

Because I didn't stick to my plan, in my third and final year at law school in the fall of 1969, I met the Clintons.

Over the ensuing years, I occasionally was in touch with both Bill and Hillary, who were married in October 1975. In 1980, after Clinton lost his reelection after his first term as Arkansas governor, I got a call from a mutual friend, Harold Ickes, whom I knew from the anti–Vietnam War movement in the 1960s. (Ickes was the son and namesake of the famous liberal New Deal–era Secretary of the Interior, one of Roosevelt's closest advisers.) My generation's Harold Ickes heard I had been elected by the Maryland state party as Democratic national committeeman and called to see if I'd support Clinton if he decided to run for chairman of the DNC. Of course, I said yes, but Clinton subsequently decided to run again for governor in 1982.

Clinton won that race and every subsequent election, and by 1990 (as previously mentioned) was named chairman of the influential centrist Democratic Leadership Council (DLC), started in 1985 by my old friend from the Muskie campaign, Al From.

The DLC's preferred presidential candidate in 1988 was thirty-nine-year-old Al Gore, a first-term senator from Tennessee. But Gore lost the nomination to Massachusetts Governor Michael Dukakis, a traditional liberal pushed even further to the left by the historic candidacy of the Reverend Jesse Jackson. During the 1988 primary season, the DLC was especially critical of Jackson, whom it viewed not so much as an inspiring success story of the Civil Rights Movement but as a more bombastic version of George McGovern. (Jackson certainly gave as good as he got: He referred to the DLC as the "Democratic Leisure Class.")

The real point for me, despite my friendship with Jackson and respect for Dukakis, is that they were too liberal for the American electorate at the time—as the subsequent election returns showed. So in 1990 From looked at the landscape of potential new leaders of the DLC. He had settled on the moderate, charismatic, and popular governor of Arkansas, who had just been reelected to his sixth term. I knew Clinton to be liberal on almost all issues, but I also believed he had the charisma and style to appeal to conservative voters.

I also knew that Clinton was very much like Al Lowenstein in resenting and opposing the "We are always right" purism of the party base. Like Lowenstein (and me), Clinton embraced the politics of persuasion and coalition building with Republican moderates and conservatives to get things done, preferring to win and effect change versus losing and self-proclaiming purist, moral righteousness.

After From convinced the DLC leadership to recruit Clinton to assume the chairmanship, the governor toured the country, spreading the group's centrist "coalition-building" message. I knew he was planning to run for president in 1992, with the risky (for a Democrat) political positioning of running in the center-left, meaning he might be vulnerable in the primaries. Which is why, aside from our Yale connections and his marriage to my law school friend, I knew I would end up supporting him. By 1992, as a DNC member from Maryland, I had an automatic vote as a delegate to the party national conventions—a so-called "superdelegate."

Carolyn and I were in Little Rock on that historic night of November 3, 1992, when I had the surreal sensation of seeing my old friends from Yale days emerge from the governor's mansion at about 10:00 p.m. local time as the nation's television networks had just announced Bill Clinton had defeated President George H. W. Bush and Ross Perot.

I felt like I was in a time warp.

It seemed like just yesterday that I had first met Hillary while we were in line to register for classes in the fall of 1969 (and Bill not long afterward).

And there they were, the two of them: Bill, soon to be inaugurated as the forty-second president of the United States, and Hillary as First Lady. I just kept thinking, *Wow!*

During the transition I was asked to lead a group of lawyers to review the list of potential cabinet selections. The first was an impressive Yale Law–educated lawyer, Zoe Baird, whom Clinton had nominated to be U.S. attorney general. I knew her husband as a Yale Law classmate. When I called to begin the background "vetting" process in late December or early January 1993, they both immediately volunteered that they had not paid Social Security withholding taxes on their nanny and her husband and that neither the nanny nor her husband had obtained their green cards from the Labor Department that allow noncitizens to work in the United States.

I realized that many people had the same problem (including me), and I was relieved to hear they had already taken steps to pay the back taxes owed and file the necessary papers with the Labor Department. Still, I was sufficiently worried about what might happen at a public Senate Judiciary Committee hearing that I called a renowned Los Angeles attorney, Warren Christopher, who headed the Clinton transition team, to fill him in.

"Chris," as the future secretary of state was called, said it was not a big enough deal to take to the president-elect. I should have heeded my instincts. A few days before Baird's Senate hearing, the information about the "nanny problem," as the media called it, came out. There were tough headlines, and not just in the conservative media. *The Washington Post*, for example, published an accusatory editorial highly critical of Zoe and her husband.

Even the friendly chairman of the Senate Judiciary Committee, Joe Biden (my old friend from my first days running for Congress), recommended withdrawal of the nomination before the scheduled confirmation hearing. That advice was not heeded, and the day after the hearing on January 23, 1993, Zoe saw no choice but to ask the Clintons—who'd been in office all of three days—to withdraw her nomination.

Soon afterward there was a media report that "White House sources" had indicated that the Baird issue was due to poor vetting. I ignored it, rationalizing that someone in the White House thought it was necessary to protect the president. But Carolyn did not react as I did.

On a Saturday afternoon, Carolyn (now a graduate of Georgetown Law School, who had participated on the vetting team) called the White House and had gotten through to Bruce Lindsey. Bruce was a close friend of President Clinton and served as his legal adviser.

"You got through to Bruce Lindsey to complain?" I asked, aghast.

She assured me she had, adding that she had "given him a piece of my mind." (I knew that experience.) Years later, when Carolyn finally had a chance to meet Bruce in person, they laughed about the conversation, Bruce conceding he had survived the scolding "but just barely."

In early February the second possible nominee for attorney general, U.S. District Court Judge Kimba Wood, also had to withdraw when she disclosed that she had not obtained papers that would complete the documentation necessary for her nanny, although it was pointed out at the time of her hire that such papers were not legally required. I was not involved in that vetting.

A few days later, White House Counsel Bernard Nussbaum called me and asked if I would vet another possible nominee, Janet Reno, the state attorney (top prosecutor) in Dade County, Florida. Bernie implied that the president had confidence in me and our prior vetting—but also that we should also be extra careful on this one.

I assured him that we would explore the Social Security, contractor, and undocumented worker issues, as well as any other potentially thorny personal issues, as best we could. I called two dozen attorneys (including

Carolyn), and they all agreed to join our vetting team and meet the next morning. We began a thorough, nearly 24/7 effort of making hundreds of calls to friends, family, and professional colleagues of Reno in Dade County and beyond. I called Janet to introduce myself. At my request she packed her bags, filled up many boxes with documents from all the cases she had supervised, and shipped them for overnight delivery to my office. The next morning she was in my law office at Patton Boggs to meet with our vetting team.

For the next few days, we made hundreds of calls, read and reviewed thousands of pages in her boxes of files, and had some very personal conversations with Janet about her social and professional life.

The worst issue I was forced to explore was published rumors that she was gay. That wouldn't be an issue today, of course, and I didn't think it should have been then. I said we shouldn't dignify her critics by looking into her private life at all. But everyone at the White House who called me—and many did—thought we should inquire, with Janet's permission, just to be prepared in case the matter surfaced. I met Janet alone and, with apologies and some embarrassment, asked her about these rumors. She laughed and said that she had read those reports and that they were a result of her being a single woman who never married. That was that. I reported her answer up the chain of command and said I was done with it.

All went well. I was immensely impressed with Janet. In the first week of February 1993, a team of White House lawyers and senior staffers came to the big conference room at Patton Boggs to hear about the results of our vetting. I gave a full report, with all the members of the vetting team adding their own details. No nanny problem. No undocumented immigrant worker problem. No personal issues.

On February 10, however, I got a call from Nussbaum. He reaffirmed that he did not care about the gay question and didn't believe the president or the First Lady cared, either, but he had gotten a call from a third party in Miami and wanted me to run down one more rumor. He told me the president was planning to announce Janet's nomination the next day in the Rose Garden, so I didn't have much time.

I called an attorney on the vetting team whom I knew well. She was an outstanding trial lawyer and a woman who would be able to ask Janet personal and detailed questions that I was too bashful or too inept to ask.

That night she met with Janet—just the two of them.

The next morning I got a call from this attorney who had spent many hours speaking with Janet. She told me she had good news and bad news. Which one did I want to hear first?

I said good news.

"She is, in my opinion, personally and professionally, definitely not gay."

"Okay," I said. Not that I cared one way or the other, and I kept repeating apologies that we were even asking or talking about the issue. "So what's the bad news?"

She laughed. "Well, it really isn't bad news per se, but it helped prove to me she wasn't gay."

"Okay, tell me," I said, puzzled.

"She fucks around!" she said.

Adding for emphasis: "With men!"

Honestly, I sighed with relief, but I still felt embarrassed that I even had to address this topic. I called Bernie Nussbaum at the White House and was put through within seconds. He apparently had been awaiting my call. I made sure he was alone.

"Well?" he asked.

I told him the good news and the bad news as it had been expressed to me. When I got to the bad news, he had to laugh. He shared my chagrin that this was even a topic to be scrutinized.

Within an hour I watched the president of the United States announce his new nominee for attorney general—Janet Reno. And there she was, beaming and so proud in the Rose Garden.

Several weeks later she was confirmed by the Senate in a unanimous 98–0 vote. We had a party for the vetting team at our home in Potomac, and Janet was the surprise guest (accompanied now by a Secret Service and security team).

As we sat with her in the living room before dinner, our big, lovable rescue dog, Dusty, without anyone noticing, headed over to Janet. He decided to go under her chair and do his business right there in the house. Within seconds, we noticed an unpleasant odor coming from under Janet's chair. And there it was—Dusty's gift to Janet.

Carolyn and I, horrified, jumped up to deal with it, but Janet was faster than we were. She waved us off as she looked under her chair and laughed. She said we shouldn't worry, that she'd had plenty of dogs and cats and was experienced at looking after them. With that, she grabbed tissues from the nearby bathroom, made several back-and-forth trips, and then finished up with a wet paper towel. Everyone in the room was mortified, but when she started laughing with an infectious belly laugh, we all laughed with her.

Noticing our embarrassment, she told Carolyn and me, "Don't worry—this is a good experience for me. After all, I am going to be doing something like this to deal with Washington, D.C., politicians!"

■ ■ ■

The Clinton administration's first term was marred by what now is generally acknowledged to be a frivolous and partisan investigation called "Whitewater." This involved the Whitewater Development Corporation, a real estate investment made by the Clintons twenty years earlier that had resulted in monetary losses to its investors, including an Arkansas savings and loan. It had nothing to do with Clinton's presidency. There was never a shred of evidence of any criminal wrongdoing by either Clinton. Yet for almost the entire first term, the nation's mainstream media, the television networks, and the White House press corps wasted their time—and the nation's time—by obsessing over this nonissue.

*The New York Times* and *The Washington Post*, both of which seemed to want to prove they could be bipartisan, virtually forced the appointment of a special prosecutor. That was when things went off the rails.

Passed as a Watergate reform, the special prosecutor law had already been proven problematic. Republicans targeted by the law complained for years that the statute was an unworkable mess. Congress could call for a special prosecutor, the attorney general then agreed, but a three-judge panel appointed the prosecutors. Too often the result was unaccountable fiefdoms run by prosecutors with Napoleon complexes who dragged out investigations for years, showed no sense of perspective, and even sought to criminalize policy differences. These complaints turned out to be valid, as a horrified Janet Reno learned while watching powerlessly as interminable special counsel investigations damaged the lives and political careers of public servants ranging from conservative lawyer Theodore Olson to charismatic liberal Democrat Henry Cisneros.

Olson's challenge to the law case went all the way to the Supreme Court, which upheld the constitutionality of the special prosecutor law (by then renamed the "independent counsel" law) on a 7–1 vote. I don't often find myself in lonely agreement with Antonin Scalia, but based on what unfolded in the Clinton presidency, Justice Scalia was prescient. "I fear the Court has permanently encumbered the Republic with an institution that will do it great harm," he wrote.

Reno, who favored the law when she arrived in Washington and played a role in getting it reauthorized, eventually came to the same conclusion. She was appalled by the conduct of several of the prosecutors appointed during her tenure, especially David M. Barrett, who was appointed to investigate whether Cisneros—appointed by Clinton as secretary of housing—had minimized, during his FBI background check, how much money he'd paid to a former girlfriend when he was mayor of San Antonio.

It turned out that Cisneros had indeed underreported the figure, but this was the very definition of a "process" crime—there was no victim—

and about as wholesome a sex scandal as you'd ever find. Cisneros, while married, fell in love with a woman named Linda Medlar, lived with her for a time, and then decided to go back to his wife. Medlar essentially lost her livelihood because of it, so Cisneros (by then working in the private sector) helped her financially. It was the stand-up thing to do. But not to the special prosecutor. Barrett took ten years investigating, at a cost of $21 million to U.S. taxpayers; wrote a four-hundred-page report; derailed Cisneros's political career permanently; and sent Medlar to prison for fudging details on a mortgage form while trying to be discreet about Cisneros. (Barrett was still investigating this insignificant case *after George W. Bush had been reelected in 2004.*)

In any event, by January 1994, the statute had lapsed, so when Republicans clamored for an "independent counsel," it fell to Reno to decide. To universal acclaim, she appointed Robert B. Fiske, a man of unparalleled integrity who in the past had demonstrated political independence as well as prosecutorial restraint. Fiske pursued the Whitewater investigation aggressively and professionally—and had added to his portfolio the tragic suicide of Deputy White House Counsel Vince Foster—when he was abruptly replaced by a three-judge panel. It was a bizarre catch-22 situation. Congress had reauthorized the independent counsel law (supported by Reno and signed by Clinton) after he was appointed, and it was universally believed in Washington that the three-judge appellate panel would keep Fiske's investigation on track. Instead, without being asked to get involved, the judges ruled that in the interest of avoiding even the "perceptions of conflict," it was replacing Fiske. This was a crock, as the identity of the new special prosecutor made clear: It was Kenneth Starr, not only a very conservative D.C. Circuit judge but also an outspoken Republican partisan.

If this were a screwball comedy of the type popular when Ken Starr (now deceased) and I were young, what we'd say about what came next would be, "Hijinks ensued."

But what unfolded over the next five years was no laughing matter. It helped set this country on a take-no-prisoners kind of politics that has Americans hating each other over whether they identify as a *D* or an *R*. As far as Whitewater goes, I'd set the record straight by pointing out that after seven years and more than $60 million, hundreds of hours of partisan Republican congressional investigations and public hearings, and thousands of column inches and sensational headlines in mainstream media, Starr and his overzealous prosecutors found no wrongdoing.

Of course, by then, Starr was going after Clinton for behavior utterly unrelated to Arkansas finances or his official duties as president. But that was all in the future.

■ ■ ■

In 1996 Clinton was ready to run for a second term against Kansas Senator Robert Dole. The economy was humming along, and the Clinton-Gore ticket seemed unbeatable. But Whitewater lingered as an issue, with attacks on Hillary becoming more and more personal, which meant I got angrier and angrier. On January 6, 1996, William Safire, one of the nation's most influential political columnists, wrote a *New York Times* column headlined "Blizzard of Lies," referring to Hillary's public claims and testimony about her role in the Whitewater real estate investment.

Despite the scurrilous headline, Safire's column did not establish a single "lie" by the First Lady. It was all innuendo. Worse, Safire, a Republican and former Nixon speechwriter, referred to Hillary as a "congenital liar."

That made me angry. As Hillary would say over the years, when Lanny gets mad at false accusations in the media, he won't give up until they are corrected. She is right, and it's especially true when it involves a friend who has been kind and supportive of me.

I wrote a rebuttal column, citing specific instances of false innuendo versus the facts, proving that Safire had been wrong. The *Times* refused to publish it.*

I circulated the piece to my friends and allies, however. As a result, I received a call from a leader of an outside group led by a former Iowa congressional candidate, Lynn Cutler, which had been set up to defend the Clintons on Whitewater. She said "someone" at the White House had forwarded my unpublished column to her. She asked if I would be willing to go on a new cable show, CNN's *Burden of Proof*, cohosted by former prosecutor and future Fox News Channel star Greta Van Susteren.

I was briefed by a deputy White House counsel, Jane Sherburne, on the facts concerning Whitewater. Two White House lawyers took the lead in prepping me for this first media appearance and from then on for dozens of others in 1996 during the presidential campaign. Their names: Mark Fabiani and Chris Lehane. The pair literally invented this concept of White House lawyers who led the media message response to partisan attacks. Fabiani and Lehane, two geniuses at media and pretty darn good lawyers, also opened the door to my going to the White House and showed me the path to inventing a law practice at the intersection of law, media, and politics to the present day. (When they left to set up a crisis management firm in California, they were known as the Masters of Disasters.)

On one occasion I was in the middle of Tennessee for a law client and was in the hotel bar having a snack when the bartender told me there was an urgent call to the hotel from the White House. I called back from a phone booth. (Cell phones were rare in those days.) Lehane and Fabiani were on the line, asking me if I could call in to CNN's 9:00 p.m.

* Two years later, in January 1998, I was invited to lunch with Safire to discuss my lingering anger at his false attack on Hillary Clinton. Remarkably, it was a friendly lunch: He conceded he had suspicions, not facts, and probably used language that was a "bit too strong." Afterward, he wrote a gracious column, at least giving me respect for my criticisms of his column and defense of the Clintons on Whitewater.

prime-time show, *Larry King Live*, to debate a Republican partisan congressman who had attacked the Clintons in the media that day on the Whitewater issue. I said I was stuck in a bar in Tennessee, but they insisted I call in within a few minutes and gave me the studio number.

So there I was in a phone booth looking at the TV behind the bartender, with Larry King interviewing me on the phone, as I debated (and some said aggressively attacked) this Republican congressman. The handful of people in the bar, especially the bartender, were in disbelief as their heads went from watching the TV screen showing my name as being on the phone with Larry King and then back to me on the phone in the booth. If it seemed surreal to them, it was the same for me.

■ ■ ■

Late in November 1996, I received a phone call that changed my life. It was White House Counsel Jack Quinn, an old friend from past (unsuccessful) campaigns going back to Walter Mondale in 1984. He told me that the president and Mrs. Clinton were looking for a replacement for the magical Fabiani-Lehane team. They needed lawyers who understood politics and media and said that my work in 1996 proved I could do the job.

When I hesitated because of the financial sacrifice entailed in withdrawing as a partner at my law firm and mentioned there were other lawyers who had media experience, Jack added, "But you have a third qualification that the First Lady wanted me to remind you of: You are an old and loyal friend."

After consulting with Carolyn and calculating the drawdown on our savings account and the losses I would sustain by leaving as an equity partner at Patton Boggs, I called Quinn back and said yes. But first I wanted to confer with another past political acquaintance. When I visited White House Press Secretary Michael McCurry in his famous West Wing office with the half-circle desk that had been inhabited by many famous predecessors, he was ready with the answer to my key question.

"So, Mike," I asked him, "if I am supposed to speak for the president to the media as a White House counsel, and you speak for the president as a press secretary, where does your job end and my job begin?"

McCurry put his legs up on the half-moon desk and smiled the mischievous grin I soon learned to be wary of.

"That's easy," he said. "Have you ever heard of the bumper sticker 'Shit happens'?"

"Yes," I answered, "what about it?"

"Well, when shit happens, you speak."

We discussed Mike's strategy of him referring all unpleasant questions about campaign finance and other legal controversies or "scandals" to me. This would allow him, he explained, to take questions only about the president's policy initiatives. He added a brilliant, counterintuitive twist: He would furnish me a list of the White House correspondents from mainstream media organizations so we could leak information to them on our timetable. Their stories would come from White House documents (mainly from former Deputy Chief of Staff Harold Ickes's files) that had been turned over under subpoena to the Republican-dominated Senate and House Oversight Committees.

Led by Tennessee Senator Fred Thompson, who had presidential aspirations for 2000, and Indiana Representative Dan Burton, the Republicans were planning nationally televised hearings in the early summer of 1997. McCurry's plan: Get the most damaging information out early, in the winter and spring of 1997, so by the time of the hearings, all the stories would be "old news," blunting their political impact.

The strategy worked better than we could have imagined. Before each televised hearing, I and my colleagues from the White House counsel's office would scoop the opening of the televised hearing by handing out multiple news clippings of the stories about the subject of the hearing, already written weeks and months ago, while reciting our mantra: "Old news, been there, done that."†

A high point for us was when Senator Thompson, frustrated at our tactics, started out a hearing by saying something like, "Today we are investigating a subject that even Lanny Davis can't call 'old news'!" When we heard him from a side room where the White House staff gathered to watch the hearings on TV, we cheered and high-fived. The final summary of the effectiveness of McCurry's preemptive "bad news" strategy was a cover story in the September 1, 1997, edition of *The New Republic* by William Powers. The cartoon on the front cover was of me, with a blown-up head, wearing oversized glasses, coming out of a cyclone, depicted as a "whirling dervish."

The headline: "The Hardest Working Man in Snowbiz." The lengthy article described our "get the bad news out ourselves" preemptive strategy. Powers ended the piece with the following:

> *[Lanny] then went off the record and gave me a fascinating and provocative answer, entirely different from what preceded*

† My White House memoir, published in 1999 after I left, described our strategy in detail, using specific examples of nasty stories that we preempted by "equal opportunity leaking," as McCurry called it.

> *it, that I can't share with you. It made me think good thoughts about this White House for a few seconds . . . maybe Lanny's secret message would have affected what I wrote. I'd been spun. And it was sort of thrilling, in a vaguely disquieting way.*

I left the job on January 31, 1998, earlier than my two-year commitment to the president and First Lady, because we were expecting our son Josh, who was born in March.

My White House memoir, *Truth to Tell*, describes the conflict I felt ten days before my scheduled departure date when I got a call from Peter Baker, then working for *The Washington Post*. Peter asked me to comment on a huge breaking story. He gave me ninety minutes to comment about the independent counsel expanding his criminal investigation of the Whitewater real estate "scandal" to include President Clinton's alleged conduct involving a former White House intern named Monica Lewinsky.

In consternation, I asked, "What does that have to do with Whitewater?" I added that I had never heard the name Monica Lewinsky before.

At home I put my hand over the telephone and said to Carolyn, sitting across the kitchen table from me, "This could be one of the worst stories President Clinton has ever faced."

"Oh, you always say that," she replied, trying to be reassuring.

This time my instincts were solid. And after I left the White House at the end of January, President Clinton's personal attorney had no choice but to limit White House officials in commenting publicly during an ongoing criminal investigation. As a result, that left me—friend, lawyer, and *former* White House counsel—to fill the vacuum as the only go-to guest on nightly cable news shows to defend Clinton from House Republican impeachment efforts.

It soon became apparent to me that friendships I had made with two of the sharpest Republican adversaries during the subsequent evening cable debates on the ensuing drama put me in a unique position to help

President Clinton. The pair was South Carolina Representative Lindsey Graham and Florida Representative Joe Scarborough. My position was that Clinton should not be the second president in U.S. history—after the partisan and illegitimate 1868 impeachment of Andrew Johnson—to be impeached. What Clinton had done, a result of a personal weakness shared by many, was not what the Founders envisioned as an impeachable offense. Most Americans shared my view—that this was a matter best left up to him and his wife.

So I decided I could quietly help the president and the Democratic leaders of the House—and I believe (and still believe) the country as a whole—by trying to persuade Representatives Graham and Scarborough to see censure as an alternative to impeachment. I opposed both but was searching for common ground. My hope was that these two anti-Clinton Republican conservatives would give me insights into the possibility of winning over enough Republicans to consider censure as an alternative to impeachment.

But as I soon learned, and the rest of America learned as well, compromise and consensus were no longer the coin of the realm in Washington. The currency was winning at all costs, demonizing one's adversary, and punishing the other side—the good of the country be damned.

## CHAPTER 21

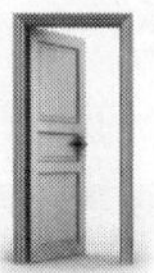

# CLINTON IMPEACHMENT: LINDSEY GRAHAM, JOE SCARBOROUGH, AND ME

We came so close, down to the final minutes on December 12, 1998, when South Carolina congressman Lindsey Graham said six words to me: "No man is above the law."

Then he turned to vote on the House Judiciary Committee for impeachment rather than censure. At that moment I could only recall the many months of quiet efforts on my own, without any official authorization from the White House, getting to know Graham personally and thinking we had become akin to friends and getting private advice from his Republican colleague, Florida Congressman Joe Scarborough. Although Scarborough was pro-impeachment, he nevertheless counseled me on how to best move Lindsey to support censure rather than impeachment.

I knew at that moment we had come so close to avoiding the historic asterisk on Bill Clinton's presidency that I deeply believed would be unjustified but indelible. I felt no satisfaction in how close we came. Close only counts in horseshoes and hand grenades, as the saying goes, and this didn't feel like horseshoes.

My personal connection to Scarborough and Graham began after the Monica Lewinsky story broke in the media in mid-January 1998, which led to immediate talk of impeachment by House Republicans and the extension of Independent Counsel Kenneth Starr's jurisdiction. I had already announced my resignation from my White House special counsel position because my wife was expecting a baby.

So after January 31, 1998, I was a private citizen again. This gave me an advantage in defending President Clinton in the media: I could do so without the president's lawyers having to be responsible for anything I said, especially if I made mistakes. I tried to check on my facts and the law, however, before speaking out. Invitations poured in from cable and broadcast producers, asking me to appear. I was happy to accept, especially because Starr's active investigation made it imprudent for his attorneys to speak publicly.

From February 1998 until the House impeachment vote on December 19, I was often on cable television or radio talk show interviews several times a day. In that process I became well acquainted with Scarborough and Graham, two of the House Republicans leading the charge on an impeachment inquiry. What developed between us was a prolonged debate about the appropriateness of what I considered the obvious and preferable alternative to impeachment proceedings: a censure resolution by both houses of Congress, signed by Clinton, along with a presidential apology.

Our conversations on impeachment versus censure almost always occurred off camera, in the hallways of CNN or other cable stations and sometimes in telephone calls I made to their offices. The two men were consistent during my separate conversations with each, on and off camera. They wanted Clinton to be held publicly and historically accountable for his conduct—and they saw impeachment as the only constitutional method to do so.

I maintained (and still do) that the personal conduct of President Clinton did not come close to meeting the standards for impeachment articulated by Alexander Hamilton, James Madison, and the other

Founders and affirmed by constitutional scholars through the years. It simply didn't rise to an egregious executive branch abuse of power, undermining the Constitution. I did not want Clinton to be unfairly stigmatized as only the second U.S. president to be impeached by the House of Representatives—the first being Andrew Johnson on February 24, 1868.*

I found Lindsey Graham to be easygoing and possessing a first-rate legal mind. He'd been a defense lawyer and a prosecutor before entering politics and had served in the JAG Corps in the United States Air Force before and after serving in Congress. But he wasn't easygoing about perjury, an issue he fixated on as the scandal unfolded.

For his part, Scarborough was mainly repulsed by what the president had done. He didn't really engage with me on the Constitution's words requiring a "high crime and misdemeanor" or the intent of the Framers. He was just too offended. I liked and respected Joe almost from the first moment we met on a CNN set. I thought he'd lost all sense of perspective in wanting to use the impeachment clause to remove an elected president for a personal failing exhibited by many men I knew (including, as I said to him, both of us). Still, I could appreciate his sharp legal mind and that he was articulate and passionate. I thought he was a good lawyer, and his charisma was palpable. (Many times, I thought, *This guy would be great on TV if he ever got out of politics.*)

Often, as we left the set, Joe would pat me on the shoulder and compliment me by telling me that if he was ever in trouble, I was the guy he'd want in his corner. "Bill Clinton is lucky to have you," he'd say.

Lucky? I didn't feel lucky. Despite his ardent support for impeachment, Joe was also willing to give me good political advice, mostly about dealing with Graham, who he explained to me was the House Republican who should be the focus of my attention. Graham was perhaps the most

---

* The House Judiciary Committee approved three articles of impeachment against Richard Nixon on July 27, 1974, but the thirty-seventh U.S. president resigned two weeks later, forestalling any further action by Congress. One of the young Democratic lawyers working for the committee was none other than Hillary Rodham.

influential member of the House Judiciary Committee, controlled by the Republicans 21–17. No Clinton impeachment resolution could get to the floor unless approved first by a majority of members on Judiciary.

So I spent most of my time trying to persuade Lindsey to support censure instead of impeachment. Perjury was the sticking point. He would not countenance a president lying under oath, which Graham had convinced himself Clinton had done. Graham was referring to Clinton's January 17, 1998, deposition in a lawsuit alleging sexual harassment brought against the president by a former Arkansas state employee named Paula Corbin Jones, whose civil case became part of Ken Starr's sweeping criminal investigation.

Starr's original portfolio was to see if any federal laws had been broken in an arcane personal investment Bill and Hillary made in the Whitewater Development Corporation, an Arkansas real estate partnership that later went bankrupt. (No wrongdoing was ever found on the part of either of the Clintons.) Both controversies involved private conduct, having nothing whatsoever to do with presidential abuse of power. The Whitewater investment (in which the Clintons lost money) was in the 1980s. Paula Jones said her encounter with Governor Clinton took place on May 8, 1991—more than twenty-one months before he became president. Jones waited to file her case in Little Rock's federal district court until May 6, 1994, two days before the statute of limitations expired.

Paula Corbin, who was twenty-seven when she went to work for the state of Arkansas, was not a political person. But the Little Rock lawyers who backed her lawsuit certainly were known Clinton adversaries. So was Steve Jones, the man she married in 1992 and who told journalists he "hated" the president. Although Paula Jones's May 6, 1994, press conference received scant media coverage, as the litigation made its way through the courts, interest in the case grew—especially after May 27, 1997, when the U.S. Supreme Court ruled unanimously that the case could proceed. Even then, the coverage was somewhat restrained, right up until the Monica Lewinsky story exploded onto the front pages and airwaves of every news outlet in America.

Clinton's testimony took place on January 17, 1998, four days before the Lewinsky matter was known to the public. The story appeared in the early edition of *The Washington Post*, published late at night on January 20, the fifth anniversary of Clinton's inauguration (although a sparsely read political blog, the *Drudge Report*, first mentioned the Lewinsky matter on January 17).

Neither the president nor his attorney, however, knew that Paula Jones's attorneys had been alerted to the fact that Starr had expanded the investigation into an alleged relationship with a young White House intern. Later, we learned that a group of Philadelphia attorneys who called themselves the "elves" knew members of the Starr team and were told about Starr's expanded investigation of Clinton's personal life. (That information was arguably definable as "grand jury information," meaning it was a crime to reveal it.)

One of those "elves" was someone named George Conway. He would subsequently marry Republican pollster Kellyanne Fitzpatrick. She, in turn, would find fame—some would say notoriety—as a senior adviser to Donald Trump. Still later, their marriage would founder when George Conway emerged as one of the most vocal and vitriolic "Never Trumpers." Conway's questionable role in the nexus between Starr and Jones's lawyers was forgotten and never mentioned by him when he became a hero to Trump opponents in the 2020s.

Thanks to the leak, Clinton was asked by Jones's attorney whether he'd had "sexual relations" with Ms. Lewinsky. Within a week or so, that question was ruled irrelevant to the Jones sexual harassment case. But the damage was done. The "perjury trap" had been sprung.

But did Bill Clinton really commit perjury? I maintained at the time, and do so to this day, that the answer is no. The evidence later cited by Starr was that the president denied having "sexual relations" or "an extramarital sexual affair" with Monica Lewinsky. But in the deposition before U.S. District Court Judge Susan Webber Wright, it was Jones's lawyers who came up with the tortured definition of sex that Clinton was responding to—and which did not cover the activity with Lewinsky that Clinton later acknowledged. Was the president being overly "lawyerly"? Well, yes, he's an attorney—in a face-off against other attorneys who were trying to get him. Was he being legalistic? Sure, but it was a legal proceeding.

Notwithstanding nighttime television jokes about the nature of sex and the endless ridicule from Republican impeachment supporters, Clinton was careful—more careful than his critics. But I could never get Graham to see it. Instead, from the moment that definition was leaked, Graham used it to state unequivocally that Clinton had committed "perjury," that is, he had shown criminal intent by inventing what he called "that absurd" definition.

Tired of Graham constantly referring to squirrely language he said was created by Clinton or his attorneys, I took the time (which apparently few others did) to read the deposition transcript when it was made public by the Jones legal team.

To repeat, because it's misunderstood to this day, I was shocked to discover that it was Jones's own attorney, James A. Fisher, who wrote and introduced the definition, not Clinton or his counsel.

Graham wrongly assumed, as did most people, that Clinton came up with this arcane definition of "sexual relations" to give him cover to mislead the courts. Graham relied on his belief that Clinton had created the definition to demonstrate Clinton's *criminal intent*, that is, perjury. When I confronted Graham with the deposition transcript showing it was Jones's lawyer who introduced the definition at the start of the deposition and not Clinton, Graham could not hide his surprise. But then he just reiterated his mantra: Clinton lied under oath, period.

The next time I was with Scarborough on TV, I showed him the passage from the transcript showing that it was Jones's attorney who had introduced the narrow definition and had, in effect, instructed Clinton to rely on it for purposes of the deposition. Scarborough, too, admitted he did not know it and seemed taken aback—but only for a moment. I could see Joe had some doubts. He hesitated. Then, like

Graham, he just repeated his belief that Clinton had lied. But he seemed less convinced.

Nonetheless, as the spring turned to summer, I sensed (and anecdotally I heard from Democratic House members) that the momentum, if not enthusiasm, to impeach Clinton over the Jones deposition was waning among many GOP members. Then another shoe dropped. On July 30, 1998, the media reported that President Clinton, contrary to the advice of most of his legal team, had agreed to testify before a federal grand jury. He had been subpoenaed by Starr. But by voluntarily agreeing to testify, Clinton wasn't acknowledging or conceding that he was forced to do so by subpoena.

I wasn't surprised to learn Clinton was willing to roll the dice. He was, in my estimation, the greatest politician of my generation. He knew that refusing to testify would be counter to the core Democratic Party value of transparency. I assume he also believed the grand jury would find him a convincing witness.

Republicans saw it differently. They were giddy. They were convinced Clinton would have no choice but to lie to the grand jury about his relationship with Ms. Lewinsky. Among the many calls I got from others, especially the media, it was universal: Almost everyone expected Clinton to lie about what had happened between him and Ms. Lewinsky (since all assumed *something* had happened).

Remarkably, I did see a reaction from Graham about Clinton's dilemma in testifying before the grand jury that I had not seen before: something approaching empathy. "That poor SOB," Graham said. The consensus was nearly universal—in the political world, in the media, among most of my friends: Bill Clinton would never tell what was perceived as the truth about what happened between himself and Monica Lewinsky.

And then he did.

■ ■ ■

On August 17, 1998, I was on the MSNBC set in Washington, D.C., waiting to go on air. I had no idea what I would say if, as I expected, President Clinton continued to deny any improper conduct with Ms. Lewinsky. I knew it would be difficult for me to convey that I believed that to be true. I just didn't know what I would say other than ducking.

I was nervous for him. I deeply felt his pain. He had to choose between hurting his wife, my longtime friend, and their daughter and endure the embarrassment of admitting that he had lied when he denied any improper relationship just seven months or so before on national television.

My other reaction was outrage at the terrible, senseless, utter loss of proportionality by the independent counsel in choosing to essentially criminalize private personal conduct. Then as I stared at the blank TV monitor, there he was. Close up. Full face. The lead prosecutor began his questioning on international live TV by stating that he knew his questions would be "uncomfortable" and adding, "I apologize for that in advance."

My heart was beating so hard and so fast that host Brian Williams must have noticed my distress.

"Are you okay, Lanny?" he asked.

I didn't answer. Just stared at the screen. Robert Bittman, a prosecutor on Starr's staff, asked the first question that went to the core of the entire proceeding. The answer would define whether an incumbent American president had committed perjury or not.

"Mr. President, were you physically intimate with Monica Lewinsky?"

President Clinton responded, "Mr. Bittman, I think maybe I can save the—you and the grand jurors a lot of time if I read a statement which I think will make it clear what the nature of my relationship with Ms. Lewinsky was . . ."

"Absolutely. Please, Mr. President."

Then Clinton testified, "When I was alone with Ms. Lewinsky on certain occasions in early 1996, and once in 1997, I engaged in conduct that was wrong. These encounters did not consist of sexual intercourse. They did not constitute sexual relations, as I understood that term to be defined in my January 17, 1998, [Paula Jones case] deposition. But they did involve inappropriate, intimate contact."

When I heard Clinton say those words, I could only imagine how much agony he had gone through and was now going through in public, before his family and the world. But I also felt relief. I and almost everyone else had underestimated Bill Clinton. He had told the truth on the only issue that mattered. As to impeachment, I now knew for Republicans it was game over.

Suddenly, in my earpiece, I heard the immediately recognizable deep baritone voice of Tom Brokaw, the famous NBC *Nightly News* anchor. "Hello, Lanny, we are coming to you now. Live." I now experienced a terrifying moment. I was about to be on television to the American people at a crucial moment in U.S. history and had absolutely no idea what I was going to say. After all these years, I can't remember exactly what I said in the twenty to thirty seconds. It was something approaching satisfaction that the president had told the truth, and I hoped and expected impeachment threats were behind us.

I was even more confident of that belief when the results of the November midterm congressional elections came in. Ordinarily, all other things being equal, the party in Congress that doesn't control the White House gains House seats—sometimes overwhelmingly, if the incumbent is suffering political difficulties. On November 3, 1998, contrary to all precedent, House Republicans suffered a *net loss of five seats*. It was incredible. It hadn't happened since 1822. To me, the lesson was clear: Republicans had overplayed their hand on impeachment. Political scientist Alan Abramowitz conducted a postelection analysis and came to the same conclusion. He attributed the GOP's poor performance in the 1998 midterms to public backlash against their excessive focus on the Lewinsky matter and Clinton impeachment effort.

Now I thought there was no way the Republicans could go forward with impeachment, given this repudiation by the voters. Once again, I was wrong. I underestimated the determination of House Republican Whip Texas Representative Tom DeLay to stay the course. He was intent on holding an impeachment vote in December before the House session was concluded. DeLay knew that would make the impeachment vote illegitimate since he would be counting the votes of "lame duck" pro-impeachment Republicans who had just been defeated for reelection by anti-impeachment Democrats less than two months before. He didn't care.

I called Lindsey Graham shortly after I heard DeLay was insisting on going forward. I asked him for the first time whether he would consider a strong censure resolution in lieu of impeachment. I expected his usual sharp negative response to letting Clinton escape impeachment. This time he hesitated. "It depends on the language," he said. Then he added, quickly puncturing my lightly filled balloon of hope: Only if he agreed in the resolution that he had committed perjury before the grand jury. I knew that was a nonstarter. Clinton might admit to a lot of things, but he would not agree to that. He had told the truth, painfully, about the essential issue. Rather than arguing with Graham, I asked him to give me some time.

I called Joe Scarborough. Yes, he saw that the November elections had dampened the enthusiasm of a lot of House Republicans, including himself, to vote on a Clinton impeachment. "Work on Lindsey Graham," he said. "I told you before—he's the pivotal vote."

Soon thereafter, I received a call from Trent Lott, the Republican leader of the Senate. He was a friend of my senior partner and mentor, Tom Boggs, at my law firm, Patton Boggs. Tom had encouraged him to call me and deliver the message: Lott thought he could get enough Republican support in the Senate to support a tough censure resolution rather than impeachment. Lott read the 1998 midterm election returns the way everyone else did. He also said that he put President Clinton's "offense" into the category of a human weakness that should be between himself and his wife and family rather than a political weapon in a partisan impeachment vote.

I had some more hope. That's not how it turned out, but from that day forward, I had high regard for Lott.

A quick flash forward: Five years later I would respond to Lott's call for advice when he faced his own political crisis. He had told a joke with racist overtones. Reverend Jesse Jackson, whom he knew had become a friend of mine, had reached out to him. He was worried about whether Reverend Jackson would exploit Senator Lott if he took the call. I assured him no, that Reverend Jackson had ministered to many people over the years, including me and Bill Clinton, and I was sure that was the reason he had called.

I called Jesse and told him about Lott's call to me. He told me he sincerely wanted to minister to him, to forgive him and help him find peace. I was in Jesse's D.C. office when Senator Lott called him. I sat there in amazement when I heard Reverend Jackson take Lott's call, listen for five minutes, interrupt every so often with "I understand," and then say, "Senator, I forgive you. Let us pray."

It was surreal, listening to Jesse Jackson pray for Trent Lott. From that day forward, the two men remained friends. I remain thankful I was there to witness that awesome prayer by Jesse Jackson for Trent Lott, two political opposites who shared the common human experience of sin and redemption.

■ ■ ■

Back in early December 1998, I called a friend in the White House. I told him about wanting to check with House Democrats about the wording of a possible censure resolution. He told me that work was already underway. He warned me of something I already knew: Clinton would agree to a lot of tough language. But he would never agree to having lied to the grand jury—because he had not.

I spoke to many Democrats on the House Judiciary Committee about language for the resolution. One was North Carolina Representative Mel Watt, a classmate from Yale Law in the class of 1970. Mel also knew Hillary Rodham during law school. No one knew about our regular conversations, with Mel giving me the same advice as Scarborough: Lindsey Graham was the key. Mel knew and liked Lindsey. I also talked many times to Florida Democrat Robert Wexler, who often joined me on CNN and other shows defending Clinton from impeachment efforts.

I talked with several other House Democrats, including Jerrold Nadler of New York, John Conyers of Michigan, and Sheila Jackson Lee of Texas.

As we approached the December 12 committee vote, I relied most heavily on Massachusetts Representative Barney Frank, a friend since our days on the 1972 Muskie campaign and a fellow Al Lowenstein acolyte. The final words of the censure resolution Democrats proposed (with the commitment from the White House that the president would sign it after approval by the Senate) were written with Graham in mind. The words stated that he had failed to uphold the "high moral standards and conduct himself in a manner that fosters respect for the truth." The resolution supported by Democrats also accused Clinton of violating the "trust of the American people."

Then came the words that I objected to but clearly were written, thinking they were needed to win over Lindsey Graham: stating that Clinton had made "*false statements* concerning his reprehensible conduct" with a "subordinate," that "*no person is above the law*," and that President Clinton, when he left office, "remains subject to *criminal* and civil penalties" (my emphasis).

I couldn't abide these words, "falsely" and "criminal." But Barney Frank and I both argued to other Democrats on the committee that we had to convince Clinton to do what was necessary to avoid impeachment.

I think it was on December 10, two days before the scheduled House Judiciary Committee impeachment vote, that I learned that the final words had been approved by the Democrats on the committee and by the Senate leadership, Republican Majority Leader Lott and Democratic Minority Leader Tom Daschle as well. Then my friend at the White House confirmed to me that Clinton had agreed—although unhappily—to sign it.

The next day, after multiple tries, I finally got through to Graham on his office phone. I asked him if he had read the Democratic final draft of the censure resolution. He said yes.

"Well?" I asked him.

"Still not enough," he said.

"Why?" I asked in consternation.

He responded quietly, respectfully, in words something like, "I have said from the beginning that Bill Clinton must own up to the fact that he played it too cute and lied to the grand jury. He still hasn't said that."

I was furious. "You would insist that he *lie about lying*?" I asked. "He told the truth to the grand jury—the painful truth about the only issue that matters. You know he did. What did you want him to do—go into graphic details?"

There was only silence on the phone. And then the phone disconnected.

The next day, which happened to be my fifty-third birthday, I showed up early before the scheduled House Judiciary Committee vote. I stood near the somewhat obscure entrance a few doors down from the hearing room, which I knew was the way members could get into the room without the media seeing them. Sure enough, I waited and finally saw Lindsey walking down the hallway, heading for that entrance. He saw me. He couldn't hide his look of dismay.

As he moved to walk past me, I tried one more time: "The resolution is tough and I think accomplishes the public accountability you always said you needed, including specifically saying he could face criminal prosecution after he leaves the presidency."

"Sorry," he said, "I feel no joy in this. But I can't escape the principle: No person in America is above the law."

*Postscript: On February 9, 2021, 8,095 days after the House vote to impeach President Bill Clinton, Graham, then a South Carolina U.S. senator, voted to acquit Donald J. Trump of inciting an insurrection and attempting to overturn the results of a presidential election. The central argument made by Democrats was that "no person is above the law"—even an ex-president.*

*After the vote the Senate Republican majority leader declared that Trump was "practically and morally responsible" for the January 6, 2021, insurrection and violence. Both Senators McConnell and Graham, however, argued that the impeachment clause of the Constitution only provided for the "removal" of a president, and thus, once a president was out of office, he could not be subject to conviction under the clause. However, seven senators in the same party as the accused president voted in favor of conviction and removal. The final vote in favor of conviction and removal of Trump was 57–43, with Graham supporting him.*

*I was not surprised that Graham had abandoned the principle that "no person is above the law," even in his floor statement justifying his vote for acquittal. I knew what was going on for him within the Trump-dominated Republican Party. And I understood.*

■ ■ ■

On December 19, 1998, the House of Representatives cast its historic votes on impeaching President Clinton. The first Republican overreach, obvious to much of the nation, was the decision, led by the Majority Whip Tom DeLay, to deny the House the chance to vote on whether to choose censure in lieu of impeachment. Had GOP leaders allowed such a vote, as DeLay conceded to me years later, censure would have passed the House overwhelmingly, and there never would have been a Clinton impeachment in the historical record.

As expected, House Republicans then voted in favor of impeaching Clinton on two counts, perjury and obstruction of justice. Both counts passed on a nearly entirely party-line vote. Graham and Scarborough voted in favor of both. The gratifying shocker for me was the House vote against impeaching Clinton for perjury in the Paula Jones deposition. After countless hours of Republicans insisting that Clinton had lied during the Jones deposition and should be impeached for doing so, the House rejected that count by a surprisingly large margin, 229–206 against. Twenty-eight Republicans voted against it.

When I heard the "nay" vote when Graham's name was called on Count II (perjury in the Jones deposition), I almost fell off my chair. After all those hours of debating both on air and off, with Graham insisting in the hallway on December 12 that he *had* to vote "yes" on the count asserting that Clinton had committed perjury in the deposition, when it came time to vote on the floor, he had voted no. And so did Joe Scarborough. Incredible!

Maybe their keen legal minds overcame their partisan instincts. After all, the question defining "sexual relations" had been created by Jones's counsel, and Clinton was instructed to rely on it.

Next came lengthy presentations by House managers in the Senate, with a majority of fifty-five Republicans in the chamber. Another shocker was that the House managers could not win a majority of one, or fifty-one votes, for either House impeachment count. Perhaps even more humiliating (and satisfying for me) was that on the supposedly strongest House impeachment count—that Clinton had lied to the grand jury—the impeachment managers lost ten Republican senators, who voted to acquit.

These ten included three former attorneys general of their states: Fred Thompson of Tennessee, Slade Gorton of Washington State, and James Jeffords of Vermont. A fourth was the famous former Philadelphia city prosecutor Senator Arlen Specter. The other six Republican no-votes were highly respected on both sides of the aisle and the national media: Rhode Island's John H. Chaffee; the two Maine senators, Susan Collins and Olympia Snowe; Virginia's John Warner; and Ted Stevens, the conservative Republican from Alaska. Probably most surprising to President

Clinton was that former Democratic Senator Richard Shelby of Alabama also voted to acquit on the grand jury perjury count. Clinton and Shelby had serious personal animus in the first two years of Clinton's first term, with many people believing that was one of the primary reasons Shelby quit the Democratic Party and became a Republican.

I felt some measure of satisfaction. After Graham's (and the mainstream media's) certitude that Clinton had lied to the grand jury, my first reaction that night to Tom Brokaw in the NBC studios had been vindicated. Clinton had told the truth about the core issue. And great lawyers, even staunch Republicans, had put the law above politics and recognized that fact.

Unfortunately the conventional wisdom took hold, wrongly, that Clinton committed perjury before the grand jury, apparently forgetting those ten Republican senators who disagreed. I think they are unsung heroes.

■ ■ ■

Weeks later, I passed Shelby in a hallway near his office and thanked him for his vote against Count I. He reminded me that he and Trent Lott had tried to convince House Republicans to accept a censure resolution and call it a day. He also told me that he thought Clinton showed guts owning up to behavior most husbands wouldn't tell their friends, much less the entire country.

Later, I called Lott, who had privately offered me advice regarding a possible censure alternative to an impeachment vote. He seemed semi-apologetic that he "had" to vote for impeachment. He told me that he believed history would be kind to Clinton based on the objective positive facts of his presidential performance—and that any stigma from the entirely partisan impeachment would be overshadowed by Clinton's impressive record of achievement.

But who decides? Elections are decided by the voters. Political legacies are more complex. Since 1948, when Harvard professor Arthur Schlesinger persuaded several of his fellow historians to help him rate the U.S. presidents, several such comparative rankings have proliferated. They range from Gallup surveys of voters, which tend to be popularity contests of recent presidents, to evaluations by historians, political scientists, or other presidential scholars. The criteria vary. Famed Princeton political scientist Fred I. Greenstein used six metrics, ranging from a president's skill as a communicator to success getting legislation through Congress. Alvin Felzenberg, another Princeton-trained academic, took this idea further and gave presidents separate rankings. Admittedly these rankings are subjective, almost by definition. (One of Greenstein's categories, for instance, is "emotional intelligence.")

But my point isn't that these rankings are imperfect. My point is that in the more recent surveys, Clinton has moved steadily up the list. As Lott and others predicted, the passage of time allowed the objective performance facts to be given more weight in such rankings.

For example, a recent survey on presidential rankings was completed in February 2024 by the Presidential Greatness Project under the auspices of the American Political Science Association, an organization described as the "foremost organization of social science experts in presidential performance."

The results of the survey, conducted from November 15 to December 31, 2003, had Clinton ranked twelfth, sandwiched between James Madison and John Adams, and just two spots below John F. Kennedy, his boyhood idol (whom Clinton met in the Rose Garden when he represented Arkansas in the Boys Nation program in 1963).†

If he'd had the advantage of sixty dependable Democratic Party votes in the Senate, as President Obama enjoyed, Clinton most likely would have been able to pass national affordable health insurance—and his presidential rankings would almost certainly be much higher.

---

† Although the order varies, Abraham Lincoln, George Washington, and Franklin Roosevelt are ranked in the top three in nearly every survey, as they were in the APSA survey. Donald Trump came in last.

In other words, objective facts about Clinton's performance as president have come to trump (no pun intended) the partisan Republican impeachment process. Facts are stubborn things, as John Adams once noted.

And here are some of the undeniable facts of Clinton's tenure as the forty-second U.S. president, which speak much louder than subjective relative rankings:

**Contemporaneous Job Approval:** One obvious criterion for evaluating presidents is how the American people judged them at the end of their tenure, when the total record can be put into perspective. On his last day in office, despite all the distractions over the previous two years from partisan impeachment efforts, Clinton held a 66 percent favorable job approval rating. This is the highest final job approval rating of any two-term president since the advent of modern polling.

The U.S. Constitution begins with three words in the preamble: "We the people." The verdict of the people on the Clinton presidency was overwhelmingly positive.

**Stewardship of the Economy:** That historically high job approval rating was largely driven by economic prosperity. As James Carville famously said, "It's the economy, stupid." A humming economy far outweighed the unpopular and partisan impeachment. Clinton's successes on the economy are recognized even by many Republican voters. The C-SPAN survey ranks Clinton fifth among the forty-four presidents on "economic management"—ahead of Dwight Eisenhower (sixth), Kennedy (seventh), Barack Obama (ninth), and Ronald Reagan (fifteenth).

Over his eight years in office: economic growth averaged 4 percent per year, compared to 2.8 percent during the prior twelve years under Ronald Reagan and George H. W. Bush; there were the most new jobs ever created under a single administration; median income went up

$6,000 in eight years (in 1999 dollars); unemployment was at its lowest level in more than thirty years—from 6.9 percent in 1993 to 4.0 percent in 2000; and there was the lowest inflation since the 1960s—averaging 2.5 percent, down from 4.7 percent in the previous Bush administration.

Over opposition from many on the progressive side of the Democratic Party, Clinton signed a historic welfare reform bill in July 1996. The result was that the number of Americans receiving public assistance dropped from 12.2 million in 1996 to 4.3 million in 2001. As respected Rutgers University history professor David Greenberg put it, "By the end of the Clinton presidency, the numbers were uniformly impressive. Besides record-high surpluses and the record-low poverty rates, the economy could boast the longest economic expansion in history; the lowest unemployment since the early 1970s; and the lowest poverty rates for single mothers, Black Americans, and the aged."

**Balanced Budget and Surplus:** This impressive economic record wasn't done with smoke and mirrors, to use a phrase from the Reagan era, or via deficit spending. Quite the contrary. Clinton took a huge risk in 1993 by pushing the Omnibus Budget Reconciliation Act, a combination of tax increases and budget cuts, through without a single Republican vote in either the House or the Senate. While it cost the Democrats in the 1994 midterm elections, handing control of the House and Senate to the GOP, many economists traced the ensuing economic boom to this legislation.

Nonetheless, Clinton worked constructively with Newt Gingrich and moderate Democrats to craft a historic budget deal in 1997. It lowered the tax rate on capital gains, implemented a $500 child tax credit, increased funding for children's health care, and raised the federal taxes on cigarettes. In hindsight, looking back more than two decades, it is perhaps one of the most impressive bipartisan economic and political achievements for a U.S. president with a Speaker of the other party.

By 1998 the federal government achieved the first budget surplus since the 1960s. *The New York Times* described the end of the deficits as "the fiscal equivalent of the fall of the Berlin Wall." In 1993, Clinton's first year in the presidency, the federal government had a $255 million deficit. That deficit dropped each year through 1997. In 1998 revenues exceeded expenditures by $69.3 million. The surplus increased each year until Clinton's final year, 2000, when the government had a surplus of $236 million. The gross domestic product (GDP) increased from $6.8 billion in 1993 to $10.5 billion in 2000, and the national debt dropped as a percentage of GDP from 48 percent to 33.27 percent in 2000.

**Political Leadership:** Clinton made history in his repositioning of the Democratic Party back to the center, where a Democrat could be elected president. Before 1992, when Clinton won, Democrats had lost four out of five presidential campaigns and lost them handily. Before 1992, pundits spoke of the GOP having an Electoral College "lock." In 1992 and 1996, Clinton won states that Democrats had long since written off as unwinnable (Louisiana, Arkansas, Missouri, Iowa, Tennessee, Arizona, Iowa, Ohio, and Florida). He also showed strength in rural America.

Here is what Professor Russell L. Riley of the University of Virginia wrote in October 2016 about Clinton's impact and legacy:

> *Clinton managed to remake the image and operations of the Democratic Party in ways that effectively undermined the so-called Reagan Revolution. His "New Democrat" Party co-opted the Reagan appeal to law and order, individualism, and welfare reform and made the party more attractive to white middle-class Americans. At the same time, the reborn party retained traditional Democratic commitments to providing for the disadvantaged, regulating the excesses of the private*

*marketplace, supporting minorities and women, and using government to stimulate economic growth.*

**Congressional Relations:** Clinton's success on the economy working with Republican conservatives is documented—on tax policies, the stimulus package, welfare reform, and trade deals that helped produce the tremendous Clinton-era economy, all of which required congressional authorization. This approval didn't happen on its own. It happened because Clinton worked so hard at it, and so skillfully.

"It's hard to think of another president who has taken on so many tough issues this early," FDR biographer William Leuchtenburg said at the time.

On September 14, 1993, Clinton succeeded in getting Gerald Ford, Jimmy Carter, and George H. W. Bush to speak in the East Room in favor of the North American Free Trade Agreement. As the audience laughed along with him appreciatively, Bush 41, whom Clinton had defeated only ten months earlier, had this to say after hearing Clinton speak: "I thought that was a very eloquent statement by President Clinton, and now I understand why he's inside looking out and I'm outside looking in."

At the outset of the legislative battle, Jerry Ford had predicted that the North American Free Trade Agreement would fail unless Clinton "gives it his all." The new president did just that, skillfully maneuvering the treaty through a skeptical Democratic Congress and getting a win without alienating his own side. Here was the assessment of George Mason University political scientist James Pfiffner:

*At the personal level, Bill Clinton was an impressive lobbyer of Congress. He took pains to court members of both parties with invitations to the White House and personal phone calls. He was quite effective at the interpersonal level, combining the personal affability of Ronald Reagan with the detailed policy expertise of Jimmy Carter. In addition, he was*

> *empathetic and could communicate that he understood and sympathized with the perspective of his listener. And he was certainly willing to compromise on substance and pass out favors in seeking votes.*

Thus, Clinton's Third Way comprised an ideological mix not seen before: progressive on social programs while insisting on more individual responsibility; moderate on cultural issues, preaching tolerance and understanding of those who were less quick to embrace significant new cultural trends. Regarding economic policy, this Third Way translated into a unique blend that put results ahead of ideology—and which proved tremendously successful: The Clinton formula included fiscal restraint on the federal budget coupled with outreach to the business community while simultaneously putting working-class Americans and their families first. The results included a balanced federal budget, vast increases in jobs, higher wages—including a higher guaranteed minimum wage and tax cuts for the middle class and working poor.

This formula worked. Clinton kept racking up legislative victories until the end of his term. House Republicans had taken out their frustrations by impeaching a man who had repeatedly bested them. Undeterred, President Clinton kept pursuing policies that put Americans to work and made our country stronger and more successful. The Senate's refusal to go along with the House is a verdict that has stood the test of time—and was affirmed contemporaneously by the American people. When the Clintons left the White House, Bill's job approval rating was higher than any departing postwar U.S. president—eclipsing the standards posted by two popular Republican predecessors, Dwight Eisenhower (59 percent) and Ronald Reagan (63 percent). Nor has it been matched since, even by Obama, who's job approval rating in a Gallup poll on his last day in office stood at 57 percent.

With all the post-2024 election soul-searching among Democratic Party leaders and at the grassroots level as well, the answer going forward seems to be obvious:

To paraphrase James Carville, it's about policies, stupid—specifically, an updated version of Clinton's Third Way policies that focuses not on identity politics, vocabulary, or ideological labels but on *solutions* that appeal to the broad center of American politics where Middle America and working families are.

"You gave me the ride of my life," Clinton told well-wishers before departing the Washington area, "and I tried to give as good as I got."

I was proud to play my small part in his success.

## CHAPTER 22

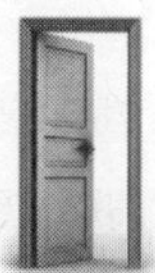

# BROTHERS FROM ANOTHER MOTHER

During my last months in the White House counsel's job, word got around through the White House grapevine that Texas Governor George W. Bush (who was angling for the Republican presidential nomination in 2000) had been a friend of mine when we were at Yale together and that we had been fraternity brothers at the Yale chapter of DKE.

At some point, President Clinton heard about it and began needling me good-naturedly as the campaign got underway. "How is *your friend* George Bush doing?" he'd ask repeatedly—as if "your friend" were part of his first name.

So I was not too surprised when I heard from Clinton the week before Bush's January 20, 2001, inauguration. I saw the telltale sign flash on my cell phone: "No Caller ID." I had a tip from a White House friend the day before that the president might want to call me to talk about "your friend" George W.

When I answered the call, I recognized the voice of one of Clinton's aides, telling me that the president had a question to ask me about Bush.

I then heard the familiar hoarse, Southern-accented voice, which gave me a quick, "Hi, Lanny, hope Carolyn is well." I was not surprised at all that he remembered her name. Then he asked me, "Got a good story to tell me about *your friend* George Bush?"

This was classic Bill Clinton: I knew he'd be meeting Bush on Inauguration Day, a few days hence. I also knew, instinctively, that he was looking for a personal connection, perhaps a personal anecdote from me, to help him form an immediate bond with Bush—especially one that would generate a good laugh between them at my expense.

What immediately came to mind was my own version of the "cue ball" story involving Calvin Hill that I recounted in chapter 9. I set the scene for Clinton: Bush handed me a white cue ball and instructed me to refuse to give it up no matter who demanded I do so, including himself—*no matter what!*

I held onto the cue ball for dear life while dozens of DKEsters shouted at the tops of their lungs for me to give it up. I refused until Bush whispered with a kind voice in my ear, "Well done, Lanny. Now it's okay to give it to me." After declining a few times as he repeated what a good job I had done and that it was okay, I gratefully handed the ball to him, only to hear him shouting into my ear, "*You butthole!*" along with everyone else in the room shouting the same at me!

Clinton chuckled and told me, "That's perfect."

To this day it pleases me to think about Clinton telling Bush that story during their historic drive together to the U.S. Capitol. It is a tradition that has been followed, with very few exceptions, since 1837. It signals the peaceful handoff of power from one current president of the United States to his successor. Knowing both of them personally, I smiled at the thought of them bonding over a story in which I was the foil.

Friends have asked me if I minded being the butt of the joke (pun intended). The truth is nearly the opposite, and I'll explain why.

On December 26, 2004—the day after Christmas and seven weeks after George W. Bush won reelection—a massive earthquake erupted beneath the Indian Ocean floor off the coast of Sumatra, causing a massive tsunami with one-hundred-foot waves barreling toward the shore. Sri Lanka, Indonesia, Thailand, and the Maldives were the hardest hit, with a death toll that exceeded 230,000. As governments around the world rushed to help, President Bush sent the U.S. Navy's Seventh Fleet to help in rescue and response efforts.

When it came time for the recovery phase, Bush turned to two of his predecessors, one a Republican and one a Democrat, to lead the effort.

At a White House event eight days after the tsunami, my former fraternity brother stood at a podium flanked by his father and Bill Clinton. The deadliest tidal wave in human history had left five million people homeless and "devastation in the region [that] defies comprehension," President Bush noted. The challenge ahead, he explained, was to raise vast sums of money to meet the humanitarian crisis.

"I have asked two of America's most distinguished private citizens to head a nationwide charitable fundraising effort," Bush said that day. "Both men, both presidents, know the great decency of our people. They bring tremendous leadership experience to this role, and they bring good hearts. I am grateful to the former presidents, Clinton and Bush, for taking on this important responsibility and for serving our country once again."

What Bush was doing seems extraordinary in our current political environment, but there is a long precedent for just such bipartisan cooperation at the highest levels of government in times of national or international emergencies. Democratic Presidents Woodrow Wilson and Harry Truman designated Republican Herbert Hoover to help with famine relief after both World War I and World War II. Jimmy Carter and Gerald Ford—who had run against each other in 1976—collaborated on two dozen projects here and abroad, traveled together extensively, and became close personal friends.

In the case of George H. W. Bush and Bill Clinton, they had opposed each other in the previous decade in a hard-fought (but not nasty) campaign won by Clinton in a three-way race. During the first year of Clinton's presidency, George H. W. Bush returned to the White House at Clinton's request (along with Jerry Ford and Jimmy Carter) to express support for the North American Free Trade Agreement. Although the elder Bush was notably gracious toward his successor on that occasion, he and Clinton hadn't interacted personally very much.

All that changed after Dubya asked them both to head up tsunami fundraising relief efforts. The two men bonded on their first flight to Asia. Their plane had only one bed, so Bush 41 suggested they take turns using it. Clinton told his eighty-one-year-old flying companion to take the bed—that he could sleep without it. This gesture "broke the ice," Clinton later recalled in a CBS *60 Minutes* interview, "and he befriended me."

"My friendship with him," Clinton added, "has been one of the great joys of my life."

It was a relationship with ripple effects, starting with George Bush's eldest son and namesake. In the case of George W. Bush and Bill Clinton, each of them had always demonstrated an ability to make human connections with people whose politics were different from theirs.

Years later, when Hillary Clinton was running for president and Bush's brother Jeb was seeking the GOP nomination in a crowded field that included Donald Trump, Dubya was asked by a reporter about his friendship with Bill Clinton—and whom he would choose in a general election matchup between Hillary and Jeb.

Bush demurred, quipping, "That would be like choosing between my brother and my sister-in-law!"

This human connection came into stark focus for me on January 20, 2021. Donald Trump did not call any mutual acquaintance of his and Joe Biden's to find some vignette to help establish common ground. He didn't even take part in the traditional ride to the Capitol. Nor did he attend Biden's inauguration—the one he had tried three weeks earlier to forestall by ginning up a riot at the Capitol.

Four years earlier, Trump had flouted convention by delivering an inaugural address that made no attempt to unite the country. Instead, he gave a tedious and angry campaign speech. Afterward, sitting in the VIP section, George W. Bush gave a terse review of Trump's angry rant to his "sister-in-law."

"That was some weird shit," he whispered to Hillary.

As I write these words, Trump had just won a second term as president and quickly began appointing one disruptive and unqualified cabinet official after another. That's his prerogative, I suppose, especially if he can bully the Senate into going along.

What has become clear to me, however, is that Bill Clinton's Third Way is not merely the best way. It's the only way. Whether they called it the Third Way or something else, it's been practiced over the years by Al Lowenstein, Jimmy Carter, Jerry Ford, both Bushes, and both Clintons. The Third Way is nothing less than a search for solutions to the nation's struggles and challenges. It is the application of what Franklin Roosevelt liked to call "American know-how" to problem-solving.

The Third Way is the American way.

CHAPTER 23

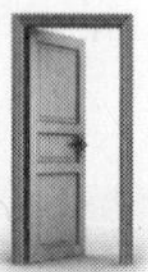

# HER TURN: HILLARY CLINTON (2000–2016)

Ever since that morning in September 1969 when I first met Hillary Rodham, I'd thought she might be our generation's first president of the United States—and the first female president.

My timetable was thrown off by her meeting, falling in love with, and marrying Bill Clinton. Of course, he went first, getting elected to several terms as governor of Arkansas and then winning two terms as president in 1992 and 1996.

Through all those years of continuing our friendship, from Little Rock to Washington, D.C., and the White House, I still waited and wondered, *When will it be my good friend Hillary's turn?*

The first time I heard about the possibility of Hillary Clinton becoming a United States senator was the evening of February 12, 1999. This was the night the Senate soundly rejected the two impeachment counts that were approved by almost entirely partisan House votes.

The celebratory event was a small gathering in the historic reception room just inside the famous white-columned North Portico entrance facing

Pennsylvania Avenue. Although the impeachment ordeal has taken its toll on the president and the First Lady, there was a feeling of elation among the loyalists in attendance because the fifty-five-member Republican Senate could not even muster a majority of fifty-one votes to convict the president, let alone the required two-thirds majority.

Later in the evening, I found myself on the outer edge of a circle of New Yorkers, most personal friends of the Clintons. In the middle of the circle, with Hillary, was legendary Congressman Charles Rangel from Harlem. He was discussing New York politics. The latest intrigue was that Senator Daniel Patrick Moynihan, a towering talent, had recently announced his retirement. Several prominent New York Democrats had already indicated their interest in replacing him. Then I heard Charlie Rangel weigh in rather loudly.

"Hillary, now it's your turn," he said. "You are going to be the next U.S. senator from the state of New York."

*Why not?* I thought.

Carolyn and I were set to leave. I said goodbye to her and could not resist.

"I hope you'll take Charlie's suggestion seriously," I said, mentioning something to her I imagine she'd already thought about: namely, that Robert F. Kennedy wasn't a New York resident, but he had spent a lot of time in New York City, and when he ran for the Senate in 1964, the "carpetbagger" charge never stuck.

She smiled and did not argue. I could see that this was not the first time she had thought about this possibility. I also knew that President Clinton, who was always in awe of her personally and intellectually ever since they fell in love in law school, would be the first cheerleader urging her to do it.

And so it began.

Within five months, on July 7, 1999, she was an undeclared (but certain) candidate and embarked on a much-publicized "listening tour," starting at the upstate farm near Oneonta that belonged to Moynihan. In subsequent days she met with small groups of farmers, citizens, and community leaders, many of them Republicans and most of them dubious about this "carpetbagger" Democrat. And she asked questions and listened to the answers, impressing the media and most voters at the time who had never met her: She was for real. She was not only smart and knowledgeable, which no one ever doubted, but also the Hillary her friends knew: nice, friendly, and warm.

When I read those reports of her "surprising" political skills and connection with voters, even in conservative Republican areas in upstate New York, I was glad that voters were seeing the Hillary Rodham that I had admired from our law school days. She had never changed.

As her Senate campaign progressed in the fall of 2000, the press reports continued to be far more positive than she had experienced before. I campaigned for her in New York one long weekend, assigned to visit numerous Long Island synagogues. I found myself not talking about issues but telling personal stories about how Hillary had been a loyal and trusted friend to me and my family. It was easy to describe the Hillary I knew: a funny, caring friend who was always thinking of you and not herself—and who was utterly authentic.

During an evening reception in New York City before departing for Washington, I was introduced to the leading candidate for state attorney general. He was friendly, funny, and very supportive of Hillary. *This guy is going to win and would have a great chance someday to be governor,* I thought. His name was Eliot Spitzer.

When I called Hillary the next day to tell her of the positive vibes I had felt, she had already heard about my personal stories of how funny she was and how, while in law school, she was unfazed by the off-color jokes told at the virtually all-male Yale Law School at the time.

The results on Election Day, November 7, 2000, confirmed her appeal. She defeated Republican Congressman Rick Lazio by a substantial margin, 55 percent to 43 percent, exceeded expectations, and ran more strongly than most had expected in the conservative Republican upstate New York counties.

I may have been the least surprised person in America when so many of the media and colleagues in the U.S. Senate learned how easy Hillary was to work with and how she did her homework and did not let previous partisan unpleasantness get in the way of being a good senator. The media took notice. Again, contrary to expectations, she was well liked by Republican Senate veterans too.

One personal anecdote sums it up. In January 2003, with Hillary two years into her first term in the Senate, I received a call from Senator-elect Lindsey Graham. He had given up his South Carolina congressional seat to run for a vacant Senate seat—and won in November 2002 by a double-digit margin, just as Hillary had in New York two years earlier.

As I described earlier in this book, I had come to know Graham during our dueling television appearances in the run-up to President Clinton's impeachment. What Graham wanted to know was whether, if he approached Hillary on the Senate floor, she would refuse to shake his hand and carry over anger from the impeachment effort.

"Of course not," I told Lindsey. "She is going to be warm and welcoming, and I predict she will want to work with you on bipartisan legislation. See if I am right."

Lindsey called me back the next day and spoke warmly about how "gracious" she was and how she had raised the topic of working together on the Senate Armed Services Committee.

Three years later in 2005, to the surprise of many but not to me, Senators Clinton and Graham collaborated on passing, *unanimously*, a Senate bill that extended access to health care to members of the National Guard and reserves, whether active duty or not.

Nor was I surprised at the friendship I observed evolving between Senator Clinton and Arizona Senator John McCain, another Republican who had become a friend over the years. I'd gotten to know McCain thanks to our mutual friendship with my close friend Connecticut

Senator Joe Lieberman. In early 2001 I bumped into Lieberman and McCain during a visit to Capitol Hill. Senator McCain couldn't wait to tell me how much he enjoyed getting to know Hillary and how "surprised" he was at how warm and "funny" she was. Joe and I exchanged knowing nods. We'd seen this reaction before.

Tough and grumpy Senate Majority Leader Robert Byrd gave Hillary the ultimate Capitol Hill compliment.

"She's a workhorse, not a show horse," Byrd told the media. His compliment surprised many Hillary critics, but for those who knew her best, it only confirmed what we had known for years. It also underscored two other points: first, how much Hillary's reputation had suffered by sublimating her own professional goals for her husband's, and second, how superficial and cruel—not to mention inaccurate—much of the media's coverage of this remarkable woman had been.

■ ■ ■

Ever since his 2004 keynote speech at the Democratic National Convention in Boston, the rare political talents of Barack Obama were apparent to me—and to much of the nation. And the night, only four years later, when he spoke about his victory in the Iowa caucuses over North Carolina Senator John Edwards and Hillary Clinton and accurately described it as a "defining moment" in our nation's history, I knew that Obama would be a very difficult opponent for Senator Clinton to defeat in her quest for the 2008 Democratic Party presidential nomination.

But the reality of the double standard applied to a female candidate was also always a factor.

Here's a vignette that illuminates that ever-present double standard. It was an exchange between me and a Hillary-critical male at the dinner table at a Wyoming ranch Carolyn and I visited each summer.

In August 2007, early in Hillary's campaign for the Democratic nomination, Hillary was viewed as the front-runner, leading in the polls and the favorite in the minds of most political pundits. On the Republican side, "America's Mayor," Rudy Giuliani, seemed to be the favorite among the same talking heads class.

Over dinner at the ranch, with the regular group of people we had come to know from repeated summer visits over the years, I was seated next to a conservative Republican from Texas. Although he had a keen sense of humor, I found it irritating that he couldn't resist reminding me of his antipathy for "*your friend* Hillary Clinton."

When he repeated once again, loudly enough so everyone could hear that he "can't stand" Hillary Clinton, I set the trap since I knew what the answer to my second question would be.

"So why do you dislike Hillary so much?"

He said what he had previously told me: "Because she is so aggressive, out there, in your face." Those exact words.

Then the trap: "And why do you like Rudy Giuliani so much?"

He responded, clueless—I am not making this up—"Because he is so aggressive, so in your face, so out there."

■ ■ ■

In 1992 Bill Clinton's presidential campaign seemed to be on the ropes before it had really gotten off the ground. Clinton was trailing former Massachusetts Senator Paul Tsongas in the New Hampshire primary, while other candidates, including Senator Bob Kerrey and former California Governor Jerry Brown, were closing fast. But Clinton campaigned virtually 24/7 and finished a close second to Tsongas, who ran virtually as a favorite son, avoiding disaster. The night of the election returns, with the primary calendar heading to more friendly territory down South, an ebullient Clinton labeled himself "the Comeback Kid."

History seemed to be repeating itself in 2008 after Hillary's devastating third-place finish in the Iowa caucuses. Suddenly her big lead in the polls in New Hampshire before Iowa disappeared, and by the next day's polling, Hillary was now down to Obama by double digits. An aura of gloom and doom enveloped her New Hampshire campaign.

Then two events occurred that—although we did not fully appreciate it at the time—altered the campaign's trajectory.

I was in New Hampshire and saw firsthand what happened to turn things around for her. The first occurred on Saturday night, January 5, at a candidates' debate in Manchester. I was sitting at the front of the meeting room, near the stage. I could see Hillary looked tired, and behind her smile, I thought I saw some anxiety.

At the end of the debate, the moderator asked each of the candidates to say what they thought of the other. The moderator commented that it seemed that many voters seemed to "like" Barack Obama more than Hillary. What would she say about how she feels about Obama?

Ouch. I was sitting near the stage.

*Come on, Hillary!* I thought, as if I was mentally trying to communicate with her. Show who you really are. Show how gracious and good-hearted you are, despite the cartoon character created by the haters, including some in the Obama campaign.

And she did.

"That hurts my feelings to hear that people don't like me, but I'll try to go on." Looking at Obama, she continued, "He's very likable . . . I don't think I am that bad."

Then it was Obama's turn, and he couldn't, or wouldn't, reciprocate. Looking toward Hillary, he responded with palpable condescension.

"You're likable . . . *enough*, Hillary."

There was an audible gasp in the audience. I heard the two women sitting next to me whispering in tones that made it clear they thought Obama had been unchivalrous.

The next day I was in Nashua knocking on doors for Hillary in Democratic precincts, and many women who answered the door volunteered how little they liked Obama's response. One said what I had already read in the morning newspapers from women in the debate audience, concerning Obama's slightly sarcastic remark: "He [Obama] reminded me of my ex-husband."

I realized Obama had made a mistake that would cost him among women.

I wasn't an eyewitness to the second incident that weekend, but I immediately heard about it. It seems Hillary was in a small café on the Saturday morning before Tuesday's primary election. She was talking to a group of female voters. When she said a few words, a woman in the audience raised her hand and asked her about her personal feelings regarding the ordeal of campaigning. She was recorded on video with a shaky voice and reported as on the verge of tears.*

The next day, on January 7, the day before the primary, I was knocking on doors again, this time in Manchester, the working-class, biggest city in the state. I was surprised to see voters wearing Obama buttons, remarking on how much they sympathized with Hillary after seeing her tear up. Again, it was clear that women were identifying with the authenticity of her emotional response, under the immense pressures she faced campaigning for president as the first serious female major party candidate. They were sympathetic.

On primary day, January 8, after spending most of the day on the telephone in Manchester making "get out the vote" calls to voters previously identified as receptive to Hillary, I decided on the spur of the

---

* Hillary was described in *New York* magazine as having "watery" eyes and as "crying." She was quoted as describing the ordeal of running in this very personal way, which was unusual for her: "I couldn't do it if I didn't passionately believe it was the right thing to do. This is very personal for me. I have so many ideas for this country, and I just don't want to see us fall backward. It's about our country. It's about our kids' future."

moment to book a plane to Washington so I could be home when the returns came in after polls closed at 8:00 p.m.

I'm embarrassed to admit that I didn't want to be there when Hillary lost, which was widely expected. I just could not bear to see her campaign crumble. I arrived at Ronald Reagan Washington National Airport at about 8:45 p.m. and passed by a television set. I was shocked at the first returns. Clinton was narrowly *ahead*. My oldest son, Seth, who was in New Hampshire knocking on doors for Obama, called me on my cell. He thought I was still in New Hampshire. "Dad, is it possible these early returns are wrong?"

As much as I hoped they showed Hillary had, in fact, become the second New Hampshire "comeback kid" in her family, I wanted to reassure my son, whom I loved with all my heart even though he was not supporting Hillary. So I told him, sharing my own doubts, that early returns are often wrong.

In fact, they foretold the upset victory to come—by a narrow margin, for sure, but still far better than losing, which probably would have knocked her out of the race. I dared to whisper the words I had not said since that night at the White House when I heard Charlie Rangel say them about urging her to run for the Senate seat: "It sure is her turn!"

But a funny thing happened on the way to the Hillary Clinton presidency: the South Carolina primary. I did not pick up what was coming when I was knocking on doors in suburban Charleston. I was getting good vibes for Hillary. But then my cell phone rang, and it was the famous civil rights leader Jesse Jackson.

Jesse had run in the primaries in 1984 and 1988, and he had won or come in a strong second in most of the Southern Democratic primary states, surprising the front-runners each time, along with most of the national media.

I had become friends with Reverend Jackson when Al Lowenstein introduced him to me in the summer of 1968, shortly after he stood next to Dr. Martin Luther King Jr. when King was assassinated. We stayed in touch and worked together for Bill Clinton during the 1992 presidential campaign. He became close to both Clintons and ministered to President

Clinton during the Monica Lewinsky episode. He had not yet endorsed Barack Obama, although I expected him to do so if there was any chance that Obama could become the first African American president.

"Just remember the math," Jesse said to me on the phone. "It's going to happen in South Carolina and all over the South."

"What's going to happen?" I asked. "What math?"

"Democratic primaries in the South are low-turnout elections, and what percentage of the vote will likely be Black?" he asked. Answering his own question, Jackson said, "It could be as high as 40 percent or more."

Then he added, "Obama is going to get 90 percent of the Black vote, just as I did. Just as JFK got that percentage of the Irish Catholic vote." He continued, "So do the math: If Blacks are 40 percent of the total primary and he gets 10 percent or more of white liberals, he wins—by a large margin."

I understood. I had followed Jackson's presidential campaigns closely. And yes, he was right: It was no different than Irish Catholics voting almost as a bloc for Kennedy. Or my fellow Jews supporting almost unanimously Joe Lieberman when he ran on the ticket as vice president with Vice President Al Gore in 2000. Tribal loyalty is not unusual in politics—or in life, for that matter. Why was anyone surprised that African Americans were proud of Obama and would overwhelmingly support him.

I was also hearing something else from African American Democrats when I canvassed Black neighborhoods—amazement that Obama had won in Iowa, a state that is nearly 90 percent white.

I heard that many times, and it did occur to me it was more than just pride that a young Black candidate had proven he could win white votes. It was that they seemed to almost believe, yes, maybe it's true, an African American could become president. "Oh my god," they seemed to be saying, "it just might be true. So we need to help him here even more."

And they did. Jesse was right on his calculations in his home state of South Carolina. But this was not only about race. This was also about

Obama being that good, because he also did well in conservative white neighborhoods. He was simply a remarkable political talent. Obama won a substantial victory over Hillary in South Carolina on January 26 (55 percent to 29 percent).

I asked Reverend Jackson to call both President Clinton and Senator Clinton to explain the math to them, which he did.

The day after the South Carolina primary, President Clinton, undoubtedly very disappointed for his wife, must have had Jesse's math equation in his mind when he made a mention of the large percentage of Obama's support among African American voters. The Obama campaign criticized President Clinton, which seemed rich to me: Progressives had delighted in calling Bill Clinton "America's first Black president" when Obama was an obscure backbencher in the Illinois legislature. Now in the heat of the moment, some overcaffeinated Obama campaign staffers were accusing Clinton of "playing the race card."

Clinton felt bad about how his comment had been construed, but the whisper campaign from the Obama camp continued. Journalists told me they were getting these comments from senior levels of the Obama campaign. I waited for Obama to denounce it. All Clinton had done was point out the reality. He had not disparaged Obama's impressive victory, nor had he impugned the proficiency of his presidential campaign or the political skills that had fueled Obama's success, including winning the Iowa caucuses.

Obama won South Carolina and went on to win the Democratic Party nomination for the reason I had first seen when he delivered his 2004 keynote speech at the Democratic Convention and in Des Moines after the caucuses: his immense political talent and charisma—and the excitement so many Americans felt, including me, that America could put the moral stain of slavery firmly in the past by electing an African American president.

At the same time, the attacks on Clinton over race infuriated me. I felt it was beneath Obama to allow his campaign operatives to even use the words "racist" and "Bill Clinton" in the same sentence, which they did in gutless "on background" conversations with journalists.

Then I made a mistake of my own. Outraged on the Clintons' behalf and offended by the many problematic remarks on race and U.S. foreign policy made by Obama's Chicago church pastor, Jeremiah Wright, I lashed out.

Obama not only stayed in Wright's congregation, but he also appointed him to a religious advisory role in the campaign. I thought it was fair game (and still do), although my decision to air the dirty laundry in *The Wall Street Journal*—the Republicans' favorite media outlet—was probably unwise.

My April 9, 2008, op-ed was published with a headline written by the *Wall Street Journal* editors: "Obama's Minister Problem." I prefaced it with some kind words about Obama in this paragraph, but it did not soften the article much at all:

> *Clearly Mr. Obama does not share the extremist views of Reverend Wright. He is a tolerant and honorable person. But that is not the issue. The questions remain: Why did he stay a member of the congregation? Why didn't he speak up earlier? And why did he reward Reverend Wright with a campaign position even after knowing of his comments?*

The next morning I had misgivings, especially when I got an angry message from my son Seth and lots of friends—even those who were pro-Clinton. The call that pained me most came from a New York lawyer friend, an African American who loved the Clintons but was supporting Obama. "How could you write this?" he asked me. "It shows how little you understand what it is like to be Black in this country."

He explained to me that the suggestion that Obama should stand up and speak out against his pastor in the one safe place for him, his church, was not only ridiculous. It was also insensitive. And I thought, as I listened to my angry friend, stupid. To this day, some members of the White House staff during Obama's two immensely successful terms as president have never forgiven me for this *Wall Street Journal* piece or for other petty criticisms I made of Obama when I appeared on television.

What was I thinking? I wasn't. I let emotion and partisanship toward my friend Hillary overrule my better judgment. And I vowed to learn a lesson from the experience, even as I carried my torch of disappointment that Hillary lost.

On August 28, 2008, the date when I thought Hillary would be nominated as the presidential candidate of the Democratic Party, I was lucky enough to be invited to join a lunch gathering by Hillary's closest friends, from childhood to postcollege. Almost all of them were women. The location was Sylvia's Restaurant, a legendary Harlem place founded by Sylvia Woods in 1962. She became known as the "Queen of Soul Food," and her restaurant became a magnet for the nation's best and most famous Black musicians.

On this day a group of accomplished women told their favorite Hillary stories, using descriptions of our friend that I knew to be true from multiple personal experiences going back forty-seven years since law school: funny, caring, warm, smart, sensitive, and empathetic. Everyone there had at least one wonderful anecdote about our friend. Perhaps inspired by the setting—a restaurant, I told them the following story.

On the day of my separation from my first wife, Elaine, I came home to my two children, my oldest daughter and younger son, waiting for me to feed them. They seemed skeptical of my ability in the kitchen.

Somehow Hillary divined my dilemma. To this day I have no idea who told her that this would be my first night to try to figure out how to make dinner. But as if in a dream, or a movie scene, the phone rang, and there was the old familiar voice. It was Hillary asking what seemed like a random question. It was anything but.

"So do you know how to make dinner?" she asked.

"I can't cook anything," I told her.

"Everybody has one dish they can make," she said. "You make that for dinner tonight. You need to eat, your kids need to eat, and the kids need to know that their father is functioning. You do something like that every day, Lanny. One foot in front of the other . . ."

I shouldn't have been surprised by the call. It was the Hillary I always knew—the person hundreds of friends and colleagues always knew and still know: loyal, caring, thoughtful.

Many such stories and memories flowed that day around the table at Sylvia's, followed invariably by laughter and, at times, tears. And I kept thinking through this remarkable lunch, How is it that so many millions of Americans claim to "dislike" Hillary Clinton, even "hate" her? These people, many of whom are women, have no idea about what she is really like or why friends like these remain devoted to her over so many years.

Although those of us at the lunch weren't yet contemplating another campaign, in due time Hillary would have another chance to run for president. It came eight years later, when she would lose to an opponent as unworthy as Obama was inspirational.

■ ■ ■

I wrote a book, published in early 2018,† showing that FBI Director James Comey's ill-advised and grandstanding October 28, 2016, gesture announcing a new "criminal" investigation of Clinton's handling of her emails while secretary of state almost certainly cost her the election against Donald Trump.

I came to this conclusion by looking at the *RealClearPolitics* polling average and the work of Nate Silver, the founder of *FiveThirtyEight*, another leading poll aggregator. Both of them showed that starting a few days before the Comey letter but more dramatically immediately after, Clinton's lead over Trump dropped steadily. In the three "blue wall" battleground states (Wisconsin, Michigan, and Pennsylvania), she went

† Lanny Davis, *The Unmaking of the President 2016* (Scribner, Simon & Schuster, 2018).

from ahead to behind on Election Day, losing each state in the final count by 1 percent or less.

I was not alone in my judgment. In May 2017 Silver published the data on the *FiveThirtyEight* website under a headline proclaiming that Clinton "probably" would have won but for the Comey letter. I did additional research when I wrote the last chapter of my book on the impact of the Comey letter and found even more data, allowing me to conclude it was more than "probable." As far as I'm concerned, the factual records show that without Comey's letter, Clinton would have defeated Trump by a substantial margin in the electoral vote.[‡]

But as I promoted the book on TV and elsewhere, I realized there was considerable Hillary fatigue in the same mainstream media that had been so tough on Trump. The reporters and television producers did not seem interested in my factual, statistical proof of the impact of the Comey letter. "C'mon, Lanny, you ignore the emails and other problems in her campaign," interviewers would say again and again. And I would respond, "Look at the statistical facts. Despite all those problems, on the day before Comey's letter was published, Hillary would have won by a substantial margin of the electoral and popular votes."

But I found myself concluding, not for the first time, that for whatever reason, including the liberal media, there was a tendency when it came to judging Hillary to put perception over reality, optics over facts. So in the middle of my media tour, I kind of gave up on trying to persuade people I was right.

Yet here I am years later, still making the argument: The math and the facts matter. (For what it's worth, Bill Clinton agrees with me. Although he's as biased as I am when it comes to his wife, the former president's record as a campaign mastermind is beyond question. And on the evening of November 21, 2024, as I was putting the finishing touches on this chapter, I spoke briefly with Bill at a Washington, D.C., book

‡ Ibid., pp. 133–156.

event for his latest memoir. The first thing he said to me was, "I wrote about your book in my book—the part where you proved Comey cost Hillary the election.")

Back in 2016 I visited Hillary in her New York office shortly after her defeat just to see how bad she must be feeling in the aftermath of the defeat and to try to cheer her up. As usual, her first question was, "How are you doing?"

When I told her not very well, she gave me advice to try meditation, as she had done and as my son Seth had advised. Then she advised me how to "deep breathe" slowly through one nostril at a time.

She was worried about me and teaching me how to deal with her defeat! Classic Hillary. More worried about others than herself.

She also urged me to stop blaming Trump voters. (The latter was a sore spot since she mentioned at the end of the campaign that "some" Trump voters—she meant the racist and misogynist ones—were "deplorable.") We both knew that comment was taken out of context and had been repeated inaccurately, over and over again, until it morphed into conventional wisdom.

I told her that I wanted to write a book on the impact of the Comey letter, and she encouraged me to do so. But then she gave me some advice. She urged me to focus on understanding why so many working-class Democrats, the heart of our party since the time of Franklin Roosevelt, voted for Donald Trump.

"Don't focus on my gender or how much you dislike Trump's rhetoric and frequent disregard for the truth," she said. "Focus on understanding why those Trump voters who used to trust the Democratic Party voted for Trump. Listen to them, and we need to figure out how to win back their trust."

Considering what would happen in 2024, Hillary was exceedingly prescient. Donald Trump's victory over Kamala Harris was made possible by the overwhelming support from working-class voters of varied ethnic backgrounds.

I left her office and resolved to write about Comey. But I also left with memories of the first time I met her and sadness that I still thought I was right ever since then: Hillary Rodham Clinton would have made a great president.

EPILOGUE

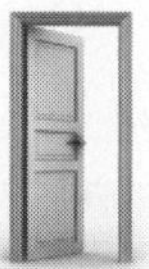

# THE 2024 ELECTION RESULTS—WHAT IF?—AND THE LIMITS OF THE THIRD WAY

I began this book with a thought experiment involving an imaginary walk through time across the Yale University campus between 1963 and 1971. I recalled the actual people I knew in those years and offered brief (fictionalized) conversations with the classmates who became future national political leaders.

The roster included two successive presidents of the United States from opposing parties, Bill Clinton and George W. Bush; future four-term U.S. Senator Joe Lieberman; future New York Governor George Pataki; and two back-to-back secretaries of state who had also been senators, Hillary Rodham Clinton and John Kerry. Also the late, great Al Lowenstein, who served in Congress and became a civil rights leader and a passionate voice in opposition to the Vietnam War.

Throughout my real-life journey, I came to see the common thread among all the individuals mentioned in the preface and others during the many decades of my journey through political history. That thread was finding shared ground among people with vastly different ideas from us—learning to listen and understand first. And then either searching for a Third Way to proceed to make incremental progress or, in the cases where compromise is too elusive, at least agreeing to disagree agreeably.

Life is often unfair, as my boyhood political hero John F. Kennedy once reminded his fellow Americans.* It's a lesson we must all learn on our own, often painfully. Bill and Hillary Clinton—God bless them—are alive and well as I write these words (on my seventy-ninth birthday), vibrantly continuing their decadeslong contributions to America's civic life. Their presence on the political scene is a continuing source of optimism for me. In sad contrast, Lowenstein still had much to offer when he was assassinated on March 14, 1980, at age fifty-one, by a mentally unbalanced former campaign worker.

Although it seems like yesterday, Lowenstein's memorial service four and a half decades ago—which I describe in chapter 11—continues to drive home in my mind the reason why he had such an outsized influence on me. Bill Buckley and Ted Kennedy both said similar words about their enduring admiration, appreciation, and even love for Al. Yet as I sat in the synagogue, I couldn't help but think how Lowenstein was hated in some quarters of both the left and the right. This realization would help me gravitate toward the presidential candidacy first of Edmund Muskie and later (and far more successfully) Bill Clinton. Clinton also took withering cross fire when he insisted on campaigning—and governing—as a "new kind of Democrat" seeking Third Way solutions to problem-solving. It's a lesson each generation of Democrats apparently must keep relearning: addressing national issues by finding common ground with conservatives and rural and working-class Americans.

I now see that this instinct was what tied me over the years to all the individuals on my "walk through time"—people with different political parties and persuasions. We sought answers, not merely influence and fame. We weren't always right. How could we be? We were often on

---

* My other boyhood idol was Willie Mays.

different sides, but the people I valued (and value still) saw the beauty in a phrase popularized by my Republican fraternity brother and future president: to be "uniters, not dividers."

■ ■ ■

Donald Trump's first year as president has revealed the limits of the Third Way concept. It is difficult, for example, to find a Third Way or common ground when it comes to coddling Vladimir Putin, the brutal Russian dictator who invaded Ukraine precisely because Ukrainians want to live in a democratic society. There is no Third Way approach to aligning America with a rapacious regime in the Kremlin that murders dissenters and political opponents.

As Tevye in *Fiddler on the Roof* put it in his "on the one hand . . . and on the other hand" conversation with God, on some issues such as Putin's dictatorship and the importance of defending democracy and the rule of law, "There is no other hand."

Other caveats became important in 2025 as well. Democrats (or Republicans and Independents) cannot in good conscience find common ground with political opponents who are making overtly racist arguments or those who fail to distinguish facts and truth versus lies. Finally, there is no Third Way approach to any president who believes he is not bound by the Constitution to respect the legislative and judicial branches of government—entities our Founders intended to be coequal.

Still, I remain convinced that those who disagree with President Trump (like myself) should not write off the millions of good and thoughtful people—our fellow Americans (and many good friends of mine)—who voted for Trump and still support him. Yes, many of them come across as bigots, fact-deniers, and conspiracy theorists. Yet we must find ways to tune out the worst of their arguments and concentrate on what we know to be true: that deep down, they want the best for their families and this country, just as we do. Maybe, just maybe, if we listen to them, we can learn something. And act as if we realize that although they don't have all the answers, neither do we.

The best way forward for Democrats—and the country as a whole—is to return to Bill Clinton's Third Way: "neither left nor right," but somewhere in the middle where solutions reside and where elections are won.

As readers of this book have seen by now, I came to this conclusion decades before Trump entered politics. Twenty-five years before these words were written, I teamed up with Mark DeMoss, a conservative Christian Republican who had introduced Mitt Romney to prominent evangelicals in the run-up to the 2008 campaign cycle. We drafted a simple "civility pledge." Consisting of only thirty words, it read:

1. I will be civil in my public discourse and behavior.
2. I will be respectful of others whether or not I agree with them.
3. I will stand against incivility when I see it.

We sent this to every member of the House and Senate and all fifty governors. My friend Joe Lieberman signed it, of course, along with two Republican House members. That's it. Exactly three politicians out of the 585 who received our plea were willing to sign the pledge.

I'm normally not one to say, "I told you so." But the way our politics have played out in the ensuing two-and-a-half decades convinces me that Mark and I were right—and that more of these men and women in public life should have been willing to put their signature to a nonbinding promise to act with decency and grace. And I still believe there are enough people in both parties, whether they voted for Trump or Harris, who still want a return to civility in politics and leaders who govern from the political center.

■ ■ ■

Now at the end of this book, which I intend to be the last book I'll write—and with the results of the 2024 election still fresh in my mind—I find myself embarking on a similar imaginary journey through time as the one from the preface. Except that this one is a what-if thought experiment. What if we rewrite history a bit, going back and asking whether doing so might have changed the outcome of the election?

So I start not with imagining a different speech in Chicago by Vice President Kamala Harris when she accepted the Democratic Party nomination for president in August 2024. Rather, let's go back to Joe Biden's inaugural address on January 20, 2021. I imagine him summarizing, even directly quoting, President Clinton's 1995 speech on the issue of illegal immigration. Here is what Biden could have said before revealing he was quoting Bill Clinton:

> *All Americans, not only in the States most heavily affected but in every place in this country, are rightly disturbed by the large numbers of undocumented immigrants entering our country. The jobs they hold might otherwise be held by citizens or legal immigrants. The public service they use imposes burdens on our taxpayers. That's why our administration has moved aggressively to secure our borders more by hiring a record number of new border guards, by deporting twice as many criminal aliens as ever before, by cracking down on illegal hiring, by barring welfare benefits to illegal aliens . . . [W]e will try to do more to speed the deportation of illegal aliens who are arrested for crimes, to better identify illegal aliens in the workplace . . . We are a nation of immigrants. But we are also a nation of laws. It is wrong and ultimately self-defeating for a nation of immigrants to permit the kind of abuse of our immigration laws we have seen in recent years, and we must do more to stop it.*

Certainly, the newly elected President Biden would have felt the wrath of the Democratic Party's most uncompromising progressive wing for taking any kind of stand on illegal immigration. This is not a hypothetical concern: In 2021, when Biden used the phrase "illegal aliens," he was swiftly condemned by what the media described as the liberal-left "advocacy groups."

Biden simply caved. In a response that was the opposite of what the media once called Clinton's "Sister Souljah moment," Biden capitulated completely to the Thought Police. By 2020, when Biden bested a large field to become our party's nominee, Democrats had been intimidated by the "advocacy groups" to the point that they didn't feel free to even speak in language Americans understand, let alone enact policies favored by large majorities of voters. Instead, Biden, who was in the process of essentially opening the southern border, issued directives to all government offices that dealt with immigration, requiring them to use the phrase "nondocumented noncitizens."

Elections can be won or lost in such symbolic moments.

I have no intention of rehashing the 2024 election in the final pages of this book, but my point is that, for Democrats, this campaign wasn't lost in the 107 days that Harris was allotted to make her case. It was lost in the three and a half years in which we forgot our own roots as the party of working-class Americans.

President Clinton, for good reason, attributed his tough stance on border security to the chairwoman of the Immigration Reform Commission. Her name was Barbara Jordan, and she was a revered hero of the Civil Rights Movement and the leading African American female member of Congress.

Barbara Jordan would have been a natural voice for Harris to invoke. But by the time of our 2024 Chicago convention, it was too late. Harris was criticized during the campaign (and even more so after it was over) for not putting any distance between herself and Biden. How exactly was that supposed to look? It was Biden who chose her as vice president after her own presidential bid floundered in 2019 and who helped steer the

Democratic presidential nomination to her when he withdrew his candidacy in the summer of 2024.

Had Biden himself focused earlier on border security, using Bill Clinton and Barbara Jordan as his North Star, the migrant crisis that lasted all four years of the Biden-Harris administration wouldn't have been such an albatross around the vice president's neck. The problem was not defective talking points or a candidate who froze under pressure. Harris inherited a set of policies and verbal straitjackets imposed by progressives that had already induced a critical mass of voters to tune Democrats out.

Along the way, the demonization of our opponents became commonplace. Do right-wing Republicans and Trump's MAGA supporters do the same thing? Absolutely, but the bar was higher for us. That's because we put it there. Democrats are tolerant, we have told ourselves for a long time. We're the party trying to save "democracy." Yet a majority of voters didn't see us as we saw ourselves in 2024. They had their reasons:

- When fair-minded Americans raised concerns about biological males competing against women and girls in sports, we shamed them as "transphobes" and bigots.
- Anyone who questioned the wisdom of a virtually open border risked being dismissed as "xenophobic" and "racist."
- Those who dared complain about the excesses of DEI were dismissed as being equivalent to "white supremacists."
- Americans, even top scientists, who questioned the efficacy of America's COVID-19 lockdowns (or who raised inconvenient truths about the origin of the virus) were silenced and accused of spreading "disinformation." A political party that had long championed free speech became the party of censorship—or "canceled" people who used the wrong vocabulary.

This was the environment Harris inherited when she accepted our party's nomination in late August. There was nothing wrong with her thirty-five-minute convention speech. She recited her upbringing in a middle-class biracial family in a diverse California neighborhood and her time after law school as a prosecutor who worked to keep people safe. She said that being an American was "the greatest privilege on Earth," extolled the virtue of an "opportunity economy," and added that "in unity, there is strength." It was an uplifting address.

Likewise, on the campaign trail, Harris vowed that, as president, she would work as hard for the people who voted against her as the people who voted for her. This might have been a winning message, especially in contrast to a Republican candidate who made no such promises and who used the ominous language of authoritarians while attacking the media, government employees, apostates in his own party, and most Democrats as "enemies of the state."

But here was the problem: Harris borrowed that language word for word from Biden, who made the same promise in 2020. Yet that is not how Americans who voted for Trump perceived the Biden presidency. Nursing our wounds in the aftermath of the election, many Democrats embraced a hoary chestnut: We hadn't done a good enough job advertising the administration's successes, we said. This is probably true. It is also missing the forest for the trees. We had a communications problem, all right, but of a much larger scale: *We forgot how to listen to voters.*

We even forgot our own successes.

During the 2024–2025 presidential transition, much of the (suddenly compliant) media gave Trump big props for his "Department of Government Efficiency," to be spearheaded by Elon Musk. But three decades earlier, President Clinton and Vice President Al Gore unveiled their "National Performance Review," which became popularly known as the "Reinventing Government" initiative.

DOGE, meet REGO. Except that ours was first, and it was done in a spirit of bipartisan cooperation with the federal workforce, not retribution and contempt. REGO worked too: Under the guiding hand of highly competent Democratic strategist Elaine Kamarck, the government was streamlined, saving billions of taxpayer dollars. But the Clinton REGO effort under Kamarck's leadership was done carefully, listening to government employees rather than abrupt firings. And that's why it turned out so well for the Clinton/Gore record.† Governments around the world instituted their own versions—and asked Kamarck to help them do it.

Finally, just suppose Vice President Harris had spoken honestly and directly on the most sensitive cultural wedge issue in the 2024 election—the treatment of transgender people. Suppose she had simply acknowledged the difficulty of the topic. This would have entailed attempting to educate conservatives about the pain many people, especially young people, experienced dealing with the inner conflict between their physical attributes and the gender they feel inside. At the same time, she would have urged her fellow Democrats to be sensitive to the fact that many Americans are fundamentally uncomfortable with their children going to a restroom alongside someone with the opposite sex's physical attributes. Or with their daughters being forced to compete against transgender athletes who possess the physical attributes and strength of men.

She might have simply said in her acceptance speech, in the vocabulary of the Third Way, "Tolerance and mutual respect need to go both ways."

■ ■ ■

In all probability, Donald Trump would have won anyway. A total of 107 days was little time to address concerns about the Democratic Party's attitudes (or Middle America's perception of those attitudes) and overcome our loss of connection with working-class voters. In any event, second-guessing Democratic Party strategy in 2024 with the 20-20 vision provided by hindsight is not the point of this chapter or this book.

---

† Lanny Davis, "DOGE Is No REGO," *RealClearPolitics*, March 4, 2025, https://www.realclearpolitics.com/articles/2025/03/04/doge_is_no_rego__152456.html.

The point is to focus on what matters—preserving our democracy—and how, to help do so, we Democrats must start by changing our attitudes toward those who disagree with us, starting with Trump voters. We must start to listen more and judge less. Democracy requires it.

I will close by relating a trip I took and a speech I made in Laramie, Wyoming, the state that gave Donald Trump the largest margin of any state in the country in 2016 (and would do so again in 2024—when 72 percent of Wyoming voters voted for the Republican ticket).

I was invited to speak to the Wyoming Bar Association. Most of the audience was pro-Trump. If I had any doubts going in, I had none after the speech when I spent almost an hour talking to individuals in the audience.

What follows is what I wrote about my experience for *RealClearPolitics* on September 11, 2023. Because it summarizes the heart of the message of this book and my journey through history and lessons learned, I have decided to republish it, with *RealClearPolitics*' permission:

**Wyoming May Vote Dark Red,**
**but It's Part of a "Purple Nation"**
By Lanny J. Davis

I had the honor last Thursday evening of being the dinner keynote guest speaker at the Wyoming State Bar meeting. Some family and friends wondered how I would be received, since I would not hide my Democratic Party loyalty and my progressive views on most issues. After all, Wyoming voters gave Donald Trump the highest popular vote percentage, at 69.9%, of any state in the 2020 presidential election. I wondered, too, how I would be received.

But we should not have worried.

I learned instead that I had much in common with the warm and friendly audience at the Wyoming bar dinner. I saw this clearly in reaction to one of my favorite true stories about my two old friends from my seven years at Yale: George W.

Bush, who was my fraternity brother while we were both undergraduates; and Bill Clinton, whom I first met shortly after I graduated from Yale Law School in 1970.

I described one day that I experienced in the White House—June 24, 2004. I attended the official unveiling of the White House portraits of President Clinton and First Lady Hillary Clinton, presided over by President George W. Bush and his wonderful wife, Laura.

The sunny historic East Room was largely divided into two sides—with ardent pro-Clinton staff alumni and friends on one side and pro-Bush, largely anti-Clinton staffers on the other.

Bush began from the podium saying: "President and Senator Clinton, welcome home . . . Over eight years . . . [you] filled this house with energy and joy . . . My congratulations to you both." When it was Mr. Clinton's turn at the podium, he said, unforgettably:

"The president, by his generous words to Hillary and me today, has proved once again that, in the end, we are held together by this grand system of ours that permits us to debate and struggle and fight for what we believe is right . . . And I hope that I will live long enough to see American politics return to vigorous debate where we argue who is right and wrong, not who is good and bad."

Suddenly, forgetting their political differences, both sides of the East Room instantly jumped to their feet and gave a thunderous ovation. President Bush stood up in the audience and gave his predecessor a virtual fist bump. Clinton returned the gesture. And the applause was even louder.

The reaction to that story among the largely pro-Trump audience in Wyoming was just as enthusiastic and warm. Another source of commonality was a willingness to be intellectually honest and consistent about constitutional principles.

For example, I mentioned in my speech that I was disappointed in the 2022 Supreme Court's decision in *Dobbs* to overturn *Roe v. Wade*, holding that there was no U.S. constitutional right to an abortion and, instead, that such policy should be left to small "d" democracy at the state government level.

Afterwards, several anti-abortion members of the audience told me they supported a national ban on abortions by Congress. But I asked: Wasn't that inconsistent with the *Dobbs* decision, which valued state governments making that decision vs. an exercise of federal mandatory powers?

I was surprised at the response by almost everyone: "You have a point, Mr. Davis."

Finally, I was heartened by the reminder that the decency instincts were still prevalent regardless of preferences to vote for Trump over Biden. Almost every Trump voter I met volunteered that they did not like Trump's personal attacks or his demonization of anyone who opposed him. They just did not like Mr. Biden's or the national Democratic Party's over-reliance on big government in Washington telling them what to do in Wyoming on too many issues.

I was reminded of Abraham Lincoln in his first inaugural speech, in 1861, predicting that the American people would ultimately be guided by the "better angels of our nature." This reinforced my belief, held for a long time, that ultimately, with some exceptions, the decency vote in our great country will prevail.

So, thank you to the Wyoming State Bar and the friendly and fair audience that heard me speak for reminding me to continue to have faith in the decency vote. And to my fellow Democrats: We cannot give up on any red state voters, including Wyoming's. We must talk to them, listen to them, respect them, and when we do, someday we might win them back.

In other words, decency and respect for other opinions and finding common ground is the objective—the heart of preserving our democracy.

And that commitment to civility and tolerance of differing opinions is the goal of this book—and being able to try hard—in business, politics, and life—to learn how to disagree agreeably and to respect and listen to others who feel differently.

To me, that is the true Third Way that can preserve our democracy and our Constitution for generations to come.

To me, the key line I kept hearing was, "You have a point, Mr. Davis."

And I was willing to say those words back. Which meant we were listening to each other even if we were disagreeing with each other. I believe that is the ultimate lesson: Civility and the ability to disagree agreeably, to treasure our diversity and appreciate our disagreements but still find common ground, are the essence, the fundamental requirement of democracy.

It is an imperfect system. How could it be otherwise? Human beings are imperfect, and if you've gotten this far in this book, you've likely realized just how human I am. Like all of us, William Jefferson Clinton was fond of various aphorisms. One of his favorites came from Benjamin Franklin. As president, Clinton would often quote Franklin as saying, "Our enemies are our friends, for they show us our faults."

The original line, written by Ben Franklin in 1756, a full generation before Franklin (and John Adams) helped Thomas Jefferson produce the Declaration of Independence, was an even steeper challenge.

"Love your enemies," Franklin advised in *Poor Richard's Almanack*, "for they tell you your faults."

I've been thinking about Ben Franklin lately. He was eighty-one years old at the time of the 1787 Constitutional Convention, two years older than I am as of this writing, and a man so universally respected that friends and acquaintances called him "Dr. Franklin."

As the convention that forged a nation came to a close in Philadelphia, Elizabeth Willing Powel, a Founding Mother, asked Franklin the key question of the age.

"Well, Doctor, what have we got: a republic or a monarchy?"

"A republic," Franklin replied, "if you can keep it."

I've come to see that *keeping it* is a challenge for each new generation of Americans and one that cannot be met unless we maintain the ability to disagree—agreeably.

■ ■ ■

**Postscript:** Shortly before this this book went to the printer, thirty-one-year-old conservative phenom Charlie Kirk was shot and killed by a stranger in an apparent assassination.

Although we probably never voted for the same candidate and I didn't agree with most of his ideas, Kirk and I agreed on one important thing: The ability to debate issues peacefully. At times I wished he had used less strident rhetoric in criticizing those he disagreed with—and he might have said the same about me. But Kirk put himself out there and put the work in, going to college campuses and saying to his youthful audiences: "Come on—debate me. Prove me wrong."

His untimely death reminded me, as it should have reminded everyone on my side of the political spectrum, that we need to get out of our bubbles of largely listening to cable networks and podcasts with whom we already agree and spend more time listening to Trump supporters and conservatives like Kirk and hearing them—and I mean *really hearing*, not half-listening and preparing counterarguments.

If we're being honest with ourselves, we know that most of Trump's voters are not bigots or practitioners of hateful speech that leads to violence. We should show tolerance for their views, as different as they are from ours. Liberals might learn something from listening to them, and by the same token, they might learning something from us—which is what this book is all about.

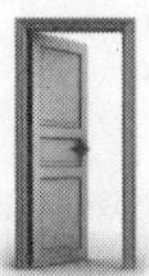

# ACKNOWLEDGMENTS

I start with the most important reason why this book was possible and the deepest gratitude of all: to the first person to whom I dedicated this book, Carolyn Atwell-Davis. She has put up with me as my wife, friend, adviser, and simply an incredibly tolerant person for more than forty years. I could not have written this book without her.

Second, thanks to my oldest son, Seth, who first suggested I write a book and "noodged" me to keep writing during the early days of the pandemic in 2019. He kept at it when I was discouraged and couldn't figure out what I wanted to write, pushed me, gave me his wisdom as a noted author, and served as a constructive critic throughout the process.

Thanks also to Naren Aryal, the head of Amplify Publishing, for his belief and trust in publishing this book and to his great team at Amplify, including executive production editor Brandon Coward, copyeditors Cypriene and Jordan, design director Josh Taggert, and marketing director Kristin Perry, as well as to Maddie Melendez, my partner and professional assistant for over fifty years and BFF (with gray hair she justifiably blames entirely on me). As Hillary Clinton has asked her on occasion, "How have you put up with this guy for so long?" Also, thanks to Maddie's and my assistant, Victoria Batts.

A few more words about Brandon. If this were a political campaign, Brandon would have had the title of campaign manager—often confronting chaos and lack of organization, wasted time, and a variety of tests of his patience, and yet somehow managing to keep the production and editing process moving smoothly to get us to the finish line.

Thank you, Brandon, for all you did for me and this book.

Thanks to an editor is often a ritual for all authors—sincere but still merely obligatory. In the case of Carl Cannon and this book, it is essential.

Aside from significantly improving upon my often verbose writing style and his deft skills as a line editor and researcher, he saw in my collections of anecdotes and adventures (and misadventures) a broader theme—the Third Way—than I had envisioned when I started writing a memoir initially intended for my family. His work in drawing that theme out made this so much more than a simple memoir—it became an important statement about politics in our time.

His influence on me personally and on the manuscript—every word, every page, and every chapter—cannot be overstated. How do I adequately express how much his advice and friendship and patience working with me and improving the quality of this book meant to me?

Honestly, I can't. But he probably could.

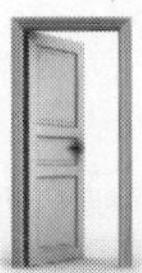

# ABOUT THE AUTHOR

**Lanny Davis** has been active in national, state, and local politics for more than fifty years and was a cofounder of the Civility Project, urging all 535 members of Congress and fifty governors to sign a pledge to act civilly (only three signed).

Throughout the 1990s he served as special counsel to President Bill Clinton and was a spokesperson for the president and the White House on matters concerning campaign finance investigations and other legal issues. In 2005, President George W. Bush appointed Davis as the only Democrat to serve on the five-member Privacy and Civil Liberties Oversight Board created by the U.S. Congress as part of the 2005 Intelligence Reform Act.

As a lawyer in private practice, he counsels individuals, corporations, and others on crisis management and legal issues.

He graduated from Yale University and Yale Law School, where he won the prestigious Thurman Arnold Moot Court Prize in his second year (a prize usually won by third-year senior law students). He also served on the *Yale Law Journal*. He is the author of six other books, including *Crisis Tales: Five Rules for Coping with Crises in Business, Politics, and Life* and *Scandal: How "Gotcha" Politics Is Destroying America*, and writes a regular column, Purple Nation, for *RealClearPolitics*, which has received bipartisan praise.

He lives with his wife, Carolyn Atwell-Davis, in the Washington, D.C., area.